T0260671

IP ADDRESS MANAGEMENT

Books in the IEEE Press Series on Network Management

Telecommunications Network Management Into the 21st Century, edited by Thomas Plevyak and Salah Aidarous, 1994

Telecommunications Network Management: Technologies and Implementations, edited by Thomas Plevyak and Salah Aidarous, 1997

Fundamentals of Telecommunications Network Management, by Lakshmi Raman, 1999

Security for Telecommunications Management Network, by Moshe Rozenblit, 2000

Integrated Telecommunications Management Solutions, by Graham Chen and Quinzheng Kong, 2000

Managing IP Networks: Challenges and Opportunities, edited by Thomas Plevyak and the late Salah Aidarous, 2003

Next-Generation Telecommunications Networks, Services, and Management, edited by Thomas Plevyak and Veli Sahin, 2010

Introduction to IP Address Management, by Timothy Rooney, 2010

IP Address Management: Principles and Practices, by Timothy Rooney, 2011

IP ADDRESS MANAGEMENT

Principles and Practice

Timothy Rooney

**IEEE Press
Series on
Network
Management**

**Thomas Plevyak and
Veli Sahin,** *Series Editors*

IEEE PRESS

A JOHN WILEY & SONS, INC., PUBLICATION

Library of Congress Cataloging-in-Publication Data:

Rooney, Tim.
    IP address management : principles and practice / Tim Rooney.
        p. cm.
    Includes bibliographical references and index.
    ISBN 978-0-470-58587-0 (cloth : alk. paper)
    1. Internet addresses. 2. Internet domain names. I. Title.
    TK5105.8835.R66 2011
    004'67'8–dc22

                                                                    2010010791

oBook ISBN: 978-0-470-88065-4
ePDF ISBN: 978-0-470-88064-7

10 9 8 7 6 5 4 3 2 1

In memory of my father, Patrick Rooney

CONTENTS

PART II DHCP

4 DYNAMIC HOST CONFIGURATION PROTOCOL (DHCP)   67

5 DHCP FOR IPv6 (DHCPv6)   90

6 DHCP APPLICATIONS   109

7 DHCP SERVER DEPLOYMENT STRATEGIES   118

PREFACE

The practice of IP address management (IPAM) entails the application of network management disciplines to Internet Protocol (IP) address space and associated network services, namely Dynamic Host Configuration Protocol (DHCP) and Domain Name System (DNS). The linkages among an IP address plan and configurations of DHCP and DNS servers are inseparable. A change of an IP address affects DNS information and perhaps DHCP as well. These services provide the foundation for today's converged services IP networks, which offer ad hoc anytime, anyplace communications.

If end-user devices such as laptops or voice-over IP (VoIP) phones cannot obtain an IP address via DHCP, they will be rendered unproductive and users will call the help desk. Likewise, if DNS is improperly configured, application navigation by name, phone number, or web address will likewise impair productivity and induce help desk calls.

Effective IPAM practice is a key ingredient in an enterprise or service-provider IP network management strategy. As such, IPAM addresses configuration, change control, auditing, reporting, monitoring, trouble resolution, and related functions as applied to the three foundational IPAM technologies

1. **IP Address Subnetting and Tracking (IPv4/IPv6 Addressing):** Maintenance of a cohesive IP address plan that promotes route summarization, maintains accurate IP address inventory, and provides an automated individual IP address assignment and tracking mechanism. This tracking of individual IP address assignments on each subnet includes those assigned by hard-coding, for example, routers or servers, and others assigned dynamically, for example, laptops and VoIP phones.

2. **DHCP:** Automated IP address and parameter assignment relevant to location and device type. This requires tracking address assignments configured on devices and setting aside dynamically allocated address pools. These address pools can be configured on DHCP servers in order to enable devices to request an IP address, and receive a location-relevant address in reply.

3. **DNS:** Lookup or resolution of hostnames, for example, www entries to IP addresses. This third key aspect of IP address management deals with simplifying IP communications for humans through the use of names, not IP addresses, to establish IP communications. After all, the mapped IP addresses must be consistent with the IP address plan.

The technologies comprising these three core functions are discussed in the first three parts of this book. The practice of IPAM in the fourth part* explains their interrelationships and practices for managing them cohesively. Most IP networks are constantly changing, with the daily demands of the business new stores are opened, offices are closed or moved, companies are acquired, and new devices and device types need IP addresses. These and other changes impacting the IP network can have major repercussions on the existing IP address plan. As the number of users and IP addresses increases, along with the number of subnets or sites, the task of tracking and managing IP address allocations, individual assignments, and associated DNS and DHCP server configurations grows in complexity.

The most common method for performing IPAM functions today entails the use of spreadsheets to track IP addresses, and text editors or Microsoft Windows to configure DHCP and DNS services. As such, IPAM concepts will be demonstrated throughout the book using sample spreadsheet data and configuration file examples as applied to a fictitious organization called IPAM Worldwide, Inc. The intent is to link the technology and configuration details to a real-world example.

CONVENTIONS

This book is typeset in 10-point Times Roman font. *Times Italic* font is used for terms introduced for the first time or to provide emphasis.

To differentiate prose from example configuration information within a DHCP or DNS server, for example, the Courier font in the following manner:

Courier plain font: Used to denote keywords or literal text within a configuration file or screen.

Courier italic font: Used to denote a parameter name that in practice is substituted for a value reflecting the denoted data element or type.

ORGANIZATION

The book is organized into four parts. The first three parts of the book focuses on each of the three core IPAM aspects, respectively: IP addressing and management, DHCP, and DNS. Part IV then integrates these three core components, describing management techniques and practice.

Part I: IP Addressing. Part I provides a detailed overview of IPv4, IPv6, and IP allocation and subnetting techniques.

Chapter 1: The Internet Protocol. Chapter 1 covers IP (IPv4) from a review of the IP header to classful, classless, and private IP addressing and discusses evolution of Internet

---

*In actuality, several constituent IPAM practices are discussed in respective technology chapters, though they are summarized in the context of overall practices in Part IV.

Protocol and the development of network address translation and private addressing as key technologies in preserving global IP address space.

*Chapter 2: Internet Protocol Version 6 (IPv6).*Chapter 2 describes the IPv6 header and IPv6 addressing, including address notation, structure, and current IANA allocations. This includes a detailed discussion of each address allocation by type (i.e., reserved, global unicast, unique local unicast, link local, and multicast). Special use addresses, including the solicited node address and the node information query address are also described. The chapter continues with a discussion of the modified EUI-64 algorithm and address autoconfiguration, then concludes with a discussion of reserved subnet anycast addresses and addresses required of IPv6 hosts.

Chapter 3: IP Address Allocation. Chapter 3 discusses techniques for IP block allocation for IPv4 and IPv6 address spaces. This includes coverage of best-fit hierarchical address allocation logic and examples, as well as sparse and random allocation approaches for IPv6. This chapter also discusses unique local address space as well as the role of Internet Registries. Block allocation is an important function of IP address management and it lays the groundwork for configuration of DHCP and DNS services.

Part II: DHCP. Part II provides an overview of DHCP for IPv4 and IPv6 and covers applications that rely on DHCP, DHCP server deployment strategies and DHCP and relevant network access security.

Chapter 4: Dynamic Host Configuration Protocol. Chapter 4 describes the DHCP protocol, including a discussion of protocol states, message formats, options, and examples. A table of standard option parameters with descriptions of each is provided.

Chapter 5: DHCP for IPv6 (DHCPv6). Chapter 5 covers the DHCPv6 protocol, including a comparison with DHCP(v4), message formats, options, and examples. A table of DHCPv6 option parameters is provided.

Chapter 6: DHCP Applications. Building on the previous two technology-based chapters, Chapter 6 highlights the end-user utility of DHCP in describing key applications that rely on DHCP, including VoIP device provisioning, broadband access provisioning, PXE client initialization, and lease limiting.

Chapter 7: DHCP Server Deployment Strategies. DHCP server deployment considerations are covered in Chapter 7, in terms of trading off server sizing, quantities, and locations. DHCP deployment options regarding distributed versus centralized approaches will be discussed, as will redundant DHCP configurations.

Chapter 8: DHCP and Network Access Security. Chapter 8 covers DHCP security considerations as well as discussion of network access security, of which DHCP is a component. A DHCP captive portal configuration example is described as is a summary of related network access control (NAC) approaches, including DHCP-based approaches, switch-based, Cisco NAC, and Microsoft NAP approaches.

Part III: DNS. Part III describes the DNS protocol, DNS applications, deployment strategies and associated configurations, and security, including the security of DNS servers and configurations and DNSSEC.

Chapter 9: The Domain Name System (DNS) Protocol. The opening chapter of Part III, provides a DNS overview, including a discussion of DNS concepts, message details, and protocol extensions. Covered DNS concepts include the basic resolution process, the domain tree for forward and reverse domains, root hints, local-host domains, and resolver configuration. Message details include the encoding of DNS messages, including the DNS header, label formatting, and an overview of International domain names. DNS Update message formatting is also discussed as is EDNS0.

Chapter 10: DNS Applications and Resource Records. Chapter 10 builds on the material in Chapter 9 to describe key applications, which rely on DNS, including name resolution, services location, ENUM, antispam techniques via black/white listing, SPF, Sender ID, and DKIM. Discussion of applications support is presented in the context of associated resource records.

Chapter 11: DNS Server Deployment Strategies. DNS server deployment strategies and trade-offs are covered in Chapter 11. DNS server deployment scenarios include external DNS, Internet caching, hidden masters/slaves, multimaster, views, forwarding, internal roots, and anycast.

Chapter 12: Securing DNS (Part I). Chapter 12 is the first of two chapters on DNS security. This chapter covers a variety of topics related to DNS security, other than DNSSEC (DNS security extensions), which is covered in its own chapter. Known DNS vulnerabilities are presented first, followed by mitigation approaches for each.

Chapter 13: Securing DNS (Part II): DNSSEC—Chapter 13 covers DNSSEC in detail. The process of creating keys, signing zones, securely resolving names, and rolling keys is discussed, along with an example configuration.

Part IV: IPAM Integration. Part IV brings together the prior three parts, discussing techniques for cohesively managing IP address space, including impacts to DHCP and DNS.

Chapter 14: IP Address Management Practices. In Chapter 14, everyday IP address management functions are described, including IP address allocation and assignment, renumbering, moves, splits, joins, DHCP and DNS server configuration, inventory assurance, fault management, performance monitoring, and disaster recovery. This chapter is framed around the FCAPS network management model, emphasizing the necessity of a disciplined "network management" approach to IPAM.

Chapter 15: IPv6 Deployment and IPv4 Coexistence. The implementation of IPv6 within an IPv4 network will drive a lengthy coexistence of IPv4 and IPv6 protocols. Chapter 15 provides details on coexistence strategies, grouped into sections on dual stack, tunneling approaches, and translation techniques. Coverage includes 6to4, ISATAP, 6over4, Teredo, DSTM, and tunnel broker tunneling approaches and NAPT-PT, SOCKS, TRT, ALG, and bump-in-the-stack or API translation approaches. The chapter concludes with some basic migration scenarios.

Norristown, Pennsylvania   Timothy Rooney
May 2010

ACKNOWLEDGMENTS

First, and foremost, I'd like to thank the following technical reviewers who provided extremely useful feedback, suggestions, and encouragement in the process: Greg Rabil (IPAM and DHCP engineer extraordinaire) and Paul Vixie (Internet guru and President of the Internet Systems Consortium).

I'd like to thank Janet Hurwitz, Alex Drescher, Brian Hart, and Michael Dooley who also provided input and feedback on this book.

I'd also like to thank the following individuals with whom I've had the pleasure to work and from whom I've learned tremendously about communications technologies and IPAM in particular: John Ramkawsky, Steve Thompson, Andy D'Ambrosio, Sean Fisher, Chris Scamuffa, David Cross, Scott Medrano, Marco Mecarelli, Frank Jennings, Jim Offut, Rob Woodruff, Stacie Doyle, Ralph Senseny, and those I've worked with at BT Diamond IP, INS, and Lucent. From my past life at Bell Laboratories, I thank John Marciszewski, Anthony Longhitano, Sampath Ramaswami, Maryclaire Brescia, Krishna Murti, Gaston Arredondo, Robert Schoenweisner, Tom Walker, Ray Pennotti, and especially my mentor, Thomas Chu.

Most of all, I'd also like to thank my family, my wife LeeAnn and my daughters Maeve and Tess, for putting up with my countless hours in writer's isolation and for supporting me throughout this process!

T. R.

PART I

IP ADDRESSING

Part I begins our discussion of the first IPAM cornerstone: IP addressing. This part covers IPv4 and IPv6 protocols as well as address block management techniques.

1

THE INTERNET PROTOCOL

1.1 HIGHLIGHTS OF INTERNET PROTOCOL HISTORY

The Internet Protocol (IP) has changed everything. In my early days at AT&T Bell Laboratories in the mid-1980s when we used dumb terminals to connect to a mainframe, the field of networking was just beginning to enable the distribution of intelligence from a centralized mainframe to networked servers, routers, and ultimately personal computers. Now that I've dated myself, a little later, many rival networking technologies were competing for enterprise deployments with no clear leader. Deployment of disparate networking protocols and technologies inhibited communications among organizations, until during the 1990s the Internet Protocol, thanks to the widespread embrace of the Internet, became the world's de facto networking protocol.

Today, the Internet Protocol is the most widely deployed network layer[*] protocol worldwide. Emerging from a U.S. government sponsored networking project for the U.S. Department of Defense begun in the 1960s, the Transmission Control Protocol/Internet

[*] The network layer refers to layer 3 of the Open Systems Interconnect (OSI) seven-layer protocol model. IP is designed for use with Transmission Control Protocol (TCP) or User Datagram Protocol (UDP) at layer 4, the transport layer, hence the term *TCP/IP protocol suite*. The OSI model and IP networking in general are discussed in the book entitled *Introduction to IP Address Management*. (Ref 11)

IP Address Management: Principles and Practice, by Timothy Rooney
Copyright © 2011 the Institute of Electrical and Electronics Engineers, Inc.

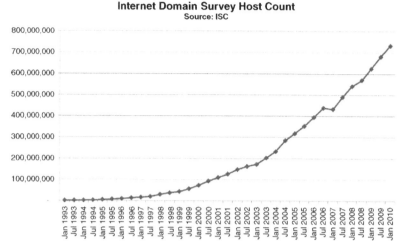

Figure 1.1. Growth of Internet hosts during 1993–2010 (3). *Source:* ISC.

Protocol (TCP/IP) suite has evolved and scaled to support networks from hundreds of computers to hundreds of millions today. In fact, according to Internet Systems Consortium (ISC) surveys, the number of devices or hosts[†] on the Internet exceeded 730 million as of early 2010 with average annual additions of over 75 million hosts *per year* over each of the past 6 years (see Figure 1.1). The fact that the Internet has scaled rather seamlessly from a research project to a network of over 730 million computers is a testament to the vision of its developers and robustness of their underlying technology design.

The Internet Protocol was "initially" defined in 1980 in Request for Comments (RFC[‡]) 760 (1) and 791 (2), edited by the venerable Jon Postel. We quote "initially" because as Mr. Postel pointed out in his preface, RFC 791 is based on six earlier editions of the ARPA (Advanced Research Projects Agency, a U.S. Department of Defense agency) Internet Protocol, though it is referred to in the RFC as version 4 (IPv4). RFC 791 states that the Internet Protocol performs two basic functions: addressing and fragmentation. While this may appear to trivialize the many additional functions and features of the Internet Protocol implemented then and since, it actually highlights the importance of these two major topics for any protocol designer. Fragmentation deals with splitting messages into a number of IP packets so that they can be transmitted over networks that have limited packet size constraints, and reassembly of packets at the destination in the proper order. Addressing is of course one of the key topics of this book, so assuring unique addressability of hosts requiring reachability is critical to basic protocol operation.

[†] The term *host* refers to an end node in the communications path, as opposed to a router or intermediate device. Hosts consist of computers, VoIP telephones, PDAs, and other such IP-addressable devices.

[‡] The Internet Protocol continues to evolve and its specifications are documented in the form of RFCs numbered sequentially. The Internet Engineering Task Force (IETF) is an open community organization with no formal membership and is responsible for publishing RFCs.

The Internet has become an indispensable tool for daily personal and business productivity with such applications as email, social networking, web browsing, wireless access, and voice communications. The Internet has indeed become a key element of modern society. And in case you're interested, the term "Internet" evolved from the lower case form of the term used by the early developers of Internet technology to refer to communications among interconnected networks or "internets."

Today, the capitalized "Internet," the global Internet that we use on a daily basis, has become a massive network of interconnected networks. Getting all of these networks and hosts on them to cooperate and exchange user communications efficiently requires adherence to a set of rules for such communications. This set of rules, this *protocol*, defines the method of identifying each host or endpoint and how to get information from point A to point B over a network. The Internet Protocol specifies such rules for communication using the vehicle of IP packets, each of which is prefixed with an IP header.

1.1.1 The IP Header

The IP layer within the TCP/IP protocol suite adds an IP header to the data it receives from the TCP or UDP transport layer. This IP header is analyzed by routers along the path to the final destination to ultimately deliver each IP packet to its final destination, identified by the destination IP address in the header. RFC 791 defined the IP address structure as consisting of 32 bits comprised of a network number followed by a local address. The address is conveyed in the header of every IP packet. Figure 1.2 illustrates the fields of the IP header. Every IP packet contains an IP header, followed by the data contents within the packet, including higher layer protocol control information.

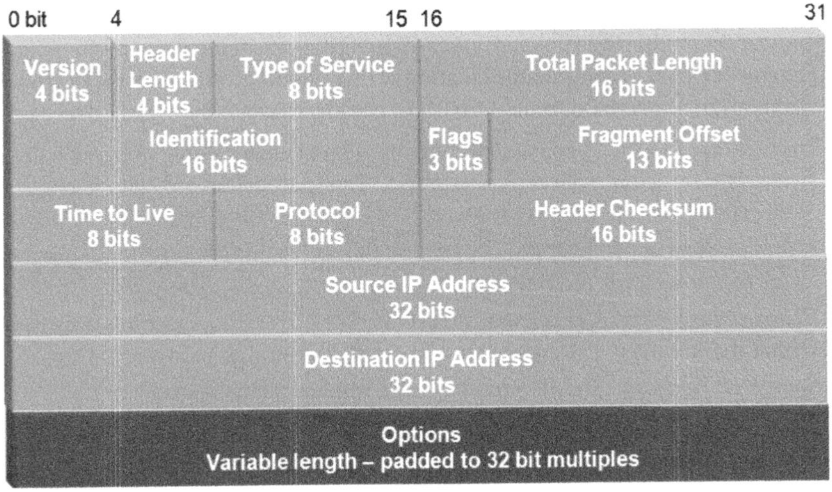

0 bit	4		15 16		31
Version 4 bits	Header Length 4 bits	Type of Service 8 bits	Total Packet Length 16 bits		
Identification 16 bits			Flags 3 bits	Fragment Offset 13 bits	
Time to Live 8 bits		Protocol 8 bits	Header Checksum 16 bits		
Source IP Address 32 bits					
Destination IP Address 32 bits					
Options Variable length – padded to 32 bit multiples					

Figure 1.2. IPv4 header fields (1).

Version. The Internet Protocol version, 4 in this case.

Header Length (Internet Header Length, IHL). Length of the IP header in 32-bit units called "words." For example, the minimum header length is 5, highlighted in Figure 1.2 as the lightly shaded fields, which consists of 5 words × 32 bits/ word = 160 bits.

Type of Service. Parameters related to the packet's quality of service (QoS). Initially defined as ToS (type of service), this field consisted of a 3-bit precedence field to enable specification of the relative importance of a particular packet, and another 3 bits to request low delay, high throughput, or high reliability, respectively.

The original ToS field has been redefined via RFC 2474, "Definition of the Differentiated Services Field (DS Field) in the IPv4 and IPv6 Header" (177). The DS field, or differentiated services field, provides a 6-bit code point (DSCP, differentiated services code point) field with the remaining 2 bits unused. The code point maps to a predefined service, which in turn is associated with a level of service provided by the network. As new code points are defined with respective services treatment by the Internet authorities, IP routers can apply the routing treatment corresponding to the defined code point to apply higher priority handling for latency-sensitive applications, for example.

Total Length. Length of the entire IP packet in bytes (octets).

Identification. Value given to each packet to facilitate reassembly of packet fragments at the receiving end.

Flags. This 3-bit field is defined as follows:

- Bit 0 is reserved and must be 0.
- Bit 1—Don't Fragment—indicates that this packet cannot be fragmented.
- Bit 2—More Fragments—indicates that this packet is a fragment, though this is not the last fragment.

Fragment Offset. Identifies the location of this fragment relative to the beginning of the original packet in units of 64-bit "double words."

Time to Live (TTL). A counter decremented upon each routing hop; once the TTL reaches zero, the packet is discarded. This parameter prevents packets from circulating on the Internet forever!

Protocol. The upper layer protocol that shall receive this packet after IP processing, for example, TCP or UDP.

Header Checksum. A checksum value calculated over the header bits only to verify that the header is not corrupted.

Source IP Address. The IP address of the sender of this packet.

Destination IP Address. The IP address of the intended recipient of this packet.

Options. Optional field containing zero or more optional parameters that enable routing control (source routing), diagnostics (trace route, maximum transmission unit (MTU) discovery), and more.

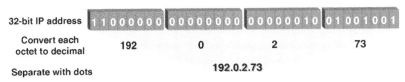

Figure 1.3. Binary to dotted decimal conversion.

It's ok if you find this IP header detail a bit droll. It's only to provide some context, but now let's focus our attention to the source and destination IP address fields and the IP addressing structure.

1.2 IP ADDRESSING

The IP address field is comprised of 32 bits. The familiar dotted decimal notation for an IP address reflects the splitting of the 32-bit address into four 8-bit octets. We convert each of the four octets to decimal, and then separate them with decimal points or "dots." This is certainly easier than calculating these 32 bits as one huge number! Consider the 32-bit IP address in Figure 1.3. We simply split this into four octets, convert each octet to decimal, and then separate the decimal representation of each octet by "dots." Hence, the term "dotted decimal."

1.2.1 Class-Based Addressing[*]

RFC 791 (2) defines three classes of addresses: classes A, B, and C. These classes were identified by the initial bits of the 32-bit address as depicted in Figure 1.4. Each class corresponded to a particular fixed size for the network number and local address fields. The local address field could be assigned to individual hosts or further broken down into subnet and host fields, as we'll discuss later.

The division of address space into classes provided a means to easily define different sized networks for different users' needs. At the time, the Internet was comprised of certain U.S. government agencies, universities, and some research institutions. It had not yet blossomed into the de facto worldwide backbone network it is today, so address capacity was seemingly limitless. The other reason for dividing address space into classes on these octet boundaries was for easier implementation of network routing. Routers could identify the length of the network number field simply by examining the first few bits of the destination address. They would then simply look up the network number portion of the entire IP address in their routing table and route each packet accordingly. Computational horsepower in those days was rather limited, so minimizing processing requirements was another consideration. A side benefit of classful addressing was simple readability. Each dotted decimal number represents one octet in binary. As we'll see later when discussing classless addressing, this is not typically the case today.

[*] Much of the remainder of this chapter leverages material from Chapter 2 of Ref. 11.

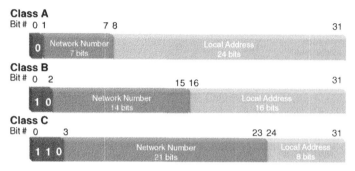

Figure 1.4. Class-based addressing.

Examining this class-based addressing structure, we can observe a few key points:

- Class A networks
  - Class A prefixes begin with binary 0 ($[0]_2$)[†] plus 7 additional bits or 8 network bits total.
  - The network address of all 0s is invalid.[‡]
  - The network address of $[01111111]_2 = 127$ is a reserved address. Address 127.0.0.1 is used for the "loopback address" on an interface.
  - This leaves us with a class A network prefix range of $[00000001]_2$ to $[01111110]_2 = 1$–126 as the first octet.
  - The local address field is 24 bits long. This equates to up to $2^{24} = 16,777,216$ possible local addresses per network address. Generally, the all 0s local address represents the "network" address and the all 1s is a network broadcast, so we typically subtract these two addresses from our local address capacity in general to arrive at 16,777,214 hosts per class A network. Thus, 10.0.0.0 is the network address of 10.0.0.0/8, and 10.255.255.255 is the broadcast address to all hosts on the 10.0.0.0/8 network.
- Class B networks
  - Class B networks begin with $[10]_2$ plus 14 additional bits or 16 network bits total.
  - The range of class B network prefixes in binary is $[10000000\ 00000000]_2$ to $[10111111\ 11111111]_2$ or networks in the range of 128.0.0.0 to 191.255.0.0, yielding 16,384 network addresses.
  - The local address field is 16 bits long for $65,536 - 2 = 65,534$ possible hosts per class B network.

[†] To differentiate a binary 0 (1 bit) from a decimal 0 (7–8 bits) in cases where it may be ambiguous, we subscript the number with the appropriate base. Don't worry; we're not digressing into chemistry with discussion of oxygen molecules with the 0_2 notation, simply "zero base 2."

[‡] Though some protocols such as DHCP use the all 0s address as a placeholder for "this" address.

- Class C networks
  - Class C networks begin with $[110]_2$ plus 21 additional bits or 24 network bits total.
  - The range of class C network prefixes is $[11000000\ 00000000\ 00000000]_2$ to $[11011111\ 11111111\ 11111111]_2$ or networks in the range 192.0.0.0 to 223.255.255.0, yielding 2,097,152 networks.
  - The local address field is 8 bits long for $256 - 2 = 254$ possible hosts per class C network.
- Class D networks (not illustrated in Figure 1.4)
  - Class D networks were defined after RFC 791 and denote multicast addresses, which begin with $[1110]_2$. Multicast is used for streaming applications where multiple users or subscribers receive a set of IP packets from a common source. In other words, multiple hosts having a common multicast address would receive all IP traffic sent to the multicast group or address. There is no network and host portion of the multicast network as members of a multicast group may reside on many different physical networks.
  - The range of class D networks is from $[11100000\ 00000000\ 00000000\ 00000000]_2$ to $[11101111\ 11111111\ 11111111\ 11111111]_2$ or the 224.0.0.0 to 239.255.255.255 range, yielding 268,435,456 multicast addresses.
- Class E networks (not illustrated in Figure 1.4)
  - Networks beginning with $[1111]_2$ (class E) are reserved.

1.2.2 Internet Growing Pains

With seemingly limitless IP address capacity, at least as it seemed through the 1980s, class A and B networks were generally allocated to whomever asked. Recipient organizations would then subdivide or subnet[*] their class A or B networks along octet boundaries within their organizations. Keep in mind that every "network," even within a corporation, needed to have a unique network number or prefix to maintain address uniqueness and maintain route integrity.

Subnetting provides routing boundaries for communications and routing protocol updates. Each network over which IP packets traverse requires its own IP network number (network address). As more and more companies sought to participate in the Internet by requesting IP address space, Internet Registries, the organizations responsible for allocating IP address space, were forced to throttle address allocations. Those requesting IP address space from Internet Registries soon faced increasingly stringent application requirements and were granted a fraction of the address space requested. In having to make do with smaller network block allocations, many organizations were forced to subnet on nonoctet boundaries.

Whether on octet boundaries or not, subnetting is facilitated by specifying a *network mask* along with the network address. The network mask is an integer number

---

[*]The term *subnet* is frequently used as a verb as in this context, to mean the act of creating a subnet.

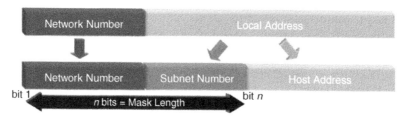

Figure 1.5. Subnetting provides more "networks" with fewer hosts per network.

representing the length in bits of the network prefix. This is sometimes also referred to as the mask length. For example, a class A network has a mask length of 8, a class B of 16, and C of 24. By essentially extending the length of the network number that routers need to examine in each packet, a larger number of networks can be supported, and address space can be allocated more flexibly. This is illustrated in Figure 1.5.

Routers need to be configured with this mask length for each subnet that they serve. This allows them to "mask" the IP address, for example, to expose only the indicated network and subnet bits within the 32-bit IP address to enable efficient routing without relying on address class. Based on this extended network number, the router can route the packet accordingly.

The network address and mask length were originally denoted by specifying the 32-bit mask in dotted decimal notation. This notation is derived by denoting the first n bits of a 32-bit number as 1s and the remaining $32 - n$ bits as 0s, and then converting this to dotted decimal.

For example, to denote a network mask length of 19 bits, you would

- create the 32-bit number with 19 1s and 13 0s: 1111111111111111111100000000 00000
- separate into octets: 11111111.11111111.11100000.00000000
- convert to dotted decimal: 255.255.224.0

For example, the notation for network 172.16.168.0 with this 19-bit mask is 172.16.168.0/255.255.224.0.

Thankfully, this approach was superseded by a simpler notation: the mask is now denoted with the network address as <network address>/<mask length>. While the notation is easier to read, it does not save us from the equivalent binary exercise! For example, the 172.16.0.0 class B network would be represented as 172.16.0.0/16. The "slash 16" indicates that the first 16 bits, in this case the first two octets, represent the network prefix.

Here's the binary representation of this network:

Network Address	Network Prefix	Local Address
172.16.0.0/16	10101100 00010000	00000000 00000000

Let's subnet this network using a 19-bit mask. Expanding this out into binary notation:

Network Address	*Network Prefix*	***Subnet*** Local Address
172.16.0.0/19	*10101100 00010000*	***000***00000 00000000
172.16.32.0/19	*10101100 00010000*	***001***00000 00000000
172.16.64.0/19	*10101100 00010000*	***010***00000 00000000
172.16.96.0/19	*10101100 00010000*	***011***00000 00000000
172.16.128.0/19	*10101100 00010000*	***100***00000 00000000
172.16.160.0/19	*10101100 00010000*	***101***00000 00000000
172.16.192.0/19	*10101100 00010000*	***110***00000 00000000
172.16.224.0/19	*10101100 00010000*	***111***00000 00000000

Notice that the class B network bits are depicted under the Network Prefix column in italic font, and we highlighted the subnet bits in larger bold italic font in the Subnet column. Using this 3-bit subnet mask, we effectively extended the network number from 16 bits to 19. By incrementing the binary values of these 3 bits from $[000]_2$ to $[111]_2$ as per the highlighted subnet bits above, we can derive $2^3 = 8$ subnets with this 3-bit subnet mask extension. Routers would then be configured to route using the first 19 bits to identify the network portion of the address by configuring the router serving such a subnet with the corresponding mask length, for example, 172.16.128.0/19, and then having the router communicate reachability to this network via routing protocols. This technique, called variable length subnet masking (VLSM), became increasingly more prevalent in helping to squeeze as much IP address capacity as possible out of the address space assigned within an organization.

The two-layer network/subnet model worked well during the first decades of IP's existence. However, in the early 1990s, demand for IP addresses continued to increase dramatically, with more and more companies desiring IP address space to publish web sites. At the then current rate of usage, the address space was expected to exhaust before the turn of the century! The guiding body of the Internet, the Internet Engineering Task Force, cleverly implemented two key policies to extend the usable life of the IP address space, namely, support of private address space [ultimate RFC 1918 (7)] and classless interdomain routing [CIDR, RFCs 1517–1519 (Ref. 4–6)]. The IETF also began work on a new version of IP with enormous address space during this time, IP version 6, which we'll discuss in the next chapter.

1.2.3 Private Address Space

Recall our statement that every "network" within an organization needs to have a unique network number or prefix to maintain address uniqueness and route integrity. As more and more organizations connected to the Internet, the Internet became a potential vehicle for hackers to infiltrate organizations' networks. Many organizations implemented firewalls to filter out IP packets based on specified criteria regarding IP header values, such as source or destination addresses, UDP versus TCP, and others. This guarded partitioning of IP address space between "internal" and "external" address spaces dovetailed nicely with address conservation efforts within the IETF.

The IETF issued a couple of RFC revisions, resulting in RFC 1918 becoming the standard document that defined the following sets of networks as "private":

- 10.0.0.0—10.255.255.255 (10/8 network)—equivalent to 1 class A.
- 172.16.0.0—172.31.255.255 (172.16/12 network)—equivalent to 16 class B's.
- 192.168.0.0—192.168.255.255 (192.168/16 network)—equivalent to 1 class B or 256 class C's.

The term *private* means that these addresses are not routable on the Internet. However, within an organization, they may be used to route IP traffic on internal networks. Thus, my laptop is assigned a private IP address and I can send emails to my fellow associates, who also have private addresses. My organization in essence has defined a private Internet, sometimes referred to as an intranet. Routers within my organization are configured to route among allocated private IP networks, and the IP traffic among these networks never traverses the Internet.[*]

Since I'm using a private IP address, someone external to the organization, outside the firewall, cannot reach me directly. Anyone externally sending packets with my private address as the destination address in the IP header will not be able to reach me as these packets will not be routed by Internet routers. But what if I wanted to initiate a connection externally to check on how much money I'm losing in the stock market via the Internet? For employees requiring access to the Internet, firewalls employing network address translation (NAT) functionality are commonly employed to convert an enterprise user's private IP address into a public or routable IP address from the corporation's public address space.

Typical NAT devices provide address pooling features to pool a relatively small number of publicly routable (nonprivate) IP addresses for use on a dynamic basis by a larger number of employees who sporadically access the Internet. The NAT device bridges two IP connections together: the internal-to-NAT device communications utilize private address space, while the NAT device-to-Internet communications use public IP addresses. The NAT device is responsible for keeping track of mapping the internal employee address to the public address used externally.

This is illustrated in Figure 1.6, with the internal network utilizing the 10/8 address space and external or public addressing utilizing the 192.0.2.0/24 space. As per the figure, if my laptop has the IP address 10.1.0.1, I can communicate to my colleague on IP address 10.2.0.2 via the internal IP network. When I access the Internet, my packets need to be routed via the firewall/NAT device in order to map my private 10.1.0.1 address to a public address, for example, 192.0.2.108. The mapping state is maintained in the NAT device and it modifies the IP header to swap out 10.1.0.1 for 192.0.2.108 for outbound packets and the converse for inbound packets.

---

[*] Technically, with the use of virtual private networks (VPNs) or tunnels over the Internet, privately addressed traffic may traverse the Internet, but the tunnel endpoints accessing the Internet on both ends do utilize public IP addresses.

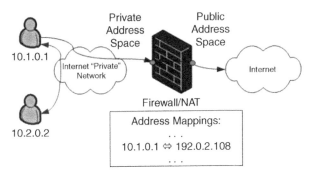

Figure 1.6. Example use of NAT to map private to public addresses.

From an addressing capacity requirements perspective, my organization only needs sufficient IP address space to support these ad hoc internal-to-Internet connections as well as Internet-reachable hosts such as web or email servers. This amount is generally much smaller than requiring IP address space for every internal and external router, server, and host. Implementation of private address space greatly reduced the pressure on address space capacity, as enterprises required far less public address space.

1.3 CLASSLESS ADDRESSING

The second strategy put into effect to prolong the life span of IPv4 was the implementation of CIDR, which vastly improved network allocation efficiencies. Like variable length subnet masking, which allows subnetting of a classful network on nonoctet boundaries, CIDR allows the network prefix for the base address block (allocated by a Regional Internet Registry or Internet Service Provider) to be variable. Hence, a contiguous group of four class C's (/24), for example, could be combined and allocated to a service provider as a single /22. This is illustrated in Figure 1.7. If the four contiguous blocks shown, 172.16.168.0/24 to 172.16.171.0/24, are available for allocation, they could be allocated as a single /22, that is, 172.16.168.0/22.

Notice that the darker shaded bits represent the network number, that is, the first 22 bits, which is identical on all four constituent networks. The remaining 10 bits represent

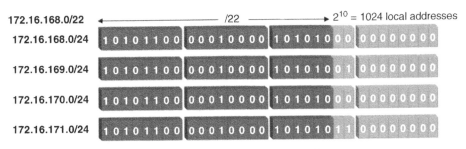

Figure 1.7. CIDR allocation example.

the local address space for host assignment. Since the network address is indicated with all 0s in the local address field, the /22 network is identified as the bit string at the top, namely, 172.16.168.0/22. As you can see, CIDR is very similar to VLSM in terms of the decimal to binary arithmetic required to calculate network addresses on nonoctet boundaries. The extra step of filling in 0s for local addresses outside nonoctet boundary masks introduces an opportunity for error. In addition, VLSM can be applied to a CIDR allocation to further increase the chance of error. But as is usually the case, there's a price to pay for more flexibility. CIDR and VLSM broke down the class walls to provide truly flexible network allocations and subnetworking.

1.4 SPECIAL USE ADDRESSES

In addition to private space, certain portions of the IPv4 address space have been set aside for special purposes or documentation. Such IPv4 address allocations include reservations for special use IP addresses, which are summarized below and defined in RFC 3330 (8) and updated in RFC 5735 (9).

Address Space	Special Use
0.0.0.0/8	"This" network; 0.0.0.0/32 denotes this host on this network
10.0.0.0/8	Private IP address space, not routable on the public Internet as per RFC 1918
127.0.0.0/8	Assigned for use as the Internet host loopback address, that is, 127.0.0.1/32
169.254.0.0/16	The "link local" block used for IPv4 autoconfiguration for communications on a single link
172.16.0.0/12	Private IP address space, not routable on the public Internet as per RFC 1918
192.0.0.0/24	Reserved for IETF protocol assignments
192.0.2.0/24	Assigned as "Test-Net-1" for use in documentation and sample code
192.88.99.0/24	Allocated for 6to4 relay anycast addresses (see Chapter 17 for further discussion)
192.168.0.0/16	Private IP address space, not routable on the public Internet as per RFC 1918
198.18.0.0/15	Allocated for use in benchmark tests of network interconnect devices
198.51.100.0/24	Assigned as "Test-Net-2" for use in documentation and sample code
203.0.113.0/24	Assigned as "Test-Net-3" for use in documentation and sample code
224.0.0.0/4	Allocated for IPv4 multicast address assignments (formerly class D space)
240.0.0.0/4	Reserved for future use (formerly class E space)
255.255.255.255/32	Limited broadcast on a link

2

INTERNET PROTOCOL
VERSION 6 (IPv6)

2.1 INTRODUCTION

During the early 1990s, the fanatical adoption of the Internet as the hottest worldwide communications vehicle led organizations throughout the world to inundate Internet Registries with IP address space requests. This surge in demand for IP address space stimulated the IETF, the engineering and standards body of the Internet, to define a new version of the Internet Protocol that would provide more addressing capacity to meet then and anticipated future address requirements. As discussed in Chapter 1, the adoption of techniques such as CIDR and private address space helped stem the flood of public address space requests; however, these strategies were expected only to prolong the availability of IPv4 address space, albeit for another 10 years or so.

The availability of IPv4 address space continues to diminish and every Regional Internet Registry (RIR) has issued notifications to the Internet community at large that IPv4 space availability is limited and will be exhausted within "a few years." RIRs are responsible for IP address allocation to Internet Service Providers, who in turn allocate space to enterprises, service providers, and any organization requiring IP address space. Ultimately, this exhaustion will impact organizations requiring public IP address space. And Microsoft's Vista™, 7, and Server 2008 products enable IPv6 by default. IPv6 may arrive sooner than you think and with Vista or 7, perhaps whether you'd like it or not!

IP Address Management: Principles and Practice, by Timothy Rooney
Copyright © 2011 the Institute of Electrical and Electronics Engineers, Inc.

Figure 2.1. IP commonality in header and packet concept.

Version 6 of the Internet Protocol* is an evolution from version 4 but is not inherently compatible with version 4. Chapter 15 describes several migration and coexistence techniques. The primary objective for version 6 was essentially to redesign version 4 based on the prior 20 years of experience with IPv4. Real-world application support added to the IPv4 protocol suite over the years was designed into IPv6 from the outset. This included support for security, multicast, mobility, and autoconfiguration.

The most striking difference in the evolution from IPv4 to IPv6 is the tremendous expansion of the size of the IP address field. Whereas IPv4 uses a 32-bit IP address field, IPv6 uses 128 bits. A 32-bit address field provides a maximum of 2^{32} addresses or 4.2 billion addresses. A 128-bit address field provides 2^{128} addresses or 340 trillion trillion trillion addresses or 340 undecillion[†] (3.4×10^{38}) addresses. To put some context around this tremendously large number, consider that this quantity of IP addresses

- averages to 5×10^{28} IP addresses per person on Earth based on a 6.5 billion population;
- averages to 4.3×10^{20} IP addresses per square inch of the Earth's surface;
- amounts to about 14 million IP addresses per nanometer to the nearest galaxy, Andromeda, at 2.5 million light years.

Like IPv4, not every single address will necessarily be usable due to subnetting inefficiencies, but a few undecillion of wasted addresses won't have much impact! Beyond this seemingly incomprehensible number of IP addresses, there are a number of similarities between IPv6 and IPv4. For example, at a basic level, the "IP packet" concept applies equally well for IPv6 as IPv4 in terms of the concept of the packet header and contents (Figure 2.1), as does the basic concept of protocol layering, packet routing, and CIDR allocations. We'll focus on the variety of defined IPv6 addresses in this chapter and discuss IPv6 subnetting and allocation techniques in the next chapter.

2.1.1 IPv6 Key Features

The IETF has attempted to develop IPv6 as an evolution of IPv4. The evolutionary strategy in migrating from IPv4 to IPv6 is intended to enable IPv6 to provide many new

---

* IP version 5 was never implemented as an official version of IP. The version number of "5" in the IP header was assigned to denote packets carrying an experimental real-time stream protocol called ST, the Internet Stream Protocol. If you'd like to learn more about ST, please refer to RFC 1819 (169).

[†] We're using the American definition of undecillion of 10^{36}, not the British definition that is 10^{66}.

features while building on the foundational concepts that made IPv4 so successful. Key IPv6 features include

- *Expanded Addressing.* 128 bits hierarchically assigned with address scoping (e.g., local link versus global) to improve scalability.
- *Routing.* Strongly hierarchical routing, supporting route aggregation.
- *Performance.* Simple (unreliable, connectionless) datagram service.
- *Extensibility.* New flexible extension headers provide built-in extensibility for new header types and more efficient routing.
- *Multimedia.* Flow label header field facilitates quality of service (QoS) support.
- *Multicast.* Replaces broadcast and is compulsory.
- *Security.* Authentication and encryption are built-in.
- *Autoconfiguration.* Stateless and stateful address self-configuration by IP devices.
- *Mobility.* Mobile IPv6 support.

2.1.2 The IPv6 Header

The IPv6 header layout is shown in Figure 2.2. While the size of both the source and destination IP address fields quadrupled, the overall IP header size only doubled. The fields in the IPv6 header are as follows:

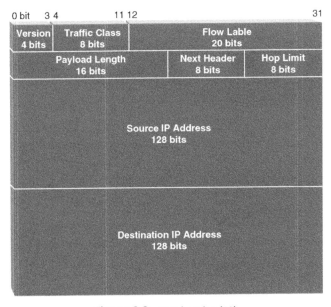

Figure 2.2. IPv6 header (10).

Version. The Internet Protocol version, 6 in this case.

Traffic Class. This field replaces the IPv4 type of service/DS header field and indicates the type or priority of traffic in order to request routing treatment.

Flow Label. Identifies the "flow" of traffic between a source and destination to which this packet belongs as set by the source. This is intended to enable efficient and consistent routing treatment for packets within a given communications session, such as those within a real-time transmission versus a best-effort data transmission.

Payload Length. Indicates the length of the IPv6 payload, that is, the portion of the packet after the base IPv6 header, in octets. Extension headers, if included, are considered part of the payload and are counted within this length parameter.

Next Header. This field indicates the type of header that follows this IP header. This may be an upper layer protocol header (e.g., TCP, ICMPv6, etc.) or an extension header. The extension header concept enables specification of source routing, fragmentation, options, and other parameters associated with the packet only when they are necessary, not as overhead on all packets as in IPv4.

Hop Limit. Analogous to the IPv4 TTL field, this field specifies the number of hops over which this packet may traverse before being discarded. Each router decrements the value of this header field upon forwarding of the packet.

Source IP Address. The IPv6 address of the sender of this packet.

Destination IP Address. The IPv6 address of the intended recipient(s) of this packet.

2.1.3 IPv6 Addressing[*]

Three types of IPv6 addresses have been defined. Like IPv4, these addresses apply to interfaces, not nodes. Thus, a printer with two interfaces would be addressed by either of its interfaces. The printer can be reached on either interface, but the printer node does not have an IP address per se.[†] Of course, for end users attempting to access a node, DNS can hide this subtlety by enabling a hostname to map to one or more interface addresses.

Unicast. The IP address of a single interface. This is analogous to the common interpretation of an IPv4 host address (nonmulticast/nonbroadcast /32 IPv4 address).

Anycast. An IP address for a set of interfaces usually belonging to different nodes, any one of which is the intended recipient. An IP packet destined for an anycast address is routed to the nearest interface (according to routing table metrics) configured with the anycast address. The concept is that the sender doesn't necessarily care which particular host or interface receives the packet, but that

---

[*] Introductory sections of this chapter are based on material from Chapter 2 of Ref. 11.

[†] Many router and server products support the concept of a "box address" via a software loopback address. This loopback address, not to be confused with the 127.0.0.1 or ::1 loopback addresses, enables reachability to any one of the device's interfaces.

one of those sharing the anycast address receives it. Anycast addresses are assigned from the same address space from which unicast addresses have been allocated. Thus, one cannot differentiate a unicast address from an anycast address by sight. Anycast in IPv4 networks has recently created a buzz in providing similar *closest routing to the intended service*, such as for DNS servers by using a shared unicast IPv4 address. This provides benefits in simplifying client configuration, in having it always use the same [anycast] IP address to query a DNS server, regardless of where on your network the client is connected. We'll discuss DNS deployment using anycast addresses in Chapter 11.

Multicast. An IP address for a set of interfaces typically belonging to different nodes, all of which are intended recipients. This of course is similar to IPv4 multicast. Unlike IPv4, IPv6 does not support broadcasts. Instead, applications that utilized broadcasts in IPv4, such as DHCP, use multicast to a well-known (i.e., predefined) DHCP multicast group address in IPv6.

A device interface may have multiple IP addresses of any or all address types. IPv6 also defines a link local scope of IP addresses to uniquely identify interfaces attached to a particular link, such as a LAN. Additional scoping can be administratively defined per site or per organization, for example, as we'll discuss later in this chapter.

2.1.4 Address Notation

Recall that IPv4 addresses are represented in dotted decimal format where the 32-bit address is divided into four 8-bit segments, each of which are converted to decimal, and then separated with "dots." If you thought remembering a string of four decimals was difficult, IPv6 will make life a little tougher. IPv6 addresses are not expressed in dotted decimal notation; they are represented using a colon-separated hexadecimal format. Jumping down to the bit level, the 128-bit IPv6 address is divided into eight 16-bit segments, each of which is converted to hexadecimal, and then separated by colons. Each hexadecimal "digit" represents four bits as per the mapping of each hex digit (0–F) to its 4-bit binary values below. Each hex digit corresponds to 4 bits with the following possible values.

$0 = 0000$	$4 = 0100$	$8 = 1000$	$C = 1100$
$1 = 0001$	$5 = 0101$	$9 = 1001$	$D = 1101$
$2 = 0010$	$6 = 0110$	$A = 1010$	$E = 1110$
$3 = 0011$	$7 = 0111$	$B = 1011$	$F = 1111$

After converting a 128-bit IPv6 address from binary into hex, we group sets of four hex digits and separate them with colons. We'll use the term *nibble* to represent a grouping of four hex digits or 16 bits; thus, we have eight nibble values separated by colons, rendering an IPv6 address appearing as shown in Figure 2.3.

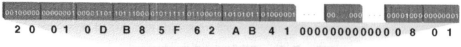

2 0   0 1   0 D   B 8   5 F   6 2   A B   4 1   0000000000000 0 8   0 1

2001:0DB8:5F62:AB41:0000:0000:0000:0801

Figure 2.3. IPv6 address: binary to hexadecimal (11).

Instead of dealing with four decimal values, each between 0 and 255, separated by dots in IPv4, IPv6 addresses consist of up to eight hexadecimal values, each between 0 and FFFF, separated by colons. There are two acceptable abbreviations when writing IPv6 addresses. First, leading zeroes within a nibble section, that is, between colons, may be dropped. Thus, the above address could be abbreviated as

$$2001 : DB8 : 5F62 : AB41 : 0 : 0 : 0 : 801$$

The second form of abbreviation is the use of a double colon to represent one or more consecutive sets of zero nibbles. Using this form of abbreviation, the above address can be further abbreviated as

$$2001 : DB8 : 5F62 : AB41 :: 801$$

Isn't that much better? Note that only one double colon may be used within an address representation. Since there are always eight nibble segments in the address, one can easily calculate how many of them are zero with one double-colon notation; however, it would be ambiguous with more than one.

Consider the address 2001:DB8:0:56FA:0:0:0:B5. We can abbreviate this address as either

$$2001 : DB8 :: 56FA : 0 : 0 : 0 : B5 \quad \text{or} \quad 2001 : DB8 : 0 : 56FA :: B5$$

We can easily calculate that the double colon denotes one nibble (8 total minus 7 nibbles shown) in the first case and three (8 minus 5 shown) in the second notation. If we attempted to abbreviate this address as 2001:DB8::56FA::B5, we could not unambiguously decode this, as it could represent any of the following possible addresses:

$$2001 : DB8 : 0 : 56FA : 0 : 0 : 0 : B5$$
$$2001 : DB8 : 0 : 0 : 56FA : 0 : 0 : B5$$
$$2001 : DB8 : 0 : 0 : 0 : 56FA : 0 : B5$$

Thus, the requirement holds that only one double colon may appear in an IPv6 address.

2.1.5 Address Structure

The IPv6 address is divided into three fields, as shown in Figure 2.4.

Figure 2.4. IPv6 address structure (12).

The global routing prefix is akin to an IPv4 network number and is used by routers to forward packets to router(s) locally serving the network corresponding to the prefix. For example, a customer of an ISP may be assigned a /48-sized global routing prefix and all packets destined to this customer would contain the corresponding global routing prefix value. In this case, $n = 48$ as per Figure 2.4. When denoting a network, the global routing prefix is written, followed by slash, and then the network size, called the prefix length. Assuming that our example IPv6 address, 2001:DB8:5F62:AB41::801, resides within a /48 global routing prefix, this prefix address would be denoted as 2001:DB8:5F62::/48. As with IPv4, the network address is denoted with zero-valued bits beyond the prefix length (bits 49–128 in this case) as denoted by the terminating double colon.

The subnet ID provides a means to denote particular subnets within the organization. Our ISP customer with a /48 may choose to use 16 bits for the subnet ID, providing 2^{16} or 65,534 subnets. In this case, $m = 16$ as per Figure 2.4. This leaves $128 - 48 - 16 = 64$ bits for the interface ID. The interface ID denotes the interface address of the source or intended recipient for the packet. As we'll discuss a bit later, the global unicast address space that has been allocated for use so far requires a 64-bit interface ID field.

One of the unique aspects of this IPv6 address structure in splitting a network ID consisting of the global routing prefix and subnet ID, from an interface ID, is that a device can retain the same interface ID independent of the network to which it is connected, effectively separating "who you are," your interface ID, from "where you are," your network prefix. As we'll see, this convention facilitates address autoconfiguration, though not without privacy concerns. But we're getting a little ahead of ourselves, so let's jump back up to the macro level and consider the IPv6 address space allocated so far by the Internet addressing authority, the Internet Assigned Numbers Authority (IANA).

2.2 IPv6 ADDRESS ALLOCATIONS

The address space that has been allocated so far by IANA is highlighted in dark gray in Table 2.1 and is discussed in the ensuing text. These allocations represent less than 14% of the total available IPv6 address space.

2.2.1 ::/3—Reserved Space

Address space prefixed with $[000]_2$ is currently reserved by the IETF. Addresses within this space that have unique meaning include the unspecified (::) address and the loopback (::1) address. The IPv6 addressing architecture specification, RFC 4291 (12), requires that all unicast IPv6 addresses, except those within this address space (that is beginning with ::/3 ($[000]_2$)), must utilize a 64-bit interface ID field, and this interface

T A B L E 2.1. IPv6 Address Allocations (13)

IPv6 Prefix	Binary Form	Relative Size of IPv6 Space	Allocation
0000::/3	000	1/8	Reserved by IETF: the "unspecified address" (::) and the loopback address (::1) are assigned from this block
2000::/3	**001**	**1/8**	**Global unicast address space**
4000::/3	010	1/8	Reserved by IETF
6000::/3	011	1/8	Reserved by IETF
8000::/3	100	1/8	Reserved by IETF
A000::/3	101	1/8	Reserved by IETF
C000::/3	110	1/8	Reserved by IETF
E000::/4	1110	1/16	Reserved by IETF
F000::/5	1111 0	1/32	Reserved by IETF
F800::/6	1111 10	1/64	Reserved by IETF
FC00::/7	**1111 110**	**1/128**	**Unique local unicast**
FE00::/9	1111 1110 0	1/512	Reserved by IETF
FE80::/10	**1111 1110 10**	**1/1024**	**Link local unicast**
FEC0::/10	1111 1110 11	1/1024	Reserved by IETF
FF00::/8	**1111 1111**	**1/256**	**Multicast**

ID field must utilize the modified EUI-64[*] algorithm to map the interface's layer 2 or hardware address to an interface ID. Thus, addresses within the ::/3 address space can have any length interface ID field, unlike the remainder of the IPv6 unicast address space, which must utilize a 64-bit interface ID field.

2.2.2 2000::/3—Global Unicast Address Space

The global unicast address space allocated so far, 2000::/3, represents 2^{125} or 4.25×10^{37} IP addresses. Given the 64-bit interface ID requirement defined in the IPv6 addressing architecture [RFC 4291 (12)], the global unicast address format as formally defined in RFC 3587 (14) is shown in Figure 2.5.

The first three bits are $[001]_2$ to indicate global unicast address space. The following 45 bits comprise the global routing prefix, followed by the 16-bit subnet ID and 64-bit interface ID, respectively. Current guidelines call for ISPs allocating /48 networks to their customers, thereby assigning global routing prefixes to customers. Each customer may then define up to 65,534 subnets by uniquely assigning values within the remaining 16-bit subnet ID field for each subnet.

---

[*] EUI-64 refers to the 64-bit Extended Unique Identifier defined by the IEEE. We'll cover the modified EUI-64 algorithm later in this chapter.

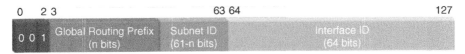

Figure 2.5. Global unicast address format (14).

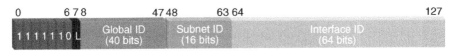

Figure 2.6. Unique local address format (15).

2.2.3 FC00::/7—Unique Local Address Space

The unique local address (ULA) space, defined in RFC 4193 (15), is intended to provide locally assignable and routable IP addresses, usually within a site. RFC 4193 states that "these addresses are not expected to be routable on the global Internet." Thus, while not as stringent as RFC 1918 in defining private IPv4 address space, the unique local address space is essentially private address space, providing "local" addressing with a high probability of still being globally unique. The format of unique local address space is shown in Figure 2.6.

The first seven bits, bits 0–6, are $[1111\ 110]_2 = \text{FC00}::/7$, which identifies a unique local address. The eighth bit, the "L" bit, is set to "1" if the global ID is locally assigned; setting the "L" bit to "0" is currently undefined, though the Internet community (IETF) has discussed enabling this setting for globally unique local addresses, assignable through Internet Registries. The 40-bit global ID field is intended to represent a globally unique prefix and must be allocated using a pseudorandom algorithm, not sequentially. In either case, the resulting /48 prefix comprises the organization's ULA address space, from which subnets can be allocated for internal use. The subnet ID is a 16-bit field to identify each subnet, while the interface ID is a 64-bit field.

An example pseudorandom approach to derive a unique global ID as described in RFC 4193 recommends computing a hash[*] of

- the current time as reported by a Network Time Protocol (NTP) server in 64-bit NTP format,
- concatenated with an EUI-64 interface ID of an interface on the host performing this algorithm.

The least significant (rightmost) 40 bits of the result of the hash operation are then populated as the global ID.

---

[*] A hash is created by performing a mathematical operation on the data to be hashed and a random value. A particular mathematical algorithm, the Secure Hash Algorithm 1 or SHA-1, is required in this case.

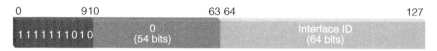

Figure 2.7. Link local address format (12).

2.2.4 FE80::/10—Link Local Address Space

Link local addresses are used only on a particular link, such as an Ethernet link; packets with link local destination addresses are not routed. That is, packets having link local addresses will not reach beyond the corresponding link. These addresses are used for address autoconfiguration and neighbor discovery, which will be discussed later. The format of link local addresses is shown in Figure 2.7.

The FE80::/10 link local prefix is followed by 54 zero bits and the 64-bit interface ID.

2.2.5 FF00::/8—Multicast Address Space

Multicast addresses identify a group of interfaces typically on different nodes. Think of multicast addresses as a scoped broadcast. All multicast group members share the same group ID and hence all members will accept packets destined for the multicast group. An interface may have multiple multicast addresses; that is, it may belong to multiple multicast groups. The basic format of IPv6 multicast addresses is shown in Figure 2.8.

The prefix FF00::/8 identifies a multicast address. The next field is a 4-bit field called "flags." The format of the multicast address depends on the value of the flags field. The scope (also affectionately referred to as "scop") field indicates the breadth of the multicast scope, whether per node, link, global, or other scope values defined below. The value of the flags and scope fields can fortunately be easily discerned by looking at the third and fourth hex digits within the address, respectively, as we'll summarize a bit later.

Flags. The flags field is comprised of 4 bits, which we'll discuss starting from right to left (12):

- The T bit indicates whether the multicast address is of transient nature or is a well-known address assigned by IANA. The T bit is defined as follows.

Figure 2.8. Multicast address format (12).

Figure 2.9. Multicast address with flag T = 0.

Figure 2.10. Multicast address with flag P = 1 (16).

o T = 0. This is an IANA-assigned well-known multicast address (Figure 2.9). In this case, the 112-bit multicast address is a 112-bit group ID field.

IANA has assigned numerous group IDs thus far.[*] For example, group ID = 1 refers to all nodes within the associated scope (defined by the scope field), group ID = 2 refers to all routers within the scope, and so on. The scope field is defined below, but example well-known multicast addresses are

- F01∷1 = all nodes on this link.
- FF02∷2 = all routers on this link.
- FF05∷1 = all nodes on this site.
- FF05∷2 = all routers on this site.

o T = 1. This is a temporarily assigned or transient multicast address. This can be an address assigned for a specific multicast session or application. An example might be FF12∷3:F:10.

- The P bit indicates whether the multicast address is comprised partly of a corresponding unicast network prefix or not. The P bit is defined[†] as follows:

o P = 0. This multicast address *is not* assigned based on the network prefix. The format of a multicast packet with P = 0 is as described above (i.e., when T = 0), with the 112-bit group ID field.

o P = 1. This multicast address *is* assigned based on the network prefix of the unicast subnet address "owning" the multicast address allocation. This enables allocation of multicast space associated with allocated unicast space for simpler administration. If P = 1, the T bit must also be set to 1. The corresponding format of a multicast packet is shown in Figure 2.10.

When P = 1, the scope field is followed by 8 zero bits (reserved), an 8-bit prefix length field, and a 64-bit network prefix field and a 32-bit group ID field. The prefix length field represents the prefix length of the associated unicast network

---

[*] Please refer to http://www.iana.org/assignments/ipv6-multicast-addresses for the latest assignments.

[†] The definition of the P bit is documented in RFC 3306 (16).

address. The network prefix field contains the corresponding unicast network prefix, while the group ID field contains the associated multicast group ID.

For example, if a unicast address of 2001:DB8:B7: :/48 is allocated to a subnet, a corresponding unicast-based multicast address would be of the form FF3s:0030:2001:DB8:B7: :g, where

- FF = multicast prefix.

- 3 = [0011]$_2$, that is, P = 1 and T = 1.

- s = a valid scope as we'll define in the next section.

- 00 = reserved bits.

- 30 = prefix length in hex = [0011 0000]$_2$ = 48 in decimal, the prefix length in our example.

- 2001:DB8:B7:0 = 2001:0DB8:00B7:0000 = 48-bit network prefix in the 64-bit network prefix field.

- g = a 32-bit group ID.

A special case of this format occurs with P = T = 1 when the prefix length field = FF and $s \leq 2$. In this case, instead of the network prefix field consisting of the unicast network address, this field will be comprised of the interface ID of the respective interface. The interface ID used must have passed the duplicate address detection (DAD) process, which is discussed later in this chapter, to assure its uniqueness. In this special case, the scope field must be 0, 1, or 2, meaning of interface local or of link local scope. This *link-scoped multicast address* format is defined as an extension of the IPv6 addressing architecture via RFC 4489 (17).

- The R bit within the flags field enables specification of a multicast rendezvous point (RP) that enables multicast group would-be subscribers to link in temporarily prior to joining the group permanently. If the R bit is set to 1, the P and T bits must also be set to 1. When R = 1, the multicast address is based on a unicast prefix, but the RP interface ID is also specified (Figure 2.11). The format of the multicast address when R = 1 is identical to the case when R = 0 and P = 1 with the exception that the reserved field is split into a 4-bit reserved field and a 4-bit rendezvous point interface ID (RIID) field.

  ○ The IP address of the RP is identified by concatenating the network prefix of corresponding prefix length with the value of the RIID field. For example, if an RP on the [unicast] network is 2001:DB8:B7: :6, the associated multicast address would be FF7s:0630:2001:DB8:B7:g, where s = a valid scope defined below and g = a 32-bit group ID.

Figure 2.11. Multicast address with flag R = 1.

o The explicit breakdown of this address is as follows:

- FF = multicast prefix.
- 7 = [0111]$_2$, that is, R = 1, P = 1, and T = 1.
- s = a valid scope defined below.
- 0 = reserved bits.
- 6 = RIID field, to be appended to the network prefix field.
- 30 = prefix length in hex = [0011 0000]$_2$ = 48 in decimal, the prefix length in our example.
- 2001:DB8:B7:0 = 2001:0DB8:00B7:0000 = 48-bit network prefix in the 64-bit network prefix field.
- g = a 32-bit group ID.
- The first flag bit is reserved and is set to 0.

Multicast Flags Summary. Who thought multicast addressing could be so complicated? But as is typically the case, with complexity comes flexibility! To summarize, the net result of the above bit stipulations yields the following valid values of the flags field as currently defined. Since the flags field immediately follows the first eight "1" bits, we denote the "effective prefix" of these first eight bits followed by the valid 4-bit flags field (Table 2.2).

TABLE 2.2. Multicast Flags Summary

Flags (Binary)	Effective Prefix	Interpretation
0000	FF00: :/12	Permanently assigned 112-bit group ID scoped by 4-bit scope field
0001	FF10: :/12	Temporarily assigned 112-bit group ID scoped by 4-bit scope field
0011	FF30: :/12	Temporarily assigned unicast prefix-based multicast address
0111	FF70: :/12	Temporarily assigned unicast prefix-based multicast address with rendezvous point interface ID
All other flags values	–	Undefined

Scope. The scope field identifies, naturally enough, the scope or "reach" of the multicast address. This is used by routers along the multicast path to constrain the reach of the multicast communications with the corresponding scope. Note that scopes other than interface local, link local, and global must be administratively defined within the routers serving the given scope in order to enforce the corresponding reach constraint. Table 2.3 summarizes valid scope values.

T A B L E 2.3. Multicast Scope Field Interpretation

Scope Field			
Binary	Hex	Meaning (Scope)	Description
0000	0	Reserved	Reserved
0001	1	Interface local	Scope consists of a single interface on a node and is useful only for loopback transmission
0010	2	Link local	Scope is only the link on which the multicast packet is transmitted
0011	3	Reserved	Reserved
0100	4	Admin local	Scope is limited to the smallest scope administratively configured. This is not based on physical connectivity or other multicast-related configuration
0101	5	Site local	Scope is limited to the site as administratively defined
0110–0111	6–7	Unassigned	N/A
1000	8	Organization local	Scope consists of multiple sites within one organizational entity as administratively defined
1001–1101	9–D	Unassigned	N/A
1110	E	Global scope	Scope is unlimited
1111	F	Reserved	Reserved

2.2.6 Special Case Multicast Addresses

Solicited Node Multicast Address. One form of multicast address that each node must support is the solicited node multicast address. This address is used during the duplicate address detection phase of address autoconfiguration and for the neighbor discovery protocol, which enables identification of IPv6 nodes on a link. The solicited node multicast address is formed by appending the low-order (rightmost) 24 bits of the solicited node's interface ID to the well-known FF02::1:FF00/104 prefix.

For example, let's say a node wishes to resolve the link layer address of the device (interface) with IP address 2001:DB8:4E:2A:3001:FA81:95D0:2CD1. Using the low-order 24 bits, D02CD1 in hex, the device would address its request to FF02::1: FFD0:2CD1 (Figure 2.12).

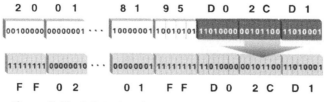

Figure 2.12. Solicited node multicast address derivation (12).

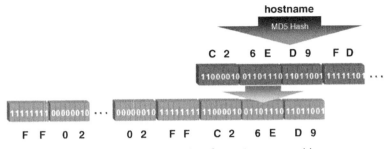

Figure 2.13. Solicited node information query address.

Node Information Query Address. The node information query address is a multicast address enabling solicitation of hostname and IPv6 and IPv4 address information from an IPv6 host (Figure 2.13). If you think this sounds like an overlap with what DNS already provides, you're correct. However, according to RFC 4620 (18), this mode of resolution "is currently limited to diagnostic and debugging tools and network management." And instead of querying a DNS server for this information, a query is issued to the node information query address.

Use of this multicast address format enables an IPv6 address to be formed based only on the hostname of the intended recipient; if the IPv6 address is already known and hostname information is requested, the IPv6 address itself may be used as the destination address. When IP address information is being requested for a known hostname, the canonical hostname[†] is hashed using the 128-bit MD-5 algorithm, and the first 24 bits resulting from the hash are appended to the FF02::2:FF00:0/104 prefix. Each node receiving a message addressed to this node information query address compares the last 24 bits in the address with the first 24 bits of a hash of its own hostname; if it matches, the recipient will reply with the requested information.

2.2.7 IPv6 Addresses with Embedded IPv4 Addresses

We will discuss IPv4 to IPv6 migration and coexistence strategies in Chapter 15, but we'll introduce the IPv4-mapped IPv6 address here (Figure 2.14). This type of address is not routable on the Internet, and is used solely by some translation schemes, and should not generally be used within an IPv6 packet on a communications link. This address

Figure 2.14. IPv4-mapped IPv6 address (12).

[†] The "canonical hostname" is technically the first "label" in the fully qualified domain name in lowercase characters. This terminology is described in detail in Chapter 9 but suffice it to say that this generally is the intended destination hostname.

format consists of 80 zero bits, followed by 16 one bits, followed by the 32-bit IPv4 address.

This address notation combines the familiar IPv4 dotted decimal format appended to the specified IPv6 prefix. Thus, an IPv4-mapped IPv6 address for 172.16.20.5 would be represented as : :FFFF:172.16.20.5.

2.3 IPv6 ADDRESS AUTOCONFIGURATION

One of the advertised benefits of IPv6 is the ability for devices to automatically configure their own IPv6 address that will be unique and relevant to the subnet to which it is presently connecting.[‡] There are three basic forms of IPv6 address autoconfiguration:

- *Stateless.* This process is "stateless" in that it is not dependent on the state or availability of external assignment mechanisms, for example, Dynamic Host Configuration Protocol for IPv6 (DHCPv6). The device attempts to configure its own IPv6 address(es) without external or user intervention.
- *Stateful.* The stateful process relies solely on external address assignment mechanism such as DHCPv6. The DHCPv6 server would assign the 128-bit IPv6 address to the device in a manner similar to DHCP for IPv4 operation. This process will be described in detail in Chapter 5.
- *Combination of Stateless and Stateful.* This process involves a form of stateless address autoconfiguration used in conjunction with stateful configuration of additional IP parameters. This commonly entails a device autoconfiguring an IPv6 address using the stateless method, and then utilizing DHCPv6 to obtain additional parameters or options such as which NTP servers to query for time resolution on the given network.

At the most basic level, the autoconfiguration of an IPv6 unicast address involves concatenating the address of the network to which the device is connected (where you are) and the device's interface ID (who you are). Let's first consider how the device determines the address of the network to which it is connected.

2.4 NEIGHBOR DISCOVERY

The process of *neighbor discovery* in IPv6 enables a node to discover the IPv6 subnet address on which it is connected. Neighbor discovery in general also enables identification of other IPv6 nodes on the subnet, to identify their link layer addresses, to discover routers serving the subnet, and to perform duplicate address detection. Discovery of routers enables IPv6 nodes to automatically identify routers on the subnet, negating the need to configure a default gateway manually within the device's IP

[‡] Note that some IPv4 protocol stacks, such as those provided with Microsoft Windows 2000 and XP, among others, perform address autoconfiguration utilizing the IPv4 "link local" address space, 169.254.0.0/16.

configuration. This discovery enables a device to identify the network prefix(es) and corresponding prefix length(s) assigned to the link.

The discovery process entails each router periodically sending advertisements on each of its configured subnets indicating its IP address, its ability to provide default gateway functionality, its link layer address, the network prefix(es) served on the link including corresponding prefix length and valid address lifetime, as well as other configuration parameters.

The router advertisement also indicates whether a DHCPv6 server is available for address assignment or other configuration. The M bit (managed address configuration flag) in the router advertisement indicates that DHCPv6 services are available for address and configuration settings. The O bit (other configuration flag) indicates that configuration parameters other than the IP address are available via DHCPv6; such information may include which DNS servers to query for devices on this link. Nodes can also solicit router advertisements using router solicitation messages, addressed to the link local routers multicast address (FF02::2).

2.4.1 Modified EUI-64 Interface Identifiers

Once a node identifies the subnet to which it is attached, it may complete the address autoconfiguration process by formulating its interface ID. The IPv6 addressing architecture stipulates that all unicast IPv6 addresses, other than those beginning with binary $[000]_2$, must use a 64-bit interface ID derived using the modified EUI-64 algorithm. The "unmodified" EUI-64 algorithm entails concatenating the 24-bit company identifier issued by the IEEE to each network interface hardware manufacturer (e.g., the initial 24 bits of an Ethernet address) with a 40-bit extension identifier. For 48-bit Ethernet addresses, the company identifier portion of the Ethernet address (first 24 bits) is followed by a 16-bit EUI label, defined as hexadecimal FFFE, followed by the 24-bit extension identifier, that is, the remaining 24 bits of the Ethernet address.

The modification required to convert an unmodified into a modified EUI-64 identifier calls for inverting the "u" bit (universal/local bit) of the company identifier field. The "u" bit is the seventh most significant bit in the company identifier field. Thus, the algorithm for a 48-bit MAC address is to invert the "u" bit and insert the hexadecimal value FFFE between the company identifier and the interface identifier. This is illustrated in Figure 2.15 using a MAC address of AC-62-E8-49-5F-62. The resulting interface ID is AE62:E8FF:FE49:5F62.

For non-Ethernet MAC addresses, the algorithm calls for use of the link layer address as the interface ID, with zero padding (from the "left"). For cases where no link layer address is available, for example, on a dial-up link, a unique identifier utilizing another interface address, a serial number, or other device-specific identifier is recommended.

The interface ID may not be unique, especially if not derived from a unique 48-bit MAC address. Thus, the device must perform duplicate address detection prior to committing the new address. Prior to completing the DAD process, the address is considered tentative.

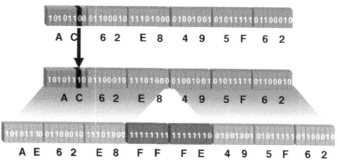

Figure 2.15. Modified EUI-64 interface ID example (11).

2.4.2 Duplication Address Detection

DAD is performed using the neighbor discovery process, which entails the device sending an IPv6 Neighbor Solicitation packet to the IPv6 address it just derived (or obtained from DHCPv6) in order to identify a preexisting occupant of the IP address. After a slight delay, the device also sends a Neighbor Solicitation packet to the solicited node multicast address associated with this address.

If another device is already using the IP address, it will respond with a Neighbor Advertisement packet, and the autoconfiguration process will stop; that is, manual intervention or configuration of the device to use an alternate interface ID is required. If a Neighbor Advertisement packet is not received, the device can assume uniqueness of the address and assign it to the corresponding interface. Participation in this process of Neighbor Solicitation and Advertisement is required not only for autoconfigured addresses but also for those statically defined or obtained through DHCPv6.

IPv6 addresses have a lifetime during which they are valid (Figure 2.16). In some cases the lifetime is infinite, but the concept of address lifetime applies to both DHCPv6 leased addresses and autoconfigured addresses. This is useful in easing the process of network renumbering. Routers are configured with and advertise a preferred lifetime and a valid lifetime value for each network prefix in their Router Advertisement messages. IP addresses that have successfully proven unique through the duplicate address detection process described above can be considered either preferred or deprecated. In either state, the address is valid, but this differentiation provides a means for upper layer protocols (e.g., TCP, UDP) to select an IP address that will likely not change during the ensuing session.

A device refreshes the preferred and valid times with each Router Advertisement message in accordance with the values advertised. When time expires on a preferred prefix, the associated address(es) will become deprecated, though still valid. Thus, the deprecated state provides a transition period during which the address is still functional but should not be used to initiate new communications. Once the valid lifetime of the address expires, the address is no longer valid for use. Should a subnet be reassigned a different network prefix, the router can be configured to advertise the new prefix, and

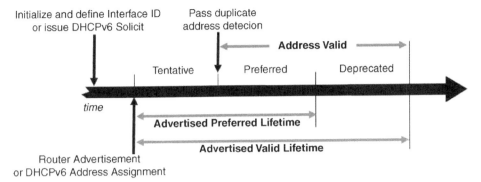

Figure 2.16. IPv6 address lifetimes (figure based on Ref. 19).

devices on the network would undergo the autoconfiguration process using the new prefix as the lifetime of the old prefix expires.

2.5 RESERVED SUBNET ANYCAST ADDRESSES

RFC 2526 (20) defines the format for reserved subnet anycast addresses. These addresses are used by IPv6 devices to route packets to the nearest device of a particular type on a specified subnet. For example, a reserved subnet anycast address can be used to send packets to the nearest mobile IPv6 home agent on a specified subnet. Since the global routing prefix and subnet ID are specified within this address type, it enables a node to locate the nearest node of the desired type on that subnet.

The format of the address takes on one of two forms based on whether the subnet prefix requires formulation of the interface ID field in modified EUI-64 format. Recall that all global unicast addresses other than those beginning with $[000]_2$ must utilize 64-bit interface IDs formulated based on the interface's link layer address and the modified EUI-64 algorithm described previously.

1. If the EUI-64 algorithm is required, the reserved subnet anycast address is formulated by concatenating the following fields (Figure 2.17):

   - 64-bit global routing prefix and subnet ID.
   - 57 bits of all 1s, except the seventh bit in this sequence (the 71st bit from the beginning, counting left to right), which is 0. This seventh bit corresponds to the "u" bit (universal/local bit) of the company identifier field in the hardware

Figure 2.17. Reserved subnet anycast address format when EUI-64 is required (20).

Figure 2.18. Reserved subnet anycast address format when EUI-64 is not required (20).

address when applying the EUI-64 algorithm. This bit is always zero in this
particular scenario to represent the "local" setting of the bit.

- 7-bit anycast ID. RFC 2526 defines a single anycast ID of hex 7E for mobile
  IPv6 home agent anycast. Other anycast ID values are reserved, though IANA
  may assign additional anycast IDs based on future IETF RFC publications.

2. If EUI-64 is *not* required based on the global routing prefix and subnet ID, then
   the network prefix length is arbitrary at n bits, followed by $121 - n$ 1 bits, followed
   by the 7-bit anycast ID (Figure 2.18).

2.6 REQUIRED HOST IPv6 ADDRESSES

RFC 4294 (21) summarizes the requirements for IPv6 nodes, a device that implements
IPv6, and for IPv6 routers. In terms of required addresses, all IPv6 nodes must be capable
of recognizing the following IPv6 addresses for itself:

- The loopback address ($::1$).
- Its link local unicast address (FE80::<interface ID> as configured via
  autoconfiguration).
- The all-nodes multicast address (FF0s::1, where s = scope).
- Unicast and anycast addresses configured automatically or manually on each
  interface.
- The solicited node multicast address for each of its unicast and anycast addresses.
- Multicast addresses for each multicast group to which the node belongs.

A router node is required to support the above addresses plus the following addresses:

- The subnet router anycast address (<subnetwork prefix>::/128, that is, interface
  ID = 0s).
- The all-routers multicast address (FF0s::2, where s = scope).
- Anycast addresses configured on the router.

Other device types such as DHCP and DNS servers must recognize scoped multicast
addresses corresponding to group IDs assigned by IANA (i.e., when flags = 0).

3

IP ADDRESS ALLOCATION

In this chapter, we will begin describing the technology and applications that serve as the foundation of the practice of IP address management. In addition, we will illustrate the technology and applications by way of example. Thus beginning with the fundamentals of IP address allocation, we'll incrementally apply each new concept to a fictitious organization called International Processing and Materials (IPAM) Worldwide (play on words intended!). IPAM Worldwide's basic organization consists of a global headquarters in Philadelphia and three major geographic headquarters spanning the world, in Europe at Dublin, in North America at Philadelphia, and in Asia at Tokyo. IPAM Worldwide has about 17,000 employees and 24 distribution centers, which also serve as branch offices, and an additional 37 offices functioning solely as branch offices. Figure 3.1 illustrates a basic location spreadsheet, highlighting each continental headquarters, and corresponding distribution centers and branch offices.

The deployment of the IP network will primarily be driven by where the users of the IP network are located per the sites listed in Figure 3.1, by the number of users at each location, by the variety of user requirements for access to information resources such as internal applications and the Internet, and by the variety of administration requirements for managing the IP network from security to auditing. Because of the variety of inputs

IP Address Management: Principles and Practice, by Timothy Rooney
Copyright © 2011 the Institute of Electrical and Electronics Engineers, Inc.

IPAM Worldwide Global Locations				
Core Sites	Region	Regional Site	Distribution Centers	Branch Offices
Philadelphia	HQ—Corporate	Philadelphia		
Philadelphia	HQ—North America	Philadelphia		
	N. America—East	Norristown	Toronto Nashua Newark Baltimore Pittsburgh Charlotte Atlanta	Providence Quincy Albany Manhattan Ocean City Reston Richmond Charleston Montgomery
	N. America—Central	Kansas City	Chicago Des Moines Memphis New Orleans Mexico City	Lisle Indianapolis Topeka Houston
	N. America—West	San Francisco	Denver Vancouver Phoenix	Calgary Albuquerque Salt Lake City Boulder Edmonton Sacramento Anaheim
Dublin	HQ—Europe	Dublin		
	Europe—West	London	Amsterdam Paris	Manchester Madrid Lyon Lisbon
	Europe—South	Rome	Rome	Nice Milan Athens
	Europe—East	Berlin	Munich Moscow	Vienna Prague Budapest Kiev
Tokyo	HQ—Asia	Tokyo	Tokyo Beijing Singapore Auckland	Seoul Osaka Singapore Manila New Delhi Sydney

Figure 3.1. IPAM Worldwide global locations and offices.

related to individual business needs, the IP network of any one organization generally looks somewhat different from that of any other. However, the techniques we discuss should be broadly applicable across a wide variety of networks, including yours.

The IT team at IPAM Worldwide has decided to deploy a high-speed backbone or core network among the organizational and geographic headquarters. Emanating from each regional headquarters office is an intracontinental wide area network (WAN) interconnecting each of the region's retail, distribution, and branch offices. Building on this basic two-layer hierarchy of core and regional networks, each branch network is further divided by geographic region. For example, within North America, they've divided the administration into three subregions: east, central, and west, and then further by major distribution center and branch office site. Likewise, the Europe region has been subdivided into west, south, and east regions.

Following this topology, the IT team has decided to mimic this structure with respect to address space, as we'll see next. Hence, a core network interconnects the regional headquarters sites, and each regional headquarters serves as an intermediary between its corresponding regional network and the core network. Each regional network interconnects its respective distribution centers and branch offices within the region. From an organizational perspective, each region has its own IT team that would like to manage its own space and associated DHCP and DNS server configuration. Figure 3.2 depicts the high-level IPAM Worldwide network topology design.

In terms of IP address space allocation, IPAM Worldwide will deploy a 10.0.0.0/8 network from the RFC 1918 private address space. Public address space, 192.0.2.0/24, has been obtained from an ISP (we'll discuss where this space comes from and ISP public address space allocation and policies later in this chapter). This public space will be allocated for Internet facing devices like web servers, email gateways, and VPN gateways for partner connections and remote employees. In addition, a portion of the public address space is reserved for deployment as a public address pool on a network address translation (NAT) firewall facing the ISP. As we introduced in Chapter 1, a NAT can be configured to perform private-to-public address conversion automatically in order to enable privately addressed (internal) hosts to access the Internet.

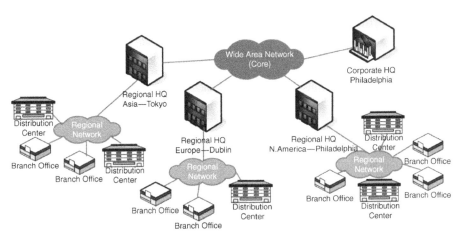

Figure 3.2. IPAM Worldwide network topology (partial).

3.1 ADDRESS ALLOCATION LOGIC[*]

Effective IP address allocation requires diligent planning and, ideally, accurate fore-casting. Knowing the IP address space requirements for every level of the network hierarchy enables optimal allocation of address space to fully meet the address capacity needs while minimizing address space waste. Of course in reality, having an accurate long-term IP address forecast is a rare luxury. Business needs drive constant change with new sites opening, some closing or moving, new IT initiatives like rolling out voice over IP, and even mergers. Beyond these strategic events that can usually be planned for proactively, organizational dynamics can drive shorter term perturbations in address capacity requirements. For example, perhaps a regional organization is conducting a wildly successful customer event, driving a surge in IP address demand, or a new project is causing a shift in IP address needs due to temporary colocation of project resources.

The bottom line is to do your best in mapping out high-level address capacity needs, add some additional "insurance" address space to the extent possible, then proactively monitor address utilization as a feedback loop to ensure the addresses allocated are being effectively utilized given the short- and long-term address-affecting events. A key function in the management of IP space, proactive monitoring can trigger the allocation or movement of address space to where it may be needed more urgently.

Of course, the intensity of proactive monitoring will be directly proportional to the utilization of the address space. If many of your networks are above 90% utilization,[†] you may need to monitor their utilization hourly or at least multiple times per day. Networks with utilization below 70% may require monitoring checks a couple times a week. Ideally, you can define thresholds and alert conditions within a monitoring or IP address management system to alleviate the need to constantly monitor your networks manually, and have the associated management system collect the information and alert you to a particular capacity utilization condition.

Beyond capacity needs, another important consideration is the allocation of IP address blocks in a hierarchical manner such that address space "rolls up" to the highest level efficiently. This practice is critical to maximizing route aggregation to reduce routing protocol traffic and routing table overhead. It's important then to consider routing topology when allocating space.

A third consideration is a more recent phenomenon: allocation per application. Due to latency or quality of service (QoS) requirements for certain applications such as voice over IP, which generally requires low latency on the order of tens of milliseconds versus data, which tolerates multisecond time latency, some network planners implement routing treatment based on application. One way to perform this is to carve out a portion of the overall address space for voice treatment with higher priority queuing for example, while separating this from the data space. Other "special need" IP applications may require further address delineation.

---

[*] Allocation logic and examples are based on analogous content in Chapter 6 of Ref. 11.

[†] Blanket percentages aren't always the best trigger for action, especially when you have different sized subnets throughout the organization. Ninety percent utilization of a subnet with 10 addresses would certainly be of higher urgency than would one with 1000 addresses.

3.1.1 Top-Level Allocation Logic

To illustrate address allocation concepts, let's apply them to IPAM Worldwide's private address block, 10.0.0.0/8. When performing top-level allocations such as this, keep in mind not only the capacity required in terms of IP addresses but also the number of subdivisions or hierarchy layers that may be ultimately necessary. In the case of IPAM Worldwide, we will define our address hierarchy layers as follows:

- Application
- Continental or core layer
- Regions
- Sites or buildings

Thus, our top-level allocation will divide our address space by application. Each application-specific allocation will then be allocated at the core router or continental level, then by region, and finally by office. Since we have four layers of allocation hierarchy, we will have to allocate along nonoctet boundaries. So let's look at this from both a CIDR network notation and the corresponding binary notation.

The binary representation of this network is shown below. The network portion of the address, whose length is identified by the /8 notation is highlighted as bold italics, while the local portion is in plain text.

Private Network   10.0.0.0/8   ***00001010*** 00000000 00000000 00000000

Before we allocate this space across the organization, let's assume that IPAM Worldwide is planning to roll out voice over IP in the near future and additional IP services later on. Let's take the next four bits of our network address and allocate equal-sized /12 networks. This would provide $2^{(12-8)} = 16$ potential high-level allocations, while providing $2^{(32-12)} > 1$ million IP addresses per allocation. Thus, we'll allocate a /12 each for the infrastructure address space, a /12 for the voice over IP address "subspace," and a /12 for the data subspace. This allocation is illustrated below with the bold italic bits once again representing the network (network + subnet) portion and normally formatted bits representing the host bits.

Private Network	10.0.0.0/8	***00001010*** 00000000 00000000 00000000
Infrastructure	10.0.0.0/12	***00001010 0000***0000 00000000 00000000
Voice	10.16.0.0/12	***00001010 0001***0000 00000000 00000000
Data	10.32.0.0/12	***00001010 0010***0000 00000000 00000000

3.1.2 Second-Level Allocation Logic

This initial application-level allocation reformats our original monolithic /8 address space into three /12 spaces aligned per application. The decision to use /12 at this level is a trade-off between the number of first-level allocations and the number of addresses available per allocation. If we had decided to allocate /11s, we would have ended up with 8 /11s total, each with over 2 million IP addresses. In IPAM Worldwide's case, having more top-level blocks available for future allocation was more of a concern than managing capacity per block, given 1 million IP addresses per /12 application block. If a particular allocation becomes exhausted, we can allocate an additional /12 block.

Block sizing decisions for second and subsequent level allocations should generally employ different logic. Instead of trading off allocation size with the number of equal-sized allocations, an optimal allocation strategy should be used. This optimal strategy entails successively halving the address space down to the size required. The key reason for this approach is that it enables you to retain larger blocks of unallocated address space as available for larger requests and alternative allocations.

If you have ever endured a company merger, you may have encountered a situation like the following that illustrates the optimal allocation motivation. Let's say IPAM Worldwide acquires a company and the network integration strategy requires an allocation of 250,000 IP addresses to the new division. To minimize confusion (and to exude networking mastery over the rival IT organization), IPAM Worldwide desires to allocate a single /14 to support 262,142 addresses.

If we've optimally allocated our address space, we may happen to have a /14 readily available (IP address master!). If we had taken a uniform approach of allocating /16s everywhere, we may be lucky to identify four contiguous /16s that comprise a /14 (lucky amateur!). If we cannot identify four contiguous /16s, we may have to assign four noncontiguous /16s; this adds four times the overhead to routing tables and routing protocol update entries (four /16s versus one /14 – rookie!). With successive halving instead of the uniform single-sized approach, a /14 is more likely to be readily available for assignment. Let's look at how this works.

If we start with our 10.0.0.0/12 infrastructure block and halve it, we end up with two /13 blocks as illustrated below. Thanks to binary arithmetic, note that associating the next "host" bit with the network enables halving of the original network. Note that the 10.0.0.0/12 network no longer exists, so we've grayed it out to illustrate this; it has been split into our two /13 networks.

Original Network	10.0.0.0/12	*00001010 0000*0000 00000000 00000000
First half	10.0.0.0/13	*00001010 00000*000 00000000 00000000
Second half	10.8.0.0/13	*00001010 00001*000 00000000 00000000

Next, let's halve the "first half" above, leaving the 10.8.0.0/13 block available for future allocation or subnetworking for infrastructure applications (or acquisitions!). We extend the network portion of the address now to the 14th bit to halve the 10.0.0.0/13 to yield two /14s as below. Note that as with the 10.0.0.0/12 network, the 10.0.0/13 network no longer exists as an entity and also has been grayed out. It has been split into the two /14s as shown below. However, the 10.8.0.0/13 network is available to the organization for further allocation as needed.

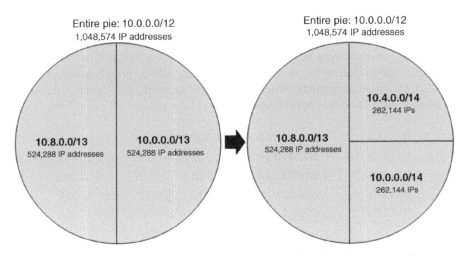

Figure 3.3. Pie chart view of address allocations (Based on [11] and [166]).

Original Network	10.0.0.0/12	**00001010 0000**0000 00000000 00000000
Original first half	10.0.0.0/13	**00001010 00000**000 00000000 00000000
First /14	10.0.0.0/14	**00001010 000000**00 00000000 00000000
Second /14	10.4.0.0/14	**00001010 00000100** 00000000 00000000
Second half	10.8.0.0/13	**00001010 00001**000 00000000 00000000

One way to visualize this halving process from an overall allocation perspective is to view the address space as a pie chart as shown in Figure 3.3. If our entire pie represents the base network, 10.0.0.0/12, then we cut it in half to render two /13s as shown on left of Figure 3.3. We can then leave one of the /13s as "available" (left half) and slice the other /13 (right half) into two /14s as shown in the right half of Figure 3.3.

Continuing to apply this logic down to a /16, we end up with the following:

Original Network	10.0.0.0/12	**00001010 0000**0000 00000000 00000000
First half (/13)	10.0.0.0/13	**00001010 00000**000 00000000 00000000
First /14	10.0.0.0/14	**00001010 000000**00 00000000 00000000
First /15	10.0.0.0/15	**00001010 0000000**0 00000000 00000000
⌐→ **First /16**	10.0.0.0/16	**00001010 00000000** 00000000 00000000
└→ **Second /16**	10.1.0.0/16	**00001010 00000001** 00000000 00000000
Second /15	10.2.0.0/15	**00001010 0000001**0 00000000 00000000
Second /14	10.4.0.0/14	**00001010 00000100** 00000000 00000000
Second half (/13)	10.8.0.0/13	**00001010 00001**000 00000000 00000000

As each "first" block is split, it creates two networks of network mask length of 1 bit longer than the original block. Now that we've performed this split, we have two /16 networks: 10.0.0.0/16 and 10.1.0.0/16 as derived above. We are also left with one /15, one /14, and one /13 shown below our two highlighted /16 blocks. These exist because the "first" set of networks were successively sliced into half, yielding a "first" network that was further subdivided and a "second" network that could be preserved for additional future allocations or assignments. The smallest "first" network, 10.0.0.0/16, is the one we can allocate as it is of the required size.

10.0.0.0/16	**00001010 00000000** 00000000 00000000
10.1.0.0/16	**00001010 00000001** 00000000 00000000
10.2.0.0/15	**00001010 0000001**0 00000000 00000000
10.4.0.0/14	**00001010 000001**00 00000000 00000000
10.8.0.0/13	**00001010 00001**000 00000000 00000000

But IPAM Worldwide requires a third /16. From which block shall we allocate this? In keeping with our recommendation to retain larger blocks, we'll take our next available network of the smallest size. In our case, from the listing above, the 10.2.0.0/15 network is available for further allocation. If we split this /15 into two /16s we have 10.2.0.0/16 and 10.3.0.0/16. We can then assign the former of these two networks as we illustrated earlier and retain the latter network as available for future assignment. The resulting pie chart is illustrated in Figure 3.4, with the allocated space.

Note that we still have many large blocks available for further allocation or assignment. Only the darker shaded wedge of the pie comprising our three /16 networks has been assigned. In relating the successive splits in the table above to the pie chart, while each "first" half block was either assigned or divided into further allocations, it yielded a corresponding "second" half block that is still free or available. Thus, the

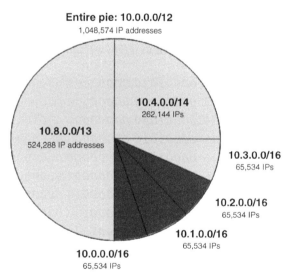

Figure 3.4. Allocation of three /16s from /12 space [Based on (11) and (166)].

resulting address allocations for IPAM Worldwide based on this initial allocation are as follows:

Original infrastructure (IS) block	10.0.0.0/12	*00001010 0000*0000 00000000 00000000
Free IS block	10.8.0.0/13	*00001010 00001*000 00000000 00000000
Free IS block	10.4.0.0/14	*00001010 000001*00 00000000 00000000
N. America IS block	**10.0.0.0/16**	*00001010 00000000* 00000000 00000000
Europe IS block	**10.1.0.0/16**	*00001010 00000001* 00000000 00000000
Asia IS block	**10.2.0.0/16**	*00001010 00000010* 00000000 00000000
Free IS block	10.3.0.0/16	*00001010 00000011* 00000000 00000000

Following similar logic with the data and voice top-level address allocations, 10.16.0.0/12 and 10.32.0.0/12 respectively, we can derive the following allocations:

Original Voice block	10.16.0.0/12	*00001010 0001*0000 00000000 00000000
Free voice block	10.24.0.0/13	*00001010 00011*000 00000000 00000000
Free voice block	10.20.0.0/14	*00001010 000101*00 00000000 00000000
N. America voice block	**10.16.0.0/16**	*00001010 00010000* 00000000 00000000
Europe voice block	**10.17.0.0/16**	*00001010 00010001* 00000000 00000000
Asia voice block	**10.18.0.0/16**	*00001010 00010010* 00000000 00000000
Free voice block	10.19.0.0/16	*00001010 00010011* 00000000 00000000
Original Data block	10.32.0.0/12	*00001010 0010*0000 00000000 00000000
Free data block	10.40.0.0/13	*00001010 00101*000 00000000 00000000
Free data lock	10.36.0.0/14	*00001010 001001*00 00000000 00000000
N. America data block	**10.32.0.0/16**	*00001010 00100000* 00000000 00000000
Europe data block	**10.33.0.0/16**	*00001010 00100001* 00000000 00000000
Asia data block	**10.34.0.0/16**	*00001010 00100010* 00000000 00000000
Free data block	10.35.0.0/16	*00001010 00100011* 00000000 00000000

The only remaining step at this core level is to allocate infrastructure space for the core routers themselves. The core network is after all a network requiring an IP subnet address and it lies "above" our intercontinental allocations. For this subnet, we'll carve out a /26 subnet. This sized subnet provides 62 host addresses, which provides sufficient capacity for growth. Let's allocate this from the smallest free infrastructure block, 10.3.0.0/16. Following similar logic just applied, we allocate the 10.3.0.0/26 network to our core backbone network. We have several free blocks available for future allocation:

Original IS block	10.3.0.0/16	**00001010 00000011** 00000000 00000000
Free IS block	10.3.128.0/17	**00001010 00000011 1**0000000 00000000
Free IS block	10.3.64.0/18	**00001010 00000011 01**000000 00000000
Free IS block	10.3.32.0/19	**00001010 00000011 001**00000 00000000
Free IS block	10.3.16.0/20	**00001010 00000011 0001**0000 00000000
Free IS block	10.3.8.0/21	**00001010 00000011 00001**000 00000000
Free IS block	10.3.4.0/22	**00001010 00000011 000001**00 00000000
Free IS block	10.3.2.0/23	**00001010 00000011 0000001**0 00000000
Free IS block	10.3.1.0/24	**00001010 00000011 00000001** 00000000
Free IS block	10.3.0.128/25	**00001010 00000011 00000000 1**0000000
Free IS block	10.3.0.64/26	**00001010 00000011 00000000 01**000000
Core Net IS block	**10.3.0.0/26**	**00001010 00000011 00000000 00**000000

3.1.3 Address Allocation Part 3

Now that we've allocated address space at the top level by application then at the core network level, each of these allocations can be subdivided further to serve requisite distribution center and branch office needs. In essence, these allocations serve as the block or pool of addresses that may be distributed for the given application within the respective region. This technique of top-down allocation ensures subsequent allocations from these initial allocations will roll-up hierarchically. Thus, our core routers can simply advertise their /16 allocations to the other core routers. Also, any special per service packet handling treatment can also be easily configured. For example, if we'd like to handle voice packets with highest priority treatment, we can configure our routers to provide such treatment for packets with source address from the respective voice space, such as 10.17.0.0/16 for Europe voice traffic (or 10.16.0.0/12 for all voice traffic). From this initial definition, further allocations can now be made further down geographical lines without affecting this treatment logic.

Let's drill into our North American data space, 10.32.0.0/16. From our location table presented earlier in Figure 3.1, we see that North American sites are organized in three regions: east, central, and west. We'd also like to allocate independent space for headquarters. Assuming our routing topology aligns with this geographical organization, we will allocate address space accordingly. Thus, a WAN may interconnect North American regional sites of Philadelphia, Kansas City, and San Francisco with head-quarters. This regional interconnection represents a "subcore" network, and similar allocation logic can be applied as was at the top level.

Let's carve up our 10.32.0.0/16 block into four regional blocks. To allocate equally, we need to divide this space into four blocks. So we need to allocate the next 2 bits ($2^2 = 4$) in the North America data space, highlighted as larger font bold italic bits in the binary representation below.

N. America data	10.32.0.0/16	***00001010 00010000*** 00000000 00000000
N. America HQ data	10.32.0.0/18	***00001010 00010010 00***000000 00000000
N. America East data	10.32.64.0/18	***00001010 00010010 01***000000 00000000
N. America West data	10.32.128.0/18	***00001010 00010010 10***000000 00000000
N. America Central data	10.32.192.0/18	***00001010 00010010 11***000000 00000000

We don't necessarily have to allocate along powers of 2 as we're showing, though this results in equal-sized allocations. We could just as easily have allocated a larger portion to the east, since it contains the most sites: 10.32.0.0/17 (East), 10.32.160.0.0/19 (Central), 10.32.192.0/19 (West), and 10.32.220.0/19 (HQ).

From this point, we can allocate from each region's space to its respective sites for addressing needs. Considering the North America West data space, 10.32.128.0/18, we can now allocate space for data applications in each of our distribution centers and branch offices. The simplest strategy for such allocation is one of *uniform* distribution, for example, each site is allocated the same sized block as we performed at the top allocation level. However, one needs to consider the number of users and data devices per site, projected growth at each site, planned new sites within the region, and application networking requirements. In the case of IPAM Worldwide, distribution centers typically house 65 employees with additional automation machinery and infrastructure requiring IP addresses totaling around 200–250. Branch offices require only about 150–200 IP devices, including associate laptops, PDAs, and other data devices serving an average employee population of 40.

In such a scenario, it makes sense to allocate at least a /23 for distribution centers, providing 510 usable IP addresses, and /24 for branch offices, providing 254 IP addresses. However, each site should be analyzed individually regarding its respective addressing requirements. In our case, we'll first allocate a /23 per distribution center and then a /24 per branch office. The following table illustrates this allocation, along with the remaining free space from the original 10.32.128.0/18 network available for future allocation.

N. America West data	10.32.128.0/18	***00001010 00100000 10***000000 00000000
San Francisco site	10.32.128.0/23	***00001010 00100000 1000000***0 00000000
Denver site	10.32.130.0/23	***00001010 00100000 1000001***0 00000000

Vancouver site	10.32.132.0/23	*00001010 00100000 10000100* 00000000
Phoenix site	10.32.134.0/23	*00001010 00100000 10000110* 00000000
Calgary site	10.32.136.0/24	*00001010 00100000 10001000* 00000000
Albuquerque site	10.32.137.0/24	*00001010 00100000 10001001* 00000000
Salt Lake City site	10.32.138.0/24	*00001010 00100000 10001010* 00000000
Boulder site	10.32.139.0/24	*00001010 00100000 10001011* 00000000
Edmonton site	10.32.140.0/24	*00001010 00100000 10001100* 00000000
Sacramento site	10.32.141.0/24	*00001010 00100000 10001101* 00000000
Anaheim site	10.32.142.0/24	*00001010 00100000 10001110* 00000000
Free space	10.32.143.0/24	*00001010 00100000 10001111* 00000000
Free space	10.32.144.0/20	*00001010 00100000 1001*0000 00000000
Free space	10.32.160.0/19	*00001010 00100000 101*00000 00000000

For our headquarters location, we'll allocate /22 networks for each of the major corporate divisions. These allocations may further be subnetted based on networking deployments.

3.1.4 Allocation Trade-Offs and Tracking

As you add layers in the address allocation hierarchy, the network portion of the address grows, shrinking the number of host bits assignable to IP devices. Each of the sites listed in the previous table has either 8 or 9 host bits available providing capacity for 254 or 510 individual IP hosts per site, respectively. Hierarchical layers enable mapping of address space to applications, regions, and ultimately, subnets, and help retain address summarization corresponding to router topology and deployments. It's a good idea to consider how much IP address capacity is needed at each site and trade this off with how many hierarchy layers are desired.

Individual IP address capacity requirements per subnet will help you derive the endpoint allocation size. Many organizations plan for allocating 254 hosts in a /24 allocation per end subnet. Multiple subnets could be allocated if needed. Using this octet boundary helps simplify translation from binary to decimal as you can see in the summary above, but it may not be feasible for your organization due to address capacity requirements. If you're required to allocate outside octet boundaries, use of an IP address management tool can probably help ensure accuracy of allocations without overlaps while conserving address hierarchy.

Whether you decide to use an IP management system or not, you must track address allocations. To illustrate one simple tracking method, we've recast our spreadsheet presented at the beginning of this chapter listing IPAM Worldwide's network locations to reflect respective block allocations. In the updated version shown below in Figure 3.5, we've listed distribution centers and branch offices together under a common Sites column, with distribution centers listed first in a lightly shaded font.

Our top-level hierarchical blocks that comprise the address supply at each hierarchy level are shown highlighted for each region to differentiate them from subnets. We followed a common allocation approach to keep things simple, allocating a /23 for each distribution center and a /24 for each branch office. We're only illustrating a small subset of the spreadsheet, but the same methodology is used for Europe and Asia sites and for voice and data applications.

A convenient side effect of this form of allocation yields the ability to easily associate an address with a location. For example, knowing that 10.0.79.0/24 is the infrastructure subnet for Albany, one could deduce that 10.16.79.0/24 is the VoIP subnet and 10.32.79.0/24 is the data subnet for Albany. This octet pattern of 10.X.Y.0 networks maps the application (octet X) and the location (octet Y) by sight. In our example, octet X is 0 for infrastructure, 16 for VoIP, and 32 for data. Octet Y is 79 for Albany in this example.

Region	Regional Site	Sites	Infrastructure Nets	VoIP Nets	Data Nets
HQ—Corp.	Phila.		**10.0.0.0/12**	**10.16.0.0/12**	**10.32.0.0/12**
HQ—N. Amer.	Phila.		**10.0.0.0/16**	**10.16.0.0/16**	**10.32.0.0/16**
		Core Net	10.3.0.0/26		
		Phila.—Exec	10.0.0.0/22	10.16.0.0/22	10.32.0.0/22
		Phila.—Fin.	10.0.4.0/22	10.16.4.0/22	10.32.4.0/22
		Phila.—Ops	10.0.8.0/22	10.16.8.0/22	10.32.8.0/22
		Phila.—Tech	10.0.12.0/22	10.16.12.0/22	10.32.12.0/22
		Phila.—Mktg	10.0.16.0/22	10.16.16.0/22	10.32.16.0/22
		Phila.—R&D	10.0.20.0/22	10.16.20.0/22	10.32.20.0/22
N. Amer—East	Norris—town		**10.0.64.0/18**	**10.16.64.0/18**	**10.32.64.0/18**
		Norristown	10.0.64.0/23	10.16.64.0/23	10.32.64.0/23

Figure 3.5. IPAM Worldwide's IPv4 block allocations (partial).

Region	Regional Site	Sites	Infrastructure Nets	VoIP Nets	Data Nets
		Toronto	10.0.66.0/23	10.16.66.0/23	10.32.66.0/23
		Nashua	10.0.68.0/23	10.16.68.0/23	10.32.68.0/23
		Newark	10.0.70.0/23	10.16.70.0/23	10.32.70.0/23
		Baltimore	10.0.72.0/23	10.16.72.0/23	10.32.72.0/23
		Pittsburgh	10.0.74.0/23	10.16.74.0/23	10.32.74.0/23
		Charlotte	10.0.76.0/23	10.16.76.0/23	10.32.76.0/23
		Atlanta	10.0.77.0/24	10.16.77.0/24	10.32.77.0/24
		Providence	10.0.78.0/24	10.16.78.0/24	10.32.78.0/24
		Quincy	10.0.79.0/24	10.16.79.0/24	10.32.79.0/24
		Albany	10.0.80.0/24	10.16.80.0/24	10.32.80.0/24
		Manhattan	10.0.81.0/24	10.16.81.0/24	10.32.81.0/24
		Ocean City	10.0.82.0/24	10.16.82.0/24	10.32.82.0/24
		Reston	10.0.83.0/24	10.16.83.0/24	10.32.83.0/24
		Richmond	10.0.84.0/24	10.16.84.0/24	10.32.84.0/24
		Charleston	10.0.85.0/24	10.16.85.0/24	10.32.85.0/24
		Montgomery	10.0.86.0/24	10.16.86.0/24	10.32.86.0/24
N. Amer.— Central	Kansas City		**10.0.192.0/18**	**10.16.192.0/18**	**10.32.192.0/18**
		Kansas City	10.0.192.0/23	10.16.192.0/23	10.32.192.0/23
		Chicago	10.0.194.0/23	10.16.194.0/23	10.32.194.0/23
		Des Moines	10.0.196.0/23	10.16.196.0/23	10.32.196.0/23
		Memphis	10.0.198.0/23	10.16.198.0/23	10.32.198.0/23
		New Orleans	10.0.200.0/23	10.16.200.0/23	10.32.200.0/23
		. . .	. . .	. . .	. . .

Figure 3.5. (Continued).

3.1.5 IPAM Worldwide's Public Address Space

Now let's look at IPAM Worldwide's public address space, 192.0.2.0/24, obtained from our ISP. We'll discuss the process ISPs use to get IP address space later in this chapter. IPAM Worldwide has an Internet connection to their chosen ISP from the Philadelphia headquarters office. While two diverse-routed local loops provide a level of access redundancy, future plans call for supporting a multihomed connection from another location, which we'll also discuss a bit later. For the time being, the 254 public IP addresses available within the /24 will be used to address Internet (externally) reachable hosts such as web and email servers, and a shared address pool to enable internal clients to access the Internet. A pair of NAT devices have been installed to enable load sharing and address translation for access by internal clients to the Internet. In reality, this /24 will likely need to be subnetted to partition Internet-reachable hosts from NAT addresses.

3.2 IPv6 ADDRESS ALLOCATION[*]

Though IPv6 addresses are represented differently than IPv4 addresses, the allocation process works essentially the same way. The main difference is in converting hexadecimal to binary and back instead of decimal to binary and back. The process of optimal assignment of the smallest available free block described above for IPv4 is an example of the best-fit allocation algorithm. Due to the vast difference in available address space, IPv6 supports not only an analogous best-fit algorithm but also a sparse allocation method. We'll also discuss a random allocation method that can be used in lieu of simple subnet numbering starting from 1 and counting up.

We'll outline each of these algorithms in this section, using the example IPv6 network 2001:DB8::/32. Note that /32 (or any)-sized global unicast allocations require prequalification with a Regional Internet Registry (RIR) as we'll discuss later in this chapter, and it's unlikely that an organization of the scale of IPAM Worldwide would receive such an allocation. However, we'll initially use this in our example to keep the number of bits from running off the page! Later we'll use a more practical /48 example allocation. The algorithm will be equivalent whether starting with a /32 or a /48, there'll just be more intermediate 0 prefix bits with the /48 network.

3.2.1 Best-Fit Allocation

Using a best-fit approach, we'll follow the same basic bit-wise allocation algorithm we used for IPv4 described earlier. After converting the hexadecimal to binary, the process is identical in terms of successive halving by seizing the next bit for the network portion of the address. For example, consider our example network 2001:0DB8::/32 below.

0010 0000 0000 0001 0000 1101 1011 1000 0000 0000 0000 0000 0000...

---

[*] This discussion of IPv6 allocations is based on Ref. 172.

Let's say we'd like to allocate three /40 networks from this space. In following the analogous IPv4 allocation example from a binary perspective, by successively halving the address space down to a /40 size shown by the larger bold italic bits below, you should arrive at the following:

*0010 0000 0000 0001 0000 1101 1011 1000 1*000 0000 0000 0000 0000...
*0010 0000 0000 0001 0000 1101 1011 1000 01*00 0000 0000 0000 0000...
*0010 0000 0000 0001 0000 1101 1011 1000 001*0 0000 0000 0000 0000...
*0010 0000 0000 0001 0000 1101 1011 1000 0001*0000 0000 0000 0000...
*0010 0000 0000 0001 0000 1101 1011 1000 00001*000 0000 0000 0000...
*0010 0000 0000 0001 0000 1101 1011 1000 000001*00 0000 0000 0000...
*0010 0000 0000 0001 0000 1101 1011 1000 0000001*0 0000 0000 0000...
*0010 0000 0000 0001 0000 1101 1011 1000 00000001*000 0000 0000...
*0010 0000 0000 0001 0000 1101 1011 1000 0000000*0 0000 0000 0000...

Here we readily have two /40 networks available (highlighted above), and translating these back into hex we have 2001:0DB8:0100::/40 and 2001:0DB8:0000::/40 (i.e., 2001: DB8::/40). After this allocation, to allocate a third /40 using the best-fit approach, we can then take the next smallest available network, in this case a /39, and split it into two /40s:

0010 0000 0000 0001 0000 1101 1011 1000 0000 0010 0000 0000 0000
0010 0000 0000 0001 0000 1101 1011 1000 0000 0011 0000 0000 0000

We split this into half by taking the next bit, yielding two /40s. We can choose one to allocate and the other will be free for future assignment. So our three /40s for allocation are 2001:DB8::/40, 2001:DB8:0100::/40, and 2001:DB8:0200::/40. The other /40, that is, 2001:DB8:0300/40, is available for future assignment. Figure 3.6 illustrates this successive halving in a pie chart form.

After allocating these three /40 networks, highlighted in Figure 3.6, the remainder of the pie is available for allocation. These available networks appear as the top six in the successive halving list above, plus the unallocated half of the former 2001:DB8:200::/39 network.

3.2.2 Sparse Allocation Method

You'll notice from the prior algorithm that by allocating a /40 from a /32, we incrementally extend the network length to the 40th bit as we did with IPv4 allocation. We then assign the network by assigning a 0 or 1 to the 40th bit as our first two /40 networks. In essence, we process each bit along the way, considering "1" the free block and "0" the allocated block. However, if we step back and consider the eight subnet ID bits that extend the /32 to a /40 as a whole, instead of incrementally halving the network, we observe that we've actually allocated our subnets by simply numbering or counting within the subnet ID field as denoted by the highlighted bold italic bits in this table:

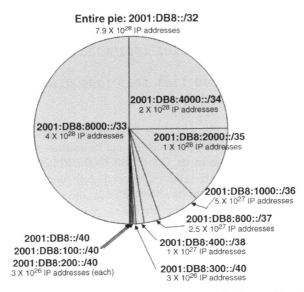

Figure 3.6. Allocation results from carving three /40 networks from a /32 network [Based on (11) and (166)].

0010 0000 0000 0001 0000 1101 1011 1000 **0000 0000** 0000 0000
0000... 2001:DB8::/40
0010 0000 0000 0001 0000 1101 1011 1000 **0000 0001** 0000 0000
0000... 2001:DB8:100::/40
0010 0000 0000 0001 0000 1101 1011 1000 **0000 0010** 0000 0000
0000... 2001:DB8:200::/40

Thus, if you knew in advance that the original /32 network would be carved uniformly into only /40-sized blocks, a simpler allocation method would be to simply increment the subnet ID bits. The next allocation of /40s would use subnet ID values of 00000011, 00000100, 00000101, and so on. In some networks, this uniformity policy of allocating /40 blocks may not apply, so the method of successive halving may be more appropriate.

On the other hand, if you are a Local Internet Registry (LIR) or ISP, a sparse allocation method may be attractive. The sparse allocation method seeks to spread out allocations to provide room for growth by allocating with the maximum space *between* allocations. The sparse algorithm also features halving of the available address space, but instead of continuing this process down to the smallest size, it calls for allocating the next block on the edge of the new half. This results in allocations being spread out and not optimally allocated. Again, the philosophy is that this provides room for growth of allocated networks by leaving ample space between allocations in the plentiful IPv6 space. Considering an example, our allocation of three /40s from our 2001: DB8::/32 space would look like as below:

0010 0000 0000 0001 0000 1101 1011 1000 `0000 0000` 0000 0000
0000... 2001:DB8::/40
0010 0000 0000 0001 0000 1101 1011 1000 `1000 0000` 0000 0000
0000... 2001:DB8:800::/40
0010 0000 0000 0001 0000 1101 1011 1000 `0100 0000` 0000 0000
0000... 2001:DB8:4000::/40

These translate as 2001:DB8::/40, 2001:DB8:8000::/40, and 2001:DB8:4000::/40 respectively. This allocation enables spreading out of address space as illustrated in Figure 3.7. Should the recipient of the 2001:DB8:8000::/40 network require an additional allocation, we could allocate a contiguous or adjacent block, 2001:DB8:8100::/40. This block will be among the last to be allocated under the sparse method, so there's a good chance it will be available. In such a case, the recipient of our two contiguous blocks could identify (and advertise) their address space as 2001:DB8:8000::/39. Note that our subnet ID bits are effectively counted from left to right, instead of the conventional right-to-left method used for "normal" counting.

RFC 3531 (22) describes the sparse allocation methodology. Because network allocations are expected to follow a multilayered allocation hierarchy, several sets of successive network bits can be used by different entities for successive allocation. For example, an Internet Registry may allocate the first macro block to a Regional Registry, who in turn will allocate from that space to a service provider, who may in turn allocate from that subspace to customers, who can further allocate across their networks. RFC 3531 recommends the higher level allocations, for example, from the registries, utilize the leftmost counting or sparse allocation, the lowest level allocations use the rightmost or best-fit allocation, and others in the middle use either, or even a centermost allocation scheme. For an organization like IPAM Worldwide, we can use the sparse

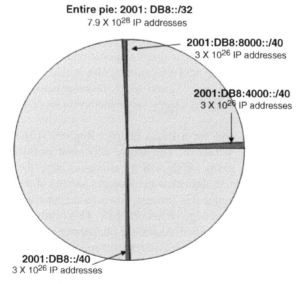

Figure 3.7. Sparse allocation example (Based on [11] and [166]).

method to allocate our intercontinental networks, leaving room for future growth at the top level. Note that while RFC 3531 addresses IPv6 allocation, we could also have allocated IPAM Worldwide's top-level IPv4 space in this manner to spread out initial allocations as 10.0.0.0/12 for infrastructure, 10.128.0.0/12 for VoIP, and 10.64.0.0/12 for data.

3.2.3 Random Allocation

The random allocation method selects a random number within the sizing of the subnetwork bits to allocate subnetworks. Using our /40 allocations from a /32, a random number would be generated between 0 and $2^8 - 1$ or 255 and allocated assuming it's still available. This method provides a means for randomly spreading allocations across allocated entities and generally works best for "same size" allocations. Randomization provides a level of "privacy" in not ordering blocks and subnets consecutively starting with "1." Be aware that random allocation may render the identification of larger contiguous blocks per our earlier merger example as well as the freeing up contiguous space for renumbering purposes more difficult. So while it makes sense to allocate sparsely at the top layer of allocation, the random or best-fit methods are more appropriate at the subnet allocation level.

3.2.4 Unique Local Address Space

While IPv6 does not have designated "private" address space, the concept of unique local address (ULA) space is essentially equivalent. By using the FC00::/7 prefix, setting the L bit to "1" (i.e., FD00::/8) indicating local assignment and assigning a random 40-bit Global ID, IPAM Worldwide can contrive a /48 network for internal use. There is some discussion among the Internet community over possibly enabling Regional Internet Registries, the organizations responsible for allocating public IP address space as we'll see next, to allocate globally unique 40-bit Global IDs. Regardless of global uniqueness, ULA destination addressed packets should not be routed outside an organization. Enforcement of this however is generally up to each organization to prohibit such packets from crossing beyond its external border routers.

3.3 IPAM WORLDWIDE'S IPv6 ALLOCATIONS

While we used a /32 for the sake of illustration when describing allocation, let's use a more realistic /48-sized block for the IPAM Worldwide example: 2001:DB8:4AF0::/48. And although IPAM Worldwide has plentiful public IPv6 space, for the sake of example, let's choose a ULA network for allocation as well: FD01:273E:90A::/48. These address blocks will be allocated hierarchically in accordance with IPAM Worldwide's geographic structure. We'll also allocate these networks using common subnet ID numbers for each location as in our earlier 10.X.Y.0 example, for pattern consistency and easier visual correlation.

In IPAM Worldwide's case, let's use sparse allocation at the core network layer. From this allocation, we can further sparsely allocate to our regions and then use a best-fit approach for our distribution centers and branch offices. While we're only running data applications over IPv6 for the time being, we should still perform an application-level allocation for application expansion or growth.

For simplicity, we will allocate on 4-bit boundaries.[*] If we use our first 4 subnet bits (bits 49–52), we have 16 possible allocations. Since we have one application as yet, we'll simply allocate four networks to represent our core networks for the "data" application. Using the sparse method, we arrive at the following allocations:

Core Allocation	Bits 49–52	Public Space Allocation	ULA Allocation
Headquarters	**0 0 0 0**	2001:DB8:4AF0::/52	FD01:273E:90A::/52
N. America	**1 0 0 0**	2001:DB8:4AF0:8000::/52	FD01:273E:90A:8000::/52
Europe	**0 1 0 0**	2001:DB8:4AF0:4000::/52	FD01:273E:90A:4000::/52
Asia	**1 1 0 0**	2001:DB8:4AF0:C000::/52	FD01:273E:90A:C000::/52

Applying a similar approach, using bits 53–56 for our next level allocations, we arrive at the following suballocations:

Subcore Allocation	Bits 53–56	Public Space Allocation	ULA Allocation
N. America—East	**0 0 0 0**	2001:DB8:4AF0:8000::/56	FD01:273E:90A::/56
N. America—Central	**1 0 0 0**	2001:DB8:4AF0:8800::/56	FD01:273E:90A:8800::/56
N. America—West	**0 1 0 0**	2001:DB8:4AF0:8400::/56	FD01:273E:90A:8400::/56
Europe—West	**0 0 0 0**	2001:DB8:4AF0:4000::/56	FD01:273E:90A:4000::/56
Europe—South	**1 0 0 0**	2001:DB8:4AF0:4800::/56	FD01:273E:90A:4800::/56
Europe—East	**0 1 0 0**	2001:DB8:4AF0:4400::/56	FD01:273E:90A:4400::/56

Within each of these /56 allocations, we can further allocate individual /64 subnet addresses for each distribution center and branch office. We'll perform this allocation using a best-fit approach and summarize a subset of our allocations in our expanded address allocation spreadsheet. IPv6 subnets in general should be allocated with /64 network prefixes. Many IPv6 features such as neighbor discovery assume (rely on) this prefix size.

For router point-to-point or back-to-back links, you may assign a /126 subnet, analogous to a /30 in IPv4 providing two host addresses. However, be aware of the setting of the "u" (universal/local, 71st bit) and "g" (individual/group, 72nd bit) bits within the interface identifier field of the IPv6 address. Setting these bits incorrectly may affect applications that access or utilize them. The "u" bit indicates that the company ID was assigned by the IEEE (1) or locally (0), and the "g" bit indicates that the address is a unicast (0) or a multicast (1). The /127 address should not be used. The /128 prefix denotes a single IP address, analogous to /32 in IPv4.

Let's add these IPv6 allocations to IPAM Worldwide's IP address spreadsheet that follows.

---

[*] We'll discuss the implications of allocating on non-4-bit boundaries, particularly on DNS, in Chapter 9.

Core Sites	Region	Regional Site	Sites	Infra. Nets	VoIP Nets	Data Nets	Public IPv6	IPv6 ULA
Philadelphia	HQ—Corp.	Philadelphia		**10.0.0.0/12**	**10.16.0.0/12**	**10.32.0.0/12**	**2001:DB8:4AF0::/52**	**FD01:273E:90A::/52**
Philadelphia	HQ—N. America	Philadelphia		**10.0.0.0/16**	**10.16.0.0/16**	**10.32.0.0/16**	**2001:DB8:4AF0::/56**	**FD01:273E:90A:8000::/52**
			Backbone Net	10.3.0.0/26			2001:DB8:4AF0:800::/64	FD01:273E:90A:800::/64
			Philadelphia—Exec	10.0.0.0/22	10.16.0.0/22	10.32.0.0/22	2001:DB8:4AF0::/64	FD01:273E:90A::/64
			Philadelphia—Finan	10.0.4.0/22	10.16.4.0/22	10.32.4.0/22	2001:DB8:4AF0:1::/64	FD01:273E:90A:1::/64
			Philadelphia—Ops	10.0.8.0/22	10.16.8.0/22	10.32.8.0/22	2001:DB8:4AF0:2::/64	FD01:273E:90A:2::/64
			Philadelphia—Tech	10.0.12.0/22	10.16.12.0/22	10.32.12.0/22	2001:DB8:4AF0:3::/64	FD01:273E:90A:3::/64
			Philadelphia—Mktg	10.0.16.0/22	10.16.16.0/22	10.32.16.0/22	2001:DB8:4AF0:4::/64	FD01:273E:90A:4::/64
			Philadelphia—R&D	10.0.20.0/22	10.16.20.0/22	10.32.20.0/22	2001:DB8:4AF0:5::/64	FD01:273E:90A:5::/64
	N. America— East	Norristown		**10.0.64.0/18**	**10.16.64.0/18**	**10.32.64.0/18**	**2001:DB8:4AF0:8000::/56**	**FD01:273E:90A:8000::/56**
			Norristown	10.0.64.0/23	10.16.64.0/23	10.32.64.0/23	2001:DB8:4AF0:8000::/64	FD01:273E:90A:8000::/64
			Toronto	10.0.66.0/23	10.16.66.0/23	10.32.66.0/23	2001:DB8:4AF0:8001::/64	FD01:273E:90A:8001::/64
			Nashua	10.0.68.0/23	10.16.68.0/23	10.32.68.0/23	2001:DB8:4AF0:8002::/64	FD01:273E:90A:8002::/64
			Newark	10.0.70.0/23	10.16.70.0/23	10.32.70.0/23	2001:DB8:4AF0:8003::/64	FD01:273E:90A:8003::/64
			Baltimore	10.0.72.0/23	10.16.72.0/23	10.32.72.0/23	2001:DB8:4AF0:8004::/64	FD01:273E:90A:8004::/64

(*continued*)

Core Sites	Region	Regional Site	Sites	Infra. Nets	VoIP Nets	Data Nets	Public IPv6	IPv6 ULA
			Pittsburgh	10.0.74.0/23	10.16.74.0/23	10.32.74.0/23	2001:DB8:4AF0:8005::/64	FD01:273E:90A:8005::/64
			Charlotte	10.0.76.0/23	10.16.76.0/23	10.32.76.0/23	2001:DB8:4AF0:8006::/64	FD01:273E:90A:8006::/64
			Atlanta	10.0.77.0/24	10.16.77.0/24	10.32.77.0/24	2001:DB8:4AF0:8007::/64	FD01:273E:90A:8007::/64
			Providence	10.0.78.0/24	10.16.78.0/24	10.32.78.0/24	2001:DB8:4AF0:8008::/64	FD01:273E:90A:8008::/64
			Quincy	10.0.79.0/24	10.16.79.0/24	10.32.79.0/24	2001:DB8:4AF0:8009::/64	FD01:273E:90A:8009::/64
			Albany	10.0.80.0/24	10.16.80.0/24	10.32.80.0/24	2001:DB8:4AF0:800A::/64	FD01:273E:90A:800A::/64
			Manhattan	10.0.81.0/24	10.16.81.0/24	10.32.81.0/24	2001:DB8:4AF0:800B::/64	FD01:273E:90A:800B::/64
			Ocean City	10.0.82.0/24	10.16.82.0/24	10.32.82.0/24	2001:DB8:4AF0:800C::/64	FD01:273E:90A:800C::/64
			Reston	10.0.83.0/24	10.16.83.0/24	10.32.83.0/24	2001:DB8:4AF0:800D::/64	FD01:273E:90A:800D::/64
			Richmond	10.0.84.0/24	10.16.84.0/24	10.32.84.0/24	2001:DB8:4AF0:800E::/64	FD01:273E:90A:800E::/64
			Charleston	10.0.85.0/24	10.16.85.0/24	10.32.85.0/24	2001:DB8:4AF0:800F::/64	FD01:273E:90A:800F::/64
			Montgomery	10.0.86.0/24	10.16.86.0/24	10.32.86.0/24	2001:DB8:4AF0:8010::/64	FD01:273E:90A:8010::/64
N. America— KC Central				**10.0.192.0/18**	**10.16.192.0/18**	**10.32.192.0/18**	**2001:DB8:4AF0:8800::/56**	**FD01:273E:90A:8800::/56**
			Kansas City	10.0.192.0/23	10.16.192.0/23	10.32.192.0/23	2001:DB8:4AF0:8800::/64	FD01:273E:90A:8800::/64
			Chicago	10.0.194.0/23	10.16.194.0/23	10.32.194.0/23	2001:DB8:4AF0:8800::/64	FD01:273E:90A:8800::/64
			Des Moines	10.0.196.0/23	10.16.196.0/23	10.32.196.0/23	2001:DB8:4AF0:8801::/64	FD01:273E:90A:8801::/64
			Memphis	10.0.198.0/23	10.16.198.0/23	10.32.198.0/23	2001:DB8:4AF0:8802::/64	FD01:273E:90A:8802::/64
			New Orleans	10.0.200.0/23	10.16.200.0/23	10.32.200.0/23	2001:DB8:4AF0:8803::/64	FD01:273E:90A:8803::/64

We're going to need longer pages if this keeps up! As we noted with the IPv4 allocations where Pittsburgh, for example, uses "site number" 73 (third octet), we can identify its IPv6 site number as 8005, the fourth colon segment. We'll make one more allocation from our public IPv6 space for our externally (Internet) accessible servers, such as DNS, web, file transfer, and email servers. Our IPv4 space was allocated using two different address spaces: private space for internal allocations and public space for external. For IPv6, we've allocated public space and ULA space internally, and we need to add an allocation for external accessibility. Let's allocate the 2001:DB8:4AF0:2000::/56 network for assignment to external hosts.

Now we have completed our initial allocation planning for IPAM Worldwide and we have recorded each allocation in our spreadsheet. Let's take a step back and discuss how public IP address space is managed and allocated to ISPs and then describe multihoming (use of multiple ISPs) in more detail.

3.4 INTERNET REGISTRIES

IP addresses must be unique on a given network for proper routing and communication.[*] How is this uniqueness ensured across the global Internet? The Internet Assigned Numbers Authority (IANA) is responsible for global allocation of IP address space for both IPv4 and IPv6, as well as other parameters used within the TCP/IP protocol, such as application port numbers. In fact, you can view these top-level allocations by browsing to www.iana.org and selecting "Internet Protocol v4 Address Space" or "IPv6 Address Space" under Number Resources (23).

IANA is, in essence, the top-level Address Registry and it allocates address space to Regional Internet Registries (RIRs). The RIRs, listed below, are organizations responsible for allocation of address space within their respective global regions from their corresponding space allotments from IANA.

- AfriNIC (African Network Information Centre)—Africa region
- APNIC (Asia Pacific Network Information Centre)—Asia/Pacific region
- ARIN (American Registry for Internet Numbers)—North America region, including Puerto Rico and some Caribbean Islands
- LACNIC (Latin American and Caribbean Internet Addresses Registry)—Latin America and some Caribbean Islands
- RIPE NCC (Réseaux IP Européens)—Europe, the Middle East, and Central Asia

The goals of the RIR system are as follows:

- *Uniqueness.* Each IP address must be unique worldwide for global Internet routing.

---
[*] As with every seemingly authoritative statement, there are exceptions! Anycast addresses are typically assigned to multiple hosts, and multicast addresses likewise are shared. This statement applies to unicast addresses.

- *Aggregation*. Hierarchical allocation of address space ensures proper routing of IP traffic on the Internet. Without aggregation, routing tables become fragmented that could ultimately create tremendous bottlenecks within the Internet.
- *Conservation*. Not only for IPv4 but also for IPv6 space, address space needs to be distributed according to actual usage requirements.
- *Registration*. A publicly accessible registry of IP address assignments eliminates ambiguity and can help when troubleshooting. This registry is called the *whois* database. Today, there are many whois databases, operated not only by RIRs but also by LIRs/ISPs for their respective address spaces.
- *Fairness*. Unbiased address allocation based on true address needs and not long-term "plans."

As you can probably guess, the allocation methods we've discussed in this chapter are similar to those employed to allocate address blocks to RIRs, and by RIRs to allocate to National or Local Internet Registries, and in turn to service providers and end users. Allocation guidelines for RIRs are documented in RFC 2050 (24). The general address allocation hierarchy is depicted in Figure 3.8. National Internet Registries are akin to Local Internet Registries, but are organized at a national level.

Back in the 1980s and early 1990s, many corporations (end users per Figure 3.8) obtained address space directly from a centralized Internet Network Information Center (NIC). However, the RIR and LIR/ISP layers were inserted during the transition to CIDR addressing to provide further delegation of address allocation responsibility. Today, most organizations obtain address space from LIRs or ISPs. The process for obtaining such address space is generally dictated by the LIR/ISP with whom you conduct business, though RIRs recommend use of consistent policies to maximize efficiency.

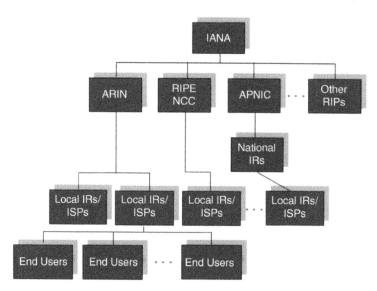

Figure 3.8. IP address allocation from the top-down (24).

As space is allocated to an ISP, the ISP may then advertise the address space on the Internet. Thus, this insertion of the LIR/ISP layer helps aggregate route advertisements on the Internet. Multiple customers served by the ISP can be summarized in one route on the Internet. If business is good and the LIR/ISP requires more address space, the LIR/ISP can request additional space from their RIR. Each RIR generally has its own defined process for fulfilling address requests, so you should consult the RIR in your region for details.

3.4.1 RIR address allocation

From an RIR perspective, RIRs *allocate* space to LIRs/ISPs, and LIRs/ISPs *assign* address space to their customers. The term *allocate* technically refers to the provision of an IP address block to serve as a "pool" of address space that can be drawn from for *assignment* to customers. Customers like IPAM Worldwide can then use the assigned address space, allocating blocks and subnets from it, and then assigning IP addresses from allocated subnets to individual hosts. The mechanics of this allocation and assignment are based on the procedures we described earlier in this chapter regarding the IPAM Worldwide hierarchical allocation examples. However, RIRs differentiate allocations from assignments because assignments comprise addresses in use, while allocations are pools for assignment that begin as unused but in theory grow in usage with a number of assignments from the allocation over time. Technically, RIRs count both allocations and assignments as in-use, but leave open the ability to audit allocated space for actual address utilization as needed to process additional allocation requests from each LIR/ISP.

To obtain address space in the first place, the LIR/ISP must demonstrate the need for utilization of 25% of the allocation immediately and 50% within 1 year[*]. This requirement applies to obtaining IPv4 space; it's a bit easier to obtain IPv6 space today. Requests for additional address space require justification via demonstration of utilization of the LIR/ISP's current allocations. In order to keep track of LIR/ISP allocations, the RIRs have each implemented electronic update mechanisms. As the LIR/ISP assigns address space, the assignment information can be communicated to the RIR using the corresponding form of electronic update. Theoretically, by the time additional address space is requested, the RIR and LIR/ISP have common allocation information against which the utilization threshold can be confirmed and approved. All RIRs allow emailing of information in specific template formats to convey allocation information. ARIN refers to this process as the Shared Whois Process or SWIP. Email templates vary by RIR and do occasionally change, so it's best to contact the RIR serving your geographic region to obtain the latest version of the template you require.

To control allocation of diminishing IPv4 address space, RIRs employ a *slow-start* allocation scheme to enable LIR/ISPs to start with a small address allocation and obtain larger allocations as their allocation performance dictates. In some instances, the LIR/ISP must obtain approval from the RIR prior to allocating from its space to an end user. RIPE, APNIC, and LACNIC RIRs utilize a construct called the *assignment window*

---

[*]Note that with rapidly diminishing availability of IPv4 space, allocation policies are rapidly evolving and tightening. Please contact your RIR for the latest allocation policies.

(AW) to control the block size allocations requiring RIR approval; AfriNIC uses a similar construct called a suballocation window (SAW). ARIN utilizes a standard /20 as its effective AW. The AW or SAW, expressed in CIDR notation, enforces boundaries constraining the maximum size of block allocations made by LIR/ISPs from their address space without approval from the corresponding RIR.

While APNIC and LACNIC enforce the AW (and AfriNIC's SAW) as the maximum allocation size without RIR approval, RIPE enables an LIR/ISP to allocate up to 400% of their AW or up to a /20 whichever is smaller. Thus, an LIR/ISP with an AW of /22 from RIPE may make individual allocations of up to /20 (remember, each bit movement to the left doubles the address space), while one with an AW of /21 may make individual allocations of up to a /19. AfriNIC, RIPE, LACNIC, and APNIC constrain the [S]AW to zero for new LIR/ISPs, requiring RIR approval of all allocations. Over time, as the LIR/ISP proves a responsible steward of address space, the [S]AW can be increased. Table 3.1 summarizes the key allocation policies employed by the RIRs today.

To enforce the aggregation goal of the RIR system, the RIR strongly recommends that each LIR/ISP contractually oblige their customers to return address space allocated to them should they decide to change service providers. This goal exists to preserve the addressing hierarchy, analogous to the addressing hierarchy we described in IPAM Worldwide's case. To illustrate the importance of this requirement, consider an ISP with a /20 allocation from a RIR. The ISP allocates a /23 to one of its customers. If the

T A B L E 3.1. RIR allocation policy summary

RIR Policy Highlights	Regional Internet Registry				
	AfriNIC (25)	APNIC (26)	ARIN (27)	LACNIC (28)	RIPE NCC (29)
Initial minimum IPv4 allocation	/22	/21	/20	/21	/21
IPv4 justification: initial/1 year	25/50%	25/50%	25/50%	25/50%	25/50%
IPv4 network utilization criteria for additional allocations	80%	80%	80%	80%	80%
RIR must be notified for allocations greater than:	Assigned SAW	Assigned AW (/19 max)	/19 (or /18 for extra large ISPs)	Assigned AW (/21 max)	/20 or 4 X AW
Initial minimal IPv6 allocation	/32	/32	/32	/32	/32
Expected LIR/ISP IPv6 assignment	/48	/48	/48	/48	/48
IPv6 HD ratio criteria for additional allocations	0.94	0.94	0.94	0.94	0.94

customer changes service providers and takes the /23 address space with them, the /23 will need to roll up on the Internet "backbone" to the new ISP, not the original ISP. The original ISP would now need to advertise not only the /20 block it had originally received but also the other /23, a /22, and a /21; that is all of its space minus the departed customer's /23. The new ISP would need to advertise its allocated blocks plus the new customer's /23. This obviously creates a rise in routing table entries on both sides and on the global Internet, defeating the goal of aggregation. Such "portable" address space is referred to as *provider independent* (PI) and is easy for customers but inefficient for Internet routing.

By requiring a return of the address space to the original ISP, the /23 can be returned to the pool to be assigned or suballocated elsewhere, and the customer will need to renumber their IP network with new address space assigned by the new ISP. The requirement that address space be returned upon changing ISPs ensures the ISP a single aggregate route advertisement and is termed *provider aggregate* (PA) space. Some organizations that obtained IP address space prior to the institution of the ISP/LIR layer in the allocation hierarchy have PI space. Now allocation of PI space is largely frowned upon in favor of PA space.

3.4.2 Address Allocation Efficiency

During the development of IPv6, much thought went into deriving the 128-bit address size. While IPv4 provides a 32-bit address field that provides a theoretical maximum of 2^{32} addresses or over 4.2 billion addresses, in reality the theoretical maximum is much less than 4.2 billion. This is due to the hierarchical allocation of address space for multiple layers of networks, then subnets, and finally hosts. RFC 1715 (Ref. 30) provides an analysis of address assignment efficiency, in which a logarithmic scale was proposed as a measure of allocation efficiency, which was defined as the H ratio:

$$H = \frac{\log_{10}(\text{number of objects})}{\text{number of available bits}}$$

With about 730 million hosts on the Internet today, today's H ratio is 0.277. The H ratio for 100% utilization of 4.2 billion IP addresses is 0.301,[*] so today's H ratio is high.

Assignment efficiency measurements for IPv6, with its massive amount of address space, is not calculated based on the H ratio; a different ratio, the HD ratio (31), is used:

$$HD = \frac{\log_{10}(\text{number of allocated objects})}{\log_{10}(\text{maximum number of allocatable objects})}$$

The "objects" measured in the HD ratio for IPv6 are the IPv6 site addresses (/48s) assigned from an IPv6 prefix of a given size. The /48 address blocks are those expected to be assigned to each end user by the LIR/ISP. So an LIR/ISP with a /32 allocation that has allocated 100 /48s would have an HD ratio of log(100)/log (65,536) = 0.415.

---

[*] 0.301, which is equal to $\log_{10}(2)$, is the maximum value of the H ratio.

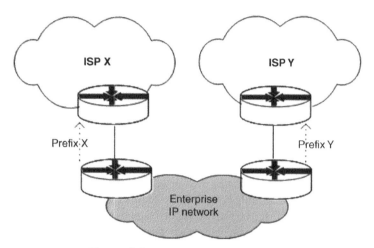

Figure 3.9. Multihoming architecture.

3.5 MULTIHOMING AND IP ADDRESS SPACE

The term *multihoming* refers to an enterprise provisioning multiple (>1) connections to
the Internet. A simple architecture is depicted in Figure 3.9. A multihoming strategy
provides several benefits:

- Link redundancy, providing continued Internet connectivity availability in the
  event of a connection outage
- ISP redundancy if multiple ISPs are used to limit exposure in the event of an ISP
  outage
- Load sharing of Internet traffic over multiple connections
- Policy and performance benefits achieved through routing of traffic based on
  congestion or based on requirements to route traffic of differing applications to
  differing links or ISPs.

Multihoming offers several attractive benefits though it does require care in configuring
routers interfacing to each ISP. As we show in Figure 3.9, the enterprise border
routers interfacing directly to their respective ISP edge routers participate in an exterior
routing protocol (e.g., BGP) to advertise reachability to the respective address blocks
(by address prefix). Thus, the enterprise router connected to ISP X will advertise
reachability to the address space provided to the enterprise by ISP X. Similarly, the
enterprise router connected to ISP Y will advertise reachability to the address space
provided by ISP Y.

These two enterprise routers also communicate with each other using an interior
routing protocol via the enterprise IP network. In this manner, loss of connectivity to an
ISP may be detected, though this is where things get interesting. To illustrate this without

going into all the routing details,[*] the following summarizes the most common multi-homing deployment options, outage impacts, and implications on IP address space:

- *Case 1.* Two or more diverse physical links to the same ISP. This "multiattached" architecture provides link redundancy but not ISP redundancy. Referring to Figure 3.9, the two ISP clouds would be collapsed into a single cloud but still with two (or more) links from the enterprise. With one ISP, prefix X = prefix Y, so this public address space allocated from the ISP may be advertised uniformly on all connections.
- *Case 2.* Two or more connections to one or more ISPs using provider independent address space. Recall that PI space in this scenario has been allocated to the organization directly and independent of ISP associations. Referring to Figure 3.9, the advertised prefix is again the same on both connections, though we could denote it as prefix Z as being independent of the ISP address space. As in case 1, the PI space may be advertised to all ISPs and allocated across the organization as needed.
- *Case 3.* Two or more connections to two or more ISPs using provider aggregate address space from each ISP. In this case, each ISP allocates address space as part of its service. Figure 3.9 reflects this scenario as is. With two independent address blocks X and Y, if the link to ISP X fails, the enterprise router connected to ISP Y will detect this by virtue of the interior routing protocol update from the enterprise router connected to ISP X. Thus, the enterprise router connected to ISP Y could now advertise reachability to prefix X. Depending on ISP Y's policies, it may or may not propagate the route because it does not fall within ISP Y's address space but ISP X's.

Another approach is to perform an indirect BGP peer update from the ISP Y-facing enterprise router to an ISP X router peer. In this manner, ISP X routers may be notified of an alternate route to reach the enterprise's address space via ISP Y. These two alternative approaches are shown in Figure 3.10 with the former shown with prefix X being advertised to ISP Y's router and the latter with prefix X being advertised to ISP X's router.

NAT gateways at each ISP connection are commonly deployed to enable address pooling, translating a given packet's internal private address into a public address based on the ISP connection proximity, for example, from prefix X or prefix Y. Barring the use of NAT gateways, enterprise border router policies should be implemented to minimize or prevent routing of traffic among internally addressed hosts via the ISP(s).

3.6 BLOCK ALLOCATION AND IP ADDRESS MANAGEMENT

In this chapter, we've discussed techniques for IP address block allocations for public and private IPv4 space and IPv6 space. From a basic management perspective, it's critical to

---

[*] Please refer to the following RFCs for the routing details around multihoming: 2260 (170), 4116 (171), 4177 (172), and 4218 (173).

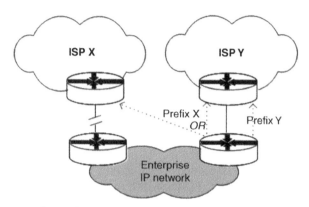

Figure 3.10. Multihoming link outage recovery.

maintain an inventory of allocations with respect to the hierarchy of allocations, in which locations of subnets have been deployed, and any additional relevant information such as a mapping of each subnet to its corresponding provisioned router or switch interface, associated Internet Registry administrative information if appropriate, trouble contact information, and other information of interest.

Many organizations responsible for block allocations use spreadsheets or simple database applications such as Microsoft Access to keep this information organized. Though performing block allocations and binary arithmetic are not natively performed with a single mouse click using spreadsheets, underlying homegrown Visual Basic or perl code, for example, can apply the logic we've reviewed in this chapter in order to perform best-fit, sparse, or random allocations and track the resulting allocations. Certainly, care must be taken to perform this accurately and to manage block allocations, moves, modifications, and deletions.

We've kept the IPAM Worldwide spreadsheet updated with each allocation to reflect our private IPv4, public IPv4 and IPv6, and ULA IPv6 address allocations. This information provides a necessary foundation for our next step, assigning individual IP addresses from respective subnets for each location. Now that each branch office and distribution center has IP subnets that aggregate up the hierarchy, we can begin the process of address assignment. We'll discuss one form of automated address assignment, DHCP, in the next part of the book, and we'll discuss other more manual methods of address assignment in Chapter 14.

PART II

DHCP

Part II covers the Dynamic Host Configuration Protocol (DHCP) for IPv4 and IPv6. Applications enabled by DHCP are covered after a technology overview, followed by deployment and security considerations.

4

DYNAMIC HOST CONFIGURATION PROTOCOL

4.1 INTRODUCTION[*]

In the early days of the Internet's existence, when hosts numbered in the hundreds, assigning an IP address to a device was fairly trivial. It was simply one of the configuration parameters entered manually on each host. This "once and done" or *static* address assignment process using a hard-coded IP address certainly was simple, but it inhibited the host's mobility among different networks or subnets. Enabling mobility required the cumbersome task of reconfiguring the host with a new IP address based on the present location or network to which connection was desired.

Nonetheless, you will likely have a set of static addresses for devices on your network that do not require mobility, such as routers, servers, IP PBXs, and so on. It's imperative to keep track of which IP addresses on allocated subnets are statically assigned, which are assigned to address pools for dynamic assignment, and which are free or reserved for future use. Maintaining a subnet IP inventory is a recommended practice to maintain a record of addresses assigned on each subnet to minimize duplicate or otherwise erroneous IP address assignments. Just make sure the inventory of static

---

[*] Initial sections of this chapter are based on Chapter 3 of Ref. 11.

IP Address Management: Principles and Practice, by Timothy Rooney
Copyright © 2011 the Institute of Electrical and Electronics Engineers, Inc.

addresses matches what's actually been provisioned on the router, server, or statically addressed device. Performing periodic baselines of address assignments through various forms of discovery or ping sweeps can help identify any mismatch as we'll discuss in Chapter 14.

4.2 DHCP OVERVIEW

The Dynamic Host Configuration Protocol (DHCP) is a client–server protocol for devices connecting to an IP network to automatically obtain an IP address. DHCP has been a tremendous time saver for IP network administrators. It enables a device to broadcast its request for an IP address, and have one or more DHCP servers within the IP network service the request without user intervention. For most end user devices such as laptops, VoIP phones, PDAs, and others, the DHCP process transpires "behind the scenes" upon device boot-up or connection to a wire line or wireless network without user intervention. DHCP also enables efficient use of IP addresses by allowing an IP address to be reused among devices within dynamically allocated address pools. A given IP address may be used by one device one day and a different device the next.

DHCP is supported as part of both IPv4 and IPv6. We'll discuss the IPv4 version in this chapter and the IPv6 version in the next. When we use the term "DHCP" in this chapter, we're referring to the IPv4 version. Defined in RFCs 2131 (32) and 2132 (33) with many additions in subsequent RFCs*, DHCP is built on the foundation of an older protocol, the Bootstrap Protocol, referred to as BOOTP. BOOTP, initially specified in RFC 951 (34), provides automation of address assignment but is restricted to preassigning a given IP address to a particular device, identified by its network interface (MAC) address. Thus, a BOOTP server is configured with a list of MAC addresses and corresponding IP addresses. DHCP incorporates this functionality with the added capability of assigning IP addresses to clients without requiring *a priori* knowledge of each client's hardware address. In effect, DHCP supersedes BOOTP, enabling backward compatibility with BOOTP clients.

DHCP supports three types of IP address allocation:

1. *Automatic Allocation.* The DHCP server assigns a permanent IP address to the client.
2. *Manual Allocation.* Like BOOTP, the DHCP server assigns a "fixed" IP address based on the particular device's hardware address.
3. *Dynamic Allocation.* The DHCP server assigns an IP address for a limited time period, after which it can be reassigned, perhaps, to a different device.

Automatic allocation may be useful for a particular set of users or devices requiring a permanent IP address assignment via DHCP, where there's no requirement for a particular user or device to have a particular IP address. In other words, you may want to set aside a number of "permanent" addresses without directly associating each IP address

---

* Please refer to the RFC Index at the back of this book for a complete list.

with a particular hardware address. This is in contrast to Manual DHCP, which associates a particular hardware address with a corresponding IP address.

Dynamic allocation is commonly used to set up address pools in DHCP servers in order to "reuse" IP addresses. Under dynamic allocation, the DHCP server leases its IP addresses to clients for a fixed period of time. In this way, the DHCP server can assign an IP address to a particular client for a given time period referred to as the lease time, and when the IP address becomes available due to the expiration of the lease or the client relinquishing the address, reassign the same address to a different client. The lease time is a configurable parameter within the DHCP server implementation.

Regardless of the DHCP address allocation type, the process by which a DHCP client obtains a lease is the same. The basic process begins with a DHCP client broadcasting a DHCPDISCOVER packet. Since the client has neither an IP address nor generally any information about the IP network, it inserts the all-zeroes address as the source address and the broadcast (all-ones) address as the destination address within the IP header. Let's assume that a DHCP server has been deployed on the same subnet to which the DHCP client is connected. Upon receiving the DHCPDISCOVER packet, the DHCP server will determine if it has an address available on this subnet on which the DHCPDISCOVER was received.

If an address is available in the pool, the DHCP server will send a DHCPOFFER packet to the client, offering an IP address and associated configuration parameters, called *options*. The DHCP client may receive more than one DHCPOFFER if multiple DHCP servers are servicing this subnet. The client will select one configuration set and broadcast a DHCPREQUEST packet, specifying the selected DHCP server whose offer it has accepted. The selected DHCP server will acknowledge the DHCPREQUEST with a DHCPACK once it has recorded the lease information in nonvolatile storage, thereby binding the IP address to the DHCP client. This basic message flow, illustrated in Figure 4.1 is sometimes referred to as the "DORA" process – Discover, Offer, Request, and Ack.

In this simple example, the DHCP server resides in the same subnet as the DHCP client. The client broadcasts the DHCPDISCOVER packet on the network. Since the DHCP server resides in the same network, it receives the broadcast and processes the packet. Knowing the network from which the broadcast originated, the DHCP server can assign an available IP address on the network. But do you have to deploy a DHCP server on every subnet? Fortunately, no; the DHCP server simply must be reachable from the subnet via the IP routing infrastructure. The router(s) receiving the DHCPDIS-COVER broadcast packet will not propagate the broadcast, as this would create

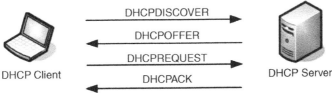

Figure 4.1. DHCP "DORA" process.

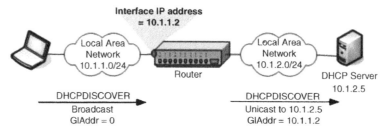

Figure 4.2. DHCP Relay (11).

excessive and needless IP traffic. Instead, the router will forward or *relay* the packet to the intended DHCP server(s). Each router configured to perform this relay function is referred to as a *relay agent*. Each relay agent must be configured with the IP addresses of each DHCP server serving the subnet. This configuration parameter, commonly referred to as the DHCP Relay address, enables the router to accept the DHCPDIS-COVER broadcast, look up the DHCP server(s) configured for DHCP Relay, and then route the DHCPDISCOVER packet via unicast directly to each DHCP server as illustrated in Figure 4.2.

In the process, the router modifies the DHCPDISCOVER packet to insert the IP address of the interface on which the DHCPDISCOVER was received into the relay agent (gateway) interface address field. This parameter enables the DHCP server to identify the subnet on which an address assignment has been requested. Note that when the gateway interface address (GIAddr) field is zero, the DHCP server assumes the subnet on which to assign the IP address is the same as that on which the DHCPDISCOVER was received (via direct broadcast).

In addition to the four-packet exchange outlined above, the IETF has adopted RFC 4039 that defines a rapid commit option, option 80. This option is modeled after the DHCPv6 equivalent defined in the next chapter, and halves the messaging requirements by enabling the server to simply send a DHCPACK in response to a DHCPDISCOVER message. The client would include the rapid commit option in its DHCPDISCOVER message. Servers responding with an address assignment would directly issue an ACK packet, also including the rapid commit option. Rapid commit functionality is desirable particularly for mobility applications such as cell phones that have limited bandwidth available. Note that each server responding will assume the address it assigned is leased, so rapid commit should be used with either short lease times or for support by a limited number of servers if normally there are many serving the same subnet.

4.2.1 DHCP message types

We've introduced the four basic DHCP message types, so let's expand on this and review the complete set of DHCP messages and their respective meanings. We often omit the "DHCP" prefix on these messages and just capitalize the first letter, but here's how they're officially defined:

- *DHCPDISCOVER.* Issued from the client to the server to solicit DHCP address assignment; the DHCPDISCOVER may include parameters or options required by the client
- *DHCPOFFER.* Issued from the server to the client indicating an IP address offer including its corresponding lease time (and other configuration parameters) to the client in response to a DHCPDISCOVER.
- *DHCPREQUEST.* Issued from the client to a server in response to a DHCPOFFER to accept or reject the offered IP address, along with desired or additional parameter settings. The DHCPREQUEST is also used by clients desiring to extend or renew their existing IP address lease.
- *DHCPACK.* Issued from the server to the client to positively acknowledge the grant of the IP address lease and associated parameter settings. The client may now begin using the IP address and parameter values.
- *DHCPNAK.* Issued from the server to the client to negatively acknowledge the DHCP transaction. The client must cease the use of the IP address and reinitiate the process if necessary.
- *DHCPDECLINE.* Issued from the client to the server, to indicate that the IP address offered by the server is already in use by another client. The DHCP server will then typically mark the IP address as unavailable.
- *DHCPRELEASE.* Issued from the client to the server to inform the server that the client is relinquishing the IP address. The client must cease the use of the IP address thereafter.
- *DHCPINFORM.* Issued from the client to the server to request non-IP address configuration parameters from the server. The server will formulate a DHCPACK reply with the associated values as appropriate.
- *DHCPFORCERENEW.* Issued from the server to the client to force a client into the INIT state* in order to obtain a new (different) IP address. Few clients have implemented support of this message.
- *DHCPLEASEQUERY.* Issued from a relay agent or other device to a server to determine if a given MAC address, IP address, or client-identifier value has an active lease and its associated lease parameter values according to the DHCP server (used primarily by broadband access concentrators or edge devices).
- *DHCPLEASEUNASSIGNED.* Issued from a server to a relay agent in response to a DHCPLEASEQUERY informing the relay agent that this server supports that address but there is no active lease.
- *DHCPLEASEUNKNOWN.* Issued from a server to a relay agent in response to a DHCPLEASEQUERY informing the relay agent that the server has no knowledge of the client specified in the query.
- *DHCPLEASEACTIVE.* Issued from a server to a relay agent in response to a DHCPLEASEQUERY with the endpoint location and remaining lease time.

---

* We'll discuss DHCP states next.

RFC 2131 defines a number of states in which the client may exist with respect to its IP address configuration using DHCP. The following states are defined:

- *INIT.* Initialization, meaning the client has neither an IP address nor any prior configuration information.
- *INIT-REBOOT.* The client initializes, though it has prior IP address information, and desires to confirm its settings.
- *BOUND.* The client and server are bound to their IP lease agreement.
- *RENEWING.* The client is attempting to renew the lease.
- *REBINDING.* The client is approaching lease expiration and is attempting to renew the lease.
- *SELECTING.* Intermediate state where the client is awaiting and evaluating DHCPOFFERs from DHCP server(s).
- *REQUESTING.* Intermediate state where the client has selected an Offer and wishes to accept it or has identified an Offer for an IP address that is already in use, in which case it sends a DHCPDECLINE to the server.
- *REBOOTING.* Client is attempting to rebind after a reboot.

The distinction between renewing and rebinding boils down to the urgency of the renewal request, with rebinding being of higher urgency, and to transport mode, with renewals being unicast and rebinding being broadcast. When a lease is initially obtained, the client sets two timers:

- T1 = 50% of the lease time by default.
- T2 = 87.5% of the lease time by default.

These timer values may be modified upon agreement between the DHCP client and the server by specifying values within corresponding options within the DHCP packet exchange. Upon expiration of the T1 timer, the client enters the renewing state and attempts to renew the lease by unicasting a DHCPRENEW message to the DHCP server from which it obtained the lease. If a DHCPACK is received, the client re-enters the bound state. If a DHCPNAK is received, the client ceases the use of the IP address and enters the INIT state. Otherwise, having not received a response, the client awaits the expiration of the T2 timer, then broadcasts a DHCPRENEW in an attempt to renew the lease. The broadcast is issued in case the original server from which the lease was obtained is down and a failover DHCP server is available to renew the lease.

Figure 4.3 depicts the state transition diagram among these DHCP client states and the respective state transition mechanisms. Note that the DHCPINFORM message is not included in the figure as this relates to non-IP address parameters. A client already configured with an IP address issues the DHCPINFORM to request additional parameter settings and the server replies with a DHCPACK indicating the requested values.

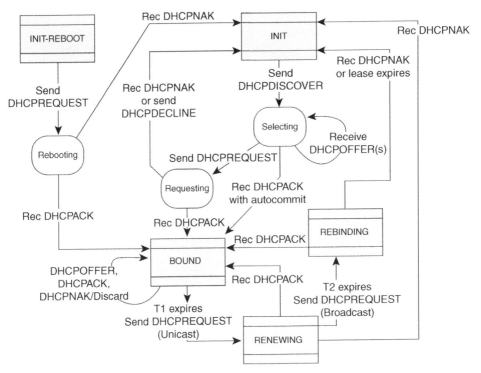

Figure 4.3. DHCP state transitions (32).

4.2.2 DHCP Packet Format

Let's examine the fields in the DHCP packet[*] and how they relate to the overall DHCP process. Figure 4.4 displays the field layout, and we'll describe each field following the figure.

DHCP packet field descriptions:

- *Operation Code.* Leveraging the BootP predecessor, the values for this field are
  - 1 = BootRequest
  - 2 = BootReply

Note that the type of DHCP message (Discover, Offer, Request, etc.) is actually defined in the options field with option number 53, DHCP message type, with the following valid values:

  - 1 = DHCPDISCOVER
  - 2 = DHCPOFFER
  - 3 = DHCPREQUEST

---

[*] A "DHCP packet" is transported over IP within an IP packet. The DHCP "application" uses the packet header format described in this chapter.

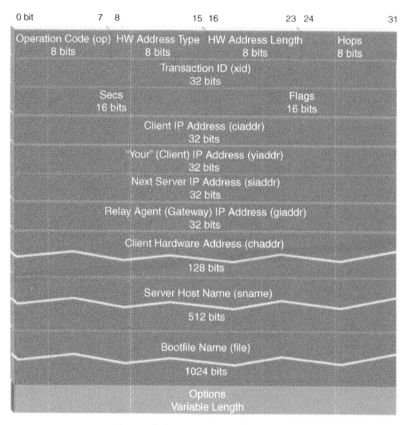

Figure 4.4. DHCP packet fields (32).

- ○ 4 = DHCPDECLINE
- ○ 5 = DHCPACK
- ○ 6 = DHCPNAK
- ○ 7 = DHCPRELEASE
- ○ 8 = DHCPINFORM
- ○ 9 = DHCPFORCERENEW
- ○ 10 = DHCPLEASEQUERY
- ○ 11 = DHCPLEASEUNASSIGNED
- ○ 12 = DHCPLEASEUNKNOWN
- ○ 13 = DHCPLEASEACTIVE
- *Hardware Address Type.* The type of hardware or MAC address, such as Ethernet, 802, and so on.
- *Hardware Address Length.* Defines the length of the MAC address in octets.

- *Hops.* Set to zero by clients, this field can be incremented by each router between the client and the server.
- *Transaction ID (xid).* A random number chosen by the client to correlate messages and responses between the client and the server.
- *Seconds (secs).* The number of seconds that have elapsed since the client began the process of obtaining an IP address or renewal.
- *Flags.* This field is used by DHCP clients that cannot receive unicast IP packets until its IP protocol software has been configured. For such cases, the client sets the first bit in this field to 1, and sets the remaining bits to 0. When set to 1, the server, if locally connected, or the relay agent will broadcast the Offer and Ack messages to the client; otherwise, the server or relay agent will send them to the unicast address specified in the yiaddr field. This bit is sometimes referred to as the broadcast bit within the Flags field.
- *Client IP Address (ciaddr).* The IP address of the client used when known by the client, for example, when in the BOUND, RENEWING, or REBINDING state.
- *Your IP Address (yiaddr).* The IP address assigned by the DHCP server for use by the client.
- *Server IP Address (siaddr).* The IP address of the "next" server to use for bootstrapping as provided by the DHCP server.
- *Gateway Interface Address (giaddr).* IP address of the interface on which the DHCP broadcast was received as populated by the relay agent.
- *Client Hardware Address (chaddr).* The link layer or hardware address of the client provided by the client.
- *Server name (sname).* DHCP server host name.
- *File.* Boot file name, null or fully qualified directory pathname.
- *Options.* Additional IP parameters such as lease time, domain name, default gateway, and subnet mask (see next section for a complete list). The first four octets of the options field are always the magic cookies of value (in hex): 63825363. This is a carryover from the original BootP specification in RFC 951 that was intended to provide a means to interpret the options, for example, for vendor-specific purposes.

4.3 DHCP SERVERS AND ADDRESS ASSIGNMENT

Each DHCP server can be configured with multiple address pools serving several different subnets in various locations. In fact, for some DHCP server implementations, the same address pool can be configured on multiple DHCP servers for redundancy. This will be discussed in more detail in Chapter 7. The DHCP server keeps track of the state of all IP addresses across all of its configured address pools. When an address is leased to a client, the server generally tracks not only the lease time for the IP address but also an identifier for the client leasing the IP address. This identifier is typically the layer 2

(MAC) address of the client, as obtained via the chaddr field, though the client identifier field, option 60, may also be used.

The use of the client identifier (client ID) option over the chaddr field was suggested to maintain an identifier for the device even if the link hardware is moved to another device. But in practice, most devices either do not provide a client ID or copy the value of the chaddr field into the client ID option.

The basic decision process typically used by DHCP servers in offering an address is based on the following:

- If the client has a leased address as recorded in the DHCP server, the server will assign this address.
- If the client previously had an address that is now expired or released but is still available, the server will assign this address.
- If the client includes an address in the Requested IP Address option, option 50, and the address is available, the server will assign this address.
- The server will assign an available address from a pool on the same subnet on which the DHCPDISCOVER broadcast was received if the GIAddr field is zero, or on the subnet indicated by the GIAddr value if nonzero. Additional criteria based on parameters within the DHCPDISCOVER packet may dictate from which pool the address gets assigned if there are multiple pools serving the subnet in question. These parameters are generically referred to as client class parameters and are discussed next.

4.3.1 Device Identification by Class

Client class parameters provide a means both for the DHCP client to provide additional information to the DHCP server and for the DHCP server to recognize clients requiring unique IP address or parameter assignments. For example, you may want to dedicate one address pool for VoIP devices and a separate pool for data devices. This may be motivated by administrative concerns or by source routing policies for voice versus data packets from the respective devices. Most DHCP servers, including those available from the Internet Systems Consortium (ISC) and Microsoft, enable specification of vendor class or user class values to match on to provide such categorization. The DHCP server can be configured to associate a particular vendor class or user class value or set of values as criteria in assigning an address from an address pool.

Let's consider an example. Recall in Chapter 3, in allocating address space for IPAM Worldwide, we allocated the subnet 10.16.128.0/23 for VoIP devices in San Francisco. Many organizations allocate a single subnet in a location and define two separate address pools for different VoIP device vendors due to differences in initialization and configuration requirements. In IPAM Worldwide's case, we'll need to define one address pool within the 10.16.128.0/23 subnet for VoIP devices for "vendor X" and a different pool within the same subnet for "vendor Y" VoIP devices. We then define two pools on IPAM Worldwide's DHCP server for each address pool, for example, the 10.16.128.20–10.16.128.250 address range and the 10.16.129.20–10.16.129.250

address range. We've shown them to be of equivalent size for simplicity, but there's no requirement that this be the case. In our IP subnet inventory, whether in a spreadsheet, database, or IP address management system, we can record these pools within these respective subnets. We should have also recorded static address assignments, for example, 10.16.128.1 for a router, 10.16.128.6 for a server, and so on.

In Figure 4.5a, we'd like to configure our DHCP server to discriminate between the VoIP phone vendors and assign addresses from different address pools. The first step is to determine what information in the DHCP packet can be used to uniquely identify each class of devices as VoIP phone or laptop. Typically, your VoIP phone provider will inform you that there is a particular string in the vendor class identifier option (option 60); let's say, originally enough this string is "vendorX" for vendor X and "vendorY" for vendor Y.

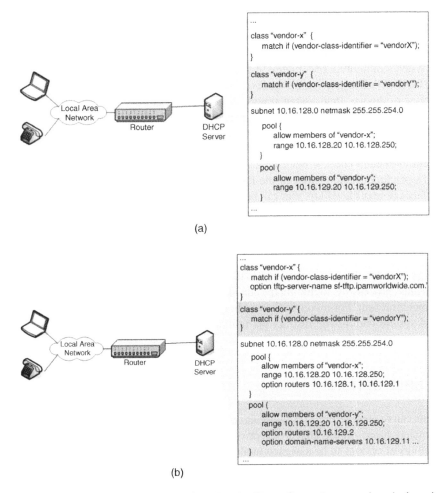

(a)

(b)

Figure 4.5. (a) Client classing example using DHCP configuration pseudocode based on Ref. [35]. (b) Specifying additional configuration information for DHCP clients by class based on Ref. [35].

We can define a class in the DHCP server for each vendor per the example in Figure 4.5a, though the syntax will depend on your DHCP server vendor (or IPAM tool). In this example, we configure the DHCP server to categorize devices sending DHCP packets with option 60 = "vendorX" as devices of the vendor-x class. Likewise, we define a class to discriminate vendor Y devices by defining the vendor class identifier option having a value of "vendorY" per the match-if clause in Figure 4.5a. In addition, a third pool could be set up as the "default" pool for clients not matching other defined client classes.

Now that we've defined our two classes, enabling the DHCP server to identify packets as originating from devices belonging to one class or the other, we can now instruct the server how to handle these requests. We can define two address pools within the respective subnet declaration, as we'd like to separate the address assignments for these two classes of devices. Within our 10.16.128.0/23 subnet, we define one address pool for vendor-x class devices as containing addresses 10.16.128.20–10.16.128.250 and a second address pool on the subnet for vendor-y class devices as containing 10.16.129.20–10.16.129.250, shaded to map to the class definition in the figure.

When configured per Figure 4.5a, the DHCP server will now examine each DHCPDISCOVER packet from devices on the 10.16.128.0/23 subnet to discern the class of device, then assign vendor X devices an address from the 10.16.128.20–10.16.128.250 pool, and assign vendor Y devices from the 10.16.129.20– 10.16.129.250 pool. Note that there may be additional parameters or option settings you may wish to define within each of these pool statements to provide configuration information according to each class of device, as we'll discuss a bit later.

Depending on the vendor of the DHCP server you deploy, there are various menu interfaces or text file editors that can be used for managing the configuration of address pools and server behavior as well as criteria you can specify to dictate address assignment logic. For example, Microsoft DHCP servers can be configured through a Windows graphical user interface (GUI), while ISC DHCP servers can be configured via text editor. However, the ISC DHCP provides more flexibility in defining client classes beyond user class and vendor class; any parameter in the packet can be examined and filtered upon for client class processing, including the chaddr field for MAC address filtering, or any other parameter present. For mixed ISC and Microsoft environments, the use of a centralized IPAM system could help abstract the individual vendor interfaces and enable configuration of both with a single interface.

4.4 DHCP OPTIONS

Clients can request settings for particular options, and servers can assign these and other parameters based on the DHCP server configuration. DHCP administrators can define groupings of options to be assigned to all or certain DHCP clients based on the client's hardware address, client class value, or other DHCP packet parameter.

As discussed in the previous section, we set up two client classes for IPAM Worldwide's San Francisco office corresponding to VoIP devices by vendor. Devices of these types will likely require different configuration parameters. For example, Cisco VoIP devices typically require option code 66 or 150, while Avaya VoIP devices require

TABLE 4.1. DHCP Options

Code	Name	Len	Meaning	Reference
0	Pad	0	None	RFC 2132 (33)
1	Subnet mask	4	Subnet mask in "IP address" format	RFC 2132 (33)
2	Time offset	4	Time offset in seconds from UTC (deprecated by RFC 4833 that specifies the use of options 100 and 101)	RFC 2132 (33)
3	Router	N	$N/4^*$ Router (default gateway) addresses	RFC 2132 (33)
4	Time server	N	$N/4$ Timeserver addresses	RFC 2132 (33)
5	Name server	N	$N/4$ IEN-116[†] name server addresses	RFC 2132 (33)
6	Domain server	N	$N/4$ DNS server addresses	RFC 2132 (33)
7	Log server	N	$N/4$ MIT Laboratory for Computer Science (LCS) UDP log server addresses	RFC 2132 (33)
8	Quotes server	N	$N/4$ "Quote of the day" server addresses	RFC 2132 (33)
9	LPR server	N	$N/4$ Line printer server addresses	RFC 2132 (33)
10	Impress server	N	$N/4$ Imagen Impress server addresses	RFC 2132 (33)
11	RLP server	N	$N/4$ Resource Location Protocol server addresses	RFC 2132 (33)
12	Hostname	N	Client hostname string	RFC 2132 (33)
13	Boot file size	2	Size of boot file in 512 byte blocks	RFC 2132 (33)
14	Merit dump file	N	File pathname to which the client should dump its core image in the event of a client crash	RFC 2132 (33)
15	Domain name	N	The DNS domain name of the client	RFC 2132 (33)
16	Swap server	N	Swap server address	RFC 2132 (33)
17	Root path	N	Path name for the client's root disk	RFC 2132 (33)
18	Extension file	N	Path name of a file containing vendor-extension information retrievable via TFTP	RFC 2132 (33)

(Continued)

TABLE 4.1. DHCP Options (*Continued*)

Code	Name	Len	Meaning	Reference
19	Forward on/off	1	Enable/Disable IP packet forwarding	RFC 2132 (33)
20	Source routing on/off	1	Enable/Disable IP packet forwarding for packets specifying nonlocal source routes	RFC 2132 (33)
21	Policy filter	N	Specifies acceptable nonlocal next hops to which IP packets may be forwarded for packets specifying nonlocal source routes	RFC 2132 (33)
22	Max datagram reassembly size	2	The maximum size datagram the client should be ready to reassemble specified as a 16-bit unsigned integer	RFC 2132 (33)
23	Default IP TTL	1	Default IP time to live value for use in outgoing packets' IP header TTL field	RFC 2132 (33)
24	Path MTU aging timeout	4	The timeout in seconds when performing path maximum transmission unit (MTU) discovery in accordance with RFC 1191; MTU discovery helps minimize packet fragmentation along the path	RFC 2132 (33)
25	Path MTU plateau table	N	A table listing MTU sizes to use when performing path MTU discovery per RFC 1191	RFC 2132 (33)
26	Interface MTU	2	The value of the MTU for this device interface	RFC 2132 (33)
27	All subnets are local	1	Indicates whether all subnets within the client's network use the same MTU as the local subnet to which the client is connected	RFC 2132 (33)
28	Broadcast address	4	Specifies the broadcast IP address for the client's subnet	RFC 2132 (33)
29	Mask discovery	1	Specifies whether the client should perform subnet mask discovery or not	RFC 2132 (33)
30	Mask supplier	1	Specifies whether the client should respond to other clients performing mask discovery	RFC 2132 (33)
31	Router discovery	1	Specifies whether the client should perform router discovery or not	RFC 2132 (33)
32	Router solicitation address	4	Specifies the IP address to which the client should direct router solicitation requests	RFC 2132 (33)
33	Static route	N	Specifies a set of static routes the client should install in its routing cache; listed as "destination network—next hop router" pairings (obsoleted by RFC 3442 defining the classless static route option, 121).	RFC 3442 (36)

34	Trailer encapsulation	1	Specifies whether the client should attempt to negotiate the use of layer 2 frame trailers (like headers but at the end of the frame payload) in ARP messages	RFC 2132 (33)
35	ARP timeout	4	ARP cache timeout in seconds	RFC 2132 (33)
36	Ethernet encapsulation	1	Specifies whether the client should use Ethernet II or IEEE 802.3 on an Ethernet interface	RFC 2132 (33)
37	Default TCP TTL	1	Default TCP time to live value	RFC 2132 (33)
38	TCP keepalive time	4	TCP keepalive interval in seconds	RFC 2132 (33)
39	TCP keepalive garbage	1	Specifies whether the client should send an octet of "garbage" within TCP keepalive messages for compatibility with older implementations	RFC 2132 (33)
40	NIS domain	N	Network Information Services (NIS) domain	RFC 2132 (33)
41	NIS servers	N	N/4 Network Information Services server addresses	RFC 2132 (33)
42	NTP servers	N	N/4 Network Time Protocol server addresses	RFC 2132 (33)
43	Vendor specific	N	Vendor-specific information	RFC 2132 (33)
44	NETBIOS Name server	N	N/4 NETBIOS Name server (aka WINS server) addresses	RFC 2132 (33)
45	NBDD server	N	N/4 NETBIOS Datagram Distribution (NBDD) server addresses	RFC 2132 (33)
46	NETBIOS node type	1	Specifies the client as a specific NETBIOS node type	RFC 2132 (33)
47	NETBIOS scope	N	Specifies the NETBIOS scope for the client	RFC 2132 (33)
48	X Window font server	N	N/4 X Window font server addresses	RFC 2132 (33)
49	X Window display manager	N	N/4 X Window display manager addresses	RFC 2132 (33)
50	Address request	4	IP address requested by the client (within a Discover message)	RFC 2132 (33)
51	Address time	4	IP address lease time requested by the client (within a Discover or Request message)	RFC 2132 (33)
52	Option overload	1	Indicates that the "sname" and/or "file" DHCP header fields contain additional DHCP option information if options to return to the client exceed the normal option space in the message	RFC 2132 (33)
53	DHCP message type	1	DHCP message type as we discussed earlier in this chapter (Discover, Offer, etc.)	RFC 2132 (33)

(Continued)

TABLE 4.1. DHCP Options (*Continued*)

Code	Name	Len	Meaning	Reference
54	DHCP server identifier	4	DHCP server identification provided in the Offer (and Request and optionally ACK, NAK) to identify the server, for example, to distinguish among multiple offers	RFC 2132 (33)
55	Parameter list	N	List of DHCP option code numbers for parameters requested by the client	RFC 2132 (33)
56	DHCP error message text	N	Text containing an error message; can be used by the server in a Nak message to the client or by the client in a Decline message; for example, this text could be included in logging details	RFC 2132 (33)
57	Maximum DHCP message size	2	The maximum DHCP message length the client is willing to accept	RFC 2132 (33)
58	Renewal (T1) time	4	Interval from address assignment time to the time the client enters the Renewing state	RFC 2132 (33)
59	Rebinding (T2) time	4	Interval from the address assignment time to the time the client enters the Rebinding state	RFC 2132 (33)
60	Vendor class identifier	N	Used by clients to specify a vendor-specific identifier	RFC 2132 (33)
61	Client Id	N	Client identifier	RFC 2132 (33)
62	Netware/IP domain	N	Netware/IP domain name	RFC 2242 (37)
63	Netware/IP option	N	Netware/IP sub options	RFC 2242 (37)
64	NIS + domain	N	NIS+ client domain name	RFC 2132 (33)
65	NIS + servers	N	N/4 NIS + server addresses	RFC 2132 (33)
66	TFTP server name	N	TFTP server name; can be used when the "sname" DHCP header field has been overloaded with other options	RFC 2132 (33)
67	Bootfile name	N	Bootfile name; can be used when the "file" DHCP header field has been overloaded with other options	RFC 2132 (33)
68	Home agent	N	N/4 Mobile IP home agent addresses	RFC 2132 (33)
69	SMTP server	N	N/4 Simple Mail Transfer Protocol (SMTP) server addresses for outgoing email	RFC 2132 (33)

70	POP3 server	N	N/4 Post Office Protocol v3 (POP3) server addresses for incoming email retrieval	RFC 2132 (33)
71	NNTP server	N	N/4 Network News Transport Protocol (NNTP) server addresses	RFC 2132 (33)
72	WWW server	N	N/4 World Wide Web (WWW) server addresses	RFC 2132 (33)
73	Finger server	N	N/4 Finger server addresses; finger servers enable retrieval of host user information regarding login name, login duration, and more	RFC 2132 (33)
74	IRC server	N	N/4 Internet Relay Chat (IRC) server addresses	RFC 2132 (33)
75	StreetTalk server	N	N/4 StreetTalk server addresses; StreetTalk was a Banyan Vines user and resource directory	RFC 2132 (33)
76	STDA server	N	N/4 StreetTalk Directory Assistance (STDA) server addresses; StreetTalk was a Banyan Vines user and resource directory	RFC 2132 (33)
77	User class	N	User class identifier	RFC 3004 (38)
78	SLP directory agent	N + 1	N/4 Service Location Protocol (SLP) Directory Agent IP address(es)	RFC 2610 (39)
79	SLP service scope	N	SLP service scope the SLP agent is configured to use	RFC 2610 (39)
80	Rapid Commit	0	Rapid Commit – requests a two-packet DHCP transaction instead of the normal four-packet DORA process for mobility or overhead-constrained applications	RFC 4039 (40)
81	Client FQDN	N	Fully qualified domain name (FQDN) – defines the client's FQDN and whether the client or DHCP server should update DNS	RFC 4702 (41)
82	Relay agent information	N	Relay agent information – additional client information supplied by the intervening relay agent	RFC 3046 (42)
83	Internet storage name service (iSNS)	N	iSNS server addresses and iSNS application information	RFC 4174 (43)
84	Unassigned	–	–	RFC 3679 (44)
85	NDS servers	N	N/4 Novell Directory Services (NDS) server IP addresses to contact for NDS client authentication and access the NDS directory repository	RFC 2241 (45)
86	NDS tree name	N	NDS tree name of the NDS repository the client should contact	RFC 2241 (45)
87	NDS context	N	NDS initial context within the NDS repository the NDS client should use	RFC 2241 (45)
88	Broadcast and multicast server (BCMCS) controller domain name	N	BCMCS domain name (FQDN) list, used to construct follow-up SRV query(ies) (BCMCS is used in 3G wireless networks to enable mobiles to receive broadcast and multicast services)	RFC 4280 (46)

(Continued)

TABLE 4.1. DHCP Options (*Continued*)

Code	Name	Len	Meaning	Reference
89	BCMCS Controller IPv4 address	*N*	*N*/4 BCMCS Controller IP address(es) (BCMCS is used in 3G wireless networks to enable mobiles to receive broadcast and multicast services)	RFC 4280 (46)
90	Authentication	*N*	Authentication option used to communicate authentication information between the client and the server in accordance with the DHCP authentication protocol	RFC3118 (47)
91	Client last-transaction time option	4	Seconds since the last DHCP transaction with the client on this lease as queried in a DHCP Lease Query message	RFC 4388 (48)
92	Associated IP option	*N*	List of IP addresses associated with the client as queried in a DHCP Lease Query message	RFC 4388 (48)
93	PXE client system	*N*	PXE client system architecture type(s) each encoded as 16-bit code, for example, Intel x86PC, DEC Alpha, EFI x86-64, and so on	RFC 4578 (49)
94	PXE client network interface	3	PXE client network interface identifier with individual octets encoded for interface type, interface major version number, and interface minor version number	RFC 4578 (49)
95	LDAP	*N*	Lightweight Directory Access Protocol servers; this option is used by Apple Computer though no governing RFC has been published	RFC 3679 (44)
96	Unassigned	–	–	RFC 3679 (44)
97	PXE client machine identifier	*N*	PXE client machine identifier with encoded type and identifier value	RFC 4578 (49)
98	User Authentication Protocol (UAP)	*N*	List of locations (URLs) for services capable of processing authentication requests encapsulated using Open Group's UAP	RFC 2485 (50)
99	Civic location	–	Location of the server, network element closest to the client or the client itself as provided by the server encoded in country-specific civic (e.g., postal) format	RFC 4776 (51)
100	Time zone	*N*	Time zone encoded as IEEE 1003.1 TZ (POSIX)	RFC 4833 (52)
101	Time zone database	*N*	Reference to a local (on the client) TZ database for lookup of time zone	RFC 4833 (52)
102–111	Unassigned	–	–	RFC 3679 (44)

112	Netinfo address	N	NetInfo parent server address: this option is used by Apple Computer though no governing RFC has been published; NetInfo is a distributed database user and resource information for Apple devices	RFC 3679 (44)
113	Netinfo tag	N	NetInfo parent server tag: this option is used by Apple Computer though no governing RFC has been published. NetInfo is a distributed database user and resource information for Apple devices	RFC 3679 (44)
114	URL	N	Uniform resource locator; this option is used by Apple Computer though no governing RFC has been published	RFC 3679 (44)
115	Unassigned	–	—	RFC 3679 (44)
116	Autoconfigure	1	Instructs the client to autoconfigure a link local address (69.254.0.0/16) or not. This can be used by the DHCP server to inform the client that it has no IP addresses to assign and that the client may or may not autoconfigure	RFC 2563 (53)
117	Name service search	N	Lists one or more name services in priority order that the client should use for name resolution: DNS, NIS, NIS +, or WINS	RFC 2937 (54)
118	Subnet selection	4	Identifies an IP subnet (address) from which to allocate an IP address to this client – overrides the GIAddr setting or DHCP server interface on which a broadcast Discover was received	RFC 3011 (55)
119	Domain search	N	List of one or more domains for configuration of the client's resolver. If the application requests a resolution for a non-FQDN host name, these domain(s) will successively be appended to the host name prior to querying	RFC 3397 (56)
120	SIP servers	N	A listing of one or more of Session Initiation Protocol (SIP) server FQDN(s) or of SIP server IP address(es). SIP is a control protocol for management of multimedia calls or sessions	RFC 3361 (57)
121	Classless static route	N	Specifies a set of static routes the client should install in its routing cache; listed as "<CIDR mask length>.<destination network> – next hop router" pairings. The destination network is enumerated only to significant octets, dropping local (nonsubnet) portions; for example, 172.16.0.0/12 would be encoded as 12.172.16 and 10.0.0.0/18 as 18.10.0.0	RFC 3442 (58)

(Continued)

TABLE 4.1. DHCP Options (*Continued*)

Code	Name	Len	Meaning	Reference
122	CableLabs client configuration	N	Specifies resource (e.g., provisioning server, DHCP server, etc.) locations, and parameters for use by cable multimedia terminal adapters (MTAs), which are customer premises devices operating over a DOCSIS cable network, providing VoIP and related multimedia services	RFC 3495 (59)
123	Location configuration information (LCI)	16	Provides the client its LCI, including latitude, longitude, altitude, and resolution of each coordinate	RFC 3825 (60)
124	Vendor-identifying vendor class	N	Enables specification of multiple vendor classes, each identified by IANA-assigned enterprise number (EN); this is useful to identify the hardware vendor, software vendor, application vendor, and so on supporting the device	RFC 3925 (61)
125	Vendor-identifying vendor-specific information	N	Set of DHCP options grouped by vendor as identified by IANA-assigned EN	RFC 3925 (61)
126–127	Unassigned	–	–	RFC 3679 (44)
128	PXE – undefined (vendor specific)			RFC 4578 (49)
Overloaded	Etherboot signature. 6 bytes: E4:45:74:68:00:00			
	DOCSIS "full security" server IP address			
	TFTP server IP address (for IP phone software load)			
129	PXE – undefined (vendor specific)			RFC 4578 (49)
Overloaded	Kernel options. Variable length string			
	Call server IP address			
130	PXE – undefined (vendor specific)			RFC 4578 (49)
Overloaded	Ethernet interface. Variable length string			
	Discrimination string (to identify vendor)			
131	PXE – undefined (vendor specific)			RFC 4578 (49)

Option	Name	Description	N	Reference
Overloaded	Remote statistics server IP address			RFC 4578 (49)
132	PXE – undefined (vendor specific)			
Overloaded	802.1Q VLAN ID			RFC 4578 (49)
133	PXE – undefined (vendor specific)			
Overloaded	802.1D/p L2 priority			RFC 4578 (49)
134	PXE – undefined (vendor specific)			
Overloaded	Diffserv code point			RFC 4578 (49)
135	PXE – undefined (vendor specific)			
Overloaded	HTTP proxy for phone-specific applications			
136	PANA agent	Identifies one or more IPv4 addresses of PANA (Protocol for Carrying Authentication for Network Access) authentication agents for use by the client for authentication and authorization for network access service	N	RFC 5192 (62)
137	LoST server	Location to service translation (LoST) server domain name; LoST protocol maps service identifiers and location information to service URLs	N	RFC 5223 (63)
138	CAPWAP access controller	Control and provisioning of wireless access points (CAPWAPs) access controller IP address(es) to which the client may connect	N	RFC 5417 (64)
139	Mobility service (MoS) IP addresses	IPv4 address(es) for servers providing particular types of IEEE 802.21 MoS	N	RFC 5678 (65)
140	MoS FQDNs	FQDN(s) for servers providing particular types of IEEE 802.21 MoS	N	RFC 5678 (65)
141	SIP user agent configuration	Session Initiation Protocol (SIP) user agent configuration		draft-lawrence-sipforum-user-agent-config-03.txt (179)
142–149	Unassigned			RFC 3942 (66)
150	TFTP server address			RFC 5859 (175)
	Etherboot			
	GRUB configuration path name			

(Continued)

TABLE 4.1. DHCP Options (*Continued*)

Code	Name	Len	Meaning	Reference
151–174	Unassigned			
175	Etherboot (tentatively assigned – June 23, 2005)			RFC 3942 (66)
176	IP telephone (tentatively assigned – June 23, 2005)			
177	Etherboot (tentatively assigned – June23, 2005)			
178–207	Unassigned			
208	PXE magic (deprecated)	4	F1:00:74:7E	RFC 3942 (66)
209	PXE configuration file	N	Configuration file name or file path name for second-stage PXE boot loading	RFC 5071 (67)
210	PXE path prefix	N	Configuration file path prefix to the file name specified in the PXE configuration file option (209)	RFC 5071 (67)
211	PXE reboot time	4	Number of seconds to wait to reboot if TFTP server is unreachable	RFC 5071 (67)
212	6rd configuration		6rd customer edge device configuration (6rd is a service provider IPv4-IPv6 technology - see Chapter 15	RFC 5969 (176)
213	LIS domain name		Location Information Server (LIS) domain name for this access network	draft-ietf-geopriv-lis-discovery-15.txt (178)
214–219	Unassigned			
220	Subnet allocation option (tentatively assigned – June 23, 2005)			
221	Virtual subnet selection option (tentatively assigned – June 23, 2005)			
222–223	Unassigned			RFC 3942 (66)
224–254	Reserved (private use)			
255	End	0	None	RFC 2132 (33)

*The $N/4$ notation refers to the use of "*N*" bytes to represent one or more IPv4 addresses, each of which is comprised of four bytes; thus for a length of *N*, the field would contain *N*/4 complete IPv4 addresses. This implies of course that *N* is a multiple of 4 in cases where the data type is IP address.

†IEN-116 = Internet Experiment Note 116; IENs were eventually merged with RFCs as TCP/IP went into production across ARPANET.

option 172. We've already described how client classes can be used to configure the DHCP server to distinguish different DHCP clients. We can now associate options for each pool, which will be provided to clients receiving addresses in the corresponding pool. An example of this is depicted in the high-level sample configuration in Figure 4.5b, which includes option declarations with the class and address pool statements to define additional parameters to be provided to clients. Alternatively, Manual DHCP address reservations enable mapping of a hardware address to a specific IP address, and associated DHCP options can also be defined for the device.

Table 4.1 lists the current set of defined DHCP options. The "code" column indicates the option code or number and the "name" column lists the corresponding option name. Note that the "Len" (length) column indicates the value of the length field within the option. The total option length is this value plus two bytes, one byte for the code and one for the length field itself.

4.5 OTHER MEANS OF DYNAMIC ADDRESS ASSIGNMENT

While DHCP provides a means for network administrators to preallocate dynamic address pools on a number of subnets and provide a mechanism to discern different device types for discriminatory assignment of an IP address and configuration parameters, there are other methods, albeit less popular, for dynamic address assignment. A common alternative method besides address autoconfiguration is the use of a Radius server to assign an IP address. Radius, or its successor protocol, Diameter, provides an authentication, authorization, and accounting (AAA) service for IP hosts attempting to access a network. The connection from a client to a Radius server is commonly performed via a Point-to-Point (PPP) or Extensible Authentication Protocol (EAP) connection, for example, when the client is attempting to access a network edge device or dial pool. The Radius server challenges the client to enter a user name and password, authenticates the entered information against its internal or external database, and finally provides access to the network by providing an IP address to the client.

While vastly simplifying the Radius protocol, the relevant concept here is that some Radius servers, or even edge router devices, can be configured with address pools from which individual IP address assignments can be made to authorized clients. In some cases, Radius servers can be configured to actually utilize the DHCP protocol to obtain an address from a DHCP server. In this case, the Radius server acts as a DHCP proxy client to obtain an IP address on behalf of, and for assignment to, the requesting client. We'll discuss some alternative DHCP server deployment strategies in Chapter 7, where we'll compare DHCP deployment on edge devices with DHCP deployment on discrete DHCP servers.

DHCP FOR IPv6 (DHCPv6)

For those devices that obtain IPv6 addresses dynamically, two main strategies are available to automate this address assignment process: client based or network server based. In Chapter 2, we introduced the concept of client-based address assignment in the form of address autoconfiguration, a process whereby a client can determine its location based on router advertisements and automatically calculate its interface identifier to derive an address. However, if during the requisite process of duplicate address detection, the host determines that its autoconfigured address is already in use, it must rederive another address or await manual intervention.

Network server-based address assignment such as DHCP enables a host to announce its presence in requesting an IP address, among other parameters, from a server in the IP network. DHCP for IPv6 addresses is referred to as DHCPv6 and is defined in RFC 3315 (68). As defined, DHCPv6 is not integrated with DHCP for IPv4. This means that DHCPv6 will support IPv6 addresses and configurations only, not additionally IPv4 addresses and parameters. It is left to future development to define this should demand dictate.

IP Address Management: Principles and Practice, by Timothy Rooney
Copyright © 2011 the Institute of Electrical and Electronics Engineers, Inc.

5.1 DHCP COMPARISON: IPv4 VERSUS IPv6[*]

DHCPv6 uses different message types and packet formatting than DHCP for IPv4, but is similar in many ways. Table 5.1 highlights these similarities and differences.

T A B L E 5.1. Comparison of DHCP for IPv4 and IPv6

Feature	DHCP for IPv4	DHCPv6
Destination IP address of initial client message	Broadcast (255.255.255.255)	Multicast to link-scoped address: All-DHCP-Agents address (FF02::1:2)
DHCP Relay support	Yes by configuring DHCP server addresses in each relay agent	Yes either by configuring DHCP server addresses in each relay agent or using the All_DHCP_Servers site-scoped multicast address (FF05::1:3)
Relay agent forwarding	Same message type code, but inserts giaddr and unicasts to DHCP server(s)	Encapsulates client message in RELAY-FORW to DHCP server(s) and RELAY-REPL from server(s)
Message to locate server to obtain IP address and configuration	DHCPDISCOVER	SOLICIT
Server message to engage client	DHCPOFFER	ADVERTISE
Client message to accept parameters	DHCPREQUEST	REQUEST
Server acknowledgment of lease binding	DHCPACK	REPLY
Client message to leasing DHCP server to extend lease	DHCPREQUEST (unicast)	RENEW (unicast)
Client message to any DHCP server to extend lease	DHCPREQUEST (broadcast)	REBIND (multicast)
Client message to relinquish a lease	DHCPRELEASE	RELEASE
Client message to indicate that an offered IP address is already in use	DHCPDECLINE	DECLINE
Server message to instruct client to obtain a new configuration	DHCPFORCERENEW	RECONFIGURE
Request IP configuration only, not address	DHCPINFORM	INFORMATION-REQUEST

[*]Initial sections of this chapter are based on Chapter 3 of Ref. 11.

5.2 DHCPv6 ADDRESS ASSIGNMENT

When a device initializes on an IPv6 subnet, it will listen for or solicit a router advertisement to determine if DHCPv6 services are available for the subnet. Recall from our discussion about neighbor discovery in Chapter 2 that the M bit within the router advertisement informs subnet devices that DHCPv6 services are available for address and parameter assignment; the O bit indicates that DHCPv6 services are available for parameter setting but not for address assignment. The DHCPv6 process begins with a client issuing a SOLICIT message, in essence requesting a "bid" from DHCP servers that can provide an IP address on the particular subnet to which the client is connected. Instead of broadcasting this initial packet as in IPv4, the SOLICIT message is sent by the client to the All_Relay_Agents_and_Servers multicast address, FF02::1:2. Note that the scope field on this multicast address, highlighted in bold (FF0**2**::1:2), applies to link local scope.

DHCPv6 servers on this subnet will receive the SOLICIT packet directly and may respond with an ADVERTISE packet, indicating a preference value. The preference value is intended to enable the client to select the server advertising the highest preference as configured by administrators. The server will also indicate if it has no addresses available on the subnet. The ADVERTISE packet will be unicast to the client if the SOLICIT had been received directly using the client's source IP address from the SOLICIT packet (most likely the client's link local address).

The client analyzes the advertisements received, and selects a server from which to request an IP address, typically with the highest preference, and issues a REQUEST message to the server. The server will then record the address assignment and reply to the client with a REPLY message as shown in Figure 5.1.

Any routers on the link configured as relay agents receiving the SOLICIT packet from a DHCPv6 client will relay the packet to one or more DHCPv6 servers. IPv6 relay agents do not require configuration of DHCP Relay addresses as in the IPv4 case, though they may enable such configuration. Instead of simply forwarding the packet to one or more DHCP servers as in IPv4, IPv6 relay agents encapsulate the original SOLICIT packet within a RELAY-FORW packet. This packet is then sent to configured DHCP servers or via multicast to the scoped All-DHCP-Servers multicast address (FF05::1:3). Analogous to the IPv4 DHCP GIAddr parameter, the link address field of the RELAY-FORW packet indicates the link on which the client requesting an IP address currently resides. This process is illustrated in Figure 5.2. This information is used by the DHCPv6 server in assigning an appropriate IP address for this link. The

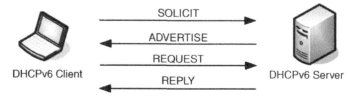

Figure 5.1. DHCPv6 address assignment.

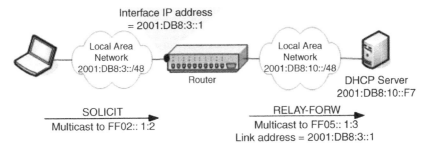

Figure 5.2. DHCPv6 Relay (11).

DHCPv6 server encapsulates its ADVERTISE message in a RELAY-REPL packet and unicasts it to the corresponding relay agent.

When the client receives a Reply packet to confirm the address assignment, the client must perform duplicate address detection to ensure no other device is already using the IP address due to autoconfiguration or manual configuration. If another device is using the assigned IP address, the client would send a Decline message to the DHCP server, indicating that the address is in use. The client can then reinitiate the DHCP process to obtain a different IP address.

In addition to the four-packet exchange outlined above, DHCPv6 features a rapid commit option. This halves the messaging requirements by enabling the server to simply REPLY to a SOLICIT packet. The client would include the rapid commit option in its SOLICIT message. Servers responding with an address assignment would issue a REPLY packet directly, also including the rapid commit option. Note that each server responding will assume that the address it assigned is leased, so rapid commit should be used either with short lease times or for support by a limited number of servers if normally there are many serving the same subnet.

As in IPv6 autoconfiguration described in Chapter 2, each nontemporary[*] IPv6 address assigned via DHCP has a preferred lifetime and a valid lifetime. After the preferred lifetime expires, the address is considered valid but deprecated. No new IP communications sessions should utilize the address while deprecated.

5.3 DHCPv6 PREFIX DELEGATION

DHCPv6 is not only used to assign individual IP addresses and/or associated IP configuration information to hosts but can also be used to delegate entire networks to requesting router devices. This form of delegation via DHCPv6 is called *prefix delegation*. This original motivation for prefix delegation arose from broadband service providers seeking to automate the process of delegating IPv6 subnets (e.g., /48 to /64 networks) to broadband subscribers in a hierarchical manner. A requesting router device at the edge of the service provider network, facing subscribers, would issue a request for address space via the DHCPv6 protocol to a delegating router. Note the terminology: this

[*] A temporary address is a short nonrenewable address.

is intended to be an inter-router protocol though a DHCPv6 server could perform the functions of the delegating router.

The prefix delegation process utilizes the same basic DHCPv6 message flow described above for address assignment per Figure 5.1: Solicit, Advertisement, Request, and Reply. Additional information within the corresponding DHCPv6 messages is used to determine an appropriate network for delegation. Like IP addresses, prefixes have preferred and valid lifetimes. The requesting router can request a lifetime extension via the DHCPv6 Renew and Rebind messages.

5.4 DHCPv6 SUPPORT OF ADDRESS AUTOCONFIGURATION

When we discussed IPv6 autoconfiguration in Chapter 2, we defined three types of autoconfiguration:

- *Stateless.* This process is "stateless" in that it does not depend on the state or availability of external assignment mechanisms, for example, DHCPv6.
- *Stateful.* The stateful process relies solely on external address assignment mechanism such as DHCPv6.
- *Combination Stateless and Stateful.* This process involves a form of stateless address autoconfiguration used in conjunction with stateful configuration of additional IP parameters.

This third combined form of autoconfiguration leverages DHCPv6 not for IPv6 address assignment, but for assignment of additional parameters, encoded as DHCPv6 options. The client can request configuration parameters via the Information-Request message, indicating which option parameter values it is seeking. A server(s) that is able to supply the desired configuration parameters will respond with a Reply message with the corresponding option parameters.

5.4.1 DHCPv6 Message Types

The following message types have been defined for DHCPv6:

- SOLICIT—message type = 1—issued by a client to locate DHCPv6 servers.
- ADVERTISE—message type = 2—issued by a server in response to a Solicit message to indicate availability of the server for DHCP service.
- REQUEST—message type = 3—issued by the client to request IP addresses and configuration parameters from a particular DHCPv6 server.
- CONFIRM—message type = 4—issued by a client to any available server to verify that the addresses assigned to it are still appropriate to its current subnet location.
- RENEW—message type = 5—issued by a client to the server from which it received its IP address to extend or renew its IP address lifetime and to update other parameters.

- REBIND—message type = 6—issued by a client to all available servers to extend its IP address lifetime and to update other parameters. This is sent after receiving no response from a prior RENEW message.

- REPLY—message type = 7—issued by a server to supply IP address and/or configuration parameters to a client in response to Solicit, Request, Renew, or Rebind messages. The server also issues this message type to clients desiring to confirm their configurations via the Confirm message and to acknowledge receipt of Release and Decline messages from clients.

- RELEASE—message type = 8—issued by a client to the server from which it received its IP address to relinquish the IP address. The client must then cease use of the IP address.

- DECLINE—message type = 9—issued by a client to inform a server that one or more addresses assigned by the server are already in use on the link on which the client resides.

- RECONFIGURE—message type = 10—issued by a server to instruct a client to reinitialize as the server has new or updated configuration parameters for the client. The client must then issue a Renew or Information-Request as instructed by the server to obtain the updated or new information.

- INFORMATION-REQUEST—message type = 11—issued by the client to obtain configuration parameters other than IP addresses from a server.

- RELAY-FORW—message type = 12—issued by a relay agent to a server or set of servers directly or via another agent to encapsulate a client-initiated or relay agent-initiated message.

- RELAY-REPL—message type = 13—issued by a server in reply to RELAY-FORW to a relay agent encapsulating a message destined for a client, which is encoded as an option within the RELAY-REPL message. The relay agent may pass the message directly or via other relay agents to the client.

- LEASEQUERY—message type = 14—issued by a device such as an access concentrator or relay agent to request lease binding information from the DHCP server for a particular client IPv6 address, DUID, relay agent, link address, or remote identifier. The IPv6 client DUID queries are for individual device lease queries, whereas the other query types facilitate bulk lease query of multiple client lease states. Bulk lease query for IPv4 is under development within the IETF.

- LEASEQUERY-REPLY—message type = 15—issued by a server to the querying device in response to a LEASEQUERY message with the lease binding information relevant to the query.

- LEASEQUERY-DONE—message type = 16—issued by a server to the querying device indicating the end of a result of a Bulk LeaseQuery.

- LEASEQUERY–DATA—message type = 17—issued by a server to the querying device to encapsulate a single DHCPv6 client's lease information when more than one client's data is provided in such results.

Figure 5.3. DHCPv6 packet format (68).

5.4.2 DHCPv6 Packet Format

The DHCPv6 packet format is very simple (Figure 5.3). It consists of an 8-bit message type, 24-bit transaction ID, and a variable-length options field. That's it! Information regarding identification and configuration of the client is placed within the options field.

However, when a relay agent is in the path between the client and the server, the relay agent modifies the message, yielding a common format for both forwarded and reply messages, as shown in Figure 5.4:

- 8-bit message type
- 8-bit hop count or the number of relay agents that have relayed this message, incremented by each along the path
- 128-bit link-address—the IPv6 address that is used by the server to identify the link on which the client is located (similar to the giaddr concept)
- 128-bit peer address—the IPv6 address of the client or relay agent from which the message to be relayed was received
- Variable length options field, including the relay message option that includes the DHCPv6 message being relayed between the client and the server

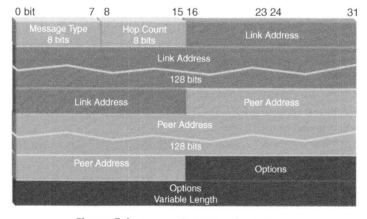

Figure 5.4. DHCP Relay packet format (68).

5.5 DEVICE UNIQUE IDENTIFIERS

Like DHCPv4, a DHCPv6 server must track the availability and assignment of IP addresses within its configured address pools and identify requestors and holders of IP addresses. DHCPv6 utilizes the Device Unique Identifier (DUID) to identify clients. DUIDs are used not only for servers to identify clients but also for clients to identify servers. The DUID is analogous to the client-identifier concept in that DUIDs are intended to be globally unique for a device, not an interface. DUIDs should not change over time, even if the device undergoes changes in hardware. DUIDs are constructed in various manners automatically by IPv6 nodes. They consist of a two-octet type code followed by a variable number of octets based on the type. The following DUID-type codes are defined as follows:

- Type = 1—link layer address plus time (DUID-LLT)
- Type = 2—vendor-assigned unique ID based on Enterprise Number (DUID-EN)
- Type = 3—link layer-based DUID (DUID-LL)

For those based on link layer address, they are to be used for *all* device interfaces, even if the hardware from which the link layer address was obtained is removed. The DUID is a device identifier, not an interface identifier.

5.5.1 DUID-LLT

The DUID-link layer address plus time format is shown in Figure 5.5. The DUID type is "1". The hardware type is the IANA-assigned value for the hardware type of the interface (see http://www.iana.org/assignments/arp-parameters for a complete list). The time field follows and represents the time that the DUID was created in seconds since midnight UTC, January 1, 2000, modulo 2^{32}. Then the hardware address of the selected interface comprises the link layer address field.

This DUID is formed by a device by selecting one interface for the use of its link layer type and address. The DUID should be stored in persistent storage on the device. The link layer address must be globally unique for its corresponding hardware type. This same DUID is then associated with each interface on the device during

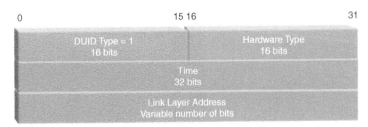

Figure 5.5. Link layer address plus time formatted DUID (68).

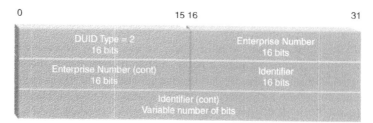

Figure 5.6. Enterprise number formatted DUID (68).

communications with the DHCP server, even if the interface upon which derivation of the DUID was based is removed. However, should the interface be removed and placed in another device, the time component of this DUID format should provide a high degree of likelihood that the DUID formulated by the new device using the same interface card will differ, should that device so choose to base its DUID on the same interface address. The DUID-LLT format is recommended for those devices that have persistent storage for storing the DUID.

5.5.2 DUID-EN

The Enterprise Number-based DUID format is assigned to the device by the vendor (Figure 5.6). The DUID consists of the DUID type "2", the Enterprise Number as assigned by IANA (see http://www.iana.org/assignments/enterprise-numbers) to the device vendor much as Ethernet interface prefixes are assigned to vendors by the IEEE. The EN is then followed by a vendor-unique identifier assigned by the vendor. This DUID must be stored in persistent storage on the device.

5.5.3 DUID-LL

The link layer address-based DUID is very similar to DUID-LLT, with the omission of the time field. The DUID Type is '3' (Figure 5.7). The hardware type is the IANA-assigned value for the hardware type of the interface (see http://www.iana.org/assignments/arp-parameters for complete list), and the link layer address field follows. Like the other forms of DUIDs, a common DUID should be associated with each

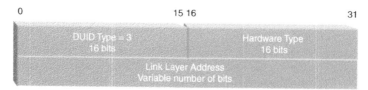

Figure 5.7. Link layer address formatted DUID (68).

interface on the device. This form of DUID is recommended for those devices that do not have persistent storage capabilities for the DUID value.

5.6 IDENTITY ASSOCIATIONS

While DUIDs are associated with all interfaces of a device and IP addresses are assigned to interfaces, you may be wondering how the device and server identify particular interfaces for a given DUID. The concept of the identity association (IA) provides this linkage between a DHCPv6 server and a client interface for individual address assignment. IAs are differentiated by type between those for temporary addresses (IA_TA), which are short-leased, nonrenewable addresses, those for nontemporary addresses (IA_NA), and those for prefix delegation (IA_PD).

Temporary address assignments assuage privacy concerns associated with auto-configured addresses based on hardware addresses (i.e., modified EUI-64 interface IDs), which do not change over time. The concern is that a given interface ID within an IPv6 address does not change unless the underlying hardware interface changes. Thus, even if the network upon which a device is connected changes from day to day, the interface ID does not. The ability to track the location of a device and thus its user becomes relatively easy, thus the concern with privacy. The use of short-lived, non-renewable address assignments via DHCPv6 using temporary addresses is one means to address this concern. Please see RFC 3041 for more background on this privacy issue.

For individual address assignment, temporary or nontemporary, each client interface has an IA, identified by an IA identifier (IAID). The IAID is represented as four octets in client–server DHCPv6 communications and is chosen by the client. The IAID must be unique among all IAIDs associated with the client and must be stored persistently across client reboots or consistently derivable upon each reboot. The client specifies its DUID and IAID for which an address is being requested from the DHCPv6 server. The DHCPv6 server assigns an IPv6 address to the IAID, along with the corresponding T1 (renew) and T2 (reboot) timer values.

IA_PDs are not necessarily associated with a device interface. Recall that the requesting router is using DHCPv6 to obtain an IPv6 network delegation. The requesting router must derive one or more IA_PDs for use within DHCPv6, and it must be persistent across reboots or consistently derivable.

5.7 DHCPv6 OPTIONS

DHCPv6 options are used to convey information relevant to the associated DHCP message, including DUIDs and IAs. Options are listed within the DHCPv6 message and have the general format as shown in Figure 5.8.

The currently defined set of DHCPv6 options are given in Table 5.2. Note that certain options may be nested, such as those associated with an IA.

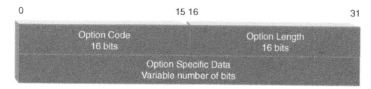

Figure 5.8. DHCPv6 options format (68).

TABLE 5.2. DHCPv6 Options

Code	Name	Meaning	Reference
1	OPTION_CLIENTID	Client identifier (DUID of client)	RFC 3315 (68)
2	OPTION_SERVERID	Server identifier (DUID of server)	RFC 3315 (68)
3	OPTION_IA_NA	Identity association for nontemporary addresses— includes the IAID, T1 time, T2 time, and additional options for the IA for nontemporary addresses	RFC 3315 (68)
4	OPTION_IA_TA	Identity association for temporary addresses—includes the IAID and additional options for this IA for temporary addresses	RFC 3315 (68)
5	OPTION_IAADDR	IA address option—specifies IPv6 addresses and associated preferred lifetime, valid lifetime, and options associated with an IA_NA or IA_TA. As such, this option may only appear as an option to the DHCPv6 message option OPTION_IA_TA or OPTION_IA_NA	RFC 3315 (68)
6	OPTION_ORO	Option request option—used by clients to list option codes for which values are requested or by servers in a Reconfigure message to indicate which options the client should request in its subsequent Renew or Information-Request message	RFC 3315 (68)
7	OPTION_PREFERENCE	Preference setting by the server to facilitate client selection of DHCP server	RFC 3315 (68)

T A B L E 5.2. DHCPv6 Options *(Continued)*

Code	Name	Meaning	Reference
8	OPTION_ELAPSED_ TIME	The amount of time since the client began the current DHCP transaction in hundredths of a second. Clients are required to use this option	RFC 3315 (68)
9	OPTION_RELAY_MSG	The DHCP message being relayed by a relay agent	RFC 3315 (68)
10	Unassigned		
11	OPTION_AUTH	Authentication information for use in reliably identifying the source of a DHCP message and to verify message integrity	RFC 3315 (68)
12	OPTION_UNICAST	Server unicast option indicates the IP address to which the client may unicast messages to this server	RFC 3315 (68)
13	OPTION_STATUS_ CODE	Status code option indicates a 2-byte status code and variable length status message. This option may be used as a DHCP message option or as an option within another DHCP message option	RFC 3315 (68)
14	OPTION_RAPID_ COMMIT	Rapid commit option enables a client to request a direct reply with an IP address and parameters, bypassing the Advertise and Request messages	RFC3315 (68)
15	OPTION_USER_CLASS	User class option—analogous to user class in DHCPv4 in assisting the server in making address assignment decisions	RFC 3315 (68)
16	OPTION_VENDOR_ CLASS	Vendor class option—analogous to vendor class in DHCPv4 in conveying the vendor or manufacturer of the device or interface to assist the server in making address assignment decisions. The vendor class option includes the IANA-assigned Enterprise Number for the vendor	RFC 3315 (68)

(continued)

T A B L E 5.2. DHCPv6 Options (*Continued*)

Code	Name	Meaning	Reference
17	OPTION_VENDOR_ OPTS	Vendor-specific information— this option includes the IANA-assigned Enterprise Number as well as one or more options, each defined with option code, length, and value	RFC 3315(68)
18	OPTION_ INTERFACE_ID	Interface ID option—used by relay agents to convey the agent's interface ID on which the client message was received. This option may only appear in RELAY-FORW messages, and when it does, it is copied by the server to the RELAY-REPL message	RFC 3315 (68)
19	OPTION_RECONF_MSG	Reconfigure message option for use in the Reconfigure message to inform the client which message type to use to reconfigure; either Renew or Information-Request	RFC 3315 (68)
20	OPTION_RECONF_ ACCEPT	Reconfigure accept option—the client uses this option if it is willing to accept Reconfigure messages from the server	RFC 3315 (68)
21	OPTION_SIP_ SERVER_D	SIP servers domain names option listing domain names of the SIP outbound proxy servers that the client can use	RFC 3319 (69)
22	OPTION_SIP_ SERVER_A	SIP servers IPv6 address list option lists the IPv6 addresses of the SIP outbound proxy servers that the client can use	RFC 3319 (69)
23	OPTION_DNS_SERVERS	DNS recursive name server option—lists IPv6 address(es) of DNS recursive name servers to which DNS queries may be sent by the client resolver in order of preference	RFC 3646 (70)
24	OPTION_DOMAIN_LIST	Domain search list option— provides a domain search list for client use when resolving hostnames via DNS	RFC 3646 (70)

TABLE 5.2. DHCPv6 Options (*Continued*)

Code	Name	Meaning	Reference
25	OPTION_IA_PD	Identity association for prefix delegation—includes the IAID, T1 time, T2 time, and additional options for the IA_PD, including the associated prefix(es) defined as option code 26	RFC 3633 (71)
26	OPTION_IAPREFIX	IA_PD Prefix option—specifies the IPv6 prefixes associated with the IA_PD, along with associated options and preferred and valid lifetimes. This option may only appear as an option to the DHCPv6 message option OPTION_IA_PD. The prefix is specified with an 8-bit prefix length and a 128-bit IPv6 prefix	RFC 3633 (71)
27	OPTION_NIS_SERVERS	Network information service (NIS) servers—ordered list of NIS servers by IPv6 address available to the client	RFC 3898 (72)
28	OPTION_NISP_SERVERS	Network information service v2 (NIS +) servers—ordered list of NIS + servers by IPv6 address available to the client	RFC 3898 (72)
29	OPTION_NIS_ DOMAIN_NAME	Network information service domain name—NIS domain name to be used by the client	RFC 3898 (72)
30	OPTION_NISP_ DOMAIN_NAME	Network information service v2 (NIS +) domain name—NIS + domain name to be used by the client	RFC 3898 (72)
31	OPTION_SNTP_ SERVERS	Simple Network Time Protocol (SNTP) servers—ordered list of SNTP servers by IPv6 address available to the client	RFC 4075 (73)
32	OPTION_ INFORMATION_ REFRESH_TIME	Information refresh option—specifies the upper bound of the number or seconds from the current time that a client should wait before refreshing information received from the DHCPv6 server, particularly for stateless DHCPv6 scenarios	RFC 4242 (74)

(continued)

TABLE 5.2. DHCPv6 Options (*Continued*)

Code	Name	Meaning	Reference
33	OPTION_BCMCS_ SERVER_D	Broadcast and multicast service (BCMCS) domain name list— list of one or more FQDNs corresponding to BCMCS server(s) (BCMCS is used in 3G wireless networks to enable mobiles to receive broadcast and multicast services.)	RFC 4280 (46)
34	OPTION_BCMCS_ SERVER_A	Broadcast and multicast service IPv6 address list—list of one or more IPv6 address(es) corresponding to BCMCS server(s). (BCMCS is used in 3G wireless networks to enable mobiles to receive broadcast and multicast services)	RFC 4280 (46)
35	Unassigned		
36	OPTION_GEOCONF_ CIVIC	Geographical location in civic (e.g., postal) format. This option can be provided by the server to relate the location of the server, the closest network element (e.g., router) to the client, or the client itself. The location information includes an ISO 3166 country code (US, DE, JP, etc.) and country-specific location information such as state, province, county, city, block, group of streets, and more	RFC 4776 (51)
37	OPTION_REMOTE_ID	Relay agent remote ID option—remote identity inserted by the relay agent in RELAY-FORW message to the DHCPv6 server. This is useful in service provider environments where the "edge" device facing the subscriber device inserts an identifier for the subscriber connection prior to relaying to the DHCPv6 server	RFC 4649 (75)

T A B L E 5.2. DHCPv6 Options (*Continued*)

Code	Name	Meaning	Reference
38	OPTION_SUBSCRIBER_ID	Relay agent subscriber ID option—subscriber identity inserted by the relay agent in RELAY-FORW message to the DHCPv6 server. This is useful in service provider environments where the "edge" device facing the subscriber device inserts an identifier for the subscriber from which the message originated, prior to relaying to the DHCPv6 server	RFC 4580 (76)
39	OPTION_CLIENT_FQDN	FQDN option—indicates whether the client or the DHCP server should update DNS with the AAAA record corresponding to the assigned IPv6 address and the FQDN provided in this option. The DHCP server always updates the PTR record	RFC 4704 (77)
40	OPTION_PANA_AGENT	This option provides one or more IPv6 address(es) associated with PANA (Protocol for Carrying Authentication for Network Access) Authentication Agents that a client can use	RFC 5192 (62)
41	OPTION_NEW_POSIX_TIMEZONE	Time zone (TZ) to be used by the client in IEEE 1003.1 format (POSIX—portable operating system interface). This format enables textual representation of time zone and daylight savings time information	RFC 4833 (52)
42	OPTION_NEW_TZDB_TIMEZONE	Time zone database entry referred to by entry name. The client must have a copy of the TZ database, which it queries for the corresponding entry to determine its time zone	RFC 4833 (52)

(continued)

T A B L E 5.2. DHCPv6 Options (*Continued*)

Code	Name	Meaning	Reference
43	OPTION_ERO	Relay agent echo request option—used by relay agents in the RELAY_FORW message to request that the DHCPv6 server echo back certain requested relay agent options, even if not supported on the server (DHCPv4 servers always echo back relay agent option (82) information, but this is not required in DHCPv6, hence this option for relay agents requiring such echo back.)	RFC 4994 (78)
44	OPTION_LQ_QUERY	The query option is used in the LEASEQUERY message to identify the query information being requested. This option includes the query type (by IA address or client ID option), link address to which the query applies, and query options	RFC 5007 (79)
45	OPTION_CLIENT_ DATA	Client data—this option contains the query response information for the requested client data within a LEASEQUERY-REPLY message. At a minimum, this option includes the client identifier (OPTION_ CLIENTID), the IA address or prefix (OPTION_IAADDR and/ or OPTION_IAPREFIX), and client last transaction time (OPTION_CLT_TIME)	RFC 5007 (79)
46	OPTION_CLT_TIME	Client last transaction time— indicates the number of seconds since the server last communicated with the client referenced by the lease query. This option is encapsulated within the OPTION_CLIENT_ DATA option within a LEASEQUERY-REPLY message	RFC 5007 (79)

TABLE 5.2. DHCPv6 Options (*Continued*)

Code	Name	Meaning	Reference
47	OPTION_LQ_RELAY_ DATA	Relay data—used in a LEASEQUERY-REPLY message to provide the relay agent information associated with the client information requested. This option includes the relay agent address from which the client's relay information was received along with the complete relayed message	RFC 5007 (79)
48	OPTION_LQ_CLIENT_ LINK	Client link—identifies one or more links on which the queried client has DHCPv6 bindings. The queried client can be identified by address or client ID	RFC 5007 (79)
49	OPTION_MIP6_HNINF	Mobile IPv6 home network information—used by the client to identify its target home network to the server (in an Information Request message)	draft-ietf-mip6-hiopt-17.txt (80)
50	OPTION_MIP6_RELAY	Mobile IPv6 relay agent—used by a relay agent to identify home network information via a RELAY-FORW message	draft-ietf-mip6-hiopt-17.txt (80)
51	OPTION_V6_LOST	Location to Service Translation (LoST) server domain name; LoST protocol maps service identifiers and location information to service URLs	RFC 5223 (63)
52	OPTION_CAPWAP_AC_ V6	Control and provisioning of wireless access points (CAPWAP) access controller IPv6 address(es) to which the client may connect	RFC 5417 (64)
53	OPTION_RELAY_ID	DHCPv6 Bulk LeaseQuery—requests lease and prefix delegation bindings for a specified relay agent identified by its DUID in this option	RFC 5460 (81)

(continued)

TABLE 5.2. DHCPv6 Options (*Continued*)

Code	Name	Meaning	Reference
54	OPTION-IPv6_ Addresss-MoS	List of IPv6 address(es) for servers providing particular types of IEEE 802.21 Mobility Services (MoS)	RFC 5678 (65)
55	OPTION-IPv6_ FQDN-MoS	List of FQDN(s) for servers providing particular types of IEEE 802.21 Mobility Services	RFC 5678 (65)
56	OPTION_NTP_SERVER	Network Time Protocol (NTP) and Simple NTP (SNTP) server address(es) and/or domain names	RFC 5908 (180)
57	OPTION_F6_ACCESS_ DOMAIN	Domain name of the Location Information Server (LIS) on this access network	draft-ietf-geopriv-lis-discovery-15 (178)
58	OPTION_SIP_UA_ CS_LIST	Session Initiation Protocol (SIP) user agent configuration	draft-lawrence-sipforum-user-agent-config-03 (179)
59	OPT_BOOTFILE_URL	URL of client boot file	draft-dhc-dhcpv6-opt-netboot-10 (181)
60	OPT_BOOTFILE_PARAM	Client bootfile parameters	draft-dhc-dhcpv6-opt-netboot-10 (181)
61	OPTION_CLIENT_ ARCH_TYPE	Client system architecture	draft-dhc-dhcpv6-opt-netboot-10 (181)
62	OPTION_NII	Client network interface for universal network device interface (UNDI) support	draft-dhc-dhcpv6-opt-netboot-10 (181)
63–255	Unassigned		

6

DHCP APPLICATIONS

The most fundamental application for DHCP is automated address assignment. We take DHCP for granted when we connect to an IP network. This basic function renders IP applications easier to use by automating initialization of the IP layer. End users need not call the help desk to obtain and enter IP addresses into their devices. DHCP not only automates IP address assignments but also enables network administrators to retain control of what IP addresses may be assigned to certain clients, even up to denying access as we'll discuss in Chapter 8. In this chapter, we'll discuss technology applications that rely on DHCP, beyond basic address assignment services. Of course, these applications that rely on DHCP therefore also rely on the DHCP configuration being consistent with the IP address plan!

This chapter highlights those applications requiring special purpose DHCP configurations, including device-specific configuration and broadband provisioning. DHCP-based access control could also be grouped within this topic, but we'll cover that in the context of security in Chapter 8 instead.

The cornerstone in supporting various applications with DHCP is the ability of the DHCP server to classify a device requesting an address and to supply an appropriate IP address and additional configuration information. This classification of clients into *client classes* enables the DHCP administrator to identify a parameter value within a particular

IP Address Management: Principles and Practice, by Timothy Rooney
Copyright © 2011 the Institute of Electrical and Electronics Engineers, Inc.

DHCP packet field or option to match on a per-DHCP transaction basis. When a client is classified, the DHCP server may then determine

- from which IP address pool to assign an address to the client (if any)
- what additional or alternative option parameter values to provide to the client.

Leading DHCP reference implementations from the Internet Systems Consortium (ISC) and Microsoft support both the vendor class identifier (option 60 for IPv4 and 16 for IPv6) and the user class identifier (option 77 for IPv4 and 15 for IPv6) options as class parameters. When these options are included in the Discover or Solicit packet, the server can use this information to identify the type of device that is requesting its configuration.

6.1 MULTIMEDIA DEVICE TYPE SPECIFIC CONFIGURATION

The most common example application we've used so far is that of multimedia device initialization, such as voice over IP (VoIP) devices. In many cases, the multimedia vendor manufacturer encodes a given vendor class identifier option value. Most vendors supply a model number and/or manufacturer name within the vendor class identifier option field. Configuring the DHCP server to recognize this particular value enables the server to supply certain DHCP options required by the client and to assign an IP address from a specific address pool. Other application-specific DHCP clients requiring particular configuration parameters may likewise be identified and configured on the basis of the value of the corresponding vendor class option.

The user class identifier option is another candidate for determining client configuration. However, since user class identifier is typically end-user settable, it is considered less reliable. Should a user outside of the user class group discover the value or setting, he or she could program his or her device accordingly. For example, using Microsoft's ipconfig utility with the/setclassid argument, it's quite easy to set the value of the user class identifier option.

In Chapter 4, we introduced an example VoIP application configuration when discussing the setting up of client classes for IPAM Worldwide's San Francisco office to differentiate VoIP devices by vendor class. Figure 4.5b, reproduced here as Figure 6.1, illustrates a simple example of configuring an ISC DHCP server to identify clients of class "vendor-y" if a DHCP packet contains a vendor class identifier option value of "vendorY." Once classified as a vendor-y device, the client would be issued an address from the 10.16.129.20–10.16.129.250 pool on the subnet with corresponding routers and DNS server options. These option values are specified along with the allowed members of "vendor-y" statement within this pool declaration.

Similarly, devices of class "vendor-x" will be identified by clients supplying a vendor class identifier option value of "vendorX." Such devices will be assigned from the 10.16.128.20–10.16.128.250 pool on the 10.16.128/23 subnet with the routers (and tftp-server-name) option values.

The ISC DHCP server supports filtering on additional class parameters, in fact, up to any packet parameter from MAC address, a subset of the MAC address, or any option

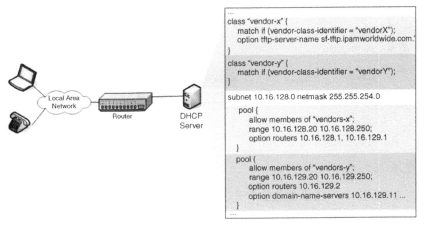

Figure 6.1. Specifying configuration information for DHCP clients by class (syntax based on Ref. 35).

value. This is convenient if a given MAC address (interface card) or MAC prefix (manufacturer) needs to be filtered and assigned certain parameters.

6.2 BROADBAND SUBSCRIBER PROVISIONING

The cable industry defined a standard for data transmission over cable, referred to as Data Over Cable Service Interface Specifications (DOCSIS®). The DOCSIS specifications, authored by CableLabs, require the use of DHCP for provisioning of customer premises equipment (CPE), such as cable modems and telephony devices. A cable operator that offers cable data or broadband Internet services must deploy DHCP servers to support the CPE provisioning process. Other broadband technologies such as digital subscriber line (DSL) and fiber may also use DHCP or Bootp, though other techniques such as PPP (Point-to-Point Protocol) are also used by these broadband technologies.

The incorporation of DHCP into the provisioning process affords the broadband operator control over IP address assignments and capacity, as well as additional configuration parameters used by CPE for initialization. DHCP can also be used to assign IP addresses from address pools corresponding to various service levels based upon the customer's subscription. Assigning an address from a given pool requires the network routing infrastructure be configured to route IP packets with such addresses only to certain networks, permit access to certain destinations, and treat packets with corresponding levels of priority and queuing.

Let's consider an example to illustrate these concepts. In Figure 6.2, three subscribers are connected to a common broadband gateway via the broadband access network. The figure depicts each subscriber with various levels of service as indicated by different shading, connected to individual ports on the broadband gateway. Depending on the broadband access technology, these may be physical ports or logical ports for shared network access.

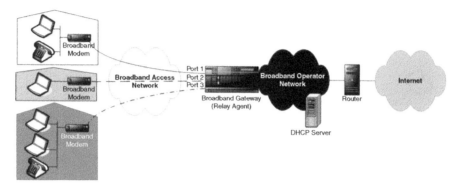

Figure 6.2. Broadband access scenario (11).

Regardless of the broadband access technology, service providers using DHCP need to base address and parameter assignment on known or trusted information. Instead of relying on the client hardware address field of the DHCP packet, which can be spoofed, service providers rely on information from the broadband gateway, which resides in the service provider's network and is considered trustworthy.

The broadband gateway, acting as a DHCP Relay agent, unicasts the DHCP packet to the appropriate DHCP server(s), inserting the GIAddr field within the DHCP packet header. The gateway also inserts the relay agent information option parameter as the last option before the null option terminator. The relay agent information option provides information such as the subscriber device hardware address or subscriber virtual circuit identifier to help the DHCP server identify the subscriber client that issued the DHCPDISCOVER packet.

This enables the DHCP server to provide, on the basis of its configuration, an appropriate number of IP addresses and/or option parameters for a given subscriber. The relay agent information option in IPv4 (option 82) is comprised of one or more suboptions, the following of which have been defined:

Suboption Code	Name	Description	RFC Ref.
1	Circuit ID	Encodes information about the connection to the subscriber. This consists of a virtual circuit identifier corresponding to the subscriber, typically corresponding to a layer 2 identifier such as an ATM virtual circuit ID, frame relay data link connection identifier (DLCI), or remote access server or switch port number	3046 (42)
2	Remote ID	Encodes information about the remote client device such as its Ethernet address, modem identifier, or caller ID for a dial-up connection	3046 (42)

(*Continued*)

Suboption Code	Name	Description	RFC Ref.
3	Reserved	Not used	—
4	DOCSIS device class	Encodes the DOCSIS device class of the cable CPE. This option is applicable to DOCSIS cable access networks and the CMTS (cable edge device) may include this suboption on the basis of this information gathered during the DOCSIS registration process	3256(82)
5	Link selection	Encodes an IP address to be used in lieu of the GIAddr field by the DHCP server when selecting a subnet address for address assignment to the client. This would apply when shared subnets* are in use	3527(83)
6	Subscriber ID	Encodes a subscriber identifier string to associate the DHCPDICSCOVER with the given subscriber's client. This is useful if the subscriber can access the network over various media where use of the circuit identifier or remote identifier would only indicate the underlying access mechanism and not the subscriber association	3993(84)
7	RADIUS attributes	Encodes RADIUS attributes per the RADIUS protocol (RFC 2865) to use by the DHCP server in making parameter assignments. These attributes are encoded as a type length value octet stream and can include the user name, passwords, access server IP/port, and others	4014 (85)
8	Authentication	Encodes authentication information as a means to provide message integrity checking on relay agent information. This encoding is similar to that used for DHCP authentication, which is discussed in Chapter 8	4030 (86)
9	Vendor-specific information	Encoded as one or more sets of vendor-specific information each consisting of a 3-tuple: IANA-registered enterprise number, length, and data	4243 (87)

(*continued*)

(Continued)

Suboption Code	Name	Description	RFC Ref.
10	Relay Agent Flags	Extensible suboption to flag conditions; one flag is defined to indicate that the relay agent received the DHCP packet via unicast (1) or broadcast (0)	5010 (88)
11	Server Identifier Override	Instructs the DHCP server to use this specified value in its Server Identifier field in its response to the client; this enables the relay agent to receive DHCPRENEW packets that it may not otherwise have visibility to, enabling the relay agent to insert other relay agent suboption values associated with the client when forwarding the DHCPRE-NEW packet to the server	5107 (89)

*Shared subnets refers to the provisioning of multiple logical subnets on a single physical subnet (router interface).

Within DHCPv6, two analogous options have been defined:

- Code 37 = Option_remote_id
- Code 38 = Option_subscriber_id

Let's consider an example DHCP server configuration using ISC DHCP syntax (35) to illustrate relay agent processing. This statement declares the class "broadband" that is based on matching the circuit ID suboption of the relay agent identification option. Here, we define a single client class but provision subclasses to identify specific instances of the broadband class. In this case, we simply define two subclasses for two corresponding values of the circuit ID suboption.

```
class "broadband" {

  match option agent.circuit-id;

}

subclass "modem" "45023" {

  [ declarations and parameters for modem devices ]

}

subclass "phone" "67032" {

  [ declarations and parameters for phone devices ]

}
```

A more scalable approach would be to utilize the class-spawning feature of the ISC DHCP implementation. We'll illustrate this along with the ability to limit the number of leases or IP addresses assignable to a subscriber. A basic level of service may promise a single IP address, while a higher level of service (and perhaps price) may include two or more. The `lease limit` statement enables this feature control within the ISC DHCP configuration file. This statement can be associated with a client class definition to specify the maximum number of leases that can be provided to clients matching this class.

Class spawning enables dynamic creation or spawning of client subclasses on the fly based on information in the DHCP packet. The `spawn with` declaration defines a spawning class with the parameter on which to base the spawn. For example, the DHCP server can be configured to spawn client classes based on each unique circuit ID relay agent suboption value. Thus, when a DHCPDISCOVER is received by the DHCP server, it analyzes the circuit ID suboption. If a class exists (was previously spawned) for the given value, the corresponding parameters and declarations are analyzed for processing; if a class with that circuit ID does not exist, the DHCP server spawns a new subclass for the given value. The example below illustrates the definition of a broadband client class with a spawning subclass based on the circuit ID that limits outstanding subscriber leases to a maximum of six using ISC DHCP syntax (35).

```
class "broadband" {

  spawn with option agent.circuit-id;

  lease limit 6;

}
```

6.3 RELATED LEASE ASSIGNMENT OR LIMITATION APPLICATIONS

The use of lease limiting and parameter setting based on relay agent information is not exclusive to broadband environments. Other applications may use the same technique assuming relay agents support the population of the relay agent information option. In such cases, using the ISC DHCP server enables address and parameter assignment as well as lease limiting based on defined classes and relay agent information parameters. This technique may be employed to throttle address assignments on certain subnets or to provide configuration parameters to devices in factory or similar applications.

6.4 PREBOOT EXECUTION ENVIRONMENT CLIENTS

Preboot Execution Environment (PXE or "Pixie") clients are devices that boot up relying on network servers instead of a co-resident hard disk. Such diskless servers and other such devices typically use DHCP to obtain an IP address and boot parameters including boot server addresses and boot file names. DHCP provides a convenient mechanism to initialize these devices without manual intervention. Historically, DHCP servers had to be configured with the MAC address of each PXE client to provide configuration information specific to the device, even if multiple PXE clients of the same "type" could leverage exactly the same boot information.

RFC 4578 (49) is an informational RFC defining a means whereby a PXE client can identify its type or architecture to the server. This information can be used by the DHCP server to identify and provide appropriate device initialization parameters. The DHCP server would need to be configured to match on particular client-provided PXE option values, then map these results to a corresponding set of configuration parameters or options to return to the client. Naturally, this is accomplished using client class processing.

Options to be included between PXE clients and the DHCP server are as follows:

- Option 93—client system architecture type—specifies the architecture type of the PXE device and must be included in all DHCP packets during the transaction
  o Intel x86PC
  o NEC/PC98
  o EFI Itanium
  o DEC Alpha
  o Arc x86
  o Intel Lean Client
  o EFI IA32
  o EFI BC
  o EFI Xscale
  o EFI x86-64
- Option 94—client network interface identifier—identifies the network interface type and version and must be included in all DHCP packets in the transaction. The only defined interface type is for universal network device interface (UNDI).
- Option 97—client machine identifier—identifies the type of machine booting. This option is encoded with a type and identifier. The only defined type, 0, indicates the identifier is encoded as a 16-octet globally unique identifier (GUID).
- Options 128–135—these options are to be requested by PXE clients and are intended for use by downloaded bootstrap programs, if needed, though they are not officially assigned for PXE use.

Be aware that PXE clients using options 128–135 may conflict with the alternative assigned meaning of these options as summarized in Chapter 4.

6.4.1 PPP/RADIUS Environments

The RADIUS (Remote Access Dial In User Service) protocol provides a means to authenticate end users attempting to connect to a network. RADIUS is a vital component of 802.1X, a popular layer 2 media access control protocol proposed within leading network admission control (NAC) offerings. RADIUS also plays a role at layer 3, especially when used in conjunction with PPP connections, commonly used with dial-up or DSL connections.

When operating at layer 3, some RADIUS servers can be configured to assign IP addresses to each client at the other end of the PPP connection. This address assignment process can be performed by configuring an address pool directly on the server or by configuring the RADIUS server to obtain an address via a DHCP server. In the latter scenario, the RADIUS server functions as a DHCP proxy on behalf of the client. The RADIUS server initiates the DHCP D-O-R-A process, issuing a DHCPDISCOVER packet. One caveat with this approach is that the RADIUS server must generate a hardware address or client identifier on behalf of each client to uniquely identify each. Otherwise, by using the RADIUS server's hardware address, the DHCP server would assume that the same client is continually rebooting and assigns the same IP address on all requests! The RADIUS server can spoof the client's hardware address using an internal mechanism but needs to map the derived address to the end client to process subsequent lease transactions like Renews and Releases. An alternative approach is to leverage the RADIUS attributes suboption of the Relay Agent Information option described earlier in order to uniquely identify each client.

6.4.2 Mobile IP

Mobile IP provides a mechanism for an IP device to retain network connectivity while moving about a local or remote IP network. This movement may occur during a communication session, not only when conducting and then terminating a session, for example, from a headquarters meeting to opening a new session at a branch office. The mobile device has a home address, corresponding to its home network, as well as a care-of address, which is obtained on serving network depending on where the mobile device is presently connected. For example, if I power up my personal digital assistant (PDA) device while out of town, I may obtain wireless service from a different service provider from the one I normally use when "at home." As long as my home provider has a service agreement with the provider I'm visiting, I should be able to obtain an address manually, via DHCP, or via autoconfiguration.

IP mobility support differs somewhat between IPv4 and IPv6, but both protocols leverage the concept of a mobile node possessing a home address, the node's address on the "home" network, and a care-of address, its address on the visited network. While not strictly a DHCP "application," we mention it here as an area for consideration with respect to address allocation and assignment strategies, not to mention access security for visiting nodes on your network.

7

DHCP SERVER
DEPLOYMENT STRATEGIES

This chapter examines deployment strategies and trade-offs for DHCP servers. Most trade-offs pit budget dollars against quantities of servers, so the most common goal is to deploy DHCP servers where end users will always be able to obtain these services in a timely manner, while minimizing the total dollars spent on servers deployed and associated server lifecycle expenses. This simply stated goal implies a need for highly available and reasonably performing services, all provided within budget constraints. Budget dollars must account not only for server purchases, but for ongoing support and maintenance, which includes server hardware upgrades, operating system (OS) patches and upgrades, as well as DHCP upgrades for new features, bug fixes, or security measures.

7.1 DHCP SERVER PLATFORMS

DHCP servers can be deployed in a variety of platforms from physical hardware servers or appliances, or as virtual servers on a virtual machine (VM) platform. When we discuss deployment options, we'll generically use the term platform, which can generally be interpreted as either one of these options in each case.

IP Address Management: Principles and Practice, by Timothy Rooney
Copyright © 2011 the Institute of Electrical and Electronics Engineers, Inc.

7.1.1 DHCP Software

The traditional model for deploying DHCP servers entails deploying a physical server supporting the recommended processing components and operating systems supported by the corresponding DHCP software vendor. Other applications may also be installed on such servers to maximize hardware utilization.

7.1.2 Virtual Machine DHCP Deployment

Virtual machines (VMs) exist for major Windows and Linux operating systems (OSs), enabling the deployment of Microsoft DHCP on Microsoft VMs and ISC on Linux VMs. Deployment on VMs saves on hardware costs, rack space and power draw, while enabling better segregation than in installing a DHCP daemon on a generic hardware server. Major appliance vendors also offer their appliance products as virtual machines, combining the benefits of VMs with the benefits of appliances, discussed next.

7.1.3 DHCP Appliances

DHCP appliances are preinstalled DHCP services on secure hardware platforms, typically Intel-based platforms with a hardened Linux operating system. Like routers, which were initially deployed as software running on general purpose hardware and evolved to special purpose hardware platforms, DHCP appliances offer an evolutionary path to self-contained hardware platforms for DHCP services. Appliances are "hardened" in that the base Linux kernel installed on the platform has been stripped of any unnecessary services. This results in a customized kernel and OS that supports only DHCP services (and other services supported by the vendor such as DNS). Underlying file system, users, permissions, and network ports should also be pared down accordingly by the appliance vendor.

Appliances offer simplified deployment with one-stop shopping, instead of having to coordinate and acquire server hardware, install the proper OS version and patch levels, then install DHCP services software. Appliances can simplify the ongoing upgrade process by prepackaging upgrades with compliant OS and services versions with corresponding hardware platforms. Depending on the vendor, these upgrades may be applied from a single centralized console, eliminating the need to physically deploy staff to perform upgrades. In addition, most vendors support centralized monitoring of deployed appliances, enabling proactive detection of outages or degradations.

Of course appliances generally cost more than general purpose server hardware, and most incorporate ISC DHCP services, which are freely available for most leading OSs at www.isc.org. In this chapter, we'll focus on deployment strategies for DHCP services, regardless of implementation on general hardware or appliances platforms.

7.2 CENTRALIZED DHCP SERVER DEPLOYMENT

The deployment of DHCP servers generally comes down to a trade-off between wide distribution of a large number of servers "closer" to clients versus narrow distribution of

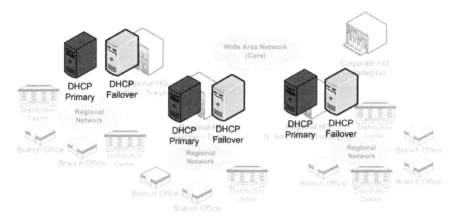

Figure 7.1. Centralized DHCP server deployment for IPAM Worldwide.

a fewer number of DHCP servers serving clients from a variety of locations. The extremes of this trade-off consist of a DHCP server on every subnet versus one or more DHCP servers centrally located serving all of the organization's clients. The key is to balance availability and reasonable performance of the DHCP service between clients and servers while remaining within budget constraints for servers and ongoing management thereof. Your deployment will likely fall between these two extremes.

Figure 7.1 illustrates the fully centralized deployment approach scenario for IPAM Worldwide. Overlaying the high-level network diagram from Figure 3.2 in Chapter 3, this scenario features the deployment of a pair of DHCP servers per region, one functioning as the primary and the other as failover or backup. All DHCP traffic must be funneled to the regional headquarters sites, imposing higher reliance on robust network connectivity to these sites from the respective regions. This architecture also implies the DHCP server hardware is sufficiently sized to meet performance and capacity requirements. Note that DHCP primary and failover servers should generally be deployed in separate physical locations for disaster resilience. An outage at one site would not interrupt all DHCP services for a region.

7.3 DISTRIBUTED DHCP SERVER DEPLOYMENT

At the other end of the deployment continuum, the decentralized deployment approach is illustrated in Figure 7.2. In this figure, a primary DHCP server is located at [nearly] every branch office and distribution center. This localizes DHCP traffic, affording deployment of less stringently sized DHCP servers. Network connectivity to the regional headquarters is still required however due to the deployment of DHCP failover servers there. These servers act as failover servers for the regional servers, though more than one per region may be required for load sharing. Consider the load and redundancy capabilities of your chosen DHCP vendor to identify viable alternative architectures for your network.

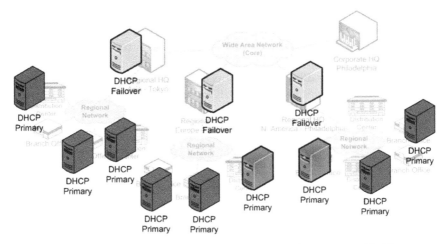

Figure 7.2. Distributed DHCP server deployment for IPAM Worldwide.

Contrasting the two extremes of Figures 7.1 and 7.2, the former requires fewer, albeit more powerful DHCP servers and rock solid network connectivity to the regional headquarters sites. The latter requires many more DHCP servers, though of more modest specifications, providing localized services with a network reachable shared backup. You may be wondering, if the network link to a site goes down, what good is having an IP address from a DHCP server? Without a redundant link, other than providing IP access to local network resources, it may indeed be of limited value. But in the centralized architecture, without distributed sites, if a link to a regional headquarters site fails, clients requiring new or renewed address leases will likewise be rendered useless. As always, the trade-off must be considered and generally a mixed approach of centralized with at least partial distribution often minimizes overall outage risk.

While the ISC DHCP server is a single-threaded application, its performance is usually sufficient for most environments. If you have several thousand DHCP clients attempting to obtain leases at about the same time however, some delays will be likely. If this occurs frequently, you may want to consider deploying additional servers and partitioning finer networks-per-server granularity to reduce the load per server. Again, this is usually not a major concern unless you are a service provider utilizing DHCP to initialize devices like customer premises modems for paying subscribers. After recovery from a neighborhood power outage, devices will come back up and inundate the DHCP server for addresses. In such environments, it probably makes sense to consider a commercial performance-oriented DHCP server.

Prepare your routers to support DHCP by configuring the IP addresses of your DHCP servers within your routers' relay agent lists. These lists within each router enable the router to terminate received DHCPDISCOVER packet broadcasts, then retransmit them as unicast packets to each configured DHCP sever IP address on its relay agent list. If you partition your network such that address pools for certain subnets are served by a given DHCP server, while those for other subnets are served by another DHCP server, make sure you configure routers serving those subnets accordingly. You could add all DHCP servers to all routers, but this will result in needless relay agent traffic, especially if you have several DHCP servers. DHCP for IPv6 networks utilizes well know multicast addresses, obviating the need to configure relay agent lists on routers, though such configuration may alternatively be performed on the relay agent to control which DHCPv6 servers are to process relayed DHCP transactions and not just any DHCPv6 server listening on this multicast address.

7.4 SERVER DEPLOYMENT DESIGN CONSIDERATIONS

Key considerations when formulating the DHCP server deployment design including the following:

- *Response Time Requirements.* Do your clients have stringent response time requirements? Most popular clients tolerate response times in the seconds, but certain applications may be more demanding. The more stringent your requirements, the more important will be server performance and perhaps client proximity.

- *Load Requirements.* Do you have certain load conditions that must be handled? For broadband service providers utilizing DHCP as a customer premises equipment initialization technology, load spikes may occur upon recovery from a residential power outage or equipment installation or reboot. For enterprise environments, such a spike could occur at the start of the workday if several associates arrive at or near the same time, though many devices will simply attempt to renew an IP address previously used by default.

- *Traffic Expectations.* Do you employ short lease times to minimize overbooking, which causes more frequent renewal attempts? Generally the shorter the lease time (the T1 and T2 times), the shorter the interval between obtaining the lease and subsequent lease renewal attempts. This drives increasing traffic on the network to and from the DHCP server(s) and must be considered when designing to the aforementioned response time and load requirements for server quantities and associated bandwidth.

- *Availability Requirements.* Do your clients positively have to be able to obtain an IP address or configuration via DHCP 24 × 7 or is the service "best effort" based? Most will answer that high availability is critical, but with devices growing increasingly multinetworked, as long as one network's address assignment mechanism is available this may be acceptable.* Mean time to repair (MTTR) is another consideration in meeting DHCP services availability objectives. Having a spare server locally can shorten MTTR while having to order a replacement will delay this process.

---

* Of course this statement assumes different DHCP services serve these different interfaces that may not be the case.

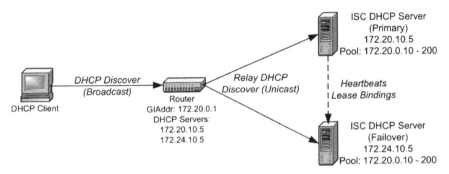

Figure 7.3. ISC DHCP failover configuration.

The first three considerations above relate to deploying sufficient quantities of servers of given lease distribution rate to meet respective performance objectives. A good starting point is to identify the number of expected DHCP clients at each site on your network. This number should account for all devices requiring DHCP, including data devices, voice devices, and all IP devices requiring DHCP at each site. Don't forget to account for "peak" quantities of users and devices so that everyone, even associates visiting on temporary basis, may obtain a valid lease.

After accounting for peak quantities of DHCP clients, consider the frequency of DHCP transactions. This will be dependent on your lease times, as well as client lease release configuration. Most clients will "remember" a prior lease and attempt to request it upon power-up, for example, when an employee returns to work the next day, though this is not always the case.

The fourth consideration listed above relates to providing high availability DHCP services for DHCP clients. Given the general importance of providing highly available DHCP service, deploying for high availability is typically recommended. Once you've designed your deployment based on performance requirements, total or selective high availability may be planned. Based on server technologies you plan to deploy, implementation of high availability will impact not only the number of servers required, but potentially your address space plan.

The ISC and the Microsoft DHCP implementations utilize vastly different approaches. The ISC server employs a failover protocol* such that for a given address pool, one DHCP server will act as the primary, while a second DHCP server will act as the backup or failover server. This basic configuration is illustrated in Figure 7.3.

Each relay agent must be configured to unicast received DHCP [for IPv4] broadcast packets to both the primary and failover DHCP servers, 172.20.10.1 and 172.24.10.1 in Figure 7.3. Recall that DHCPv6 relay agents can likewise be configured with DHCPv6 server addresses or may utilize a well-known site-scoped multicast address, FF05::1:3. The DHCP servers utilize a failover protocol such that the primary sends heartbeat

---

* The ISC implementation was based on RFC draft specifications by the IETF, which were largely tabled. However, the IETF is endeavoring to redefine the DHCP failover protocol and ISC plans to implement the new version while also supporting the current RFC draft-based implementation.

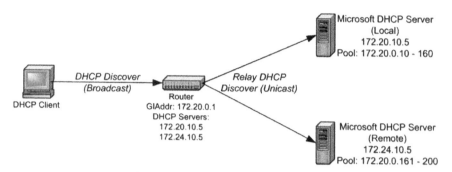

Figure 7.4. Split scopes configuration.

messages as well as lease binding information to the failover server. The failover server utilizes user-settable parameters to determine that the primary is down and begins processing the unicast DHCP packets from the relay agent(s). Thus, clients are able to continue receiving IP address and parameter assignments despite the primary server being down. Upon recovery, the primary server obtains the current lease database from the failover server, then assumes its role as primary once again.

The Microsoft approach does not employ an interserver protocol like DHCP failover. Instead, by deploying two DHCP servers with complementary address pools, *not the same address pools*, either server can process DHCP transactions without worry of duplicate assignment. Microsoft recommends using the "80-20 rule" in configuring 80% of the address pool on a "local" server and 20% on a "remote" server. In this way, most of the DHCP transactions will be handled by the local server assuming the client will receive the first offer from the local server and accept it. This configuration is illustrated in Figure 7.4, where we have split our 172.20.0.10-200 pool using the 80/20 guideline.

Like the ISC failover configuration in Figure 7.3, each relay agent needs to be configured with both local and remote Microsoft DHCP server addresses. Each DHCP server is configured with an address pool for the relevant subnet, 172.20.0.0, but with nonoverlapping contents. In this example, we've used the same total pool size for the pair of Microsoft DHCP servers as was used in the ISC example in Figure 7.3. Since both servers are required to meet the capacity needs, you may end up with an inability to meet IP address demands should one fail. Another alternative is to configure the local DHCP server with 100% of the required local capacity and allow overflow of extra addresses to the remote server for backup. In this manner, the local server can handle 100% of the capacity, and the remote can assist with a portion of those additional clients when the local server is unavailable. Referring to Figure 7.4, the local server could be configured with address pool 172.20.0.10-200 and the remote server with 172.20.0.201-254. This additional capacity can range up to 100% of the required capacity, providing 100% redundancy at the expense of doubling the required address space. While popularized by Microsoft, the split scope approach may be used with various vendor DHCP servers.

From a security perspective, implementations of DHCP authentication have not been broadly commercialized. Thus, little practical security exists for securing the

DHCP transaction itself. This may not be of major concern for enterprise networks, where DHCP is provided for internal use, but this may be problematic if users unknowingly start a DHCP service on their machines. Most users probably don't have a DHCP server installed but those with [self-perceived] IT expertise may.

For service provider networks using DHCP to initialize customer premises equipment, the use of the service provider gateway or edge device can provide some assurance as to the validity of the DHCP client for address assignment. Tying DHCP into the provisioning process can help correlate a DHCP client with a paying subscriber identifier to minimize theft of service.

DHCP itself can be used as a means to "secure" network access by determining whether a given DHCP client meets acceptance criteria for admission to the network by virtue of IP address assignment by the server. This provides a form of network access control, though it does not protect against IP address spoofers. Configuring DHCP for access control security is discussed in the next chapter.

7.5 DHCP DEPLOYMENT ON EDGE DEVICES

Most router vendors provide a DHCP service as a component of their router platforms. This may lead one to question whether a separate server is needed to support DHCP services. As with most design questions, the answer is, "it depends." Small environments with a few sites with local routers serving up to 100 or so monolithic clients each may be well served by configuring the router to provide DHCP services. However, larger organizations or those requiring more advanced DHCP services, for example, for discriminating voice versus data clients for address and option parameter assignment, would be better served deploying discrete (nonrouter-integrated) DHCP servers.

The advantages of running DHCP on a router device include the following:

- *Lower Hardware Cost.* No need to procure a server or set of servers.
- *Single User Interface.* The same command line interface can be used to configure the router and the DHCP server, and no relay agent configuration is needed.
- *"Fewer Moving Parts."* One less communication link and server required to perform DHCP functions, which in general can increase the overall solution reliability.

The main disadvantages of running DHCP on a router are as follows:

- *Options Support.* Most router-based DHCP servers are primitive, supporting address assignment but little in the way of options support.
- *Client Class Support.* Major vendors do not support client classes, which are required for discriminatory address/option assignment to different devices, for example, VoIP versus data devices.

- *No Failover.* If a router fails, you've probably lost connectivity in any case but if there are two routers serving a subnet for redundancy a split scopes approach would have to be employed, increasing management complexity.
- *No Centralized Management.* Router-based DHCP services are configured via command line and unless a centralized tool is employed, each router DHCP server must be configured manually with respect to the IP addressing plan; less likely support is possible if multiple router vendor products are in use.

8

DHCP AND NETWORK ACCESS SECURITY

Security is at or near the top of every IP planner's list of networking concerns. IP address management-related security topics are no exception. There are a number of security threats to DHCP information and in its communications with those requesting information. In addition, given the role of DHCP in disseminating IP addresses for access to the network, the DHCP service itself plays a key role in providing a basic level of network access control (NAC) by virtue of its inherent function. Will you configure DHCP to provide an IP address to any device that requests one or will you configure a more discriminating policy? This chapter will delve first into the area of network access control with discussion of common strategies for deploying prudent address assignment policies. Then we'll discuss DHCP information and communications security tactics.

8.1 NETWORK ACCESS CONTROL[*]

The term NAC has been hyped in recent years, but the underlying concept is fundamental: identify who is attempting to access your network prior to providing such access. Various techniques are available offering various levels of access control. We'll start by

[*] Material in this chapter is based on Chapter 9 of Ref. 11.

IP Address Management: Principles and Practice, by Timothy Rooney
Copyright © 2011 the Institute of Electrical and Electronics Engineers, Inc.

analyzing DHCP-based access control, which admittedly is among the weaker approaches to NAC. We'll then touch on more wide-reaching techniques.

8.1.1 Discriminatory Address Assignment with DHCP

Let's focus first on DHCP services and some approaches to implement discriminatory address assignment. There are several levels of policies or controls most DHCP solutions provide for discrimination of "who's asking" for an IP address via DHCP. The first is to simply filter requests by an available form of client identifier such as the MAC address of the client requesting an address. Recall that the MAC address is found in the client hardware address (chaddr) field of a DHCPv4 packet. DHCPv6 device identifiers consist of the Device Unique ID (DUID) and identity associations (IAs) that identify each client and interface, respectively.

If the DHCP server has a list of acceptable (and/or unacceptable) device identifiers, it can be configured to provide a certain IP address and associated parameters to those clients with an acceptable identifier, and either no IP address or a limited function IP address to those without an acceptable device identifier. By *limited function IP address*, we mean that the network routing infrastructure is preconfigured to route IP packets with such source IP addresses to only certain networks, such as to the Internet only, or even nowhere. An IP packet with source address A may be routable across the enterprise, while one with source address B may be routable only to the Internet, for example.

This type of IP address and configuration assignment is also possible by filtering on the client class of the device requesting an IP address, as we discussed in Chapter 4. Certain clients, such as VoIP phones, provide additional information about themselves when requesting an IP address in the vendor class identifier field of the DHCP packet. The user class identifier field may also be used. The DHCP server can be configured to recognize user classes and/or vendor classes of devices on your network to provide additional information to the DHCP server when requesting IP address and configuration parameters. Addresses can be assigned from a certain pool and/or additional configuration parameters can be assigned to the client via standard or vendor-specific DHCP options.

Another level of discriminating IP address assignment is possible by authenticating the user of the machine requesting an IP address. This function can be used in conjunction with device identifier and client class discrimination described above. For example, if a client with an unknown or unacceptable device identifier attempts to obtain an IP address, one option is to completely deny an address; another option is to require the user of the client to login via a secure access web portal page.

This enables easier capture of new device identifiers for legitimate users of your network. (Those users sometimes pop in new interface cards!) Solutions ranging from perl scripts such as NetReg (90) to sophisticated integrated software solutions are available to direct such users to a login/password requesting web page. A simple lookup against a database of legitimate users then allows access or denial of the client to a production IP address. These systems typically work in accordance with the packet flow shown in Figure 8.1.[*]

---

[*] DHCPv4 process is shown, but a comparable flow could be employed with DHCPv6.

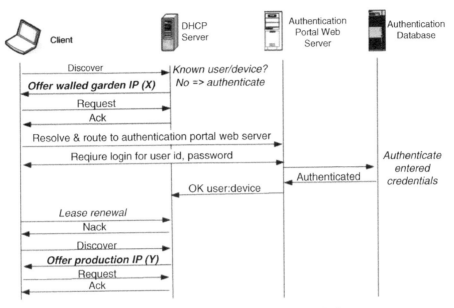

Figure 8.1. Basic DHCP captive portal flow (11).

Walking through this flow, the process begins with a device connecting to the network, attempting to obtain an IP address via DHCP. The DHCP server, employing device identifier or client class-type filtering discussed above, determines if the device is a known user device.[*] If the device is known or is otherwise already authenticated, the DHCP process may continue with an Offer for a production IP address, followed by a Request and Ack. However, if the device is not known or is required to be authenticated, the DHCP server can still provide an IP address by completing the DORA process; but the IP address assigned in this case would be a *captive portal, walled garden,* or *quarantined* IP address.

These terms refer to the fact that the IP address assigned to the client will only be routed to the subnet or VLAN that has the authentication web server and associated servers running. This quarantined VLAN enables IP communications but only to this restricted set of devices. This cordons off the device from infiltrating the rest of the network until the corresponding user can be authenticated. The routing infrastructure must be configured to route packets with a source address from the quarantined address pool to the quarantined VLAN and/or the client must be configured with the classless static route option. Thus, address X as shown in Figure 8.1 is a member of the quarantined VLAN, on which only limited network resources are available. Figure 8.2 illustrates an example network topology of this captive portal configuration.

Now when the user opens up a web browser, he/she can type in any web address. A *limited configuration* DNS server is required on the quarantined VLAN, limited in the sense that it will resolve any and every query to the IP address of the authentication web

---

[*] In some cases, even known user devices may require periodic reauthentication as a security precaution.

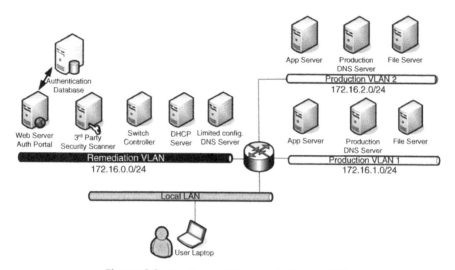

Figure 8.2. Captive portal network diagram (11).

server. Thus, no matter what web address is entered in the web browser, the web address is resolved by the captive portal web server. The authentication web server presents the login page. You may have seen something similar to this if you travel and use a hotel's broadband or wireless service. Once the requested credentials are entered, which for an enterprise environment would typically comprise a user ID and a password, the web page can call a CGI script to pass the entered credentials to a back-end database. This authentication database could be an LDAP server, a Windows Domain Controller, a Radius server, or other form of authentication data store.

Based upon the results of the authentication, the requesting device would then be deemed authorized or not, and if authorized, optionally what class of authorization is granted. The class of authorization provides more granularity than a simple boolean "authorized or not," where different authorized users can be assigned a different production IP address, which in turn can provide access to different network resources. For example, basic level users may be granted access to a basic set of resources, while advanced level users may be granted access to additional resources, for example, IT resources. Once again this requires the routing topology be configured with multiple source-routed or VLAN segments, with these networks and corresponding routing plan mapped to DHCP server configurations in terms of associating address pools with service levels.

The manner in which the production IP address is assigned follows from expiration or denial of renewal of the quarantined IP address. The quarantined IP address lease time is generally configured as a short lease time ($\sim$1–5 min). This enables the device to attempt to renew quickly. Should the device still be in the process of authentication, its renewal attempt would be ACK'd, extending the lease. Once authentication is completed successfully, the authentication system updates the DHCP server to add the client MAC address to the "known" or "allow" pool. The renewal attempt for the quarantined address would then be NAK'd, enabling a fresh DORA process to provide a "production" IP address (address Y in Figure 8.1). Should the device fail authentication, the renewal can be NAK'd and subsequent address attempts denied; alternatively, the quarantined address renewal attempt can be granted in order to provide access only to resources on the quarantined network if desired.

Beyond these device and user identification measures based on device identifiers, client classes, and user authentication, this general flow can also provide additional validation on the machine requesting the IP address. The DHCP process can be used to invoke an external security scanning system like Nessus, or another third-party application to scan the requesting client for viruses, or to validate the use of acceptable virus protection software. This device-scanning step can be used alone or in conjunction with the device identification measures to provide a robust access security solution via DHCP.

One example network configuration for DHCP-based secure access is depicted in Figure 8.2. The DHCP server shown in the diagram would be configured with a number of client class sets. We refer to the client class as the matching criteria in the DHCP packet, and link this to client class set mapping to the associated network accessibility. For example, we would need a client class set for at least each of the following in our example:

- Captive portal network (remediation VLAN)
- Production network 1
- Production network 2

Think of these client class sets as bins into which individual clients are placed based on the linking of their authentication state to the device's client class. Thus, client class members would be categorized by the DHCP server in accordance with defined client classes as they appear on the network and users authenticate. These client classes would generally map to pool definitions on the DHCP server as shown in the following simple example ISC server configuration (35). Note that additional options can be defined for each of the pools to provide additional configuration granularity to clients falling into each set or pool.

```
subnet 172.16.0.0 netmask 255.255.252.0 {
# subnet level options here...
  pool{                                       #captive portal pool
    range 172.16.0.10 172.16.0.254;
    option domain-name-servers 172.16.0.5;    #limited config DNS server
    default-lease-time 150;                   #short lease time
    allow unknown clients;                    #clients not predefined.
  }
pool {                                        #Prod Net 1
    range 172.16.1.10 172.16.1.254;
    option domain-name-servers
```

```
   172.16.1.5;                        #production DNS server
   default-lease-time 14400;          #normal lease time
   deny unknown clients;              #clients must be predefined.
   allow members of "net1";           #client class net1 allowed
 }
pool {                                 #Prod Net 2
   range 172.16.2.10 172.16.2.254;
   option domain-name-servers
   172.16.2.5;                        #production DNS server
   default-lease-time 14400;          #normal lease time
   deny unknown clients;              #clients must be predefined.
   allow members of "net2";           #client class net2 allowed
 }
}
```

Based on the results of the authentication process, the authentication server must be able to update the DHCP configuration to place the client into the appropriate bin or class. Thus, if the device is successfully authenticated for access to production network 2, the authentication portal needs to add the specific device's client class value (e.g., MAC address) to the client class group for production network 2 ("net2" class in the example above). This update may be performed, for example, using the ISC DHCP server OMAPI interface (requires version 3.1 or above). This client class declaration can define class-specific options on the DHCP server to provide to the client, for example, default gateway, DNS server, along with any other option.

The captive portal VLAN may only consist of "unknown clients," a designation configurable with the ISC DHCP server. The captive portal network (the remediation VLAN in the figure) is deployed, including the limited configuration DNS server, web server as the authentication portal, with access to an authentication database, and optionally a security scanning server and any other required preaccess services.

More than one DHCP server may be deployed for high availability and/or for scaling for larger networks. This approach does complicate things, as the DHCP server configurations need to be consistent on both servers to route unknown clients or clients requiring authentication to the captive portal net.

8.2 ALTERNATIVE ACCESS CONTROL APPROACHES

You may be thinking that the DHCP-based approach is fine for clients utilizing DHCP; but what about those "clever users" who figure out the subnet address and then manually encode a static IP address on their machines to access the network? These clever users may after all be those of most concern from a secure access perspective. In addition, for devices using IPv6 stateless autoconfiguration, no DHCP interaction is required for address assignment.

There are three basic alternative approaches for enabling detection and associated remediation action of devices without relying on the DHCP-based approach. We'll talk about leading networking vendor NAC approaches in the next section.

- DHCP LeaseQuery
- Layer 2 switch alerting
- 802.1X

8.2.1 DHCP LeaseQuery

If most or all addresses on a subnet are configured using DHCP by policy, that is, each IP address *should* have a corresponding DHCP lease, then the LeaseQuery approach may be used. The DHCP LeaseQuery is a DHCP protocol message that enables an edge router to query the DHCP server regarding the lease status of a particular device or set of devices. This provides some assurance that a device attempting to communicate via the router has not spoofed an address that should have been assigned by the DHCP server.

When the router receives IP traffic within a layer 2 frame from a particular MAC address, for example, it can issue a DHCP LeaseQuery message to its configured DHCP servers (i.e., in its role as relay agent). If a DHCP server had previously provided a lease for the client, it will respond to the router, and the router will give the green light and route the device's packets. If not, the device does not have a lease and the router can drop the device's packets. The router can cache this information as well so that the LeaseQuery rate is not exceeding high. Of course, this form of access control applies only when all clients on a subnet use DHCP such as in broadband access networks, not when other statically addressed devices communicate on the subnet.

8.2.2 Layer 2 Switch Alerting

Another approach takes advantage of SNMP-enabled switches to issue an SNMP trap upon a link up state on one of its ports and to accept port-level VLAN configurations. This alerting capability along with SNMP writable configuration information can enable gatekeeper-like functionality by dynamically identifying devices attempting to access the network and configuring the switch to provision the port to a particular VLAN. A third-party system or product would be needed to process traps, make decisions on appropriate VLAN assignments, and configure the switch accordingly.

Let's look at how this would work. If we consider the process of a device connecting to a network from the beginning, the device "boots up" on the network from layer 1. Thus, the physical layer/electrical connectivity is first attained; then the data link layer is initialized whereby layer 2 frame synchronization occurs. Then layer 3 follows, with the issuing of a DHCP packet, for example, or directly issuing IP packets if a static address is configured at layer 3. As the data link layer initializes (prior to layer 3), the switch to which the device is connected will deem the "link up" and issue a trap. Because the trap is sent prior to layer 3 initialization, this scheme can identify both statically addressed and DHCP-addressed devices.

Traps would be directed to a system that can identify the link up state, ascertain the link layer (MAC) address of the newly connected device, and then determine whether the device requires authentication or validation. This determination can be made via a MAC address database within the system that identifies known or acceptable MAC addresses and differentiates these from unknown or known unacceptable MAC addresses. The system would associate these two or perhaps more MAC address categorizations with corresponding VLAN assignments, which would then be programmed on the corresponding switch for the given port. The connected device would then be connected to the assigned VLAN. You can probably see the analogy to the DHCP scenario we discussed using client classes. In this case, the third-party system uses its database and configures the layer 2 switch using SNMP or other means instead of assigning an IP address using DHCP.

For quarantined or captive portal access, the VLAN assignment would lead only to the authentication network. For those passing authentication and/or device validation, the system could reassign the MAC address to the acceptable list and then configure the switch accordingly to change the ports VLAN association. Depending on the authentication method, client software may or may not be required. For web-based login/password, it may not be necessary to configure each of your client computers with authentication clients. However, if Radius, or other challenge/response authentication strategies are employed, client software will be necessary.

8.2.3 802.1X

IEEE 802.1X is a protocol specification enabling edge device capture of new access attempts, with the use of Radius authentication and dynamic switch port configuration. You may have used Radius in the days of prebroadband Internet dial up, which used the Point-to-Point protocol at layer 3. 802.1X, developed by the IEEE 802.1 working group focused on layer 2 protocols, is as you'd expect, a layer 2 protocol. Like the switch-based authentication strategy discussed in the previous section, this approach operates at layer 2, prior to the device getting a layer 3 (IP) address via DHCP. And 802.1X is based on standards, which theoretically enables the use of different vendors' products as components within the overall solution.

As depicted in Figure 8.3, 802.1X requires a client or agent called a *supplicant*, which interacts with an *authentication server* by way of an *authenticator* (e.g., switch). Upon initial connection to a network, the supplicant utilizes the Extensible Authentication Protocol (EAP) over 802.1X to initiate a connection request to the network access device. The switch can be configured to block all traffic by default except EAP packets from unauthenticated ports.

The access switch to which the device is connected at the data link layer transmits the EAP traffic to the authentication (i.e., Radius) server. The Radius server, in turn, challenges the client for an ID and password. Upon successful authentication, the Radius server communicates with the edge device to enable access to the associated device's port.

8.2.4 Cisco Network Admission Control

Cisco's Network Admission Control (NAC) offering (91) is based primarily on 802.1X. It requires a Cisco Trust Agent (CTA) optionally with a Cisco Security Agent installed on each end user device (Figure 8.4). The Trust Agent contains a Radius client. Upon initial

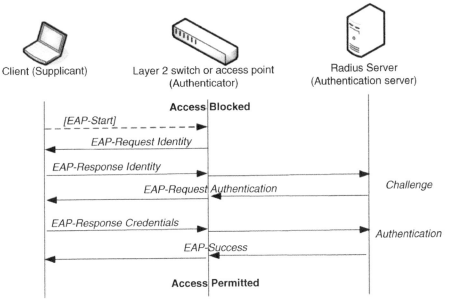

Figure 8.3. 802.1X authentication.

connection to a network, the CTA utilizes the Extensible Authentication Protocol over 802.1X or UDP to initiate a connection request to the network.

The network access device, typically a switch to which the device is connected at the data link layer, transmits the EAP traffic to the Cisco access control server (ACS), which provides Radius services. This Radius component, in turn, challenges the client for an ID and a password. A third-party validation solution may be invoked to scan the device

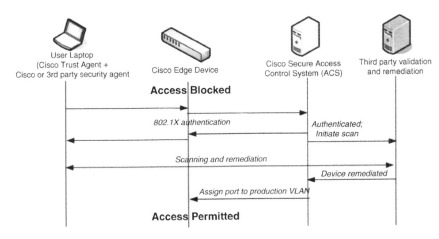

Figure 8.4. Cisco NAC basic flow.

attempting to gain access. Upon successful authentication and validation, the ACS communicates with the edge device to enable access to the associated device's port.

8.2.5 Microsoft Network Access Protection

Microsoft introduced Network Access Protection (NAP) (92) to enable administrators to ensure computers accessing a network have appropriate software installed at or above a specified version and is supported in Microsoft Vista™ or 7 client as well as Windows Server 2008 implementations. Microsoft supports an API to enable other vendors to support NAP technologies. NAP primarily emphasizes device compliance and health, and as a by-product, access control. That is, NAP is intended to enable network administrators to validate device compliance with current software releases upon network access, and not inherently to prevent access by malicious attackers. Nonetheless, NAP does entail denial of access pending health status verification with its three key functions:

- *Health Policy Validation.* Upon a network access attempt, a device's "health state" is obtained and compared with the administrator's defined "health policies." If the device complies with the specified health policies, the device is permitted unrestricted access; if the device is not compliant, the device can be provided restricted access or full access if in monitoring-only mode.
- *Health Policy Compliance.* Noncompliant devices can optionally be automatically upgraded upon access attempt. If in monitoring-only mode, the device will enjoy full network access. In restricted access mode, the device will have only restricted network access until compliance is achieved.
- *Limited Access.* Administrators can constrain the scope of network accessibility to noncompliant devices.

Microsoft Vista clients contain a NAP client that communicates with a NAP Policy Server (NPS), part of Microsoft Windows Server 2008, during an attempt to access a network. The NPS enforces the compliance policies and is consulted during access attempts over a variety of technologies, including IPSec, 802.1X, VPN, Radius, and DHCP. IPSec is the strongest form of policy enforcement and consists of a Health Registration Authority (HRA), which issues X.509 certificates to compliant NAP Enforcement Clients (ECs) based on compliance verification by the NPS.

The 802.1X access flow follows that described above for 802.1X, with the addition of the NAP Policy Server validating the device's compliance. VPN, Radius, and DHCP access components include a NAP Enforcement Server (ES) and a NAP EC that communicate regarding policy compliance during access attempts to the network via the respective technologies (Figure 8.5).

The client device, or NAP client, contains a NAP Agent, as well as Microsoft-provided and API-accessible System Health Agents (SHAs) and NAP ECs in support of additional applications. Likewise, the NPS features an API for corresponding System Health Validators (SHVs). When attempting to access the network, the NAP client will provide a Statement of Health (SoH) to the NPS via the corresponding access server; for

Figure 8.5. Microsoft NAP components (92).

example, the HRA, VPN server, DHCP server, and others. The access server passes this on to the NPS, which validates the policy compliance and either permits or restricts access based on the access technology and NAP policies. Full or restricted access is conveyed to the NAP EC on the client for enforcement, though other network configuration such as router access lists or static routes may also be required.

8.3 SECURING DHCP

8.3.1 DHCP Threats

Within enterprise environments, most threats to DHCP are posed by internal (i.e., intraorganizational) clients. DHCP servers should not be reachable by external clients by simply not deploying DHCP servers on external subnets nor relaying DHCP packets from external sources. For service providers that initialize subscriber devices using DHCP, whether cell phones, cable or fiber routers, and so on, threats to DHCP service can by definition originate externally to the network. In short, all organizations using DHCP are vulnerable. The degree of vulnerability and the impacts of compromise should drive the response in the form of securing DHCP to minimize such impacts. We'll look at the major forms of attack next.

Like all network services, DHCP is vulnerable to denial of service (DOS) attacks. When an attacker floods a given server with requests too numerous for the server to handle, the server may spend all its cycles attempting to deal with the flood and not on legitimate client requests; thus, these legitimate clients go unserved, and service is denied to them.

Another type of attack involves a rogue client attempting to obtain a valid IP address and configuration to access the network. This could be malicious, for example, theft of broadband service, or merely accidental, for example, a visitor plugging into the wall jack in the conference room.

A third form of attack features a rogue DHCP server that responds to lease requests from clients with incorrect IP address and/or option parameter information. This "man in the middle" type of attack may attempt to set improper configuration parameters on the client, such as the default gateway or DNS server address(es) to use. Note that with IPv4, a rogue DHCP server attack is generally only applicable when the server is on the same subnet as the client; relay agents presumably would be configured to relay DHCP packets to authorized DHCP servers. A remote rogue DHCPv6 server may be reachable via the DHCP multicast address.

The client may receive DHCPOFFERs from both the legitimate DHCP server(s) and the rogue server. Many clients will select the first offer that includes its requested parameters. If the rogue server is on the same subnet as the client, and legitimate servers are not, then it's likely the rogue server may be able to specify the IP configuration of the client.

8.3.2 DHCP Threat Mitigation

Protection against DOS attacks should be implemented in a broader context beyond just DHCP. Other potential targets within an organization, including DNS servers or web servers, imply that a gateway-based or packet filtering approach be considered to protect all servers with a common solution. Such a solution typically involves packet filtering and threshold limiting of the number of outstanding packets in process, though care must be taken with DHCP since most clients' transactions are funneled through DHCP Relay agents, concentrating packets from a given set of source addresses.

Mitigation steps for the threat of unknown clients accessing the IP network by illicitly obtaining an IP address from DHCP requires identification of clients based on various access control techniques we discussed at the beginning of this chapter.

Rogue DHCP servers may be difficult to detect, especially for clients on the same subnet as the rogue server. But both ISC and Microsoft implementations provide means to mitigate rogue servers. For ISC, use the `authoritative` directive, which configures the server to issue a DHCPNAK if a client requests a lease for an address for which the server is authoritative yet for which the server has no record. Microsoft requires DHCP servers to be authorized within Active Directory; thus, when a Windows DHCP server boots, it verifies its authorization in Active Directory before processing DHCP packets.

8.3.3 DHCP Authentication

The IETF has defined DHCP authentication in RFC 3118 (47) as a mechanism providing validation of the sender and receiver of DHCP packets via the use of shared tokens or keys. A token is simply a fixed value that is inserted into the DHCP Authentication option field. The receiver of the packet examines the token and if the token matches its configured token, the packet is accepted; otherwise, it is dropped. This method provides weak endpoint authentication and no message verification. The use of shared keys can provide stronger endpoint authentication with message verification. However, shared keys must be configured on each client, with each client's key configured on each DHCP server through which the client obtains leases. The DHCP Authentication specification does not define the mechanism for key distribution. Mobile clients, for example, would need to be configured with tokens for each DHCP server with which they may interact and vice versa.

Here's how DHCP authentication works. The client creates an HMAC-MD5 hash of its DHCPDISCOVER packet and signs it using the shared key. The resulting digest is placed in the DHCP Authentication option and transmitted within the DHCPDISCOVER packet to the server. For the purposes of the hash computation, the hash portion of the DHCP Authentication option must be set to zero. The DHCP server would then compute a hash of the received message utilizing the shared key associated with the client (identified by the secret ID field of the DHCP Authentication option). The server zeroes out the hash value, hops, and GIAddr fields for the purposes of the hash computation. If the calculated hash matches that transmitted in the original DHCP Authentication option, the client and the contents of the packet are considered authenticated. The DHCP server utilizes the same shared key to compute the hash value of its DHCP Authentication option when it prepares its DHCPOFFER and future packets to the client.

There have been very few implementations of DHCP Authentication. The challenges of key management and processing delays due to hash computation have been deemed too heavy a price to pay for the perceived benefits. Security of the DHCP service then typically falls on DHCP server administrators to monitor servers and react to threats as they occur.

PART III

DNS

DNS provides an automated lookup facility to ease the use of IP networks for humans. While the most common lookup function provided by DNS is for resolving names to IP addresses, DNS supports a wide variety of applications as we'll see in Chapter 10, after we discuss DNS protocol basics in Chapter 9. We'll discuss deployment and security in the remaining chapters of Part III.

9

THE DOMAIN NAME SYSTEM (DNS) PROTOCOL

9.1 DNS OVERVIEW—DOMAINS AND RESOLUTION[*]

DNS is the third cornerstone of IPAM and a foundational element of IP communications. DNS provides the means for improved usability of IP applications, insulating end users from typing IP addresses directly into applications like web browsers. Certainly, to communicate over an IP network, an IP device needs to send IP packets to the intended destination IP device; and as we have seen, the IP packet headers require source and destination IP addresses. DNS provides the translation from a user-entered named destination, for example, web site address, to its IP address.

As a network service, DNS has evolved from simple host name-to-IP address lookup utility to enabling very sophisticated "lookup" applications supporting voice, data, multimedia, and security applications. DNS has proven extremely scalable and reliable

---

[*] Initial sections of this chapter are based on Chapter 4 of Ref. 11.

IP Address Management: Principles and Practice, by Timothy Rooney
Copyright © 2011 the Institute of Electrical and Electronics Engineers, Inc.

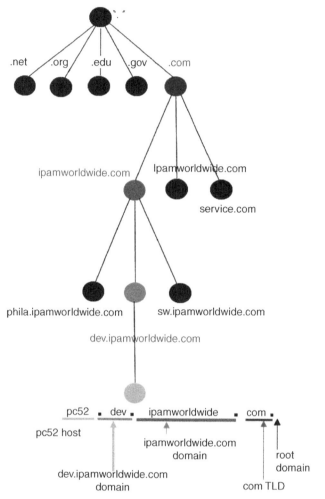

Figure 9.1. Domain tree mapping to a fully qualified domain name (11)

for such lookup functions. We'll discuss how this lookup process works after first introducing how this information is organized.

9.1.1 Domain Hierarchy

The global domain name system is effectively a distributed hierarchical database. Each "dot" in a domain name indicates a boundary between tiers in the hierarchy, with each name in between dots denoted as a *label*. The top of the hierarchy, the "." or root domain provides references to top-level domains, such as .com, .net, .us, .uk, which in turn reference respective subdomains. Each of these top-level domains or TLDs is a child of the root domain. Each TLD has several children domains as well, such as ipamworld-wide.com with the ipamworldwide domain beneath the com domain. And these children may have children domains and so on.

As we read between the dots from right to left, we can identify a unique path to the host we are seeking. The text left of the leftmost dot is generally* the hostname, which is located within the domain indicated by the rest of the domain name. A *fully qualified domain name* (FQDN) refers to this unique full [absolute] path name to the node or host within the global DNS data hierarchy. Figure 9.1 illustrates a fully qualified domain name mapping to the tree-like structure of the DNS database. Note that the trailing dot after .com. explicitly denotes the root domain within the domain name, rendering it fully qualified. Keep in mind that without this explicit FQDN trailing dot notation, a given domain name may be ambiguously interpreted as either fully qualified or relative to the "current" domain. This is certainly legal and easier shorthand notation, but just be aware of the potential ambiguity.

9.2 NAME RESOLUTION

To illustrate how domain information is organized and how a DNS server leverages this hierarchical data structure, let's take a look at an example name resolution. Let's assume I'd like to connect to a device named pc52 per the example in Figure 9.1. Thus I enter the host domain name, pc52.dev.ipamworldwide.com. as my intended destination. The application into which I type this domain name (e.g., email client and web browser) utilizes the sockets†application programming interface (API) to communicate with a portion of code within the TCP/IP stack called a *resolver*. The resolver's job in this instance is to translate the web server name I typed into an IP address that may be used to initiate IP communications.

The resolver issues a query for this hostname to my local DNS server, requesting the server provide an answer. The IP address of this local DNS server is configured either manually‡ or via DHCP using the domain servers option (option 6 in DHCP and option 23 in DHCPv6). This DNS server will then attempt to answer the query by looking in the following areas in the specified order and as illustrated in the Figure 9.2.

We often refer to this DNS server to which the resolver issues its query as a *recursive server*. "Recursive" means that the resolver would like the DNS server to try to find the answer to its query if it does not know itself. From the resolver's viewpoint, it issues one query and expects an answer. From the recursive DNS server's perspective, it attempts to locate the answer for the resolver. The recursive server is the resolver's "portal" into the global domain name system. The recursive server accepts recursive

---

* Some environments allow dots within hostnames that is relatively uncommon though permissible.
† This API call is from the application to the TCP/IP layer of the protocol stack. The gethostbyname sockets/ Winsock call initiates this particular process.
‡ We'll review how to perform this manual configuration a little later in this chapter.

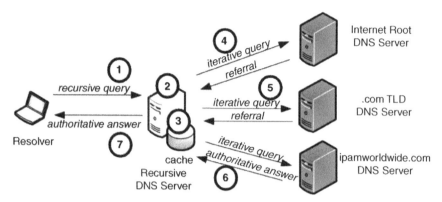

Figure 9.2. Recursive and iterative queries in name resolution (11)

queries directly from client resolvers and performs the steps outlined below to obtain the answer to the query on behalf of the resolver.

1. The resolver initiates a query to the recursive DNS server. The resolver knows which DNS server to query based on configuration via manual entry or via DHCP.

2. The queried server will first search its configured data files. That is, the DNS server is typically configured with configuration and resource record information for which it is *authoritative*. This information is typically configured using text files, a Windows interface or an IPAM system. For example, your company's DNS servers are likely configured with resolution information for your company's IP devices. As such, this is authoritative information. If the answer is found, it is returned to the resolver and the process stops.

3. If the queried server is not authoritative for the queried domain, it will access its cache to determine if it recently received a response for the same or similar query from another DNS server during a prior resolution task. If the answer for pc52. dev.ipamworldwide.com. resides in cache[*], the DNS server will respond to the resolver with this nonauthoritative information and the process stops. The fact that this is not an authoritative answer is generally of little consequence, but the server alerts the resolver to this fact in its response.

4. If the queried DNS server cannot locate the queried information in cache, it will then attempt to locate the information via another DNS server that has the information. There are three methods used to perform this "escalation."

    a. If the cache information referenced in step 3 indicates a partial answer to the query, it will attempt to contact the source of that information to locate the ultimate source and answer. For example, a prior query to another DNS

---

[*] Cache entries are temporary and are removed by DNS servers based on user configuration settings as well as advertised lifetime of a resource record.

server, server A, may have indicated that DNS server A is authoritative for the `ipamworldwide.com` domain. The initially queried DNS server may then query DNS server A for information leading to resolution of `pc52.dev.ipamworldwide.com.`

b. If the cache does not provide relevant information, and the queried recursive server is configured to forward, the server will forward the query as configured in its configuration or zone file. We'll cover the details on this configuration later.

c. If no information is found in cache, the server cannot identify a referral server, or forwarding did not provide a response* or is not configured, the DNS server will access its *hints* file. The hints file provides a list of *root name servers* to query in order to begin traversing down the domain hierarchy to a DNS server that can provide an answer to the query.

Note that by issuing queries to other DNS servers to locate resolution information, the recursive server itself performs a resolver function to execute this lookup. The term *stub resolver* is commonly used to identify resolvers, like those within end user clients, that are configured only with which recursive name servers (NSs) to query.

5. Upon querying either a root server or a server further down the tree based on cached information, the queried server will either resolve the query by providing the IP address(es) for `pc52.dev.ipamworldwide.com.` or will provide a referral to another DNS server further down the hierarchy "closer" to the sought fully qualified domain name. For example, upon querying a root server, you are guaranteed that you will not obtain a direct resolution answer for `pc52.dev.ipamworldwide.com.` However, the root name server will refer the querying DNS server to the name servers that are authoritative for `com.` The root servers are "delegation-only" servers and do not directly resolve queries, only answering with delegated name server information for the queried TLD.

6. The recursive server *iterates*† additional queries based on responses down the domain tree until the query can be answered. Continuing with our example, upon querying the name server that is authoritative for `com.`, the answer received will be a referral to the name server that is authoritative for `ipamworldwide.com.`, and so on down the tree. Ultimately, a DNS server that is authoritative for the zone of relevance to the query should be located. The authoritative DNS server will read the corresponding zone information for a *resource record* of the type being queried. The server will pass the resource record(s) to the querying (recursive) DNS server.

---

* If the `forward only` option is configured, the resolution attempt will cease if the forwarded query returns no results; if the `forward first` option is configured, the process outlined in this paragraph ensues, with escalation to a root server.

† These "point-to-point" queries are referred to as iterative queries.

7. When the answer is received, the recursive DNS server will provide the answer to the resolver and also update its cache and the process ends. If an answer cannot be found, the recursive server will also cache this "negative" information as well for use in responding to similar queries.

In summary, the resolution process entails (a) finding a name server with authoritative information to resolve the query in question and (b) querying that server for the desired information. In our example, the desired information was the IP address corresponding to the domain name pc52.dev.ipamworldwide.com. This "translation" information mapping the queried domain name to an IP address is stored in the DNS server in the form of a resource record. Different types of resource records are defined for different types of lookups. Each resource record contains a "key" or lookup value and a corresponding resolution or answer value. In some cases a given lookup value for a given type may have multiple entries in the DNS server configuration. In this case, the authoritative DNS server will respond with the entire set of resource records, or *RRSet*, matching the queried value (name), class and type. We'll discuss resource records in detail in the next chapter.

The bottom line is that DNS servers are configured at all levels of the domain tree as authoritative for their respective domain information, as well as where to refer queriers further down the domain tree. In many cases, these servers at different levels are administered by different organizations. Not every level or node in the domain tree requires a different set of DNS servers as an organization may serve multiple domain levels within a common set of DNS servers.

While the top three layers of the domain tree typically utilize three sets of DNS servers under differing administrative authority, the support of multiple levels or domains within an organization on a single set of DNS servers is a deployment decision. This decision hinges primarily on whether administrative delegation is required or desired. For example, the DNS administrators for the ipamworldwide.com domain may desire to retain administrative control of the dev.ipamworldwide.com. domain, but to delegate eng.ipamworldwide.com to a different set of administrators and name servers. This leads us to a discussion regarding the distinction between zones and domains.

9.3 ZONES AND DOMAINS

The term *zone* is used to differentiate the level of administrative control with respect to the domain hierarchy. In our example, the ipamworldwide.com zone contains authority for the ipamworldwide.com and dev.ipamworldwide.com domains, while the eng.ipamworldwide.com zone retains authority for the eng.ipamworldwide.com domain as illustrated in Figure 9.3.

By delegating authority for eng.ipamworldwide.com, the DNS administrators for ipamworldwide.com are agreeing to pass all resolutions for eng.ipamworldwide.com (and below in the domain tree for any subdomains of eng.ipamworldwide.com) to DNS servers administered by personnel operating the eng.ipamworldwide.com zone. These eng.ipamworldwide.com

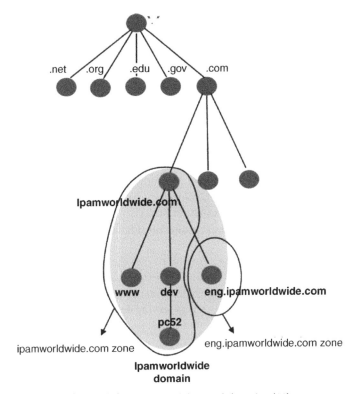

Figure 9.3. Zones as delegated domains (11).

administrators can manage their domain and resource records and any children auton-omously; they just need to inform the parent domain administrators (for `ipamworld-wide.com`) where to direct queries they receive as resolvers or other DNS servers attempt to traverse down the domain tree seeking resolutions.

Thus, administrators for the `ipamworldwide.com` zone must configure all resource records and configuration attributes for the `ipamworldwide.com` zone, including subdomains within the `ipamworldwide.com` zone such as the `dev.ipamworldwide.com` domain. At the same time, `ipamworldwide.com` admin-istrators must provide a delegation linkage to any child zones, such as `eng.ipam-worldwide.com`. This delegation linkage is supported by entering name server (NS) resource records within the `ipamworldwide.com` zone file, which indicate which name servers are authoritative for the `eng.ipamworldwide.com` delegated zone. These NS records provide the continuity to delegated child zones by referring resolvers or other name servers further down the domain tree. Corresponding A or AAAA records called *glue records* are also usually defined to glue the resolved NS host domain name to an IP address to enable direct addressing of further queries.

The shading in Figure 9.3 indicates that the `ipamworldwide.com` domain contains the `ipamworldwide.com` node plus all of its children, highlighting this level of responsibility for ipamworldwide.com and "below." The ipamworldwide.com DNS administrators are responsible for maintaining all DNS configuration information for the ipamworldwide.com zone as well as referrals to DNS servers serving delegated child zones. Thus, when other DNS servers around the world are attempting to resolve any name ending in ipamworldwide.com on behalf of their clients, their queries will require traversal of the ipamworldwide.com DNS servers and perhaps other DNS servers, such as those serving the eng.ipamworldwide.com zone.

The process of delegation of the name space enables autonomy of DNS configuration while providing linkages via NS record referrals within the global DNS database. As you can imagine, if the name servers referenced by these NS records are unavailable, the domain tree will be broken at that point, inhibiting resolution of names at that point or below in the domain tree. If the eng.ipamworldwide.com DNS servers are down, authoritative resolution for eng.ipamworldwide.com *and its children* will fail. This illustrates the requirement that each zone must have at least two authoritative DNS servers for redundancy.

Thus, the administrators for the ipamworldwide.com zone will configure their DNS servers with configuration and resolution information for the ipamworldwide.com and dev.ipamworldwide.com domains; they will also configure their servers with the names and addresses of DNS servers serving delegated or child zones. They need know nothing further about these delegated zones; just who to contact so a referral can be sent to the querying recursive DNS server.

DNS server configuration information consists of server configuration parameters and declarations of all zones for which the server is authoritative. This information can be defined on each server that is authoritative for a given set of zones. Additions, changes and deletions of resource records, the discrete resolution information within each zone configuration file, can be entered once on a *master* server, or more correctly, the server that is configured as master for the respective zone. The other servers that are likewise authoritative for this information can be configured as *slaves* or *secondaries*, and they obtain zone updates by the process of *zone transfers*. Zone transfers enable a slave server to obtain the latest copy of its authoritative zone information from the master server. Microsoft Active Directory-integrated DNS servers support zone transfers for compatibility with this standard process, but also enable DNS data replication using native Active Directory replication processes.

9.3.1 Dissemination of Zone Information

Given the criticality of the DNS service in resolving authoritatively and maintaining domain tree linkages, DNS server redundancy is a must. Different DNS server vendors take different redundancy approaches. Microsoft replicates DNS information among a set of domain controllers when DNS information is integrated into Active Directory, an architectural foundation of the Windows Server products. The ISC BIND implementation supports DNS information replication through a hub-and-spoke model. Configuration changes are made to a *master* DNS server as mentioned above. Redundant DNS servers are configured as *slaves* or *secondaries*, and they obtain zone updates by the process of *zone transfers*. Zone transfers enable a slave server to obtain the latest copy of its authoritative zone information from the master server. Microsoft Active Directory-integrated DNS servers also support zone transfers for compatibility with this standard process.

Versions of zone files are tracked by a zone serial number that must be changed every time a change is applied to the zone. Slaves are configured to periodically check the zone serial number set on the master server; if the serial number is larger than its own value defined for the zone, it will conclude that it has outdated information and will initiate a zone transfer. Additionally, the server that is master for the zone can be configured to *notify* its slaves that a change has been made, stimulating the slaves to immediately check the serial number and perform a zone transfer to obtain the updates more quickly than awaiting the normal periodic update check.

Zone transfers may consist of the entire zone configuration file, called an absolute zone transfer (AXFR) or of the incremental updates only, called an incremental zone transfer (IXFR). In cases where zone information is relatively static and updated from a single source, for example, an administrator, the serial number checking with AXFRs as needed works well. These so-called *static zones* are much simpler to administer than their counterpart: *dynamic zones*. Dynamic zones, as the name implies, accept dynamic updates, for example, from DHCP servers updating DNS with newly assigned IP addresses and corresponding domain names. Updates for dynamic zones can utilize IXFR mechanisms to maintain synchronization among the master and multiple slave servers.

With BIND 9, journal files on each server provide an efficient means to track dynamic updates to zone information. These journal files are temporary appendages to corresponding zone files and enables tracking of dynamic updates until the server writes these journal entries into the zone file and reloads the zone. Many server implementations load the zone file information into memory along with incremental zone updates, which are also loaded into memory for fast resolution. We'll discuss more details about server and zone configuration later in the chapter, but first let's consider a different kind of domain tree structure.

9.3.2 Reverse Domains

Until now, we've introduced the common name-to-IP address resolution process, locating a DNS server authoritative for a name resolution, which then responds authoritatively to the query. Another popular form of query is for IP address-to-name resolution. This "reverse" form of resolution is commonly used as a security check when establishing virtual private network (VPN) connections or for general IP address-to-hostname lookups. Given an IP address, how does a DNS server traverse the domain tree to find a host domain name? Special top-level domains are defined for IP address-based domain trees within the *Address and Routing Parameter Area* (arpa) domain: in-addr.arpa. is defined for IPv4 address-to-name resolution and ip6.arpa. is for IPv6 address-to-name resolution[*].

---

[*] Technically, these are both children of the .arpa. TLD

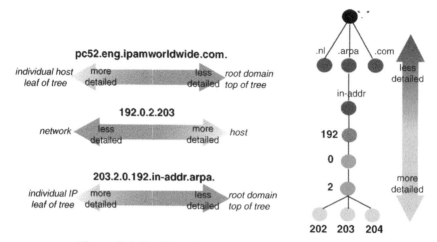

Figure 9.4. IP address (reverse) domain tree mapping (11).

The only wrinkle in organizing IP addresses within a domain tree results from mapping an IP address, which reads left-to-right as less detailed (network) to more detailed (IP host), while reading a domain name left-to-right reads more specific (specific host, domain) to less specific (root). Therefore, the IP address is reversed to enable representation within the domain hierarchy, reading left-to-right as more specific to less specific. This is illustrated in Figure 9.4.

You may notice that the mapping of dotted decimal notation enables mapping of reverse domains to octet-boundary-based network allocations. For example, if we've been allocated a "class C" network as our public space, 192.0.2.0/24, it is easy[*] to visualize the leaves of the `in-addr.arpa.` domain tree depicted above mapping to individual hosts. And like resolution of hostnames, traversal of the `in-addr.arpa.` domain tree follows a similar process to locate authoritative resolution of address-to-name queries. The pointer or PTR resource record provides a mapping from address to host, as we'll discuss in the next chapter.

But what if we had been allocated a subnet on non-octet boundaries? For example, if we had allocated a /23 instead of a /24, the network address might have been denoted 192.0.2.0/23. This /23 is in effect comprised of the 2 /24 networks: 192.0.2.0/24 and 192.0.3.0/24. The two reverse domains corresponding to these octet-normalized network addresses, `2.0.192.in-addr.arpa.` and `3.0.192.in-addr.arpa`, would need to be configured within DNS to allow reverse lookups of hosts within this /23 network.

If the allocated subnet was smaller than a class C network, a more complex representation and zone file configuration is required. Let's say for example that we allocate a subnet for a remote office as 192.0.2.0/25. If we try to represent the corresponding reverse domain as `2.0.192.in-addr.arpa`, this would encompass

---

[*] Of course "easy" is a relative term, but once you get accustomed to reverse domains, at least such classful networks are easily visualized as reverse domains.

the desired half but also the "other half" of the 192.0.2.0/24 network, namely the 192.0.2.128/25 network. But this other half could be allocated to a different organization having its own DNS authority. In that case, who would administer the classful reverse zone since it's split across two authorities? The solution is to indicate that portion of the fourth octet to which the subnet applies in the reverse zone name.

RFC 2317 (93) specifies the use of the CIDR notation within the `in-addr.arpa` zone name. Thus, literally reversing the numbers between the dots of the allocated subnet, we arrive at the following: for network 192.0.2.0/25, the corresponding reverse domain is `0/25.2.0.192.in-addr.arpa.`* The "other half" of this class C would be `128/25.2.0.192.in-addr.arpa.` Subnets of smaller sizes would follow a similar notation, using the fourth octet of the network address, followed by/<network size>, followed by the remaining three octets from the IP address, reversed, then appended with `in-addr.arpa.`

But when a resolver issues a query, it will be for a particular address (PTR record) in the form of `185.2.0.192.in-addr.arpa.`, so how do we map this query to the appropriate zone file, `128/25.2.0.192.in-addr.arpa` in this case? The solution calls for the use of canonical name (CNAME) records in the parent (`2.0.192.in-addr.arpa.`) zone to selectively point to the proper delegated zone, each of which may be administered by separate DNS administrators. A CNAME record serves as an alias for a given record, directing the querier to then query for the alias name. In this case a CNAME record for each individual IP address needs to be created to map to a corresponding RFC 2317 style reverse zone, enabling the delegation of subsets of records to different subzone administrators.

Let's look at how this would work in our example case. Within the parent zone file corresponding to this `2.0.192.in-addr.arpa.` zone, we would configure the following[†]:

```
2.0.192.in-addr.arpa. IN SOA dns.ipamworldwide.com.
admin.ipamworldwide.com. ( 1 2h 30m 1w 1d )


$ORIGIN 2.0.192.in-addr.arpa.          //implicit
0/25  IN NS dns.A1.ipamworldwide.com.  //authoritative servers
      IN NS dns.A2.ipamworldwide.com.  // for 0/25
1     IN CNAME 1.0/25.2.0.192.in-addr.arpa.
2     IN CNAME 2.0/25.2.0.192.in-addr.arpa.
3     IN CNAME 3.0/25.2.0.192.in-addr.arpa.
. . .
127   IN CNAME 127.0/25.2.0.192.in-addr.arpa.
```

---

* While RFC 2317 specifies slashes within these domain names, many DNS administrators substitute dashes in order to associate zone names with zone file names, which cannot contain slashes. Hence we could denote this zone as 0-25.2.0.192.in-addr.arpa defined in zone file db.0-25.2.0.192.in-addr.arpa. We'll stick to the RFC 2317 format here, but dashes work just as well.

[†] DNS configuration file examples in this book utilize BIND DNS format (144).

```
128/25 IN NS dns.B1.ipamworldwide.com.   //authoritative servers
       IN NS dns.B2.ipamworldwide.com.   // for 128/25
129    IN CNAME 129.128/25.2.0.192.in-addr.arpa.
130    IN CNAME 130.128/25.2.0.192.in-addr.arpa.
131    IN CNAME 131.128/25.2.0.192.in-addr.arpa.
...
254    IN CNAME 254.128/25.2.0.192.in-addr.arpa.
```

Based on standard domain tree traversal, when the querying name server queries the DNS server authoritative for the `2.0.192.in-addr.arpa.` zone, the file above on the corresponding DNS server provides not a resolution, but a next step, pointing the desired IP address answer to another FQDN via a CNAME record. So far in the process, a query for the hostname for IP address 192.0.2.185 would result in a CNAME pointing to `185.128/25.2.0.192.in-addr.arpa`. We also know who to ask to resolve this query because two NS records are listed as authoritative for the associated domain, `128/25.2.0.192.in-addr.arpa.`, namely `dns.B1.ipamworldwide.com` and `dns.B2.ipamworldwide.com`.

The corresponding `128/25.2.0.192.in-addr.arpa.` zone file on these servers would contain the following:

```
128/25.2.0.192.in-addr.arpa.   IN   SOA   dns.B1.ipamworldwide.com.
admin.ipamworldwide.com. ( 1 2h 30m 1w 1d )

128/25.2.0.192.in-addr.arpa. IN NS dns.B1.ipamworldwide.com.
128/25.2.0.192.in-addr.arpa. IN NS dns.B2.ipamworldwide.com.

129.128/25.2.0.192.in-addr.arpa.   IN   PTR   public1.ipamworldwide.
com.
130.128/25.2.0.192.in-addr.arpa.   IN   PTR   public2.ipamworldwide.
com.
131.128/25.2.0.192.in-addr.arpa. IN PTR www.ipamworldwide.com.
```

Or in abbreviated format using "relative" domain names:

```
@ IN SOA dns.B1.ipamworldwide.com. admin.ipamworldwide.com. ( 1 2h 30m
1w 1d )
// Implicit $ORIGIN 128/25.2.0.192.in-addr.arpa.

   IN NS dns.B1.ipamworldwide.com.
   IN NS dns.B2.ipamworldwide.com.
129  IN PTR public1.ipamworldwide.com.
130  IN PTR public2.ipamworldwide.com.
```

```
131  IN PTR www.ipamworldwide.com.

. . .

185  IN PTR server-x.ipamworldwide.com.
```

Querying this zone file for this referenced CNAME alias, to `185.128/25.2.0.192.in-addr.arpa.`, we find our PTR record pointing to the associated hostname server-x.ipamworldwide.com, completing the resolution.

For non-octet bounded networks larger than class C networks (i.e., /9 - /15 and /17 - /23), domain alias (DNAME) records can be used. For example, the 172.16.0.0/14 network could be allocated and delegated to an administrator in the engineering group. Reverse queries on this network can be referred to the engineering group's DNS server, dns[1-2].eng.ipamworldwide.com per the following example, configured within the `172.in-addr.arpa.` zone file:

```
16/14.172.in-addr.arpa. IN NS   dns1.eng.ipamworldwide.com

16/14.172.in-addr.arpa. IN NS   dns2.eng.ipamworldwide.com

16.172.in-addr.arpa.    IN DNAME 16.16/14.172.in-addr.arpa.

17.172.in-addr.arpa.    IN DNAME 17.16/14.172.in-addr.arpa.

18.172.in-addr.arpa.    IN DNAME 18.16/14.172.in-addr.arpa.

19.172.in-addr.arpa.    IN DNAME 19.16/14.172.in-addr.arpa.
```

These entries delegate the reverse lookups for all four /16 networks comprising the engineering group's /14 to the their DNS servers as indicated by the first two records shown above. The next four records map these four /16 reverse domains to this delegated 16/14.172.in-addr.arpa. domain.

We've essentially inserted an artificial layer in the reverse tree to serve as a consolidation point. Thus, to resolve the PTR record for a host with IP address 172.18.45.94, the resolving name server would traverse down the 172.in-addr.arpa. tree. The next node down, 18.172.in-addr.arpa., has a domain alias of 18.16/14.172.in-addr.arpa. by virtue of the DNAME lookup. Next, by querying the dns1.eng.ipamworldwide.com DNS server, which is authoritative for the 16/14.172.in-addr.arpa. zone, we resolve the corresponding PTR entry within this zone:

```
94.45.18.172.in-addr.arpa. IN PTR host.eng.ipamworldwide.com.
```

9.3.3 IPv6 Reverse Domains

IPv6 reverse domain mapping is a bit more cumbersome. As with IPv4, the IPv6 address must be reversed, maintaining its hexadecimal format. But the IPv6 address must first be "padded" to the full 32-hex digit representation; that is, the two forms of abbreviation discussed in Chapter 2 must be removed by including leading zeroes between colons and filling in double-colon-denoted implied zeroes. Figure 9.5 illustrates an example of the

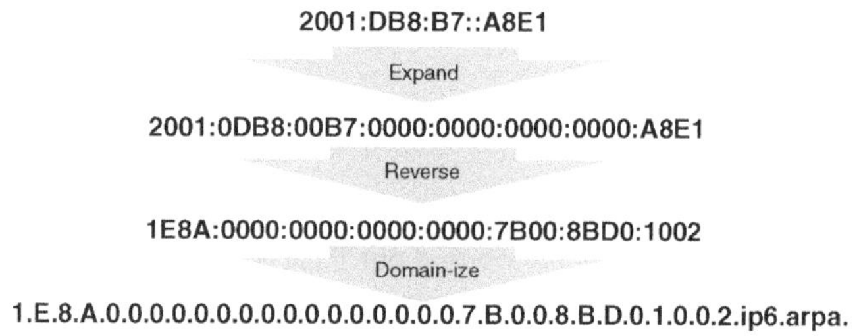

2001:DB8:B7::A8E1

Expand

2001:0DB8:00B7:0000:0000:0000:0000:A8E1

Reverse

1E8A:0000:0000:0000:0000:7B00:8BD0:1002

Domain-ize

1.E.8.A.0.0.0.0.0.0.0.0.0.0.0.0.0.0.0.0.7.B.0.0.8.B.D.0.1.0.0.2.ip6.arpa.

Figure 9.5. IPv6 address to reverse domain mapping.

process for the IPv6 address 2001:DB8:B7::A8E1. The address must be expanded or padded and the digits reversed. Then, this result must be "domain-ized" by removing the colons, inserting dots between each digit, and appending the ip6.arpa. upper level domains.

Figure 9.6 illustrates the logic in reversing the IPv6 address in order to be represented in a domain hierarchy as read left-to-right as more specific to less specific. This is directly analogous to Figure 9.4, which illustrates this concept for IPv4 addresses. The full 32-hex digit representation used in Figure 9.6 provides a unique, though lengthy, traversal down the `ip6.arpa.` domain tree (not shown).

Note that this example illustrates the reverse domain representation for a full 128-bit IPv6 address. Subnets can have corresponding reverse domain definitions as in IPv4. For a /64 allocation, only the first 64 bits (16-hex digits) would be included. Thus, for the host above, its /64 subnet reverse zone notation would be defined as

```
0.0.0.0.7.B.0.0.8.B.D.0.1.0.0.2.ip6.arpa.
```

Notation for reverse domains of IPv6 networks allocated on non-nibble boundaries was not formally addressed in RFC 2317; however, the same techniques specified in the RFC can be mapped to IPv6 reverse zones corresponding to non-nibble bounded IPv6 block allocations. Let's illustrate this by example. Say the North America team desires to allocate four /54 blocks from its 2001:db8:4af0:8000::/52 block, namely 2001:

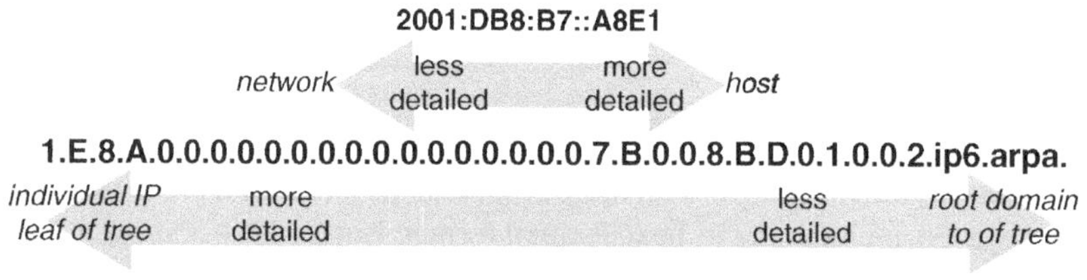

2001:DB8:B7::A8E1

network   less   more   host
           detailed   detailed

1.E.8.A.0.0.0.0.0.0.0.0.0.0.0.0.0.0.0.0.7.B.0.0.8.B.D.0.1.0.0.2.ip6.arpa.

individual IP   more   less   root domain
leaf of tree   detailed   detailed   to of tree

Figure 9.6. The IPv6 reverse domain notation.

db8:4af0:8000::/54, 2001:db8:4af0:8400::/54, 2001:db8:4af0:8800::/54, and 2001: db8:4af0:8c00::/54. Using CNAME resource records to refer queriers to servers responsible for these corresponding reverse zones, the 8.0.f.a.4.8.b.d.0.1.0.0.2.ip6.arpa zone file would look something like

```
8.0.f.a.4.8.b.d.0.1.0.0.2.ip6.arpa. IN SOA dns.ipamworldwide.com.
admin.ipamworldwide.com. ( 1 2h 30m 1w 1d )
```

```
$ORIGIN 8.0.f.a.4.8.b.d.0.1.0.0.2.ip6.arpa. //implicit
0/54  IN NS dns.A1.ipamworldwide.com.  //authoritative servers
       IN NS dns.A2.ipamworldwide.com.  // for 2001:db8:4af0:8000::
       /54
0     IN CNAME 0.0/54.8.0.f.a.4.8.b.d.0.1.0.0.2.ip6.arpa.
1     IN CNAME 1.0/54.8.0.f.a.4.8.b.d.0.1.0.0.2.ip6.arpa.
2     IN CNAME 2.0/54.8.0.f.a.4.8.b.d.0.1.0.0.2.ip6.arpa.
3     IN CNAME 3.0/54.8.0.f.a.4.8.b.d.0.1.0.0.2.ip6.arpa.

4/54  IN NS dns.B1.ipamworldwide.com.      //authoritative servers
       IN NS dns.B2.ipamworldwide.com.      // for 2001:db8:4af0:
       8400::/54
4     IN CNAME 4.4/54.8.0.f.a.4.8.b.d.0.1.0.0.2.ip6.arpa.
5     IN CNAME 5.4/54.8.0.f.a.4.8.b.d.0.1.0.0.2.ip6.arpa.
6     IN CNAME 6.4/54.8.0.f.a.4.8.b.d.0.1.0.0.2.ip6.arpa.
7     IN CNAME 7.4/54.8.0.f.a.4.8.b.d.0.1.0.0.2.ip6.arpa.

8/54  IN NS dns.C1.ipamworldwide.com.  //authoritative servers
       IN NS dns.C2.ipamworldwide.com. // for 2001:db8:4af0:8800::/54
8     IN CNAME 8.8/54.8.0.f.a.4.8.b.d.0.1.0.0.2.ip6.arpa.
9     IN CNAME 9.8/54.8.0.f.a.4.8.b.d.0.1.0.0.2.ip6.arpa.
a     IN CNAME a.8/54.8.0.f.a.4.8.b.d.0.1.0.0.2.ip6.arpa.
b     IN CNAME b.8/54.8.0.f.a.4.8.b.d.0.1.0.0.2.ip6.arpa.

c/54  IN NS dns.D1.ipamworldwide.com.  //authoritative servers
       IN NS dns.D2.ipamworldwide.com. // for 2001:db8:4af0:8c00::/54
c     IN CNAME c.c/54.8.0.f.a.4.8.b.d.0.1.0.0.2.ip6.arpa.
d     IN CNAME d.c/54.8.0.f.a.4.8.b.d.0.1.0.0.2.ip6.arpa.
e     IN CNAME e.c/54.8.0.f.a.4.8.b.d.0.1.0.0.2.ip6.arpa.
f     IN CNAME f.c/54.8.0.f.a.4.8.b.d.0.1.0.0.2.ip6.arpa.
```

Following standard domain tree traversal, when the querying name server queries the DNS server authoritative for the `8.0.f.a.4.8.b.d.0.1.0.0.2.ip6.arpa.` zone, the file above on the corresponding DNS server provides not a resolution, but a next step, pointing the desired IPv6 address answer to another FQDN via a CNAME record. So far in the process, a PTR query requesting the hostname for IP address 2001: db8:4af0:8d03::f6 results in a CNAME pointing to `d.c/54.8.0.f.a.4.8.b.d.0.1.0.0.2.ip6.arpa.` We also know who to ask to resolve this query because two NS records are listed as authoritative for this domain, namely `dns.D1.ipamworldwide.com` and `dns.D2.ipamworldwide.com`.

The corresponding `d.c/54.8.0.f.a.4.8.b.d.0.1.0.0.2.ip6.arpa.` zone file on these servers would contain the following:

```
c/54.8.0.f.a.4.8.b.d.0.1.0.0.2.ip6.arpa. IN SOA dns.D1.ipamworld-
wide.com. admin.ipamworldwide.com. ( 1 2h 30m 1w 1d )

      IN NS dns.D1.ipamworldwide.com.
      IN NS dns.D2.ipamworldwide.com.

1.0.b.0.0.0.0.0.0.0.0.0.0.0.0.0.3.0.c   IN PTR public1.ipamworld-
                                            wide.com.
0.2.0.a.4.0.0.0.0.0.0.0.0.0.0.0.3.0.c   IN PTR public2.ipamworld-
                                            wide.com.
f.c.0.0.0.0.0.0.0.0.0.0.0.0.0.0.3.0.d   IN PTR www.ipamworldwide.
                                            com.
. . .
6.f.0.0.0.0.0.0.0.0.0.0.0.0.0.0.3.0.d   IN PTR server-y.ipamworld-
                                            wide.com.
```

Querying this zone file for this referenced CNAME alias, that is, `6.f.0.0.0.0.0.0.0.0.0.0.0.0.0.0.3.0.d.c/54.8.0.f.a.4.8.b.d.0.1.0.0.2.ip6.arpa.`, we find our PTR record pointing to the associated hostname server-y.ipamworldwide.com, completing the resolution.

9.3.4 Additional Zones

Root Hints. We mentioned a *hints file* during the overview of the resolution process. This file should provide a list of DNS server names and addresses (in the form of NS, A and AAAA resource records) that the server should query if the resolver query cannot be resolved via authoritative, forwarded, or cached data. The hints file will typically list the Internet root servers, which are authoritative for the root (.) of the domain tree. Querying a root server enables the querying server to start at the top to begin the traversal down the domain tree in order to locate an authoritative server to resolve the query. The contents of the hints file for Internet root servers may be obtained from www. internic.net/zones/named.root, though BIND and Microsoft DNS server implementations include this file with their distributions.

As we'll discuss in Chapter 11, some environments may require use of an internal set of root servers, where Internet access is restricted by organizational policy. In such cases, an internal version of the hints file can be used, listing names and addresses of internal root servers instead of the Internet root servers. The organization itself would need to maintain the listing of internal root servers, as well as their requisite root zone configurations.

Localhost Zones. Another zone file that proves essential is the localhost zone. The localhost zone enables one to resolve "localhost" as a hostname on the given server. A corresponding in-addr.arpa. zone file resolves the 127.0.0.1 loopback address. A single entry within the 0.0.127.in-addr.arpa zone maps address 1 to the host itself. This zone is required as there is no upstream authority for the 127.in-addr.arpa domain or subdomains. Likewise, the IPv6 equivalents need to be defined for the corresponding IPv6 loopback address, ::1. The localhost zone simply maps the localhost hostname to its 127.0.0.1 or ::1 IP address using an A and AAAA record, respectively.

9.4 RESOLVER CONFIGURATION

Like DHCP transactions, DNS resolution occurs behind the scenes and involves a client and server. Ideally, end users don't even know it happens; they type in a web address and connect! The resolver software must be configured regarding which DNS server(s) to query for resolution. Thus, unlike DHCP that requires no initial client configuration (since it simply broadcasts or multicasts to a well-known address), DNS does require some basic client configuration prior to use. This initial configuration may be performed manually or by obtaining this information from a DHCP server.

Figure 9.7 illustrates the configuration of a Microsoft Windows resolver in terms of manually defining the DNS server to query or the use of DHCP to obtain DNS server addresses automatically.

Microsoft Windows enables entry of multiple DNS servers to query within its graphical interface. Notice there are two entries in the "brute force" method shown on the screen on the right of Figure 9.7, one for preferred and another for alternate. Clicking the Advanced tab enables entry of more than two and in particular order. We recommend having *at least* two DNS servers configured for the resolver so should a DNS server be out of service, the resolver will automatically query an alternate server. If the "Obtain DNS server address automatically" radio button is selected, as shown in Figure 9.7, the resolver will obtain a list of DNS servers via DHCP.

On Unix or Linux-based systems, the /etc/resolv.conf file can be edited with to configure the resolver. The key parameter in this file is one or more nameserver statements pointing to DNS servers, but a number of options and additional directives enable further configuration refinement as described below. The italicized text should be

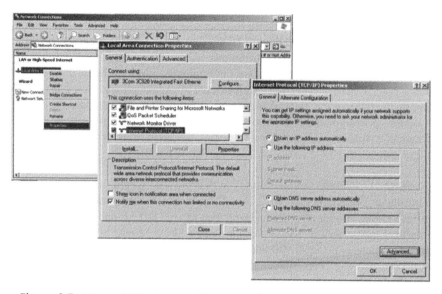

Figure 9.7. Microsoft Windows configuration of IP address DNS servers to query.

replaced by actual data referenced, for example, *domain* should be replaced with a DNS domain name.

- nameserver *IP_address*. The IP address of a recursive DNS server to query for name resolution; multiple nameserver entries are allowed and encouraged. The nameserver entry instructs the resolver where to direct DNS queries.
- domain *domain*. The DNS domain where this host (on which this resolver is installed) resides. This is used when resolving relative hostnames, as opposed to fully qualified host domain names.
- search *domain(s)*. The search list of up to six domains in which to search the entered hostname for resolution. Thus if we type in www for resolution, the resolver will successively append domains configured in this parameter in an attempt to resolve the query. If the entry search ipamworldwide.com. exists in resolv.conf, entry of www will result in a resolution attempt for www. ipamworldwide.com.
- sortlist *address/mask list*. Enables sorting of resolved IP addresses in accordance with the specified list of address/mask combinations. This enables the resolver to choose a "closer" destination if multiple IP addresses are returned for a query.
- options. Keyword preceding the following that enables specification of corresponding resolver parameters including the following:
  - debug. Turns on debugging.
  - ndots *n*. Defines a threshold for the number of dots within the entered name required before the resolver will consider the entered name simply a hostname

or a qualified domain name. When considered a hostname, the hostname will be queried as appended with domain names specified within the `domain` or `search` parameter.

o `timeout` *n.* Number of seconds to wait before timing out a query to a DNS server.

o `attempts` *n.* Number of query attempts before considering the query a failure.

o `rotate`. Enables round robin querying among DNS servers configured within the `nameserver` directives. Queries will be sent to a different server each time and cycled through.

o `no-check-names`. Turns off name checking of entered hostnames for resolution. Normally, underscore characters are not permitted for example, so setting this option enables query processing to proceed without validation of the entered hostname.

o `inet6`. Causes the resolver to issue a query for a AAAA record to resolve the entered hostname before attempting an A record query.

`search` and `options` settings can also be overridden on a per process basis via corresponding environment variable settings.

9.5 DNS MESSAGE FORMAT

9.5.1 Encoding of Domain Names

So far, we've discussed the organization of DNS information into a domain hierarchy as well as the basics of how a client or resolver performs resolution by issuing a recursive query to a DNS server that in turn iterates the query in accordance with the domain hierarchy (or forwarding) to obtain the answer to the query. Next we'll dig deeper into the DNS query and general message format, but first we'll first introduce the representation of domain names within DNS messages. Domain names are formatted as a series of *labels*. Labels consist of a one byte length field followed by that number of bytes/ASCII characters representing the label itself. This sequence of labels is terminated by a length field of zero indicating the root "`.`" domain. For example, the series of labels for `www.ipamworldwide.com.` would look like the following in ASCII format, where length bytes are highlighted in darker shading in Figure 9.8.

Starting at the upper left, the value "3" of the first length byte indicates that the following three bytes comprise first label, "`www`". The fifth or next byte after this is our next length byte, which has a value of "13" (0xD), which is the length of "`ipamworldwide`." After this label, the following byte of value "3" is the length of "`com`." Finally, the zero-value byte indicates the root "`.`" domain, fully qualifying the domain name. Note that the darker shaded bytes in the figure are encoded as length bytes to differentiate them from host or domain name characters containing numbers. The first

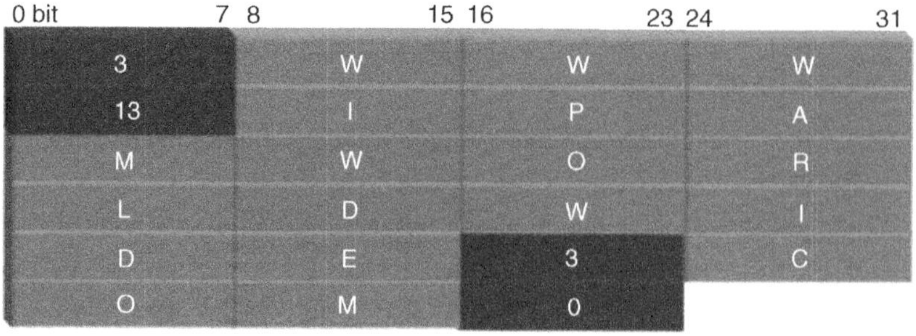

0 bit	7 8	15 16	23 24	31
3	W	W	W	
13	I	P	A	
M	W	O	R	
L	D	W	I	
D	E	3	C	
O	M	0		

Figure 9.8. DNS labels.

byte in a name will almost always[*] be a length byte followed by that number of bytes representing the first label, immediately followed by another length byte to eliminate ambiguity.

9.5.2 Name Compression

A given DNS message may contain multiple domain names, and many of these may have repetitive information, the `ipamworldwide.com.` suffix for example. The DNS specification enables message compression in order to reduce repetitive information and thereby reduce the size of the DNS message. This works by using *pointers* to other locations within the DNS message that specify a common domain suffix. This domain suffix is then appended at the point of location referenced by the pointer.

Let's say for example, that our query for www.ipamworldwide.com. returns a pair of DNS servers that can be queried for more information: `ns1.ipamworldwide.com.`, and `ns2.isp.com.` The `ipamworldwide.com.` portion of these domain names is common to the query and one of the answers, while only the `.com` portion is common to the question, first answer and the second answer. Thus, the message is formulated by fully specifying the domain name `www.ipamworldwide.com.` as illustrated above in Figure 9.8. Then when specifying `ns1`, instead of fully specifying `ns1.ipamworldwide.com`, only `ns1` is specified, followed by a pointer to the `ipamworldwide.com.` suffix earlier in the message. When identifying `ns2.isp.com`, the `ns2.isp` labels are specified, followed by a pointer to the `.com` suffix within the message.

How do DNS resolvers and servers differentiate a pointer from a standard label length byte? The DNS standard stipulates that each label may be of length 0–63 bytes. In binary, this is 000000000 to 00111111. Thus, the first two bits, $[00]_2$ in this case, identify the byte as a standard length byte, indicating the length of the following label. A pointer is identified by setting the first two bits to $[11]_2$, and is comprised of two

---

[*] As we'll discuss next, the length byte may alternatively consist of a two-byte pointer or a DNS extensions label.

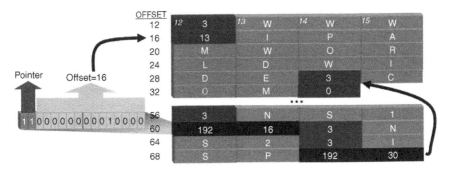

Figure 9.9. Name compression with pointers.

bytes, where the $[11]_2$ bits are followed by 14 bits identifying the offset in bytes from beginning of the DNS header. The first byte of the DNS message header is considered byte 0, and as the message is created, pointers are defined pointing to byte offsets from this point.

Let's look at how this maps out from our prior example. Let's say that beginning 12 bytes from the DNS header, we've included the domain name, www.ipamworld-wide.com. Now, later in the message, beginning at byte 56 from the beginning of the header, we would like to encode responses ns1.ipamworldwide.com and ns2.isp.com.

Figure 9.9 indicates how this would look. The first portion is as we discussed earlier, with length bytes (dark shading) followed by the respective number of name bytes (light shading). At byte position 56 in our example, the ns1 portion of the name is encoded normally, using a label length of "3", followed by ns1. However, the next byte is not a standard length byte but a pointer "double-byte" as it begins with $[11]_2$ and is shown as shaded black in the figure. The value encoded in the 14-bit offset field of the pointer is "16", indicating that the portion of the domain name starting at an offset of 16 bytes from the start of the DNS header should be appended to the ns1 label already specified. The first row of bytes in the figure below enumerates the individual byte offsets (italics), and byte 16 is the length byte of value "13", followed by encoding for ipamworldwide, followed by a length byte of value "3", then com, then. (length byte of value "0"). Concatenating this together, we arrive at the result: ns1.ipamworldwide.com.

Returning to the next domain name after processing the pointer, we find encoding for ns2.isp followed by a pointer to byte offset 30[*], which points to the length byte of "3", followed by com., completing the domain name as ns2.isp.com. Considering just these three example domain names, the number of bytes in the message occupied by domain names can be compressed from 59 to 39 bytes.

---

[*] Note that pointer double bytes shown above in black are displayed with their byte-wise decimal number representation, which in our example conveniently displays the offset in decimal in the second byte. But just to state the obvious, don't rely on just this second byte when parsing a pointer, as a pointer value can range from 0 to $2^{14} = 16,384$, which at this maximum value the decimal representation would be 255-255.

9.5.3 International Domain Names

DNS resolvers and servers communicate hostname queries and responses in ASCII-formatted messages. Configuration information is stored in ASCII[*] text files. Unfortunately, while ASCII characters have been defined to effectively represent the English language, they do not enable formatting of characters from other languages, especially those using a non-Latin-based alphabet. This limitation certainly impacts the ease-of-use of IP applications in countries where people do not use the English language. RFC 3490 (94) is a standards track RFC that addresses this limitation[†].

The RFC is entitled, Internationalizing Domain Names in Applications (IDNA). The "in applications" qualifier in the title insinuates the involvement of applications in this process. Indeed, the onus is placed on the application, such as a web browser or email client, to convert the user's native language entry into an ASCII-based string that can be communicated to a DNS server for resolution. This ingenious approach enables application level support of international character sets for end users without affecting the DNS protocol (or other ASCII-based IP protocols like SMTP). Existing DNS servers can be configured to resolve these ASCII-encoded domain names as they would for native ASCII-based domain names.

International character sets are encoded as Unicode characters. The Unicode standard "provides a unique number for every character, no matter what the platform, no matter what the program, no matter what the language," according to the Unicode Consortium web site (www.unicode.org). Every character is represented as a unique 2–3 byte hexadecimal number. RFC 3490, and its related RFCs 3491 (95), 3454 (96), and 3492 (97), describes the process of converting a Unicode-based domain name to an ASCII-formatted domain name. Note that technically, the domain labels are each converted, not the "domain name."

To resolve international domain names, a DNS server must be configured with resource records encoded in ASCII format, specifically Unicode-mapped ASCII characters referred to as *punycode*. The output of the punycode algorithm results in an ASCII string, which is then prefixed with the ASCII Compatible Encoding (ACE) header, `xn--`. Thus, within the DNS infrastructure, domains denoted as xn--<additional ASCII characters> are likely punycode representations of an international domain name. The application, for example, web browser, is responsible for converting the user-entered URL into Unicode format, then into punycode. The punycode domain name is passed to the resolver on the client for resolution via DNS using ASCII characters. The punycode algorithm is specified in RFC 3492 and several web sites are available for performing conversions for entry into DNS.

Consider an example (98): let's consider a web server host address in the żdźbło.com domain. as `www.żdźbło.com`. The domain name contains diacritics and has characters outside of the ASCII character set. The web browser in which this URL is entered would

---

[*] RFC 2673 (182), initially a standards track RFC, defined the use of binary data within DNS names but RFC 3363 (183) reverted RFC 2673 to experimental status.

[†] Note: RFC 3490 which defines "IDNA2003", has been updated by RFCs 5890-4 (184–188), referred to as "IDNA2008", each version denoted by the year specification work began. There are some differences between these versions but material in this section generally applies to both.

convert this to ASCII characters or punycode as `www.xn--dbo-iwalzb.com`. A corresponding A or AAAA record entry in DNS for the `www.xn--dbo-iwalzb.com`. host would enable the end user to enter a native language URL while utilizing the existing base of DNS servers deployed throughout the world to identify and connect via the IP address of the destination web server. The net result is that these DNS messages sent on the wire are encoded in ASCII characters.

9.5.4 DNS Message Format

Now let's look more closely at the format of DNS messages used to perform this overall resolution function, incorporating the label formatted domain names we discussed earlier. DNS messages are transmitted over UDP by default, using port 53. TCP can also be used on port 53. The basic format of a DNS message is illustrated in Figure 9.10.

- The message header contains fields that define the type of message and associated information, including the number of records for each of the following fields.
- The Question section specifies the information being sought via this message.
- The Answer section contains zero or more resource records that answer the query specified in the Question section.
- The Authority section contains zero or more resource records referring to name servers authoritative for the given answer or pointing to delegated name servers down the domain tree to which a successive iterative query may be issued.
- The Additional section contains zero or more resource records that contain supplemental information related to the question but are not strictly answers to the question.

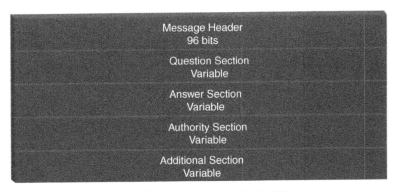

Figure 9.10. DNS message fields (99).

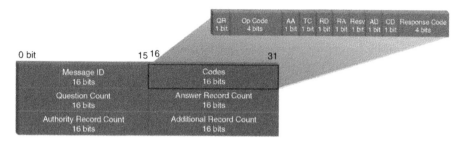

Figure 9.11. DNS message header (99).

Message Header. The DNS message header is included on every DNS message and conveys what type of message is enclosed as well as associated parameters as illustrated in Figure 9.11.

The message header is comprised of six 16-bit fields:

- *Message ID*. Also referred to as transaction ID, an identifier assigned by the resolver and copied in replies from the DNS server to enable resolver correlation of responses with queries.
- *Codes*. Message codes germane to this message. We'll examine these code fields next.
- *Question Count (QDCOUNT)*. The number of questions contained in the Question section of the DNS message.
- *Answer Record Count (ANCOUNT)*. The number of resource records contained in the Answer section of the DNS message.
- *Authority Record Count (NSCOUNT)*. The number of resource records contained in the Authority section of the DNS message.
- *Additional Record Count (ARCOUNT)*. The number of resource records contained in the Additional section of the DNS message.

The following codes bits have been defined:

- *QR (Query/Response)*. This flag indicates that this message is a query (0) or a response (1).
- *Opcode*. The operation code for this message. Presently, the following values have been defined:
  - o 0 = Query
  - o 1 = Reserved (formerly inverse query, now retired)
  - o 2 = Server status request
  - o 3 = Reserved
  - o 4 = Notify—enables a master zone server to inform a slave zone server with the same zone (and for a slave to acknowledge) that a change has been made to

the zone data. For Notify messages, the Authority and Additional sections are not used and respective record counts in the DNS header should be set to 0.

   o 5 = Update—enables a client or DHCP server to update zone data on a DNS server. For Update messages, the interpretation of DNS message fields and corresponding header fields differs from that described above. The message format for Update messages is described in the next section.

   o 6–15 = Unassigned.

- *AA (Authoritative Answer).* When set, this message contains an authoritative answer to the question. This means the response was derived from a DNS server that was configured with the zone's information. If it is not set, the answer was derived from a nonauthoritative DNS server, likely cached information from a prior query. Where multiple answers are provided, this flag pertains to the first record in the Answer section. When set by the client on the query, this indicates that an authoritative answer (not cached) is required.

- *TC (Truncated Response).* This code indicates that this message was truncated for transmission. This is generally due to the packet length restriction of UDP packets, the default transport layer protocol used by DNS.

- *RD (Recursion Desired).* This flag indicates that the querier would like the DNS server to iteratively resolve the query, traversing the domain tree as necessary. Most resolvers set this flag to indicate a query as a recursive query, while a DNS server will generally not set this flag when querying other servers.

- *RA (Recursion Available).* This flag indicates that recursive query support is available from this DNS server.

- *Reserved or Z bit.* Reserved (0).

- *AD (Authentic Data).* Used within the context of DNS security extensions (DNSSEC), this bit is set by a name server to indicate that information within the Answer and Authority sections is authentic, meaning it has been authenticated.

- *CD (Checking Disabled).* Used within the context of DNSSEC, this bit enables a DNSSEC resolver to disable signature validation in a DNSSEC name server's processing of this particular query.

- *Response Code (RCODE).* Provides result status to the client. The currently defined response codes are summarized in Table 9.1. Note that given the 4-bit RCODE field, decimal values 1–15 are encoded within the DNS header RCODE field.

   The DNS extensions (EDNS0, discussed later in this chapter) OPT resource record adds a capacity for 8 additional RCODE bits, bringing the total to 12 bits (up to decimal value 4095) when used in combination with the header RCODE bits.

You'll notice two interpretations of the decimal value 16. BADVERS is the interpretation when encoded within the OPT resource record while BADSIG is the result when encoded within a TKEY or TSIG resource record.

TABLE 9.1. DNS Message Response Codes[a] (106)

Decimal	Hex	Name	Description	Reference
RCODE				
0	0	NoError	No errors	RFC 1035 (99)
1	1	FormErr	Format error—server unable to interpret the query	RFC 1035 (99)
2	2	ServFail	Server failure—server problem has prevented processing of this query	RFC 1035 (99)
3	3	NXDomain	Nonexistent domain—domain name does not exist	RFC 1035 (99)
4	4	NotImp	Not implemented—query type not supported by this server	RFC 1035 (99)
5	5	Refused	Query refused—server refused the requested query, for example, refusal of a zone transfer request	RFC 1035 (99)
6	6	YXDomain	Name exists when it should not as determined during DNS update prerequisite processing	RFC 2136 (100)
7	7	YXRRSet	RRSet exists when it should not as determined during DNS update prerequisite processing	RFC 2136 (100)
8	8	NXRRSet	RRSet that should exist does not as determined during DNS update prerequisite processing	RFC 2136 (100)
9	9	NotAuth	Server is not authoritative for the zone listed in the zone section of the DNS Update message	RFC 2136 (100)
10	A	NotZone	Name used in the prerequisite or update section of a DNS Update message is not contained in zone denoted by the zone section of the message	RFC 2136 (100)
11–15	B–F	Available for assignment		
16	10	BADVERS	Unsupported (bad) OPT RR version	RFC 2671 (101)
16	10	BADSIG	TSIG Signature Failure	RFC 2845 (102)
17	11	BADKEY	Key not recognized	RFC 2845 (102)
18	12	BADTIME	Signature out of the valid server signature time window	RFC 2845 (102)
19	13	BADMODE	Invalid TKEY Mode—requested mode not supported by this server	RFC 2930 (103)
20	14	BADNAME	Nonexistent or duplicate key name	RFC 2930 (103)
21	15	BADALG	Algorithm not supported	RFC 2930 (103)

TABLE 9.1. (*Continued*)

RCODE				
Decimal	Hex	Name	Description	Reference
22	16	BADTRUNC	Bad truncation—Message Authentication Code (MAC) too short	RFC 4635 (104)
23–3840	14-F00	Available for assignment		
3841–4095	F01-FFF	Reserved for private use		RFC 5395 (105)

*a*If you consult the IANA web site (www.iana.org/assignments/dns-parameters), you'll notice values above 4095. Technically these are not RCODEs but reflect the 16-bit error field within the TSIG and TKEY meta resource record types, providing a capacity up to 65,535 for these two resource record types.

Question Section. The Question section within the DNS message format contains, as you might have guessed, the question that is being asked for this query. This section can contain more than one question, as identified by the number referenced in the QDCOUNT header field. Each of these questions has the following format (Figure 9.12).

The QNAME field contains the domain name, formatted as a series of labels. The QTYPE field indicates the query type, or for what purpose is this question being asked. Any resource record type may be included, which we will cover in detail the next chapter. However, there are some QTYPE values that are unique to requesting zone transfers for example that are presently defined including the following (Table 9.2).

The QCLASS field indicates for which class this query is being made, for example, IN for Internet class, the most common class. Classes essentially enable management of parallel namespaces. Currently defined QCLASSes (and DNS CLASSes) in general are defined in Table 9.3.

Answer Section. The Answer section contains zero or more answers in the form of resource records. The number of answers is specified in the ANCOUNT header field. We'll discuss the different types of resource records in the next chapter, and they all share a common generic format as defined in Figure 9.13.

The Name field, also called the Owner name field, is the lookup name corresponding to this resource record (corresponding to the lookup value or QNAME in the original question).

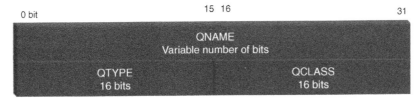

Figure 9.12. Question section format (99).

TABLE 9.2. DNS QTypes[a] (106)

QTypes Only	Query Purpose	QType ID (decimal)	IETF Status	Defining Document
*	All resource records	255	Standard	RFC 1035
MAILA	Mail agent resource records	254	Experimental	RFC 1035
MAILB	Mailbox resource records	253	Obsolete	RFC 1035
AXFR	Absolute zone transfer (entire zone)	252	Standard	RFC 1035
IXFR	Incremental zone transfer (changes only)	251	Proposed Standard	RFC 1995

[a]In addition to RRTypes in Table 12.1 that may be used as QTypes.

The Type field indicates the type of information that is provided for this name. For example, a type of A means that this resource record provides IPv4 address information for the given name. Resource record types are covered in the next chapter and are summarized in Table 10.1.

The Class field represents the namespace class, such as IN for Internet. Valid classes are displayed in Table 9.3.

The TTL or Time-to-Live field provides a time value in seconds with respect to the valid lifetime of the resource record. The receiver of this information may cache this information for TTL seconds and may use it reliably. However, upon expiration of the TTL, the cached information should be discarded and a new query issued.

TABLE 9.3. DNS Classes (106)

	CLASS			
Decimal	Hexadecimal	Name	Description	Reference
0	0	Reserved	Reserved	RFC 5395
1	1	IN	Internet	RFC 1035
2	2	Unassigned	N/A	IANA
3	3	CH	Chaos	RFC 1035
4	4	HS	Hesiod	RFC 1035
5–253	5-FD	Unassigned	N/A	IANA
254	FE	NONE	None	RFC 2136
255	FF	*(Any)	Any class (valid as QCLASS but not on resource records)	RFC 1035
256–65,270	100-FEFF	Unassigned	N/A	IANA
65,280–65,534	FF00-FFFE	Reserved for private use		RFC 5395
65,535	FFFF	Reserved	Reserved	RFC 5395

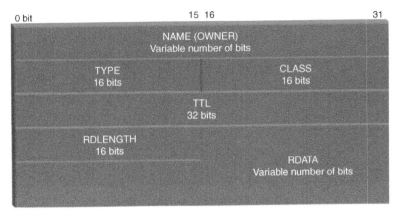

Figure 9.13. Answer section format (99).

The RDLength field indicates the length in bytes of the results (RData) field. The RData field contains the corresponding information of the specified Type in the identified Class, for the given Owner. The RData field has a variable format as we shall see when examining the wide variety of resource record types.

Authority Section. The Authority section contains $NSCOUNT$ number of answers in the form of resource records of the same format as discussed in the Answer section. Generally only NS (name server) resource records are valid within the Authority section, though most name servers return an SOA record in this section if the queried name server is authoritative but the answer section is empty. This section also contains information about other name servers that are authoritative for the queried information. This information is used by the querying resolver or more likely, recursive name server, to determine the next name server to query in traversing the domain tree to find the ultimate answer.

Additional Section. The Additional section contains $ASCOUNT$ number of answers in the form of resource records, which provide additional or related information to the query, in the same format as discussed in the Answer section.

9.5.5 DNS Update Messages

Update messages enable a client, DHCP server, or other source to perform an update (add, modify, or delete) of one or more resource records within a zone. While Update messages utilize the same basic format as DNS messages just described, the interpretation of some of the fields varies. Update messages, denoted with Op Code = 5 in the DNS message header, are encoded as follows (Figure 9.14).

Contrast this format with that for non-Update DNS messages depicted in Figure 9.10. The message header is of the same format as that of "normal" DNS messages, though the interpretation of the remaining sections differs.

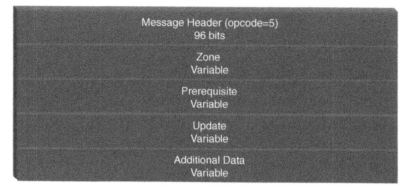

Figure 9.14. DNS Update message format (100).

The Zone section identifies the DNS zone to be updated by this Update message. The Prerequisite section enables the specification of conditions that must be satisfied in order to perform the update successfully. The condition and type of condition are determined by the value of each resource record-encoded parameter within the Prerequisite section. The following table defines how DNS update prerequisites are interpreted based on the values of the Owner, Class, Type and RData fields within the Prerequisites section.

Owner	Class	Type	RData	Prerequisite Interpretation
Match	ANY (255)	ANY	Empty	The matching owner name is in use in this zone
Match	ANY (255)	Match	Empty	An RRSet with matching owner and type exists (value independent, i.e., any RData match)
Match	NONE (254)	ANY	Empty	The matching owner name is not in use in this zone
Match	NONE (254)	Match	Empty	An RRSet with matching owner and type does not exist in this zone
Match	Same as Zone Class	Match	Match	An RRSet with matching owner, type, and RData exists in this zone (value dependent, i.e., RData match)

The Update section contains the resource records to be added to or deleted from the zone using a similar encoding as used in the Prerequisite section as follows.

Owner	Class	Type	RData	Update Interpretation
Owner to add	Same as Zone Class	RR type	RR RData	Add this resource record(s) of the specified owner, type, and RData to the zone's RRSet

(Continued)

Owner	Class	Type	RData	Update Interpretation
Owner to delete	ANY (255)	RR type	Empty	Delete the resource records of the specified owner and type
Owner to delete	ANY (255)	ANY	Empty	Delete all resource records of the specified owner name
Owner to delete	NONE (254)	RR type	RR RData	Delete the resource record(s) of the specified owner, type, and RData from the zone

The Additional Data section contains resource records related to this update, for example, out of zone glue records.

Consider an example of an Update message received with the prerequisite and update fields encoded as follows:

Field	Owner	Class	Type	RData
Prerequisite	host.ipamworldwide.com.	IN	DHCID	H8349a +)3jELeA==ES1
Update	host.ipamworldwide.com.	IN	A	10.0.0.200

The Update section contents will only be considered only if the prerequisite condition is met. In this case, the prerequisite condition is that the `host.ipamworldwide.com. IN DHCID H8349a + )3jELeA==ES1` record exists in the zone, that is, prerequisite type RRSet with matching owner, type, and RData (value dependent). If it does exist, then the `host.ipamworldwide.com. IN A 10.0.0.200` resource record from the Update section will be added to the zone. If not, the update will not be performed.

This particular example illustrates how the ISC DHCP server performs dynamic updates of DNS data upon assigning an IP address, in this case 10.0.0.200 to host.ipamworldwide.com. The DHCID record provides a hash of the host's hardware address receiving the IP address to uniquely identify the host. The prerequisite condition for updating the address record provides a means to assure that only the original holder of this A record can modify it, minimizing naming duplication or hijacking.

9.5.6 DNS Extensions (EDNS0)

Thus far in our discussion of the DNS message header, one may observe that all code bits are assigned but one, and additional response code assignments have been required by necessity. In addition, many hosts can process larger multipart UDP packets than the originally specified size limit of 512 bytes. As a result of these limitations, as well as the desire to add additional domain name label types, DNS extensions were defined in RFC 2671 (101).

RFC 2671 defines version 0 of extension mechanisms for DNS, which is denoted EDNS0. The RFC addresses the above constraints by defining the following extensions:

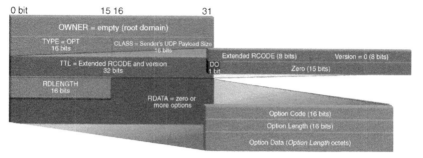

Figure 9.15. EDNS0 format (101).

- A new domain label type is defined to denote DNS extensions. As we discussed, the first two bits of the domain label uniquely identify the label as a length byte (first two bits $= [00]_2$) or as a pointer (first two bits $= [11]_2$). The extended label type has been assigned $[01]_2$ as its first two bits.
- EDNS0 defines a pseudoresource record, the OPT record (i.e., RRType = OPT). The OPT record is placed in the Additional section by the resolver or server to advertise its respective capabilities. The OPT resource record is used to advertise capabilities of the sender (client or server) to the recipient, and only one OPT record should be present.

The OPT pseudoresource record is encoded as follows, enabling specification of the sender's UDP packet size and additional response code bits (Figure 9.15).

The OPT record should never appear in a zone file. Thus, while the OPT pseudoresource record utilizes the same wire format as other resource records, the definition of standard fields has been modified to provide only extension information. The NAME field is zero for the OPT record. The TYPE is OPT, and the CLASS field indicates the maximum size of the sender's UDP payload. The 32-bit TTL field is divided into three fields:

- *Extended Response Code.* Adds 8 bits to the 4-bit RCODE in the DNS message header to provide 12 bits total.
- EDNS version number.
- *Extended Header Flags.* Bit 0 is currrently defined as "DNSSEC Answer OK" meaning that the querying server is capable of processing DNSSEC resource records. The remaining 15 bits of the extended header are currently reserved.

The RDLength field indicates the length of the RData field, which consists of a set of zero or more options, each encoded with an option code, option length, and option value.

One option has been officially defined thus far via RFC 5001 (191): the name server identifier (NSID) option. This option, defined with option code $= 3$, enables a resolver to request and a server to provide its identity as defined by the server administrator as its name, IP address, pseudorandom number, or other character string (configurable in

BIND using the `server-id` statement). This EDNS0 option is useful for debugging in environments where many servers share a common IP address, such as in deployments of anycast addressing or with load balancers. Two additional options, Long-Lived Query[*] (LLQ; option code = 1) and Update Lease Life[†] (UL; option code = 2) are currently on hold as RFCs and have not been officially published regarding these settings.

9.5.7 Resource Records

This chapter has covered the organization of DNS data and traversal of the domain tree, as well as the format of messages to do so. Once we've navigated the tree and located a DNS server authoritative for the information for a domain, how do we actually get the lookup information we're seeking for a particular purpose or application?

Resource records associated with the given domain provide the means to map the question to an answer. The type of resource record defines the desired result type, for example, the A resource record type will provide an IPv4 address as an answer while the AAAA type will provide an IPv6 address. The answer may be "the final answer" or information that can be used to obtain the desired answer via additional queries or other means.

---

[*] A Long-Lived Query is a mechanism for a resolver to request receipt of notification of zone information changes; something like a DNSNOTIFY for clients.

[†] The Update Lease Life mechanism would enable a DHCP server to inform the DNS server within a DNS Update message of the corresponding client's lease length in seconds for new and renewed leases.

10

DNS APPLICATIONS AND RESOURCE RECORDS

10.1 INTRODUCTION

DNS inherently lends itself well to "translating" a given piece of information into another related piece of information. This resolution process is the very reason for DNS's invention, and it has been extended beyond resolving hostnames into IP addresses and vice versa to support a broad variety of applications. Virtually any service or application that requires translation of one form of information into another can leverage DNS.

Each resource record configured in DNS enables this lookup function, returning a resolution answer for a given query. The DNS server parses the query from the Question section of the DNS message,[*] seeking a match within the corresponding domain's zone file for the query's QNAME, QCLASS, and QTYPE. Each resource record has a Name (aka Owner) field, Class (Internet class is assumed if not specified), and Type field. The RData field contains the corresponding answer to the query. The resource record type defines the type and format of the question (owner/name field) and corresponding answer (RData field). In some instances, multiple resource records may match the queried name, type, and class. In such cases, all matching records, called a *Resource Record Set* (*RRSet*), are returned in the Answer section of the response message.

---

[*] Refer to Figure 9.12.

IP Address Management: Principles and Practice, by Timothy Rooney
Copyright © 2011 the Institute of Electrical and Electronics Engineers, Inc.

Most, but not all, new applications require new resource record types to enable definition of application-specific information, and these new resource record types are standardized via the IETF RFC process. This chapter describes the various forms of information that are stored in DNS along with the applications they support. A resource record summary is provided at the end of the chapter for reference.

10.1.1 Resource Record Format

First let's review the format of a resource record. When responding to a query for information, a DNS server will place the resource record information in the Answer section of a DNS message. The "on-the-wire format" dictated by the DNS protocol was introduced in Figure 9.13 in the context of the format of the DNS message Answer section, and is reproduced here as Figure 10.1 for convenience.

When representing resource records in zone files, all of these fields may be entered except the RDLength field, which is inserted when the resource record information is placed in a DNS message by the DNS server. The textual representation of a resource record generally follows a common convention shown below. Most resource records are defined with the following general fields, though many have subfields within the RData field as we shall see later in this chapter!

| Owner | Time to Live | Class | Type | RData |

Owner (Name). This field matches the information being queried.

Time to Live(TTL). The number of seconds for which the information contained in this resource record is valid for servers and resolvers caching this information. After the TTL expires, the resource record information must be removed from the name server and resolver cache. The TTL can be specified on a per resource record basis or if omitted, a zone level default TTL value is used ($TTL).

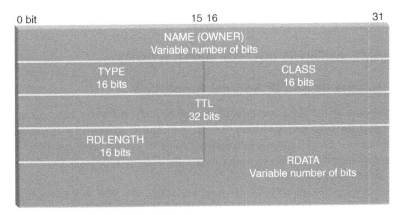

Figure 10.1. DNS resource record wire format (99).

Class. The Class of the resource record, usually IN for Internet.

Type. The type of resource record corresponding to the type of information being sought.

RData. The "record data" or answer portion corresponding to the information being sought by matching the Owner (Name), class, and type field contents.

Now that we've covered the basic format, we're ready to jump into specific applications and the resource records that support them. As we review these resource record types, we'll review the interpretation of each type and provide an example. We'll cover those that have been "officially" accepted by the IETF, that is, they've been published in an RFC; however, publication as an RFC does not guarantee universal implementation of the resource record type across all resolvers and servers. We'll point out some of those that may be new or experimental versus those ol' reliables that have been around for years.

For each record type we'll discuss in this chapter, the resource record fields and examples are displayed using a common format. The first row or table header, specifies the base fields defined above for each record type. The second row displays the interpretation of these base fields for the particular type in question. An example resource record of the given type is displayed in the third row and optionally successive rows as summarized below.

Resource record fields
Resource record field data types
Sample resource record(s)

Note that we will use the term "domain name" to refer to the name of a DNS domain, while the term "host domain name" will refer to the DNS name of a host. The host domain name may be defined with the zone file as fully qualified (FQDN) or simply a hostname interpreted in the context of the "current domain." The current domain is that defined in the zone declaration of the named.conf file, unless otherwise changed within the zone file using a $ORIGIN statement.

10.2 NAME–ADDRESS LOOKUP APPLICATIONS

10.2.1 Hostname and IP Address Resolution

First and foremost, the most common DNS application is hostname resolution, looking up a host domain name and obtaining its corresponding IP address. Two resource record types are supported for IP address lookups, one for IPv4 and the other for IPv6 addresses. The corresponding reverse record utilizes a common record type for both IPv4 and IPv6, the Pointer (PTR) record type.

When managing a mixed IPv4–IPv6 network, note that DNS will strongly influence which protocol will be used to reach a given destination host. For example, if I wish to access a web site, my resolver may first attempt to retrieve an A record for the given web site address. Upon failing to obtain an IPv4 address, it may then attempt an AAAA record lookup with success. Assuming my browser (TCP/IP stack) supports IPv6, the connection will be made over IPv6. Unbeknownst to me, I'm using IPv6! Certain IPv4–IPv6 transition technologies explicitly force dual protocol lookups (A and AAAA) in DNS. We'll cover these technologies and the overall impact of DNS on IPv4–IPv6 networks in Chapter 15.

A—IPv4 Address Record. The A record is a common resource record type used to map a queried host domain name to an IPv4 address. The format follows the standard convention per the example below. Hosts may have multiple A records to provide load balancing or mapping of a hostname to multiple devices and/or interfaces.

Owner	TTL	Class	Type	RData
Host domain name	TTL	IN	A	IPv4 address
www.ipamworldwide.com.	86400	IN	A	10.100.0.99

AAAA—IPv6 Address Record. The AAAA ("quad-A") record provides an IPv6 address based on lookup of a host domain name. Formatted and processed similarly as the A record for hostname to IPv4 address lookup, the RData field includes an IPv6 address which can be abbreviated using standard IPv6 abbreviation conventions.

Owner	TTL	Class	Type	RData
Host domain name	TTL	IN	AAAA	IPv6 address
www.ipamworldwide.com.	86400	IN	AAAA	2001:DB8:3A::21:A450:1

PTR—Pointer Record. The PTR resource record provides mapping from an IP address to a FQDN. The PTR record is used to map both IPv4 and IPv6 addresses. The IPv4 version of the PTR includes the IP address reversed and concatenated with "in-addr. arpa." as the owner field and the corresponding FQDN as the RData field. The IPv6 version is formed by writing out the IPv6 address in its hexadecimal colon format, with all zeroes included; that is, fill in leading zeroes and double-colon shortcuts. Then drop the colons, reverse the digits, then concatenate with "ip6.arpa."

Owner	TTL	Class	Type	RData
IP address in reverse domain format	TTL	IN	PTR	Host domain name
1.32.65.10.in-addr.arpa.	86400	IN	PTR	sf1.ipamworldwide.com.
1.0.0.1.0.0.0.0.0.0.0.0.0.0.0.0.0.0.0.0.0.0.0.0.0.0.0.8.B.D.0.1.0.0.2.ip6.arpa.	86400	IN	PTR	sf1.ipamworldwide.com.

The IPv4 address in this example corresponds to 10.65.32.1, while the IPv6 address is 2001:0DB8:0000:0000:0000:0000:0000:1001 or 2001:DB8::1001 in abbreviated form.

10.2.2 Alias Host and Domain Name Resolutions

The CNAME resource record type enables lookup of a host domain name by alias name. CNAME lookups return not an IP address, but a host domain name that must then be queried for its IP address, though most DNS servers responding to a CNAME query will include the corresponding A and/or AAAA record within the Additional section of the DNS response message. Meanwhile, the DNAME record provides a similar aliasing function for domains. As we discussed in the previous chapter, CNAME and DNAME records are useful in handling non-octet bounded reverse domains.

CNAME—Canonical Name Record. The CNAME record enables creation of alias names for hosts. The owner field contains the alias name being looked up, and the RData field yields the canonical host domain name. This host domain name would then need to be resolved to obtain the host's corresponding A and/or AAAA record.

Owner	TTL	Class	Type	RData
Alias host domain name	TTL	IN	CNAME	Canonical host domain name
w3.ipamww.com.	86400	IN	CNAME	www.ipamww.com.

Note that it is not legal to configure a CNAME RData field as pointing to another CNAME owner field in order to chain records. This RData field must point directly to an A/AAAA resource record owner name. The owner name of each CNAME record must also be unique; a single alias cannot resolve to multiple answers. CNAME records prove instrumental for mapping reverse domains as we discussed in Chapter 9.

DNAME—Domain Alias Record. The DNAME resource record, defined in RFC 2672 (107), enables mapping of an entire subtree of the domain name space to another domain. The major motivation for developing the DNAME record was to simplify DNS impacts of IP network renumbering. For example, if the company running the ipamww.com domain was acquired by acquired.com, the ipamww.com namespace could conceivably be "moved" beneath acquired.com with the addition of a DNAME record illustrated below.

Owner	TTL	Class	Type	RData
Alias domain name	TTL	IN	DNAME	Target domain name
ipamww.com.	86400	IN	DNAME	ipamww.acquired.com.

Resolvers seeking hosts within the ipamww.com domain subtree would be directed to seek the same hostnames under ipamww.acquired.com domain. Note that this scenario requires the resource records and subdomains of ipamww.com to be ported to their corresponding zone files within the acquired.com domain subtree. RFC 2672 stipulates that the DNAME owner (ipamww.com. in this case) zone must not have any subdomains nor contain any resource records besides the DNAME and possibly CNAME resource records.

10.2.3 Network Services Location

IP devices booting on a network often need to find specific services for device initialization. While DHCP provides some level of service location via specification of certain option values such as TFTP server IP addresses, DNS provides a services location mechanism using the services location resource record type (SRV). The SRV record provides a means for non-DHCP clients or for clients seeking services after initialization to locate servers providing requested services.

If you've worked with Microsoft clients and domain controllers since the introduction of Windows 2000, you're probably very familiar with SRV records. When Windows domain controllers boot up, they perform a dynamic DNS (DDNS) update for their A and SRV records, enabling them to effectively advertise services availability. These records are also easily recognized by underscores within the owner field. The SRV record owner field is comprised of a concatenation of a particular service, which is available via a particular protocol (TCP or UDP), for a given domain. The service name is prefixed with an underscore, as is the protocol value. The underscores were added to eliminate collisions with valid domain names. While technically not a valid host domain name character per the DNS RFC 1035, Microsoft, and BIND servers can be configured to tolerate the underscore character via the check-names option parameter. While a common example of the use of SRV records, SRV records are certainly not limited to Windows applications, though adoption beyond Windows applications has been limited thus far.

SRV—Services Location Record. The SRV record is used to enable resolver clients to identify servers offering particular services such as LDAP, Kerberos, and others. This record is critical for Microsoft Windows clients in locating Windows Domain Controllers.

Owner	TTL	Class	Type	RData			
Service encoding	TTL	IN	SRV	Priority	Weight	Port	Target host domain name
_ldap._tcp.ipamww.com.	86400	IN	SRV	10	0	389	ldap.ipamww.com.

The owner field is comprised of a concatenation of a particular service, which is available via a particular protocol (TCP or UDP), for a given domain. The RData field includes a priority field, which instructs clients to use numerically lower priority targets when multiple SRV records are returned.

The weight field is used to further prioritize records with the same priority. The port is the TCP or UDP port number to use to access the given service and the target is the host domain name of the server running the specified service.

If not also returned as additional information by the DNS server, the client may request corresponding A or AAAA records for hosts specified as targets to complete the resolution process. A couple of examples follow.

```
_ldap._tcp.ipamww.com. 86400 IN SRV 10 5 389 ldapeast1.ipamww.com.
_ldap._tcp.ipamww.com. 86400 IN SRV 10 10 389 ldapeast2.ipamww.com.
_ldap._tcp.ipamww.com. 86400 IN SRV 20 1 389 ldapeast3.ipamww.com.
```

In the three sample SRV records above, the second record would be used first. It shares the lowest priority number (10) as the first record, but it has a higher priority field (10) than the first record (5). The third record would be used last, as it has a larger priority value despite its lower weight.

The port, 389 in the examples above, is the TCP or UDP port number of the given service and the target is the hostname of the server running the specified service. If not also returned in the Additional section of the message from the DNS server, the client may request corresponding A or AAAA records for hosts specified as respective targets to complete the resolution process. Semantically, we didn't need to spell out the owner fields on the second two records assuming they were listed sequentially within the zone file, but we did so to emphasize that these three records would be returned for an SRV query for _ldap._tcp.ipamworldwide.com.

AFSDB—DCE or AFS Server Record (Experimental). The AFSDB record was defined in RFC 1183 (108) and was intended to enable location of a server, particularly for AFS (a registered trademark of Transarc Corp. and originally Andrew File System) and for the Open Software Foundation's Distributed Computing Environment (DCE).

Owner	TTL	Class	Type		RData
Cell domain name	TTL	IN	AFSDB	Subtype	Host domain name
ipamworldwide.com.	86400	IN	AFSDB	1	afsdb1.ipamworldwide.com.

The RData field consists of

- Subtype field, which identifies the AFS 3.0 volume location server for the cell domain name (subtype = 1) or the DCE directory services server for the given cell domain name (subtype = 2).
- Host domain name field identifies the server hostname.

The AFSDB resource record is not widely used, as the SRV resource record type provides generic server location functionality within DNS and in fact RFC 5864 (189) specifies the use of SRV records for AFS.

WKS—Well Known Service Record (Historic). This resource record type identifies the well-known services such as FTP, telnet, and others that are available on a particular IP address using a particular protocol (TCP or UDP) for a host. This record is not generally used, as the SRV record provides similar functionality.

Owner	TTL	Class	Type	RData		
Host domain name	TTL	IN	WKS	IPv4 address	Protocol	Services
server.ipamww.com.	86400	IN	WKS	10.0.199.35	TCP	SMTP FTP

10.2.4 Host and Textual Information Lookup

The TXT record is one of the workhorse resource record types, often used as an interim resource record in support of specific applications pending standardization and implementation. The TXT record enables lookup of a generic reference name, for example, a domain name, host domain name, or other owner values, and returning arbitrary textual information. Most recently, the TXT record has been used for interim support of DDNS update uniqueness checking (now the DHCID record type) and for spam-reducing applications (the SPF record type), both covered later in this chapter.

TXT—Text Record. The text record enables the association of up to 255 bytes of arbitrary binary data with a resource record. It has proven very versatile in providing interim support of new services.

Owner	TTL	Class	Type	RData
Reference name	TTL	IN	TXT	Arbitrary text data
txt.cfo.ipamww.com.	86400	IN	TXT	"CFO Office (610) 555-1212"

HINFO—Host Information Record. The RData field of the HINFO resource record enables lookup of a host's processor and operating system.

Owner	TTL	Class	Type	RData	
Host domain name	TTL	IN	HINFO	CPU	Operating system
sf1.ipamww.com.	86400	IN	HINFO	VAX 770/11	UNIX

HIP—Host Identity Protocol Record (Experimental). The HIP resource record type supports the experimental host identity protocol (HIP), which essentially abstracts the association of a hostname with an IP address by inserting a "host identity" layer in the resolution process. This enables association of a domain name with a host identity, which is then associated with one or more IP addresses. An application or upper

layer protocol can look up a host via the HIP resource record and obtain the host identifier
(in the form of a public key) and other host identity information, including the IP address
of the host or of a rendezvous server through which to connect to mobile devices.

Owner	TTL	Class	Type	RData					
Host domain name	TTL	IN	HIP	HIT Len.	PK Alg.	PK Len.	HIT	Public key	RVS
hiphost.ipamww. com.	86400	IN	HIP	16	2	24	Iil...	8L9d...	rs.ipamww. com.

The RData fields are defined as

- *HIT Len.* Length in bytes of the Host Identity Tag (HIT); this field is inserted by
  the server for wire transmission and is not displayed within a zone file.
- *PK Alg.* The algorithm used to generate the Public key
  - 0 = no key is present
  - 1 = DSA formatted key
  - 2 = RSA formatted key
- *PK Len.* Length in bytes of the public key; this field is inserted by the server for
  wire transmission and is not displayed within a zone file.
- *HIT.* The Host Identity Tag, a 128-bit hash of the host identifier.
- *Public Key.* The public key associated with the host that can be used to validate
  signed messages from the host.
- *RVS (optional).* One or more rendezvous server host domain name(s) for connecting with mobile devices.

RP—Responsible Person Record. The RP resource record enables association
of an email address and other text information with a node in the domain tree, whether an
end host or domain. The RData field contains an email address, formatted without the @
sign; instead, a dot is substituted for the @ sign. The second field of the RData field
indicates a record for which additional text information can be found as an additional
lookup.

Owner	TTL	Class	Type	RData	
Host domain name	TTL	IN	RP	Email address	TXT pointer
payroll.ipamww.com.	86400	IN	RP	cfo.ipamww.com.	cfo-contactinfo.ipamww.com.

In this example above, we've used an RP record to associate the payroll server with our
CFO, reachable at cfo@ipamww.com (substitute "." for "@" in email address field). The

TXT pointer field points to a resource record containing additional information, such as the following example:

```
cfo-contactinfo.ipamww.com. 86400 IN TXT "CFO Office (610)-555-1212"
```

10.2.5 DNS Protocol Operational Record Types

Two "administrative" resource record types enable specification of zone authority information (the SOA record) and delegation name servers for this and child domains (NS). These record types are instrumental to the efficient operation of keeping DNS data in synch within a zone and of keeping delegation chains in effect down the domain tree.

SOA—Start of Authority Record. One and only one SOA record is required for each zone and follows the initial default TTL ($TTL) statement if present within the zone file. The SOA record defines the domain name for which this zone is authoritative, along with additional zone maintenance information. The SOA record is composed of the following fields.

Owner	TTL	Class	Type			RData				
Domain name	TTL	IN	SOA	mname	Contact	Serial number	Refresh interval	Retry interval	Expire interval	Negative cache
ipamww. com.	86400	IN	SOA	ns1. ipamww. com.	admin. ipamww. com.	3945	2h	30m	1w	1d

- Domain name for which this zone file contains authoritative information.
- TTL, time to live.
- Record class (IN for Internet).
- Record type (SOA).
- *Master DNS Server Name (MNAME).* The name of the DNS server that is master for this domain (zone).
- Domain contact email address (replace "@" with "." so that admin@ipamworldwide.com is written admin.ipamworldwide.com. Note that email addresses with dots prior to the @ sign should be prefixed with a backslash. Thus, super.admin@ipamww.com would be encoded as super\.admin.ipamww.com.
- *Serial Number of the Zone.* Incremented with every change to zone data—enables slave servers to identify changes to zone data.
- *Refresh Interval.* Time period for slaves to query the master for zone updates.
- *Retry Time.* If unable to reach the master, the slave will wait this amount of time to retry to reach the master.

- *Expire Time.* If unable to reach the master after this amount of time expires, the slaves will delete the zone information and no longer consider itself authoritative, thereby expiring its authority for the zone.
- *Negative Caching TTL.* Time duration to maintain cache of negative responses from other servers; for example, a specified domain or record doesn't exist.

An example SOA record for our ipamww.com zone file might look like
ipamww.com. IN SOA dns1.ipamww.com dnsadmin.ipamww.com (

```
1     ; serial number
2h    ; refresh interval of 2 hours
30m   ; retry after 30 minutes
1w    ; expire after 1 week
1d)   ; negative caching TTL of 1 day.
```

NS—Name Server Record. The NS record enables lookup of an authoritative name server for a given zone. NS records are the key to distributing the DNS database. In delegating a child domain to another administrative authority, the child domain administrator must be running at least two name servers for redundancy. While traversing the domain tree, these NS records enable the queried name server along the resolution path in the domain tree to respond with a referral to another name server further down the tree, which has more information about the intended destination. Each zone must also declare at least two NS records for its authoritative name servers as well.

Owner	TTL	Class	Type	RData
Domain name	TTL	IN	NS	Name server domain name
ipamworldwide.com.	86400	IN	NS	ns1.ipamworldwide.com.

Note that the name server hostname in the RData field should have a corresponding A or AAAA record to complete the required resolution to a reachable IP address. This is referred to as a "glue" record in that it "glues" the resolution of the authoritative name server hostname for the desired domain to the IP address of that name server.

10.2.6 Dynamic DNS Update Uniqueness Validation

DHCID—Dynamic Host Configuration Identifier Record. Dynamic DNS enables the updating of DNS information with DHCP clients' assigned IP address information. Thus, a DHCP server on behalf of the client or the client itself can update DNS with the client's IP address and hostname association via A/AAAA and PTR[*] records. It is quite possible that the same hostname/FQDN may be claimed by multiple

---

[*] Associating client identification information with PTR records is not currently specified in the DHCID RFC.

DHCP clients, or that a client may claim a hostname already assigned to a predefined (e.g., statically addressed) device.

The DHCID record provides client identification information in DNS to uniquely associate the particular DHCP client with the hostname/FQDN being updated by the DHCP server. The DHCID record would be defined in the Prerequisite section of the DNS Update message to verify the record "owner" for updating. Please refer to the DNS Update section of the previous chapter for more details and an example of this prerequisite processing.

The DHCID record uses the same owner field as the corresponding A or AAAA record. The RData portion of the record is formed by performing a one-way secure hash using the SHA-256 algorithm over the following concatenated fields:

- *Identifier Type Code* (2 bytes). Identifies the information within the DHCP packet that was used in creating this hash. Possibilities include client hardware address, client identifier option, or device unique identifier (DUID).
- *Digest Type Code* (1 byte). Identifies the hash algorithm. The RFC defines values of 0 (reserved) or 1 (SHA-256) though IANA maintains a registry for future value assignments.
- Digest of the data from the DHCP packet as identified by the identifier value concatenated by the client's FQDN.

Owner	TTL	Class	Type	RData		
Host domain name	TTL	IN	DHCID	Identifier Type	Digest Type	SHA-256 hash of {identifier type, fqdn}
w3.ipamww.com.	86400	IN	DHCID	A1B87Y2/AuCcg8e93aQcjl...		

10.2.7 Telephone Number Resolution

DNS has proven very versatile and can even be used to map telephone numbers into IP addresses, which is useful for VoIP applications or related telephony over IP applications. The ENUM (E.164 telephone number mapping) service has been defined to support such resolution. ENUM supports the mapping of telephone numbers, in ITU E.164 format, into uniform resource identifiers (URIs).[*] This mapping is performed primarily using the Naming Authority Pointer (NAPTR) resource record type.

Note that most enterprise IP PBX systems provide their own directories to map intra-PBX phone numbers to destination phones' IP addresses, so ENUM is not commonly implemented in such environments. However, VoIP service providers have a vested

---

[*] A URI is an Internet identifier consisting of a uniform resource name (URN) and a uniform resource locator (URL). A simple example: for URL http://ipamworldwide.com and URN file.txt, the corresponding URI is http://ipamworldwide.com/file.txt.

interest in assuring calls remain on their or their partners' IP and access networks to the maximum extent, to reduce call handling costs paid to nonpartner network providers, or worse, competitors. And ENUM is key to enabling such call routing by virtue of telephone number mapping or resolution. That is not to say that you won't see ENUM within enterprise networks. ENUM provides resolution to multiple destinations with preference settings, which may find use within reachability or contact management type applications.

As just mentioned, the NAPTR resource record provides translation of telephone number information into destination uniform resource identifiers. Currently defined in RFC 3403 (109), NAPTR records were initially defined to provide a means to iteratively resolve an arbitrary string into a URI for the Dynamic Delegation Discovery System (DDDS). Some background on DDDS is provided in RFC 3402 (110), but it initially stemmed from the desire to define a resolution process that could enter with a resource name (e.g., a particular application or piece of data) which in itself, contains no network location information, and resolve it to a destination resource identifier by applying a series of iterative rules from a database. This separation of the specification of the resource name from the process to locate or resolve it facilitates the making of changes and redelegations of resources without impacting the end user application's naming convention.

This effort expanded beyond resolving resource names to supporting resolution of generic lookup strings, and evolved into the DDDS, using DNS as one form of the rules database. The NAPTR record enables the specification of such rules within DNS, sometimes using multiple NAPTR records to fully complete the resolution process. Each NAPTR record translates a given entry string, that is, a valid DNS domain name, into a rule that can be applied to the string to derive the next string to lookup. This process iterates until a terminal rule is reached and the final result is returned to the requesting application.

NAPTR records are the building blocks of E.164 telephone number mapping service for service provider voice over IP services. RFC 3761 (111) provides the "application specific" interpretation of NAPTR fields for the ENUM application. A NAPTR record can be used to lookup a destination telephone number, and resolve the number to a destination, for example, a Session Initiation Protocol (SIP) server, email address, or other URI-formatted destination. NAPTR records also support the ability to define regular expressions, which supply logical rules as "next steps" for the resolver to locate the intended destination.

E.164 is an International Telecommunications Union (ITU) standard for formatting telephone numbers. "Fully qualified" telephone numbers, meaning they are globally unique given the country code prefix followed by a country-specific telephone number format, are represented with a plus sign prefix, such as + 1-610-555-1234. Much like reverse domains for IP addresses, formatting a telephone number requires a similar convention of reading the resource record from left to right as more specific to less specific. This convention requires reversal of the fully qualified telephone number (dropping the plus sign) and separating each digit with "dots" as illustrated below.

Note the use of the .arpa top-level domain. Similar to ip6.arpa and in-addr.arpa domain structures, the e164.arpa domain is a "reverse" domain in that it enables lookup

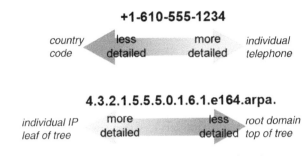

Figure 10.2. Telephone number mapping to domain structure.

of a structured numerical value, a phone number. Like other .arpa lookups, the domain structure is organized top to bottom as generalized-to-specific, or country code-to-telephone line number. Thus, the fully formatted E.164 telephone number is reversed, each digit is separated with dots, and the e164.arpa. domain suffix is appended as illustrated in Figure 10.2.

This structure lends itself well to segmentation of telephone number space. For example, the domain 1.e164.arpa refers to all country code 1 telephone numbers and could be delegated to such a number authority. Likewise 44.e164.arpa could be delegated to the U.K. telephone numbering authority. Within each of these domains, further delegation may be accomplished in accordance with the numbering plan for the country. For example, within the United States, an area code represents the next logical administrative delegation point, followed by exchange. Thus, the administrators for 1.e164.arpa may delegate the 0.1.6.1.e164.arpa zone to the numbering administrator for the 610 area code, who may in turn delegate 5.5.5.0.1.6.1.e164.arpa to those responsible for the 555 exchange within the 610 area code.

NAPTR—Naming Authority Pointer Record. The NAPTR record provides translation of a string[*] or telephone number information into destination uniform resource identifiers. The NAPTR record utilizes the e164.arpa. domain naming convention described above within its owner field to serve as the lookup format for telephone numbers. Unfortunately, this so far is only the easy part! The NAPTR record contains a number of additional subfields with its RData field. The additional subfields are described below, with examples provided for the ENUM application of NAPTR records.

- *Order Field.* Specifies the order in which multiple records within the RRSet are to be processed; lower numbered order records are processed first.
- *Preference Field.* Specifies the order in which records with equal "order" values are to be processed; lower numbered preference records are processed first.
- *Flags.* Provides information about the "next lookup" in the resolution process. Thus far, four flag values have been defined, though the Flags field can be empty:

---

[*] "Strings" refer to text or data strings. Fortunately, this is not the "string theory" of DNS!

○ "u" The output of the regular expression field of this record is a uniform resource identifier; that is, this is a terminal resolution.

○ "s" Next lookup should be for SRV records.

○ "a" Next lookup should be for A, A6, or AAAA records.

○ "p" Next lookup is protocol specific according to the protocol specified in the Services field.

- *Services.* This field encodes the services that are available based on the application in question. This field includes the type of resolution provided, a " + " sign or colon, followed by the protocol value, for example, http, sip, mailto, ftp, tel, among others.[*] Examples of types or resolution include

○ I2L. URI to URL.

○ N2L. Uniform Resource Name (URN) to URL.

○ E2U. ENUM service to URI.

- *Regular Expression.* An encoded expression that is to be evaluated. The syntax of this field is a sed-style expression.

- *Replacement.* An alternative "next lookup" fully qualified domain name in the absence of a regular expression.

Owner	TTL	Class	Type				RData		
Domain name	TTL	IN	NAPTR	Order	Pref	Flags	Services	Regexp	Replacement
me.ipamww. com.	86400	IN	NAPTR	10	5	"s"	"N2L + http"	" "	www.ipamww. com.
4.3.2.1.5.5.5. 0.1.6.1. e164.arpa.	86400	IN	NAPTR	10	20	"u"	"E2U + sip"	"!^.*$!sip:me@ ipamww.com.!"	

Let's look more closely at the two example NAPTR records above. The first example provides a rule for resolution of me.ipamww.com. The Flags field value of "s" indicates to the resolver that the next lookup should be a query for SRV resource records. The Services field indicates a URN-to-URL service using HTTP protocol. Since the regular expression field is blank, the replacement field is used as the result of the resolution process.

The second example highlights an ENUM application example, where a lookup of a telephone number can be resolved. The "u" flag indicates that the result of the regular expression provided will be a URI, which can then be resolved to an IP address. The Services field indicates ENUM services using the SIP protocol. The regular expression field is comprised of two subfields, encapsulated with the " ! " character. The first field

[*] Please consult http://www.iana.org/assignments/enum-services for the currently assigned services values for ENUM.

contains "^.*$" and is interpreted as "match from the start of the line (^) to the end of the line ($), zero or more (*) characters (.)"; that is, match the entire Owner field. The second portion of the regular expression contains "`sip:me@ipamworldwide.com`" which is returned as the result of our regular expression. The Replacement field is not used in this case.

The resulting URI, `sip:me@ipamworldwide.com` would then initiate a DNS query for an address (A or AAAA) record for `ipamworldwide.com`. Note that some DNS servers may return relevant A or AAAA records as additional information in the query response containing the NAPTR records. The resulting IP address would be used as the destination address to initiate the sip session to the "`me`" user.

10.3 EMAIL AND ANTISPAM MANAGEMENT

Spam email or unsolicited bulk email, has been a nuisance since the dawn of the Internet, though in the early days it was highly frowned upon. Nevertheless, with the explosive growth of the Internet, the volume of spam emails has seemingly grown even faster. A variety of techniques exist to combat spam, many of which involve the use of DNS. To understand how DNS can help reduce spam, we'll first look at the anatomy of an email transmission including the role of DNS in email delivery, then review the use of DNS in various antispamming solutions.

10.3.1 Email and DNS

An email typically originates from one person and is sent to one or more recipients. Each email address is formatted as a mailbox@maildomain. The mailbox commonly refers to the name of the person or owner of a mailbox or email account, while the maildomain, typically the company or Internet provider name, is the destination domain for delivery to the corresponding mailbox or mail exchanger. Emails are composed using an email client, such as Microsoft Outlook, Eudora, or web-based clients such as yahoo and google. Regardless, when sent by the originator, the client connects to a Simple Mail Transfer Protocol (SMTP) server (using the SMTP protocol) to send the email. Like a default router for email, the SMTP server is responsible for forwarding the email to its destination.

The SMTP server must resolve the maildomain to an IP address for transmission of the message. Naturally this is done using DNS with a lookup for the mail exchanger (MX) record type, as well as the corresponding A or AAAA record types.

MX—Mail Exchanger Record. The mail exchanger record is used to locate an email server or servers for a particular domain. If I send an email destined to tim@i-pamworldwide.com, my SMTP server will use DNS to find the host(s) that can receive emails for users in the ipamworldwide.com domain. More than one MX record may be created per domain, and each can be defined with a different preference value. Use of the preference field enables the sending SMTP server to prioritize the destination host to which it will forward the email for the given domain, and if unavailable to a second (and third, etc.) choice destination. The lower the preference value, the more preferred the listed destination. In the example below, we have two MX records for the ipamworldwide.com domain. The destination smtp1 is preferred (lower preference) over smtp2. However, if smtp1 is unavailable, this mechanism provides a backup server for email delivery.

Owner	TTL	Class	Type		RData
Email destination domain	TTL	IN	MX	Preference	Mail server host domain name
ipamworldwide.com.	86400	IN	MX	10	smtp1.ipamworldwide.com.
ipamworldwide.com.	86400	IN	MX	20	smtp2.ipamworldwide.com.

Note that the mail server host domain name within the RData field must have a corresponding A or AAAA record to complete the required resolution to a reachable IP address. Many DNS servers supply these address records within the Additional section of the MX query response.

Upon resolving the destination mail server, the SMTP server sends the message to the destination using the SMTP protocol. The ultimate destination server, to which recipient email clients connect, must support Post Office Protocol (POP) or Internet Message Access Protocol (IMAP) to enable client retrieval of the email message. Thus, when your email client performs a "send/receive," it utilizes SMTP to send outgoing messages to its configured SMTP server and POP or IMAP to retrieve incoming email messages from the configured POP/IMAP server(s).

Figure 10.3 highlights a very simple SMTP transaction between two servers, when my friend Mike sends me an email. On the left of the figure, Mike composes an email to tim@ipamworldwide.com using his email client and sends it. His configured SMTP server forwards the message to the destination server, as resolved by the MX record(s) for ipamworldwide.com. His SMTP server initiates a TCP connection on port 25 with the resolved destination server.

Once the TCP session is established, the SMTP application utilizes the session to handshake and process the message. The envelope portion of the message begins with the HELO (or EHLO, enhanced HELO), which conveys the sending entity's identity. The MAIL FROM statement indicates the source of the message, followed by the RCPT TO statement indicating the destination mailbox. At this point in the exchange, the recipient server may refuse to accept the message and close the connection if the destination mailbox is unknown or blocked, or if the "from address" is prohibited. Otherwise, the transaction continues and the data or message portion* is transmitted. The receiving mail exchanger stores the email message or forwards it to the server on which the destination mailbox resides.

The store-and-forward approach used by the received email server may also be used by intermediate email gateways (aka message transfer agents) to provide multihopped email delivery. As mentioned above, the resolution of a destination mailbox domain to

---

* Note that the message portion of an email consists of a header and the body. As a point of reference, RFC 2821 (163) defines the SMTP specification, while RFC 2822 (164) defines the Internet message format for email, defining valid header and data syntax.

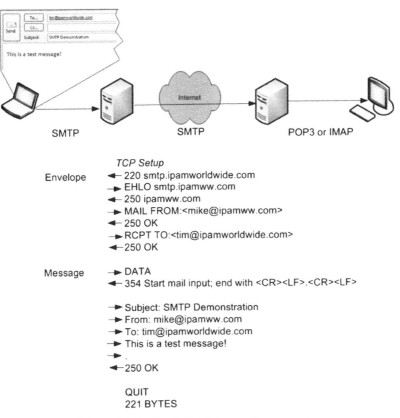

Figure 10.3. Simple SMTP transaction example.

multiple MX records implies this ability to identify a "destination" mail server, which may or may not be the final destination from which the intended recipient retrieves the email. The MX record preference field provides control over the relative preference of incoming mail servers or gateways, while providing selection from among multiple choices based on availability and performance.

Figure 10.4 illustrates a two-step email delivery scenario using SMTP. In this scenario, I'm sending the same email as shown in Figure 10.3. However, in this case, perhaps the intended destination server, smtp.ipamworldwide.com is busy and refuses a direct connection. Having resolved both the ipamworldwide.com server and an mta-gateway.com server via a DNS MX query, my outgoing mail server will attempt to send the email to the second choice, mta-gateway.com.

In accepting the SMTP transmission from my mail server, the mta-gateway.com server effectively agrees to forward the email to the ultimate destination on my behalf. The transaction between my mail server and the mta-gateway.com server completes before the second leg of transmission is attempted. SMTP uses a store-and-forward approach, not synchronous relaying of each message.

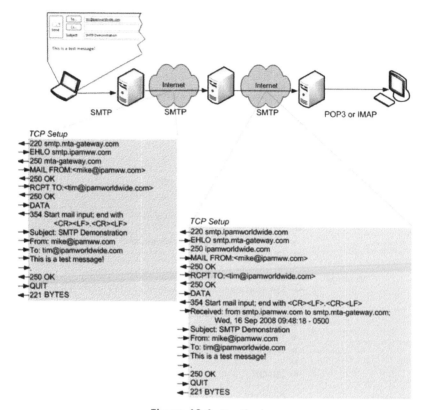

Figure 10.4. Email relay.

The first leg of the transmission looks very similar to that of Figure 10.3, except for the difference in the SMTP server. The second leg of the connection is also similar, except once again for the SMTP endpoints. The other difference is the insertion of the *Received:* line within the header portion of the data section of the mail. Each intermediate SMTP server which forwards the message prefixes a "Received" line indicating its domain name and corresponding time stamp. This enables tracing of the email from the destination back to its path. The RCPT TO line remains the same in both segments, indicating the mailbox to which errors in delivery should be sent.

As footnoted above, the message portion of an email consists of a header and the body. Each header field consists of a word followed by a colon and a value. The header contains a variety of data including the following:

- *Originator Fields.* From, sender, reply-to, orig-date;
- *Destination Fields.* to, cc, bcc;
- *Identification Fields.* Message-id, in-reply-to, references, msg-id, id-left, id-right, no-fold-quote, no-fold-literal;
- *Informational Fields.* Subject, comments, keywords;

- *Resent Fields* (informational fields relating to the reintroduction[*] of a message into the Internet, for example, by an emailing service). Resent-date, resent-from, resent-sender, resent-to, resent-cc, resent-bcc, resent-msg-id; and
- *Source Trace Information.* Trace, return, path received, name-val-list, name-val-pair, item-name, item-value.

We have summarized the basic email process and types of information that may be included in a given email message because different antispam techniques utilize different information sources in validating the sender as a legitimate or acceptable sender of emails. We'll discuss those techniques that utilize DNS to perform this validation next.

10.3.2 White or Black Listing

The use of white or black listing (190) provides a simple means for the recipient email server to lookup a sender's IP address via DNS and to validate its legitimacy. This lookup is typically formed by reversing the IP address of the source IP address of the email message, just as is done in forming PTR records. Note that the source IP address being analyzed is that from which the email was received directly, perhaps an email gateway, which may or may not be the original transmitter. However, the intent of such listing is to identify such senders of email by IP address as legitimate or not.

In this scenario, the reversed IP address is appended with a given domain name, typically that of the black list provider. The "host domain name" thus formed by this concatenation is queried in DNS using the A resource record query type, not PTR. The query answer is interpreted based on whether the record was found, in which case often an IP address within the 127/8 block is returned, and on whether the list publishes known spammers (black or block list) or known nonspammers (white list).

For example, upon receiving an email message with a source IP address of 192.0.2.95, my email server formulates an A record query for hostname 95.2.0.192. spamblacklist.org, assuming my chosen black list provider publishes lookups within the spamblacklist.org domain. Upon receiving a reply with answer (IP address) 127.0.0.5, my email server classifies the email as spam and rejects it. On the other hand, if NXDOMAIN is returned for the query, the email may be permitted. A white list service, publishing known genuine email server addresses would render the opposite interpretation based on the DNS lookup.

10.3.3 Sender Policy Framework (SPF)

The Sender Policy Framework is currently defined with RFC 4408 (112) under experimental status. SPF enables an organization to publish its own list of authorized outgoing email server addresses, a self-published white list, though with substantially more sophistication. Under SPF, the received email message's envelope information is

---

[*] Reintroduction is not forwarding. The transmission of an email with the *original sender* information instead of that of the transmitter is considered reintroduction. Forwarding uses the mailbox doing the forwarding as the sender.

examined, and an SPF DNS query from the recipient is based upon the sender, the sender's domain, as well as the source IP address. Upon receipt of an email message, the recipient email server would issue a query for an SPF resource record for the source domain name. The SPF record is encoded as a string of "mechanisms" that are used to process the source IP address from which the email originated, the domain portion of the MAIL FROM or HELO identity, and the sender from the MAIL FROM or HELO identity.

SPF—Sender Policy Framework Record. The Sender Policy Framework attempts to provide validation of what hosts are configured to send email for a given domain. That is, SPF seeks to eliminate spam emails from spoofed domains. A recipient email host can look up the SPF records for the sender's domain to verify that the sending email host matches those authorized by the sender. SPF version 1 or SPF classic as it is also called, is documented in RFC 4408 and utilizes the SPF resource record. Domain administrators can configure DNS with email hosts mapping to each host's mailfrom and SMTP HELO identities. SenderID is a related spam detection technique that also uses the SPF resource record type, though it analyzes different information from an incoming email message. We'll cover SenderID a bit later.

Note that due to actual implementations of SPF using TXT records prior to IETF publication of RFC 4408, most implementations will use both SPF and TXT records for backward compatibility, though an SPF compliant resolver will discard the TXT records if both TXT and SPF records are returned. The format of the SPF record is identical to that of the TXT record; however, a particular syntax is employed for SPF applications instead of arbitrary text. The syntax includes a version string ($v = spf1$ for SPF, $spf2.0$ for SenderID covered next) followed by a space, then one or more terms that define qualifiers on resource record types or IP network addresses, modifiers, and even macros.

Owner	TTL	Class	Type	RData
Domain name	TTL	IN	SPF	Version, directives, and/or modifiers
smtp.ipamww.com.	86400	IN	SPF	v = spf1 + ip4:192.0.2.32/30 –all
smtp.ipamww.com.	86400	IN	SPF	spf2.0 pra + ip4:192.0.2.32/30 –all

Mechanisms. Mechanisms enable specification of the match criteria within the SPF (or TXT) record, which a receiving email server can query to validate the sender of a given email message. Mechanisms are defined within the SPF record's RData field after specification of the SPF version, currently version 1, "$v = spf1$." Mechanisms are evaluated left to right. If a mechanism passes based on evaluation of the mechanism, the verification passes; otherwise, the next mechanism is tested until a pass or fail is found or no further mechanisms are defined.

Each mechanism can be defined with a qualifier, a prefix that instructs the mail or spam filter server how to interpret a given "match":

- $+ =$ pass (default). Consider this mechanism a pass, if this mechanism matches.
- $- =$ fail. Consider this mechanism a fail, if the mechanism matches.

- ~ = soft-fail. Consider this mechanism somewhere between neutral and fail, if this mechanism matches; this interpretation would not fail this check outright if it matched, but would hold it for closer scrutiny.
- ? = neutral. Consider this mechanism neutral, if this mechanism matches.

Qualifiers may be used with the following resource record check based mechanisms to define the interpretation of a given mechanism as shown in the examples following:

- a = lookup the A record for the source domain (from the MAIL FROM or HELO identity); if it matches the source IP address of the message, this mechanism matches. This can be scoped to a specific domain and/or number of CIDR bits to compare in the addresses as illustrated in the following examples:
  - o + a = pass, if the A record query for the source domain matches the source IP address.
  - o -a:ipamworldwide.com = fail, if an A record query for ipamworldwide. com matches the source IP address.
  - o ~a/24 soft-fail, if the first 24 bits of the IP address retrieved via A record lookup of the source domain matches the first 24 bits of the source IP address.
- mx = lookup the MX record for the source domain (from the MAIL FROM or HELO identity); for each MX lookup resolved, look up the corresponding A record; if it matches the source IP address of the message, this mechanism passes. As with the a mechanism, the mx mechanism can be scoped to a specific domain and/or number of CIDR bits to compare in the addresses as illustrated in the following example:
  - o + mx:ipamworldwide.com/28 = pass, if an A record associated with a MX record lookup is returned where the first 28 bits match the first 28 bits of the source IP address of the message.
- ptr = lookup the PTR record (up to 10) corresponding to the source IP address of the email message; then compare two things with each domain name returned in the PTR lookup:
  - o Check that the domain name returned matches the source domain of the email message.
  - o Check that the corresponding A or AAAA record returns an IP address matching the source IP address.

    If both conditions hold, this mechanism passes. This mechanism can be further scoped by a domain name, which can be used to filter multiple returned PTR-lookup domain names as illustrated in the following examples:
  - o -ptr: fail, if a domain name returned during the PTR lookup of the source IP address matches the source domain and if the A/AAAA domain name corresponding to the domain name returned during the PTR lookup matches the source IP address of the email.

- o +ptr:ipamworldwide.com: pass, if a domain name returned during the PTR lookup of the source IP address matches the source domain while falling within the ipamworldwide.com domain and if the A/AAAA domain name corresponding to the domain name returned during the PTR lookup matches the source IP address of the email.
- ip4 = verify that the source IP address matches the IPv4 address specified; this mechanism may be qualified by CIDR length as illustrated in the following example:
  - o ?ip4:192.0.2.32/30. Neutral, if the source IP address of the message falls within 192.0.2.32-192.0.2.35.
- ip6 = verify that the source IP address matches the IPv6 address specified; this mechanism may be qualified by prefix length as illustrated in the following example:
  - o +ip6:2001:db8:f02b:2a::/64. Pass, if the source IP address of the message falls within the 2001:DB8:F02B:2A::/64 network.
- exists:*domain_name* = lookup the A record (not AAAA) corresponding to the *domain_name*; this mechanism matches if any answer (IP address) is provided (this mechanism must be scoped with a domain name to match as illustrated in the following example).
  - o exists:ipamworldwide.com: matches, if an A record lookup for the ipamworldwise.com domain returns an IP address.
- include:*domain_name* = recursively evaluate the domain_name to leverage its SPF policies, for example, to utilize the policy of a domain from multiple ISPs or from other domains from which you send email.
- all = matches everything; often used as the final parameter as −all to fail if no prior mechanism matches.

Modifiers. Modifiers may be specified within SPF records to provide additional information. Modifiers are name-value pairs, two of which have yet been defined:

- redirect = *domain_name*: enables "aliasing" of SPF records, for example, to apply a common SPF processing record to multiple domains. This provides a convenience for ongoing change management: change the processing in one record, minimizing errors, and maximizing consistency. In the following example, the MX record check for the ipamworldwide.com domain would apply to the hq and euro subdomains as well.

```
hq.ipamww.com. IN SPF ''v=spf1 redirect=_spf.ipamworldwide.com''
euro.ipamww.com. IN SPF ''v=spf1 redirect=_spf.ipamworldwide.com''
_spf.ipamworldwide.com. IN SPF ''v=spf1 +mx:ipamworldwide.com -all''
```

The redirect can be used explicitly as in the above example, or as a "last resort", for example, listed as the rightmost mechanism.

- $exp = domain\_name$: explanation, which defines the domain for which a TXT record lookup must be done to identify the string to be presented as results upon a mechanism match failure.

Macros. Technically, the *domain_name* for any of the above mechanisms and modifiers need not be an explicitly defined (hard coded) domain, but one that can be defined using macros to dynamically formulate a domain name based on the message envelope under evaluation. Even the TXT record fetched by processing an exp modifier may be populated with macros. Macros are identified using the percent sign (%). The following macros have been defined

- `%{s}` = the sender's email address
- `%{l}` = the local part of the sender's email address
- `%{o}` = the domain of the sender's email address
- `%{d}` = the current domain, usually the same as the sender's domain but may also have been processed, for example, via the include mechanism
- `%{i}` = the source IP address of the message sender
- `%{p}` = the validated domain name via PTR lookup of the source IP address of the message sender
- `%{v}` = the literal string "in-addr" if the source IP address is an IPv4 address and "ip6" if the source IP address is IPv6
- `%{h}` = the domain part of the HELO/EHLO identity
- `%%` = the literal %
- `%_` = space " "
- `%-` = a URL-encoded space, for example "%20"

The following macros are available for use in the TXT record referenced by an exp mechanism and may not be used elsewhere:

- `%{c}` = the SMTP client IP address
- `%{r}` = the domain name of the host performing the SPF check
- `%{t}` = the current time stamp.

Macro transformers enable use of a subset of the results of a macro, for example, by specifying an integer quantity of domain name labels, or the reversal of the results of a macro, for example, reversing an IP address. Reversal is performed by adding an r into the macro curly brackets.

Macro Examples. Consider the example of Figure 10.3, where Mike (mike@ipam-ww.com) sends me an email to tim@ipamworldwide.com from my SMTP host on IP addresses 192.0.2.32. Using this and other information from the figure, we can define the macro values for this email transmission as

- `%{s}=mike@ipamww.com`
- `%{l}=mike`
- `%{o}=ipamww.com`
- `%{d}=ipamww.com`
- `%{d3}=ipamww.com`
- `%{d2}=ipamww.com`
- `%{d1}=com`
- `%{i}=192.0.2.32`
- `%{ir}=32.2.0.192`
- `%{v}=in-addr`
- `%{h}=ipamww.com`
- `%{ir}.%{v}._spf.%{d}=32.2.0.192.in-addr._spf.ipamww.com`

SPF provides a powerful macro language to granularly articulate email policies for your organization. However, it is an experimental protocol, as is a close cousin, Sender ID.

10.3.4 Sender ID

Another experimental mechanism for identifying potential spam email is called Sender ID. The Sender ID algorithm seeks to identify whether a given email from a given SMTP client at the given source IP address is authorized to send the email. Like SPF, Sender ID can examine the sender, sender domain, and source IP address of the email message based on the MAIL FROM field. Unlike SPF, Sender ID can also or alternatively verify the sender and sender domain based on message header information. Sender ID, like SPF, utilizes the SPF resource record type, as defined in the previous section with a few modifications:

- the version string ("v = spf1") is replaced with "spf2.0";
- Sender ID includes a scope for the record: "mfrom" indicates the mailfrom entity as in SPF, and/or "pra" the *purported responsible address*, discussed next; and
- modifiers are extended from the SPF definition to enable positional context as an alternative to the SPF-defined global context. That is, a modifier can affect a preceding mechanism, unlike SPF where a modifier is always applied globally.

The scope field is used to derive the sender and sender domain for validation (i.e., the MAIL FROM entity and/or the PRA). The purported responsible address, PRA, scope relates to the identity of the sender closest to the receiving email system. The PRA algorithm examines the message header, not the envelope, and seeks a sender address by examining the following headers in order, taking the first address found:

- Resent–Sender header
- Resent–From header
- Sender header
- From header

A single valid sender mailbox address (i.e., of the form mailbox@maildomain) found in one of these headers is the PRA. In the simple cases illustrated in Figures 10.3 and 10.4, the purported responsible address would be mike@ipamww.com as derived from the "From" header value. In the case where a third party is used to transmit email on behalf of a legitimate sender, the "Resent–From" or other header value would be used. The term "purported" is used since the algorithm relies on information supplied in the message header, which is supplied by the sender.

There is a bit of controversy around Sender ID versus SPF, which is one of the reasons why both techniques are deemed experimental. For example, Sender ID processing of "v = spf1" (SPF) records could result in valid messages being deemed spam. Hopefully, an agreeable unified approach can be derived in the future.

10.3.5 Domain Keys Identified Mail (DKIM)

DKIM specifies a means for a sender of email to cryptographically sign an email message such that recipients may validate it upon receipt via retrieval and application of the sender's domain key. DKIM utilizes digital signatures, which enable the originator of a given set of data (an email message in this case) to sign the data such that those receiving the data and the signature, along with a corresponding public key for deciphering the signature, can perform data origin and integrity verification. DKIM employs an asymmetric key pair (private key/public key) model. In such a model, the email message and selected header fields are encrypted with a private key and can be validated by decrypting the data with the corresponding public key. The private key and public key form a key pair. The mathematical details are very complex but conceptually, the private/public key pairs provide a means for holders of the public key to verify that data was signed using the corresponding private key. This provides authentication that the data verified was indeed signed by the holder of the private key. Digital signatures also enable verification that the data received matches the data published and was not tampered with in transit.

Referring to Figure 10.5, the data originator, shown on the left of the figure, generates a private key/public key pair and utilizes the private key to sign the data. The first step in signing the data is to produce a hash of the data, sometimes also referred to as a digest. Hashes are one-way functions[*] to scramble data into a fixed length string for simpler manipulation, and represent a "fingerprint" of the data. This means that it is very

---

[*] A one-way function means that the original data is not uniquely derivable from the hash. One can apply an algorithm to create the hash, but there is no inverse algorithm to perform on the hash to arrive at the original data.

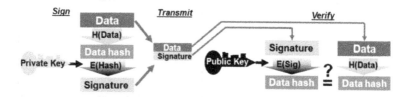

Figure 10.5. Digital signature creation and verification process.

unlikely that another data input could produce the same hash value. Thus, hashes are often used as checksums but don't provide any origin authentication (anyone knowing the hash algorithm can simply hash arbitrary data). Common hash algorithms include HMAC-MD5, RSA-SHA-1, and RSA-SHA-256. DKIM not only uses RSA-SHA-256 by default but also supports RSA-SHA-1. The hash is encrypted using the private key to produce the signature. The encryption algorithm is fed the hash and the private key to produce the signature.

Both the message and its associated signature are transmitted to the recipient. A new email header field, dkim-signature, has been defined to store the DKIM signature with information on retrieving the public key. Based on our prior review of how SMTP works, you may be wondering how modification of envelope data and insertion of headers affect the signature. DKIM offers a "simple" or strict form of canonicalization and a "relaxed" form. The simple form tolerates very little modification while the relaxed form permits white space replacement and header line rewrapping without impacting the signature validity.

DKIM Signature Email Header Field. The recipient must extract the signature from the `dkim-signature` header field. The dkim-signature field also contains the following:

- the DKIM version (e.g., $v = 1$)
- the algorithm used to generate the signature (e.g., `a = rsa-sha256`)
- signature (e.g., `b = dqdVx0fAK9...`)
- hash of the canonicalized message body (`bh = 7Dkw0eE35Jlkjexcmpol...`)
- canonicalization method (`c = relaxed`)
- the signing domain identifier—the domain of the signing entity (e.g., `d = ipam-worldwide.com`)
- user or agent on whose behalf the message is signed (`i = rooney@ipam-worldwide.com`)
- the selector or key reference within the domain (allows multiple keys per domain which aids in key rollover and more granular signatures) (e.g., `s = europe`)
- enumeration of the header fields that were signed (e.g., `h = from:to:subject:date`)

- additional optional information, including query methods to use to retrieve the public key. The default (and currently only) query method, `q = dns/txt`, instructs the recipient to perform a DNS query of querytype "txt" to retrieve the public key that corresponds with the private key that was used to sign the message. Another optional field of interest, the `i =` tag provides the identity of the user or agent on whose behalf this message was signed.

DKIM TXT Record. Using the query method q = dns/txt, the recipient performs a DNS query for a TXT record within the signing domain. The Question section of the query is formulated by concatenating the selector value (s = value), the string "_domainkey" and the specified signing domain (d = value). Using the example where s = europe and d = ipamworldwide.com as specified in the dkim-signature field of an incoming email, a TXT query for europe._domainkey.ipamworldwide.com would be issued. The RData portion of the corresponding TXT record includes one or more tags similar to the dkim-signature field

- DKIM version (v = DKIM1)
- Granularity of the key, which if specified, must match the local part of the user or agent (i=) flag in the dkim-signature header (g = *)
- Hash algorithm(s) accepted (e.g., h = sha256)
- Key type (k = rsa)
- Notes for human consumption (n = updated_key)
- The public key (p = Dkjeijf8d98Kz...)
- Service type (s = email)
- Flags indicating such things as the compliance rules among the i = tag in the dkim-signature header and the d = domain tag (encoded in the TXT record as t = s), as well as whether this domain is testing DKIM (t = y).

The only required tag is the p tag, the public key. An example TXT record follows

```
europe._domainkey.ipamworldwide.com IN TXT
("v=DKIM1; p=Dkjeijf98Kz...")
```

Upon retrieving the public key, the recipient computes a hash of the received message body and signed header fields, as did the originator. The recipient applies the hash algorithm to the received signature using the originator's public key. The output of this decryption, the original data hash, is compared with the recipient's computed hash of the data. If they match, the data has not been modified and the private key holder signed the data.

If an incoming email message contains a dkim-signature header field, it's clear that the sender is using DKIM and has signed the message. But if an incoming email message does not contain a dkim-signature header field, does this mean that the sender does not sign messages? This in fact could create an opening for a SPAM attacker issuing unsigned email messages from a spoofed source domain. DKIM relies on publication of Author Domain Signing Practices (ADSP), which enables a recipient email server to determine whether the message from a given domain by policy should be signed and if so, by whom and with what signature(s).

A recipient determines the sending domain's signing practices by issuing a query for Qtype = TXT and Qname = _adsp._domainkey.*signing-domain-identifier*, where *signing-domain-identifier* is again the d = value. The corresponding TXT record indicates whether email from this domain is always signed, may be signed, and is always signed and any unsigned email should be discarded. Please refer to RFC 5617 (113) for details.

10.3.6 Historic Email Resource Record Types

These resource record types were defined in the early days of DNS and are no longer used. We list them here purely for historical significance.

MR—Mail Rename Record. The MR resource record type translates email to an alias or list into an individual (or multiple, one per MR record). In the simplest sense, it provides an alias for a mailbox name.

Owner	TTL	Class	Type	RData
Emailbox alias name	TTL	IN	MR	Emailbox name
cfo	86400	IN	MR	finance

MB—Mailbox Record. The MB record is defined in RFC 1035 and enables association of a user ID with the desired host containing the user's email box.

Owner	TTL	Class	Type	RData
Email ID	TTL	IN	MB	Mailbox hostname
joe	86400	IN	MB	smtp.ipamworldwide.com.

MG—Mail Group Member Record. RFC 1035 defined the MG resource record to enable association of email users with a user group.

Owner	TTL	Class	Type	RData
Email group name	TTL	IN	MG	Email ID
finance	86400	IN	MG	joe

MINFO—Mailbox/Mailing List Information. The MINFO record was also defined in RFC 1035 and was intended to provide mailbox and mailing list information. It provides two email box addresses one to request addition to the mailing list and another to report errors.

Owner	TTL	Class	Type	RData	
Mailbox name	TTL	IN	MINFO	Requests mailbox	Errors mailbox
newsalerts	86400	IN	MINFO	hostmaster	majordomo

10.4 SECURITY APPLICATIONS

10.4.1 Securing Name Resolution—DNSSEC Resource Record Types

Chapter 13 is devoted to the topic of DNS security extensions (DNSSEC), so we will summarize the DNSSEC required resource record types for completeness within this chapter. We'll provide the full context and description of DNSSEC in Chapter 13.

DNSKEY—DNS Key Record. The DNSKEY resource record is used in DNSSEC to publish public keys used for validating signatures on zone information. The server signs its authoritative resource record sets within a zone using a private key and the corresponding public key is published in the zone file in the form of the DNSKEY record. Two types of keys are published: a zone signing key (ZSK), which signs resource record data and a key signing key (KSK) which signs the ZSK. The resolver can use this public key to validate a given RRSet's signature.

Owner	TTL	Class	Type	RData			
Key name	TTL	IN	DNSKEY	Flags	Protocol	Algorithm	Key
ipamww.com.	86400	IN	DNSKEY	256	3	5	AweE8F(le…

In this example, the RData fields are interpreted as follows:

- the Flags field provides information on the type and status of the key. Currently defined values for the Flags field are as follows.
  - o Bit 7. This key is a zone signing key (Decimal $= 256$)
  - o Bit 8. Revoke this Key
  - o Bit 15. This key is a key signing key (Decimal $= 1$)
  - o Other bits. Unassigned
- the Protocol field must have a value of "3" indicating DNSSEC (this is the only value currently defined).
- the Algorithm has a value of "5" in the example above, indicating the RSA-SHA-1 algorithm. Algorithms currently supported are encoded as follows:
  - o Value $= 1$. RSA/MD5, which is not recommended according to RFC 4034

    o Value = 2. Diffie–Hellman

    o Value = 3. DSA*/SHA-1

    o Value = 4. Reserved for Elliptic Curve

    o Value = 5. RSA-SHA-1, which is mandatory according to RFC 4034

    o Value = 6. DSA-NSEC3-SHA-1—an alias for algorithm 3, but with the qualifier that NSEC3 records instead of NSEC records are used

    o Value = 7. RSA-SHA-1-NSEC3-SHA-1—an alias for algorithm 5, but with the qualifier that NSEC3 records instead of NSEC records are used

    o Value = 8. RSA-SHA-256

    o Value = 10. RSA-SHA-256

    o Value = 12. GOST R 34.10-2001

    o Value = 252. Indirect

    o Values = 253-254. Private

    o Values = 0, 123-251, 255. Reserved

    o Other values. Unassigned.

- the Key is the public key.

DS—Delegation Signer Record. RFC 4034 (114) defines the DS resource record type, which essentially extends the chain of trust to a signed delegated domain (zone). The DS resource record enables a parent zone to authenticate its child zone's public Key Signing Keys (DNSKEY record for the KSK). As such, each DS record refers to a specific (by key tag) DNSKEY resource record in the delegated child zone. Authenticating the DS record enables clients to authenticate the child zone's DNSKEY.

Owner	TTL	Class	Type	RData			
Delegated domain	TTL	IN	DS	Key tag	Alg.	Type	Digest
child.ipamww.com.	86400	IN	DS	32284	5	1	75CF28D3OQ35...

The Algorithm field identifies the algorithm field on the corresponding DNSKEY record. The DS record refers to a DNSKEY record by including a digest (hash) of the DNSKEY RR in the Digest field; the [Digest] Type field indicates the algorithm utilized to construct the digest.

DLV—DNSSEC Lookaside Validation Record. Specified in RFC 4431 (115), the DLV resource record is used within DNSSEC for publishing trust anchors outside of the normal DNS domain tree hierarchy, that is, the chain of trust. The DLV record is structured identically to the DS record in that it identifies a "proxy parent zone" and it thus authenticates the "child" zone's public key signing key records (DNSKEY).

---

*DSA = U.S. Government Digital Signature Algorithm.

Lookaside validation is intended to provide an alternative upstream trust anchor, such as dlv.isc.org, in the absence of root and TLD zone signings.

Owner	TTL	Class	Type				RData
DLV domain	TTL	IN	DLV	Key tag	Alg.	Type	Digest
ipamww.com.dlv_reg.net.	86400	IN	DLV	32284	5	1	90df80DF89lLe...

NSEC—Next Secure Record. The NSEC resource record type provides two sets of information. The set of NSEC RRs in a zone forms a chain of authoritative owner names in the zone and indicates which authoritative RRSets exist in the zone. The NSEC resource record contains the next owner name that identifies associated authoritative owner names within the chain, as well as the set of RR types present at the NSEC resource record's owner name.

Owner	TTL	Class	Type	RData	
RRSet Owner	TTL	IN	NSEC	Next RRSet Owner	Type Bit Maps
ns1.ipamww.com.	86400	IN	NSEC	ns2.ipamww.com.	A NS RRSIG NSEC

The Next RRSet Owner field contains the next owner name in the canonical ordering of the zone that has authoritative data or contains an RRSet of type NS defining a delegation point. This provides authenticated denial of existence of resource records between the RRSet identified within the NSEC Owner field and the Next RRSet Owner RData field. The Type Bit Maps field identifies the resource record types that exist at this NSEC resource record's owner name. Within this field, if a bit $= 1$, then the RRType corresponding to this bit number exists. Thus if bit 1 is 1, corresponding to RR Type $= 1$ or A record, then an A RRSet is present. Fortunately, the text representation of this is in the familiar resource record type mnemonic.

NSEC3—NSEC3 Record. The NSEC resource record provides authenticated denial of existence for RRSets, but it also enables easy enumeration of RRSets in the zone, which can be considered an information security risk. In other words, a curious or malicious querier could attempt to resolve a bogus name and receive the pair of resource record owner names surrounding the queried hostname.

Like NSEC, the NSEC3 record provides authenticated RRSet denial of existence, but obfuscates the chain of RRSets in the zone. This obfuscation renders the footprinting of a zone's contents much more computationally intensive. Instead of pointing to the new owner name field, NSEC3 points to the next hashed owner name field in hash order. And the salt value that is appended to each owner name prior to hash generation further complicates the generation of hashed owner names by someone attempting to footprint the zone.

For each RRSet in the zone, the owner field is hashed using the specified hash algorithm applied to the owner name concatenated with the salt field iteratively <Iterations> + 1 times. The following pseudocode states this in another way:

```
x = {RRSet owner field concatenated with Salt value}
y = H (x)      a hash of x as defined in the prior statement
for (i = Iterations value; i > 0; i-) {
    y = H (y)
}
```

Owner	TTL	Class	Type					RData				
Hashed RRSet Owner	TTL	IN	NSEC3	Hash Alg.	Flags	Iterations	Salt Len.	Salt		Hash Len.	Next Hashed Owner Name	Type Bit Maps
jAdfJE; ...	8640	IN	NSEC3	1	0	2	8	a808f6ce 1a950b1c		18	kOLse7...	A RRSIG NSEC3

The RData fields for the NSEC3 record are defined as follows:

- *Hash Algorithm.* The algorithm used to construct the hash value; valid values are
  - Reserved
  - 1 = RSA-SHA-1
  - 2-255. Unassigned
- *Flags.* Consisting of a set of eight boolean flags, the Flags field has currently a single flag defined (bit 0). If bit 0 is set, this indicates that this record covers one or more unsigned delegation records. This Opt-Out flag enables "opting out" of securing delegations to unsigned zones (i.e., validating the non-existence of a child zone's DS record).
- *Iterations.* Specifies the number of additional applications of the hash function.
- *Salt Length.* Included in the wire format but not presented in the resource record text format, this field indicates the length in bytes of the Salt field (valid values = 0–255).
- *Salt.* The value of the Salt field is appended to the RRSet owner prior to application of the hash function and is represented in case-insensitive hexadecimal.
- *Hash Length.* The length in octets of the next hashed owner name field, included on the wire but not represented in resource record text format.
- *Next Hashed Owner Name.*
- *Type Bit Maps.* This field defines the resource record types defined for this owner within the zone and is encoded in the same manner as the corresponding field in the NSEC record.

NSEC3PARAM—NSEC3 Parameters Record. The NSEC3PARAM record type defines the parameters needed to compute hashed owner names and hence the corresponding NSEC3 records within the zone upon signing. The NSEC3PARAM record is used by the server to identify negative answers in response to a query. Thus, when a query arrives for a nonexistent RRSet within the zone, the server applies the NSEC3PARAM parameters to hash the queried owner name in order to provide an appropriate NSEC3 response, that is, between which two hashed RRSets does this queried owner name fall? Only one NSEC3PARAM record should be present within the zone file. The NSEC3PARAM record is also used by the server when signing new or changed RRSets automatically.

The RData fields have identical meanings as corresponding fields within the NSEC3 RData fields.

Owner	TTL	Class	Type	RData				
Domain name	TTL	IN	NSEC3PARAM	Hash Alg.	Flags	Iterations	Salt Len.	Salt
ipamww.com.	86400	IN	NSEC3PARAM	1	0	2	8	a808f6ce1a950b1c

RRSIG—Resource Record Set Signature Record. The Resource Record Set Signature resource record contains the digital signature associated with a given RRSet. This signature, along with the zone's public [zone signing] key, are used to authenticate the corresponding RRSet's integrity and origin.

Owner	TTL	Class	Type	RData							
RRSet Owner	TTL	IN	RRSIG	Type Cov.	Alg.	Labels	Orig. TTL	Expire	Inception	Key tag	Signer	Signature
ftp1.ipamww. com.	86400	IN	RRSIG	A	5	3	86400	2008051 5133509	2008011 5133509	27783	ipamww. com.	N78E...

The RData fields within the RRSIG record are defined as follows:

- *Type Covered.* The resource record type of the corresponding owner and class signed by this signature. This field is the standard resource record type discussed for resource records throughout this chapter. In the example above, the A (address) resource record type indicates that A records with name = ftp1.ipamww.com (Owner field) of class IN are signed with this RRSIG record.
- *Algorithm.* The algorithm used in generating the data hash for comparison with the received signature. This field is encoded in the same manner as the Algorithm field of the DNSKEY resource record type.
- *Labels.* Indicates the number labels. Recall that labels refer to the text representation of domain names, with a label for each name "between the dots." Thus, www.ipamworldwide.com has three labels. This field is used to reconstruct the

original owner name used to create the signature in the case where the owner name returned by the server has a wildcard label (*).

- *Original TTL.* The TTL of the signed RRSet as defined in the authoritative zone, used to validate a signature. This field is needed because the TTL field returned in the original response is normally decremented by a caching resolver and use of that TTL value may lead to erroneous calculations.

- *Signature Expiration.* The date and time of the expiration of this signature expressed as either the number of seconds since January 1, 1970 00:00:00 UTC or in the form of YYYYMMDDHHmmSS where

  o YYYY is the year
  o MM is the month, 01–12
  o DD is the day of the month, 01–31
  o HH is the hour in 24 h notation, 00–23
  o mm is the minute, 00–59
  o SS is the second, 00–59
  o Signatures are not valid after this date/time.

- *Signature Inception.* The date and time of the inception of this signature formatted in the same manner as the Signature Expiration field. Signatures are not valid before this date/time.

- *Key Tag.* Provides an association with the corresponding DNSKEY resource record that can be used to validate the signature.

- *Signer's Name.* Identifies the owner name of the DNSKEY resource record (i.e., the domain name) that is to be used to validate this signature.

- *Signature.* The cryptographic signature covering the resource record set defined by this RRSIG owner, class, and covered type fields and this RRSIG RData fields (excluding this Signature field).

10.4.2 Other Security-Oriented DNS Resource Record Types

TA—Trust Authority Record. While an RFC does not exist defining the TA resource record, IANA has assigned it a value, so we'll mention it here. The TA resource record is identical in format to the DS record type including RData fields for key tag, algorithm, digest type, and digest. Use of the TA record enables a resolver to have a resource record signature validated by a known trust authority even if the root zone has not been signed (it has now been signed!). This functionality is now provided using the DLV record.

CERT—Certificate Record. RFC 4398 (116) defines the CERT record as a means to store certificates and certificate revocation lists (CRLs) in DNS. Certificates provide a means to identify an organization, server, individual, or other entity and associate a public key with that identity. The public key can be used to authenticate the sender's identity and to encrypt and decrypt communications and validate message integrity.

Certificates are hierarchical and can be used to validate up to a known trusted entity (Certificate Authority). CRLs are lists of certificates, which have been revoked due to expiration or manual revocation.

CERT records containing certificates are stored in DNS to enable resolvers to obtain certificates via DNS instead of from a destination certificate server. The CERT resource record has the following format.

Owner	TTL	Class	Type	RData			
Domain name	TTL	IN	CERT	Certificate Type	Key tag	Algorithm	Certificate or CRL
ipamww.com.	86400	IN	CERT	PGP	436	3	A4df480DFC9lLa...

The owner field identifies the entity to which the certificate applies when a certificate is included in the RData portion of the record. If a CRL is included in the RData section, the owner name should contain the domain name related to the issuing authority. The RData portion contains the following subfields

- Certificate Type such as X.509/PKIX, PGP, and others
- Key tag, which is used to streamline the identification of relevant certificates to those of matching key tags
- Algorithm. The algorithm used in generating the key, which is encoded in the same manner as the Algorithm field of the DNSKEY resource record type.
- The certificate or CRL

IPSECKEY—Public Key for IPSec Record. The IPSECKEY resource record type, defined in RFC 4025 (117), provides a means to store a public key in DNS for use with IPSEC. This resource record enables a client seeking to establish an IPSec tunnel to a remote host to identify a means to authenticate the remote host and to determine whether to connect directly to the host or connect via another node acting as a gateway. IPSECKEY resource records are associated with the intended remote host's IP address or host domain name. IP addresses are stored in the .arpa. reverse domain space. The format of the IPSECKEY resource record is as follows.

Owner	TTL	Class	Type	RData				
IP address in .arpa. domain or host domain name	TTL	IN	IPSECKEY	Prece- dence	Gateway Type	Algorithm	Gateway	Public key
1.0.12.10. in-addr.arpa.	86400	IN	IPSECKEY	10	1	2	10.100.1.2	Adf4C9lL...

The RData field contains the following fields:

- *Precedence.* Used to prioritize multiple records within a common RRSet, using the lowest precedence first.
- *Gateway Type.* Indicates the format of the Gateway field.
  - o 0 = no gateway is present
  - o 1 = IPv4 address
  - o 2 = IPv6 address
  - o 3 = FQDN
- *Algorithm.* The format of the Public Key field.
  - o 0 = no key is present
  - o 1 = DSA formatted key
  - o 2 = RSA formatted key
- *Gateway.* Identifies a gateway to which an IPSec tunnel can be established to reach the remote host (identified by the owner field). The interpretation of this field is governed by the Gateway Type field.
- *Public Key.* The key generated using the algorithm specified in the Algorithm field.

KEY—Key Record. The KEY record was defined with the initial incarnation of DNSSEC, but was superseded by the DNSKEY resource record. However, prior to the release of DNSSEC*bis*, the KEY record was also utilized to store public keys associated with the SIG(0) record. The KEY record has the same format as the DNSKEY record.

Owner	TTL	Class	Type	RData			
Key name	TTL	IN	KEY	Flags	Protocol	Algorithm	Key
K3941.ipamww.com.	86400	IN	KEY	256	3	1	12S9X-weE8F(le...

KX—Key Exchanger Record. The KX record enables specification of an intermediary that can supply a key on behalf of another host. In other words, if intending to perform key negotiation with x.ipamworldwide.com, the KX record could point to the y.ipamworldwide.com host domain name with whom key exchange negotiation should ensue. A preference field enables specification of multiple alternate domains of varying preference for key negotiation.

Owner	TTL	Class	Type	RData	
Host domain name	TTL	IN	KX	Preference	Key exchanger host domain name
x.ipamworldwide.com.	86400	IN	KX	10	y.ipamworldwide.com.
x.ipamworldwide.com.	86400	IN	KX	20	z.ipamworldwide.com.

SIG—Signature Record. The SIG resource record has been superseded by the RRSIG record within the scope of DNSSEC, though the SIG record is still in use for digitally signing DNS updates and zone transfers outside the scope of DNSSEC. That is, you don't need to deploy DNSSEC to enable transaction signatures of updates and zone transfers. Such transactions can be signed using shared secret keys via TSIG (Transaction Signature) records or by using private/public key pairs via SIG(0), where corresponding public keys are stored as KEY records. The notation SIG(0) refers to the use of the SIG resource record with an empty (0) Type Covered field. In such cases, RFC 2931 (118) recommends setting the owner field to root, the TTL to 0, and class to ANY as shown in the example below.

The SIG record is formatted identically to the RRSIG record, with the exception of the formatting of the Expiration Date and Inception Date fields; for the SIG record, these fields are not formatted by date per the RRSIG record and are instead formatted as an incremental integer, enumerated as the number of seconds since January 1, 1970 00:00:00 UTC. This counter will rollover to 0 and continue counting after the counter exceeds 4.29 billion seconds (a little over 136 years).

Owner	TTL	Class	Type	RData							
RRSet Domain	TTL	IN	SIG	Type Cov.	Alg.	Labels	Orig. TTL	Expire	Inception	Key tag	Signer	Signature
.	0	ANY	SIG	0	3	3	86400	2008051 5133509	2008011 5133509	26421	ipamw w.com.	Zx9v...

SSHFP—Secure Shell Fingerprint Record. The Secure Shell (SSH) Protocol enables secure login from a client to a server and other secure network services over an insecure IP network. The security of the connection relies upon the user authenticating him- or herself to the server as well as the server authenticating itself to the client via Diffie–Hellman key exchange. If the public key is not already known by the client, a fingerprint of the key is provided by the server for verification by the user. Storage of this key fingerprint in DNS provides a means for the client to lookup and verify the fingerprint out of band via a "third party." The lookup requires use of DNSSEC to secure the lookup process and assure message integrity. The SSHFP resource record is the record type used to store these SSH fingerprints.

Owner	TTL	Class	Type	RData		
Host domain name	TTL	IN	SSHFP	Algorithm	Fingerprint type	Fingerprint
srv21.ipamww.com.	86400	IN	SSHFP	2	1	8Fd7q90D + fd...

The RData portion of the SSHFP record includes the following fields:

- *Algorithm.* Currently defined values are
  - 0 = Reserved

- o 1 = RSA
- o 2 = DSA
- *Fingerprint Type.* Currently defined values are
- o 0 = Reserved
- o 1 = SHA-1
- Key Fingerprint

10.4.3 Geographical Location Lookup

GPOS—Geographical Position Record. The GPOS resource record type, originally defined in RFC 1712 (119), has been superseded by the LOC resource record type. GPOS encoded the longitude, latitude, and altitude of a host as shown below.

Owner	TTL	Class	Type	RData		
Host domain name	TTL	IN	GPOS	Longitude	Latitude	Altitude
srv1.ipamww.com.	86400	IN	GPOS	39.582	-75.801	128.2

LOC—Location Resource Record. This type of resource record enables encoding of latitude, longitude, and altitude information about the respective host. RFC 1876 (120) defines the LOC record, which obsoletes the GPOS resource record type. The RData field for the LOC record presents each coordinate in the three dimensions

- *Latitude.* Degrees [minutes [seconds]] "N" or "S"
- *Longitude.* Degrees [minutes [seconds]] "E" or "W"
- *Altitude.* Altitude in meters
- Precision of each measure as diameter of "sphere of error" in meters

Owner	TTL	Class	Type	RData			
Host domain name	TTL	IN	LOC	Latitude	Longitude	Altitude	Precision
srv-97.ipamww.com.	86400	IN	LOC	39 58 N	75 38 W	128	50 m

In the example above, the hostnamed srv-97.ipamww.com is located at $39°58'$ N latitude, $75°38'$ W longitude, is 128 m above sea level, all within a sphere of error with diameter 50 m.

10.4.4 Non-IP Host-Address Lookups

ISDN—Integrated Services Digital Network Record (Experimental). The ISDN type enables association of an ISDN address to a host. The ISDN address is the form of a telephone number, as defined by the International Telecommunications Union standard E.164. The subaddress field is optional.

Owner	TTL	Class	Type	RData	
Host domain name	TTL	IN	ISDN	ISDN Address	Subaddress
isdnhost.ipamww.com.	86400	IN	ISDN	16105551298	318

NSAP—Network Service Access Point Record. The NSAP resource record enables translation of a hostname or FQDN to a Network Service Access Point (NSAP) address. NSAP is the notation for a network device that supports the ISO Connectionless Network Protocol (CLNP). Without getting into the details of NSAP addresses, which never really caught on, the NSAP resource record functions equivalently to an A record for IPv4 and AAAA for IPv6. It provides a destination address for a queried hostname.

Owner	TTL	Class	Type	RData
Host domain name	TTL	IN	NSAP	NSAP Address
nsap-host.ipamww.com.	86400	IN	NSAP	47.0005.09.d78d01.1010.0ffe.0011...00

NSAP-PTR—Network Service Access Point Reverse Record. The NSAP-PTR record type performs the equivalent pointer record functionality for NSAP addresses, linking an NSAP address suffix to a host domain name. The nsap.int domain serves as the corresponding reverse TLD. As with IP address based pointer records, the NSAP address must be reversed, and dots inserted between each digit. Finally, the nsap.int. suffix is added.

Owner	TTL	Class	Type	RData
NSAP Address Reversed	TTL	IN	NSAP-PTR	Host domain name
0.0...1.1.0.0.e.f.f.0.0.1.0.1.1.0.d.8.	86400	IN	NSAP-PTR	nsap-host.ipamww.com.
7.d.9.0.5.0.0.0.7.4.nsap.int.				

PX—Pointer for X.400. The PX resource record is defined in RFC 2163 (121) and is intended to provide a mapping between DNS domain names and an X.400 address for email address mapping. X.400 is an OSI standard for messaging or email, though today most systems use the Simple Mail Transfer Protocol. This resource record type is useful for networks containing SMTP-to-x.400 email gateways, referred to as MIXER (MIME Internet X.400 Enhanced Relay) gateways. The X.400 address is formatted using the Originator/Recipient (O/R) convention.

Owner	TTL	Class	Type			RData
Domain name	TTL	IN	PX	Preference	DNS domain	X.400 mapping
ipamww.com.	86400	IN	PX	10	ipamww.com.	O = company.PRMD-netx.ADMD.C = tv.

X25—X.25 PSDN Address Record (Experimental). This is an experimental resource record and is not widely used, as X.25 packet switched data networks (PSDNs) are not widely in-use today. It has a number of possible applications

- document the addresses to use in static configurations of IP-to-X.25 and SMTP-to-X.25;
- automatically associate an IP address to PSDN address; and
- configure names to X.25 PSDN addresses.

It also provides a function similar to ARP for wide area nonbroadcast networks.

Owner	TTL	Class	Type	RData
Host domain name	TTL	IN	X25	PSDN Address
x25-host.ipamww.com.	86400	IN	X25	31161700956

RT—Route Through. The Route Through resource record was defined in RFC 1183 (108) and is used to denote a proxy or alternative destination to which to route traffic for hosts without a direct network link. Multiple route through hosts can be identified, each with associated preference values, much like the MX resource record.

Owner	TTL	Class	Type		RData
Host domain name	TTL	IN	RT	Preference	Proxy Hostname
host.ipamww.com.	86400	IN	RT	10	proxy.ipamww.com.

10.4.5 The Null Record Type

NULL. The NULL resource record type is experimental and enables specification of up to 65,535 bytes of "anything." It is usually ignored and not widely used.

Owner	TTL	Class	Type	RData
Host domain name	TTL	IN	NULL	Up to 65,535 bytes of "anything"
host.ipamww.com.	86400	IN	NULL	"Ignore this NULL resource record!"

10.5 EXPERIMENTAL NAME–ADDRESS LOOKUP RECORDS

10.5.1 IPv6 Address Chaining—The A6 Record (Experimental)

Given the sheer length of IPv6 addresses, the IETF had considered an iterative approach to resolving hostnames to IPv6 addresses. The A6 record, defined in RFC 2874 (122), intended to map a host domain name to a portion (or all) of an IPv6 address, with pointers for the resolver to iteratively resolve the remainder of the IPv6 address to its full 128 bits. This enabled resolution of the host domain name by starting most commonly with the interface ID, then adding in the appropriate subnet ID, and global routing prefix, essentially resolving the hostname address moving from right to left. The intent was to simplify renumbering of IPv6 networks that may be necessary due to network maintenance, changing of ISPs, or other reasons. Changing the subnet ID for a number of hosts was as simple as changing one record, instead of each host's record.

However, due to the complexity in accurately configuring DNS with the appropriate linkages (and preventing open linkages), this resource record type was changed to experimental status. To illustrate this, the example below illustrates the A6 resource record and how three successive queries would be used to fully resolve. Note that more or fewer linkages could be defined based on individual preference.

Owner	TTL	Class	Type		RData	
Host domain name	TTL	IN	A6	Prefix Length	Address Suffix	Prefix Name
ftp-sf.ipamww.com.	86400	IN	A6	64	::A05F:0:0:2001	sf-net.ipamww.com.
sf-net.ipamww.com.	86400	IN	A6	48	0:0:0:8400::	na-west.ipamwwe.com.
na-west.ipamww.com.	86400	IN	A6	0	2001:DB8:4AF0::	

Note that the RData portion of the A6 resource record contains three subfields. The prefix length indicates the number of offset bits from the start of the address to begin inserting the address suffix bits. Thus, the first listed A6 record with owner field "ftp-sf.ipamww. com." indicates a prefix length of 64 bits, specifying the interface identifier of ::A05F:0:0:2001.

The prefix name field provides a linkage to a second lookup to continue building the entire 128-bit address. In this case, we are linked to the "sf-net.ipamww.com." prefix name, which points to an A6 record with owner field, "sf-net.ipamww.com." The corresponding A6 record indicates a 48-bit prefix length with IPv6 address, 0:0:0:8400::. Note that the full IPv6 address notation is used, including the restriction of a single double colon. This record then points to the na-west.ipamww.com. A6 record, which completes our formulation of the IPv6 address for resolution with its zero offset. Figure 10.6 illustrates this process.

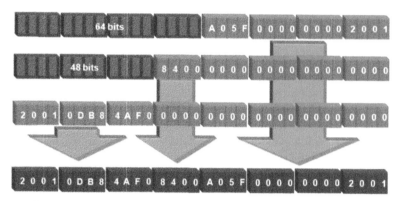

Figure 10.6. Iterative derivation of an IPv6 address using A6 records.

10.5.2 APL—Address Prefix List Record (Experimental)

While A and AAAA records are used to resolve host IP addresses, the APL record seeks to resolve address prefixes or subnet addresses. The following example illustrates a scenario of advertising a set of address ranges associated with a domain or host. The RData portion of the APL record consists of an optional negation character (!), the address family as defined by IANA[*] followed by a colon, then the address in CIDR notation (network/prefix length).

Owner	TTL	Class	Type	RData
Host domain name	TTL	IN	APL	Address Family:Address/Prefix
sf-ftp.ipamww.com.	86400	IN	APL	1:10.0.128/18, !10.16.128.0/18
				2:2001:DB8:4AF0:8400::/56

In the above example, address prefixes associated with sf-ftp.ipamww.com.com are 10.0.128.0/18 for IPv4, not 10.16.128.0/18 for IPv4 and the prefix 2001: DB8:4AF0:8400::/56 for IPv6.

10.6 RESOURCE RECORD SUMMARY

Table 10.1 summarizes the currently defined set of resource records in alphabetical order by resource record type (RRType—also corresponds to valid QType when a querier seeks this type of information from DNS, that is, within the Question section of a DNS message). While not all resource records are IETF standards or even defined within the IETF, most of those that have been assigned an RR Type ID number by IANA are listed here. Current IETF status is provided along with the defining document, which can be accessed for more details.

---

[*]Address family values are maintained by IANA, see http://www.iana.org/assignments/address-family-numbers. Relevant to our example, IANA has assigned family number 1 to IPv4 and 2 to IPv6.

TABLE 10.1. Resource Record and Query Type Summary

RRType (or QType)	RR Purpose (i.e., RData Contents)	RR Type ID	IETF Status	Defining Document
A	IPv4 address for a given hostname	1	Standard	RFC 1035 (99)
AAAA	IPv6 address for a given hostname	28	Draft Standard	RFC 3596 (123)
A6	IPv6 address or portion thereof for iterative IPv6 address resolution for a given hostname	38	Experimental	RFC 2874 (122)
AFSDB	Server hostname for a given AFS and DCE domain	18	Experimental	RFC 1183 (108)
APL	Address prefix lists for a given domain	42	Experimental	RFC 3123 (124)
ATMA	Asynchronous Transfer Mode (ATM) address for a host	34	Not Submitted	ATM Name System Specification by the ATM Forum (125)
CERT	Certificate or Certificate Revocation List	37	Standards Track	RFC 4398 (116)
CNAME	Alias hostname for a host	5	Standard	RFC 1035 (96)
DHCID	Associates a DHCP client's identity with a DNS name	49	Standards Track	RFC 4701 (126)
DLV	Authoritative zone signature for a trust anchor	32769	Informational (DNSSEC)	RFC 4431 (115)
DNAME	Alias domain name	39	Proposed Standard	RFC 2672 (107)
DNSKEY	Authoritative zone signature within a chain of trust	48	Standards Track (DNSSEC)	RFC 4034 (114)
DS	Signature for delegated child zone	43	Standards Track (DNSSEC)	RFC 4034 (114)
GID	Group ID	102	RESERVED	IANA-Reserved
GPOS	Lat./long./altitude for a given host - superseded by LOC	27	Experimental	RFC 1712 (119)
HINFO	CPU and OS information for a host	13	Standard	RFC 1035 (99)
HIP	Host Identity Protocol	55	Experimental	RFC 5205 (127)
IPSECKEY	Public key for a given DNS name for use with IPSec	45	Proposed Standard	RFC 4025 (117)

(continued)

TABLE 10.1. Resource Record and Query Type Summary (*Continued*)

RRType (or QType)	RR Purpose (i.e., RData Contents)	RR Type ID	IETF Status	Defining Document
ISDN	Integrated Services Digital Network (ISDN) address and subaddress for a given host	20	Experimental	RFC 1183 (108)
KEY	Superseded by DNSKEY within DNSSEC but still used by SIG(0) and TKEY	25	Proposed Standard	RFC 2536 (128)
KX	Intermediary domain to obtain a key for a host in given domain	36	Informational	RFC 2230 (129)
LOC	Lat./long./altitude and precision for a given host	29	Uncommon	RFC 1876 (120)
MB	Mailbox name for a given email ID	7	Experimental	RFC 1035 (99)
MD	Mail delivery host for a given domain	3	Obsolete	RFC 1035 (99)
MF	Host that will accept mail for forwarding to a given domain	4	Obsolete	RFC 1035 (99)
MG	Mail group mailbox name for a given email ID	8	Experimental	RFC 1035 (99)
MINFO	Mailbox names for sending account requests or error reports for a given mailbox name	14	Experimental	RFC 1035 (99)
MR	Alias for a mailbox name	9	Experimental	RFC 1035 (99)
MX	Mail exchanger for email host resolution	15	Standard	RFC 1035 (99)
NAPTR	Uniform resource identifier for a generic string used for DDDS, ENUM applications	35	Standards Track	RFC 3761 (111)
NS	Name server for a given domain name	2	Standard	RFC 1035 (99)
NSAP	Network Services Access Point address for a host	22	Uncommon	RFC 1706 (130)
NSAP-PTR	Hostname for a given NSAP address	23	Uncommon	RFC 1706 (130)
NSEC	Authenticated confirmation or denial of existence of a resource record set for DNSSEC	47	Standards Track (DNSSEC)	RFC 4034 (114)

TABLE 10.1. Resource Record and Query Type Summary (*Continued*)

RRType (or QType)	RR Purpose (i.e., RData Contents)	RR Type ID	IETF Status	Defining Document
NSEC3	Authenticated denial of existence of a resource record set for DNSSEC (without trivial zone enumeration obtainable with NSEC)	50	Standards Track (DNSSEC)	RFC 5155 (131)
NSEC3 PARAM	NSEC3 parameters used to calculate hashed owner names	51	Standards Track (DNSSEC)	RFC 5155 (131)
NULL	Up to 65,535 bytes of anything for a given host	10	Experimental	RFC 1035 (99)
NXT	Superseded by NSEC	30	Obsolete (DNSSEC)	RFC 3755 (132)
PTR	Hostname for a given IPv4 or IPv6 address	12	Standard	RFC 1035 (99)
PX	X.400 mapping for a given domain name	26	Uncommon	RFC 2163 (121)
RP	Email address and TXT record pointer for more info for a host	17	Experimental	RFC 1183 (108)
RRSIG	Signature for a resource record set of a given domain name, class and RR Type	46	Standards Track (DNSSEC)	RFC 4034 (114)
RT	Proxy hostname for a given host that is not always connected	21	Experimental	RFC 1183 (108)
SIG	Superseded by RRSIG within DNSSEC; used by SIG(0) and TKEY	24	Proposed Standard	RFC 2536 (128)
SOA	Authority information for a zone	6	Standard	RFC 1035 (99)
SPF	Sender Policy Framework enables a domain owner to identify hosts authorized to send emails from the domain	99	Experimental	RFCs 4408 (112), 4409 (133)
SRV	Host providing specified services in a domain	33	Standards Track	RFC 2782 (134)
SSHFP	Secure Shell fingerprints enables verification of SSH host keys using DNSSEC	44	Standards Track	RFC 4255 (135)

(*continued*)

TABLE 10.1. Resource Record and Query Type Summary (*Continued*)

RRType (or QType)	RR Purpose (i.e., RData Contents)	RR Type ID	IETF Status	Defining Document
TXT	Arbitrary text associated with a host	16	Standard	RFC 1035 (99)
UID	User ID	101	RESERVED	IANA-Reserved
UINFO	User Info	100	RESERVED	IANA-Reserved
UNSPEC	Unspecified	103	RESERVED	IANA-Reserved
WKS	Services available via a given protocol at a specified IP address for a host SRV RR more commonly used today	11	Standard	RFC 1035 (99)
X25	X.25 PSDN	19	Experimental	RFC 1183 (108)

11

DNS SERVER DEPLOYMENT STRATEGIES

This chapter[*] examines deployment strategies and trade-offs for DNS servers. DNS servers generally enable a more role-oriented deployment than DHCP and our discussion will relate configurations to particular roles (external resolution, caching, internal, etc.). Of course the usual trade-offs between budget dollars and proliferation of servers closer to end users applies for DNS as it does for DHCP.

As with DHCP deployments, DNS deployment designs should account for high availability, performance, and security. Using a component building block approach to DNS server deployment in order to segment name space and resolution responsibility can help achieve these general objectives, and we'll discuss such an approach throughout this chapter. Keep in mind that there is no cookie cutter DNS deployment in defining a "one size fits all" architecture. However, by defining role-based server configurations as deployment building blocks, you can select which are applicable to your environment's scale and policies.

---

[*] Much of the content of this chapter is based on conversations with and private documentation by Alex Drescher (165).

IP Address Management: Principles and Practice, by Timothy Rooney
Copyright © 2011 the Institute of Electrical and Electronics Engineers, Inc.

11.1 GENERAL DEPLOYMENT GUIDELINES

Some general principles to keep in mind include the following:

- Deploy a master and at least two slaves as authoritative for any given zone or set of zones.
- For Microsoft Windows DNS server deployments, deploy multiple domain controllers for each domain.
- Deploy authoritative servers on different subnets and ideally, different locations for site-diverse high availability.
- Deploy authoritative servers "close" to clients/resolvers for better performance and less network overhead. For external servers, deploy close to Internet connections; for internal servers, deploy nearer to higher density employee areas.
- For master servers, consider deploying a redundant hardware solution.
- Separate DNS servers should be deployed to handle external queries versus internal queries. By external queries, we mean those queries originating from outside the organization, for example, the Internet. Internal queries are those originating from within the organization.
- Consider separating servers responsible for resolving authoritative data from those responsible for resolving recursive queries on behalf of stub resolvers.

11.2 GENERAL DEPLOYMENT BUILDING BLOCKS

This section provides an overview of common DNS deployment scenarios in terms of component building blocks. We will break down these building blocks into four major categories based on from where a query originates (query source) and on the scope of information being queried (query scope). We define the query source as above, with external queries originating from the public Internet, while internal queries originate from within your organization. The query scope also follows this general breakdown, with external scope dealing with Internet-reachable resolution data and internal encompassing intr-aorganization resolution information. The following table summarizes this categorization using very original category names.

	Query Scope	
Query Source	External	Internal
External	External–External	External–Internal
Internal	Internal–External	Internal–Internal

In addition, we'll discuss a few nonrole-specific scenarios that apply across any building block scenario. These may apply to one or more categories as they provide special resolution or availability features.

A summary of categorized building block scenarios follows:

- *External–External Category.* This category consists of a DNS deployment to resolve queries originating from the Internet for your public (external) resolution information. If you have an Internet connection for a web site, email or for other publically available Internet applications, this category must be addressed in your deployment strategy.

  o *External DNS Server Deployment.* This building block scenario seeks to provide robust name resolution functionality for external clients seeking legitimate name resolutions for the organization's public resources, such as web servers, email servers, and the like, while minimizing exposure to those seeking to attack the DNS infrastructure or infiltrate it for attack purposes. Deployment of external DNS servers features a hidden master server with a number of slave servers. As we'll see, these servers should never be queried by a resolver directly; only by recursive name servers resolving on behalf of resolvers.

- *External–Internal Category.* This category includes queries from outside the organization seeking resolution for internal hosts and resources. Besides providing partners access with a subset of "internal" resolution information, this category should generally be prohibited. DNS server deployment for this category (for partner access) should mimic the external DNS scenario under the External– External Category, though perhaps deployed as a parallel per-partner implementation.

- *Internal–External Category.* This category consists of handling internal queries requesting Internet resource resolution.

  o *Internet Caching DNS Servers.* Internet caching servers are internal DNS servers that cache Internet resolutions for use by internal DNS servers on behalf of internal resolvers. Caching servers can be deployed as a function of or independently of internal resolution DNS servers. In the former case, authoritative servers for internal name space simply escalate queries to Internet root servers down the domain tree to resolve queries, building up a cache of resolved data. The latter case, using independent caching servers, enables other internal-resolving DNS servers to be configured to funnel queries for external data through these caching servers. Doing so enables more control over which servers make external queries while enabling them to build up a substantial cache over time.

- *Internal–Internal Category.* This category deals with internally originating queries for internal resolution information.

  o *Internal Resolution DNS Servers.* DNS servers are required to resolve queries for internal destinations from internal hosts. These DNS servers are configured with authoritative information for the internal name space. Any Internet or irresolvable host queries can be funneled to caching (Internal–External) servers. As with external master DNS servers, internal master DNS servers should be "hidden" for added security and information integrity.

o *Departmental DNS Servers.* For larger organizations, some business units or entities may desire to run their own name subspace within the organization's name space. This scenario features delegation of name space internally but is otherwise a replica of the internal resolution DNS server's case, though for a subset of the internal name space.

o *Internal Root Servers.* Internal root servers can be configured as the authoritative root of the internal name space for resolution of internal queries.

- *General Cross-Role Deployment Configurations.* This category may apply across multiple deployment scenarios.

o *Stealth Slave DNS Servers.* While hidden master deployments are discussed in the external and internal deployment scenarios, another "hiding" approach is to hide slave servers. Masters are generally hidden from direct resolution queries from resolvers as well as other name servers; stealth slaves are available for name resolution from resolvers but are hidden from other name servers requesting iterative queries.

o *Split View DNS Servers.* Deployment of multiple "versions" of a domain can be useful for limiting access to privileged name resolution information. The views feature of BIND 9 enables deployment of multiple views or versions of a domain. The views feature is not currently supported by Microsoft DNS.

o *Anycast Servers.* Anycast addresses enable the assignment of a single IP address to multiple DNS servers. This enables the use of a common IP address to which to send queries for increased performance and availability. The routing protocol in use in the network performs the routing to the nearest server with the anycast IP address.

Based on the size of your organization (and budget), you may choose to deploy an external–external set of DNS servers and an internal–internal set. This is the minimum deployment configuration, though many organizations also deploy dedicated internal-external servers. Larger or more sophisticated deployments may feature elements of other categories as well. The advantage of this building block approach is simplicity and modularity, enabling selective deployment scenarios based on your environment.

11.3 EXTERNAL–EXTERNAL CATEGORY

This category relates to deployments for responding to queries from external sources for the organization's public resolution information.

11.3.1 External DNS Servers

Once again, "external" refers to servicing DNS queries from outside or external to the organization, that is, from the Internet. Resolution services must be provided for general

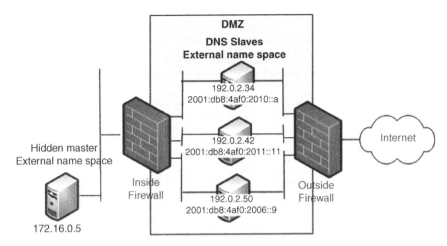

Figure 11.1. External DNS building block example.

access to the organization's web site, email, and other applications, but care must be taken to secure the information integrity of these external servers, given their inherent exposure and potential vulnerability in serving external clients. The recommended approach is to deploy two or more slave DNS servers to service external requests, and to configure these servers with IPv4 and IPv6 addresses. These slave servers may be directly on an external subnet exposed to the Internet, or behind a "first line" firewall within a DMZ, as shown in Figure 11.1.

We've configured each DNS server as dual stack (IPv4 and IPv6) to enable reachability via either protocol. We've placed each external DNS server on its own subnet since we carved up our 192.0.2.0/24 network for external hosts such as these DNS servers. In this case, we're illustrating three /29 subnets on which these servers are deployed: 192.0.2.32/29, 192.0.2.40/29, and 192.0.2.48/29. We've allocated three IP addresses from three /64 subnets derived from our 2001:DB8:4AF0:2000::/56 "external" IPv6 allocation.

Figure 11.1 illustrates a hidden master DNS server deployed behind a DMZ internal firewall and should not be directly query-able from external clients. Since this master server maintains the "master configuration" from which the slave servers transfer, its information integrity must be safeguarded. For this reason, this master DNS server should be configured as hidden, meaning that it cannot be identified by querying other DNS servers. Hiding the master DNS server reduces the risk of an attacker identifying the master server, then attempting to infiltrate its configuration. Imagine the potential impact and embarrassment if an attacker changed your www record to an illicit web site! The mechanics of hiding a master name server entail excluding NS and glue records for the server in this and the parent domain zone file and modifying the master server name ("mname") field of the SOA record in each zone db file. External facing zones are generally static zones, with no dynamic updates, so modifying the mname field can be performed safely in such cases.

Make sure the NS and glue records configured in your parent's domain point to the external slave DNS servers, not the master. This should be arranged through your ISP or domain registrar. For the example in the figure above, you could supply the following NS/glue record information to your parent (e.g., ISP) domain administrator:

```
ipamworldwide.com. 86400 IN NS  extdns1.ipamworldwide.com.
ipamworldwide.com. 86400 IN NS  extdns2.ipamworldwide.com.
ipamworldwide.com. 86400 IN NS  extdns3.ipamworldwide.com.
extdns1.ipamworldwide.com. 86400  IN  A  192.0.2.34
                           86400  IN  AAAA 2001:db8:4af0:2010::a
extdns2.ipamworldwide.com. 86400  IN  A  192.0.2.42
                           86400  IN  AAAA 2001:db8:4af0:2011::11
extdns3.ipamworldwide.com. 86400  IN  A  192.0.2.50
                           86400  IN  AAAA 2001:db8:4af0:2006::9
```

Note that external DNS servers should be deployed on different subnets and on different ISP connections if available, or have your ISP also run a slave server on your behalf. We can restrict DNS queries on our ISP connection firewalls as shown in the examples in Tables 11.1–11.2. We've consolidated the rule for our three /29 subnets into a single /27 for simplicity. In terms of firewall configuration, these are simply guidelines; your policies may be more stringent. Similar allow-* option settings (e.g., allow-query) in BIND or Windows DNS can be defined as access control lists (ACLs) for each server as well as we'll illustrate later in the chapter.

As just mentioned, these servers should be deployed in multiple locations if possible to maximize availability. If you have dual Internet connections, it's recommended that external slaves be deployed in a similar configuration at or near each connection point. Figure 11.2 illustrates a multihomed external DNS configuration. In this configuration, IPAM Worldwide's external DNS servers are accessible via either ISP, over multiple physical links and on differing subnets within the DMZ.

TABLE 11.1. Example Outside Firewall Rules for DNS Messages

Message and Direction	Control	Source Address	Source Port	Destination Address	Destination Port
DNS queries from the Internet	Allow	Any	>1023	192.0.2.32/27, 2001 :db8:4af0:2000/56	53
Responses to DNS queries	Allow	192.0.2.32/27, 2001 :db8:4af0:2000/56	53	Any	>1023
All others	Deny	Any	Any	Any	Any

TABLE 11.2. Example Inside Firewall Rules for DNS Messages

Message and Direction	Control	Source Address	Source Port	Destination Address	Destination Port
Queries from slaves to master (e.g., refresh queries)	Allow	192.0.2.32/27	>1023	172.16.0.5	53
Responses from master to slaves	Allow	172.16.0.5	53, 1053	192.0.2.32/27	>1023
All others	Deny	Any	Any	Any	Any

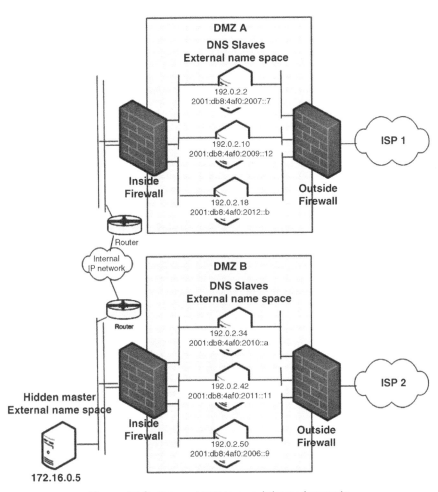

Figure 11.2. External DNS in a multihomed scenario.

Heeding these additional recommendations will also help maintain security of external DNS servers and the information they're resolving.

- Run DNS in a chroot'd jail. This reduces exposure to the server platform and related services that could provide a stepping stone to other attack targets by limiting file system access to a limited set of functionality, not the full root access on the server. This "change root" or chroot configuration runs named in a specified subdirectory, not the root directory. Should an attacker gain access to named, they will have gained access only to the chroot'd directory, not the root directory where access to all file system resources is available. Most appliance products are preconfigured to run DNS in a directory system "jail."
- Keep up with the latest versions of BIND or Microsoft DNS software and subscribe to the bind-announce email list at isc.org or Windows update. Email notifications are sent out upon detection of security vulnerabilities with associated remediation steps and patches. In addition, monitor operating system vulnerabilities that are reported for the platform(s) on which you are running DNS.
- Recursive queries must be disabled. This will enable these servers to process only iterative queries, that is, from other DNS servers, not resolvers. These servers must not perform DNS queries on behalf of anyone. This reduces the processing load of supporting recursive queries and more importantly, reduces the exposure to cache poisoning or denial of service attacks against these servers.
- Configure access control lists on zone transfers as we'll illustrate below.
- Disable dynamic updates and notify's for these external zone(s) if possible. If external name space data changes frequently and requires dynamic updates, restrict update and notify messages between the master and its slaves.
- Configure transaction signature (TSIG) keys to sign zone transfers and updates between the master and slaves as we'll illustrate next. This provides data originator authentication.
- Configure the port number on the master server on which to send notify messages to the slaves if notify is required. This requires specification of the corresponding port on the internal firewall.
- Configure the port number on the slave servers on which to obtain zone transfers from the master. This enables specification of the corresponding port on the internal firewall.
- Secure the rndc control channel by configuring listen-on address/port, allow from, and keys statements. You may even want to disable rndc on these servers.
- Set the version option to a bogus setting. There's no need to communicate what version of BIND you're running and it may provide attackers information on how best to attack the server, especially if you aren't keeping up with newer releases.

11.4 EXTERNAL–INTERNAL CATEGORY

This category comprises external hosts querying information regarding internal (non-public) resolution information. In general divulging information about internal hosts is undesirable and a potential security risk. Even interconnected partners should only have access to guarded information, certainly not the entire internal name space.

11.4.1 Extranet DNS Server Deployment

Inter-partner connections are typically configured as virtual private network (VPN) connections over the Internet or a private network and typically involve a "partner DMZ" or firewall between the partner space and the internal network. The DNS deployment architecture for this category, shown in Figure 11.3, mirrors that of the External–External category though the resolution data configuration is somewhat different. Depending on what resolution data may be divulged to a given partner, the DNS server queried by partner clients must be configured accordingly with such data. Thus, the concept of hidden master and visible slaves supporting no recursion per the External DNS scenario applies.

The partner-specific resolution information may be defined as an "extranet" name space, contained within respective zone files configured on these DNS servers. Additionally implementing views on the DNS servers serving the partner link enables per-partner resolution information if multiple partners access a common DNS server. We'll talk about DNS view configurations a little later but they allow the DNS server to answer queries depending on "who's asking," for example, for Partner A the ftp hostname may resolve differently than the ftp hostname for Partner B.

Each partner's DNS resolution process should be configured to reach these DNS servers to resolve information you wish to divulge about your network. We'll cover this from the complementary perspective of configuring our servers to resolve information for our partner's resolution data in the Internal–External category section.

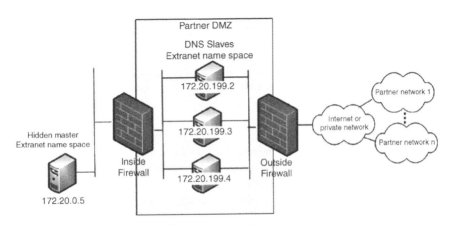

Figure 11.3. Extranet DNS deployment.

11.5 INTERNAL–INTERNAL CATEGORY

11.5.1 Internal Resolution DNS Servers

We'll review a variety of configurations for deploying DNS servers for internal resolution, including a variety of master/slave configurations, caching servers, extranet access servers, and internal root servers.

Internal DNS Servers. Internal DNS servers should be deployed to resolve queries from internal clients for internal host information. We can refer to them as internal TLDs, "top-level domains" since they will be the masters of the top level of the internal name space, for example, ipamworldwide.com., and may delegate subdomains to other internal DNS servers as we'll describe later. The internal master DNS server may be deployed as a hidden master. It's generally a good idea to control the information integrity of master servers by hiding them, as internally initiated attacks account for a large percentage of network security breaches.

Deploying a sufficient number of slave servers, which of course are also authoritative for their respective zone information, enables resolution of client queries, while offloading the master servers to handle only configuration updates. If a master DNS server fails, slaves will continue to resolve queries, but a lengthy outage can compromise the validity and certainly timeliness of the slaves' zone data. The slaves will continue supporting this zone data until the `expire time` is exceeded, after which the server will no longer consider itself authoritative for the zone. Dynamic updates will also not be possible if the master server is down.

An important consideration for Microsoft client environments with client-driven dynamic updates when attempting to hide a master DNS server is that Microsoft clients rely on the MNAME field to identify the master server to update. In this case, using BIND DNS servers, you can still hide the master by changing the MNAME field to point to a legitimate slave server, and configuring the `allow-update-forwarding` option to forward updates to the primary master. In general, we recommend against having clients directly update DNS in favor of having your DHCP servers perform this function. The fewer the entities that can update DNS, the tighter access security can be configured and the fewer the variety of update sources will be able to impact DNS data integrity.

The use of DHCP servers is generally necessary anyway to provide dynamic addressing to laptops, desktops, printers, VoIP phones, and other IP devices. Given that most if not all of these device types will require entries in DNS corresponding to their respective assigned addresses, we need to allow updating of DNS from our DHCP servers. Since we have a hidden master, we could configure the DHCP servers to update a slave DNS server. This server can be deployed with hardware redundancy to minimize any outage time where DNS cannot be updated for DHCP clients.

Figure 11.4 shows an example four-server deployment for our internal ipamworldwide.com name space. As described in the architecture overview, internal client resolvers should be configured with at least two DNS servers. Any number of additional slaves can be deployed in branch offices or remote sites to balance the query load.

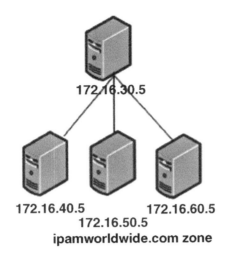

172.16.30.5

172.16.40.5   172.16.60.5
172.16.50.5
ipamworldwide.com zone

Figure 11.4. Internal DNS servers for internal clients.

11.5.2 Internal Delegation DNS Master/Slave Servers

In larger organizations, subdomains can be delegated to particular departments or divisions. Continuing our example, we've created a finance.ipamworldwide.com domain as nondelegated. This means that the configuration and resource records associated with the finance.ipamworldwide.com domain is included in its parent zone file for ipamworldwide.com.

For other departments, separate DNS administrators may desire to manage their own domain information. Let's consider an example. If the Engineering department desires to run DNS for the eng.ipamworldwide.com domain, the team managing the internal top-level domain, ipamworldwide.com, the parent of eng.ipamworldwide.com may allocate a new delegated domain, that is, zone. The NS and glue records for the DNS servers authoritative for this new zone need to be configured on both the authoritative servers themselves and on those authoritative for the parent zone, ipamworldwide.com. Technically, the eng.ipamworldwide.com zone is authoritative for these NS (and glue) records, not the parent, but the parent must configure them to provide referrals down the domain tree.

Likewise, the associated reverse domain(s) could be maintained within the Engineering organization. Let's assume they've been allocated the 172.20.0.0/15 address space from the organization's private space. Note this space does not fall on octet boundaries. Thus, two reverse domains will be required. Since the 172.20.0.0/15 space is comprised of the 172.20.0.0/16 and the 172.21.0.0/16 space together, we'll create these two octet-boundary-based reverse domains: 20.172.in-addr.arpa and 21.172.in-addr.arpa.

Figure 11.5 depicts the example server deployment. As you can see, it looks exactly like that of the internal TLD DNS servers with a master and several slave servers. This is the common deployment configuration of authoritative BIND-based DNS servers.

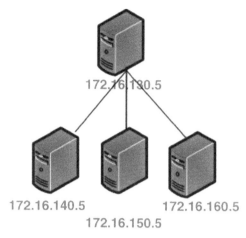

eng.ipamworldwide.com zone
20.172.in-addr.arpa zone
21.172.in-addr.arpa zone

Figure 11.5. Internal name space delegation.

11.5.3 Internal Root Servers

Each of the internal DNS server configurations described so far declare the root (.) zone as type hint, pointing to the root-hints.txt file. So far, we've assumed this file contains the Internet root server NS and A/AAAA records to enable scaling of the domain tree for external information resolution. In environments where Internet access is limited, prohibited, or otherwise generally unavailable, a set of internal root servers can be deployed to authoritatively resolve or more likely, refer queries otherwise not resolved by local recursive servers.

These internal root servers effectively replace the Internet root servers in the organization's other servers' hints files. In other words, these internal root servers are the ultimate authority and last chance for name resolution for internal clients. Thus, this configuration eliminates reliance on Internet name servers, but limits resolution to that information contained within the root servers and their delegated domain servers.

In this configuration, we can use the same configuration files defined above for our internal DNS servers. But we need to define the hints file (root-hints.txt in our case) with a listing of the internal root servers instead of the standard Internet root servers. The hints file contains only NS and glue records for the root servers. If we use a simple example of three root servers, our referenced hints file might look like

```
.                              IN  NS    root1.ipamworldwide.com.
root1.ipamworldwide.com.       IN  A     172.16.1.1
                               IN  AAAA  2001:db8:4af0:f1::1
```

```
.                                    IN   NS    root2.ipamworldwide.com.
root2.ipamworldwide.com.             IN   A     172.18.1.34
                                     IN   AAAA  2001:db8:4af0:a::1


.                                    IN   NS    root3.ipamworldwide.com.
root3.ipamworldwide.com              IN   A     10.251.0.5
                                     IN   AAAA  2001:db8:4af0:c001::1
```

The configuration file on each of the root servers might look like the following:

```
acl internal-nets { 10.0.0.0/8; 172.16.0.0/12; 2001:db8:4af0::/48; };
options {
  recursion no;                          // iterative queries only
  allow-query { internal-nets; }; // allow from internal nets
  allow-notify { none; };            // disallow notify processing
  allow-transfer { none; };          // disable zone transfers
  allow-update { none; };            // disable updates
};


zone "." {
  type delegation-only;
  file "db.dot";
};
```

Each root server is a *delegation-only* type server, as denoted within the root zone declaration block at the bottom of the example configuration file above. The delegation-only type is a special form of type master that only responds with referrals, not answers. Such a multimaster configuration in BIND is possible for static zones like this that change infrequently. Any modifications to the root zone implies a new or modified top-level domain assignment and must be made by updating the db.dot file on each root server. There are no dynamic updates, notify's, or zone transfers. All changes must be made by administrator modification of the db.dot file and requires a coordinated loading of the modified zone file on all masters to place it into service synchronously.

The following illustrates a portion of the example db.dot file, which contains resolution data for the internal root zone.

```
$TTL 1d
. IN SOA dns1.ipamworldwide.com. dnsadmin.ipamworldwide.com (
             1         // serial number
```

```
                    2h        // refresh interval of 2 hours

                    30m       // retry after 30 minutes

                    1w        // expire after 1 week

                    1d );     // negative caching TTL of 1 day

ipamworldwide.com.            IN NS dns1.ipamworldwide.com.

                              IN NS dns2.ipamworldwide.com.

                              IN NS dns3.ipamworldwide.com.

                              IN NS dns4.ipamworldwide.com.

partner.net                   IN NS dns-par1.ipamworldwide.com.

                              IN NS dns-par2.ipamworldwide.com.

. . .

16.172.in-addr.arpa           IN NS    dns1.ipamworldwide.com.

                              IN NS    dns2.ipamworldwide.com.

. . .

0.f.a.4.8.b.d.0.1.0.0.2.ip6.arpa IN NS dns1.ipamworldwide.com.

                                 IN NS dns2.ipamworldwide.com.

. . .

dns1.ipamworldwide.com.         IN   A   172.16.40.5

dns2.ipamworldwide.com.         IN   A   172.16.50.5

. . .

dns-par1.ipamworldwide.com.     IN   A   172.20.199.2

dns-par2.ipamworldwide.com.     IN   A   172.20.199.3
```

Referrals to other DNS servers we've configured previously enable authoritative resolution of queries. Here, any queries falling within ipamworldwide.com, including eng.ipamworldwide.com, will be sent to our internal authoritative servers. Note that we do not include the 172.16.30.5 server in this list as this is a hidden server.

Any resolutions requiring external, for example, partner extranet DNS servers would require corresponding entry in the hints file as well to refer to internal partner-facing servers. In our example above, access to the partner.net domain and subdomains would be referred to authoritative DNS servers dns-par1.ipamworldwide.com or dns-par2.ipamworldwide.com. As we'll discuss under the next category, these servers may be configured as *stub* servers for the partner.net zone; alternatively, direct referral to the partner.net DNS servers may be used on these entries within the root zone file. The bottom line is that these root servers can delegate top-level domains to other DNS servers, which must in turn be configured to resolve authoritatively for the corresponding domains and subdomains.

11.5.4 Stealth Slave DNS Servers

Stealth slave DNS servers as so called due to the lack of NS and glue records for the server in the parent zone as we just observed for the 172.16.30.5 server in the previous section; hence, this hidden name server is not identified via NS queries. We've used this configuration to hide a master server, but this can equally apply to slave servers. Thus, when traversing the domain tree, other DNS servers will not query this hidden server for resolution, as it will not be "advertised" in the parent zone's referrals.

This type of configuration may be deployed for a slave server in order to reduce inter-server traffic or to control such traffic to a fixed combination of resolvers and other servers. Local resolvers can be configured to query a stealth slave server. Other than removing the stealth slave server's NS and glue records, the configuration is equivalent to that of a normal slave server.

11.5.5 Multi-tiered Server Configurations

Deploying hidden masters can help reduce attack exposure to the server that is master for a set of zones. This enables resolvers and other servers to query slave servers, which are also authoritative for configured zones. But in some cases, it is desirable to add a third layer to supplement the two-tier master-slave model. This upper level tier would feature a master DNS server, perhaps master for all internal name space that can in effect provide the true master database of DNS information for an organization. This scenario is illustrated in Figure 11.6.

Let's call this top-level DNS server a Tier 1 server. It is configured with all zones as type master. Our former master servers, 172.16.30.5 and 172.16.130.5, which we'll refer to as Tier 2 servers, are now configured as slaves, pulling zone transfers from our Tier 1 master. The set of original slave servers, at Tier 3, remain as such and continue to pull zone transfers from their respective Tier 2 servers. These Tier 2 servers, though slaves, are configured within the `masters` statement of each Tier 3 server's zone statements. Thus, no changes are required in the configuration of our Tier 3 servers. However, our Tier 2 servers must be modified as slaves for each configured zone with the Tier 1 server identified as each zone's master. The Tier 1 server is referred to as the *primary master* in this configuration, as this is the server on which zone updates may be made directly, with zone transfers to Tier 2 and Tier 3 successively to update all authoritative servers accordingly.

11.6 INTERNAL–EXTERNAL CATEGORY

This category of deployment scenarios addresses DNS resolutions for information external to an organization by resolvers within the organization.

11.6.1 Hybrid Authoritative/Caching DNS Servers

Most authoritative recursive DNS servers cache resolution information they receive during the query resolution process, on behalf of resolvers, so most authoritative

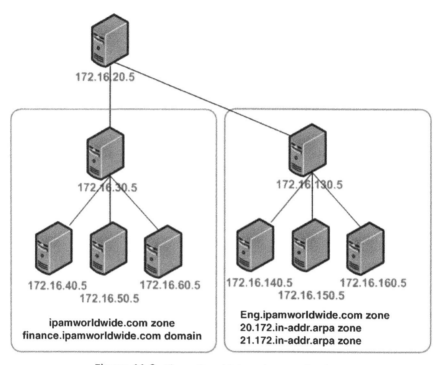

Figure 11.6. Three-tiered internal server structure.

servers are technically "hybrid" servers. The internal server configurations we've discussed so far fall into this scenario: they attempt to resolve from authoritative information and failing that, escalate to Internet (or internal) root servers. For small to modest sized organizations with a handful of internal DNS servers, this configuration works well.

A concern arises however if several (defined by personal tolerance but about 10 or more) such servers perform these Internet queries. DNS resolutions require IP traffic outbound from the organization to the Internet, which may increase exposure from a security policy perspective. And many servers may issue redundant queries for the same resolution information, reducing efficiencies. Therefore, our next section highlights the use of a set of dedicated caching servers through which all outbound queries can be issued.

11.6.2 Dedicated Caching Servers

Dedicated caching servers can serve as funnel points to resolve queries from internal hosts for information outside of the internal name space. Our internal servers will resolve ipamworldwide.com. queries for internal clients, but Internet web sites and email addresses will require resolution using DNS servers supporting respective name

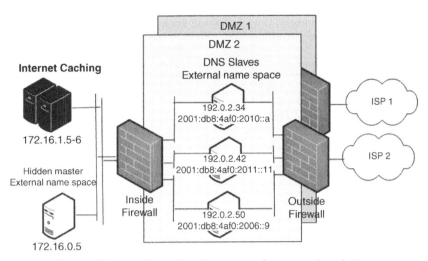

Figure 11.7. Addition of caching servers for external resolution.

spaces. The deployment of dedicated caching servers helps reduce outbound queries and simplifies configuration of firewalls for Internet DNS queries from internal sources. Other name servers within the organization will *forward* queries to these caching name servers when they are unable to resolve directly from authoritative configuration or their own cache.

Dedicated caching servers should be deployed in a high availability configuration, due to the reliance on this server for resolving Internet queries on behalf of internal hosts. Since these caching servers will frequently send and receive Internet traffic, they should be deployed close to Internet connections. Adding this to our previous external DNS figure, Figure 11.7 illustrates deployment of a high availability pair within the internal network but relatively close to the Internet connection. If you have two diverse Internet connections, it's a good idea to deploy a server or pair near each connection, though only one pair is shown in Figure 11.7.

While the external servers resolve queries for your public information for external queriers, the caching servers resolve external information on behalf of your internal clients. The Internet Caching name servers' IP addresses need to be added to the firewall permit lists to enable resolution of Internet hostnames for internal clients. The use of one or a small number of such name servers enables specification of only these few addresses instead of every DNS server address within the organization that would otherwise execute iterative queries.

Since the server is caching responses for all internal clients, the resolution efficiency tends to be higher as the server will be more likely to have query response information in its cache over time. However, vulnerability to cache poisoning and the use of inaccurate or malicious resolution information can create misdirected application connections. Make sure your firewall does not derandomize UDP port numbers used in outbound DNS queries. Also consider configuring DNSSEC validation options (trusted keys) on these

T A B L E 11.3. Example Updated Outside Firewall Configuration for DNS Messages

Message and Direction	Control	Source Address	Source Port	Destination Address	Destination Port
DNS queries from the Internet	Allow	Any	>1023	192.0.2.32/27	53
Responses to DNS queries	Allow	192.0.2.32/27	53	Any	>1023
Internet caching server queries	Allow	NAT {172.16.1.5}	>1023	Any	53
Responses to Internet caching server queries	Allow	Any	53	NAT {172.16.1.5}	>1023
All others	Deny	Any	Any	Any	Any

T A B L E 11.4. Example Updated Inside Firewall Configuration for DNS Messages

Message and Direction	Control	Source Address	Source Port	Destination Address	Destination Port
Queries from slaves to master (e.g., refresh queries)	Allow	192.0.2.32/27	>1023	172.16.0.5	53
Responses from master to slaves	Allow	172.16.0.5	53, 1053	192.0.2.32/27	>1023
Internet caching server queries	Allow	172.16.1.5	>1023	Any	53
Responses to Internet caching server queries	Allow	Any	53	172.16.1.5	>1023
All others	Deny	Any	Any	Any	Any

servers as we'll discuss in Chapter 13. The firewall example configuration we discussed earlier could be updated as shown in Tables 11.3 and 11.4. We use "NAT{172.16.1.5}" to denote the IP address resulting from NAT'ing the caching server's IP address. One such entry should be made for each server.

Important aspects of the caching DNS server configuration include the following:

- As a caching server, the server is not authoritative for any zones. The only zone file to configure (or simply include) on this server is the root-hints.file.
- Allow queries from internal sources only.
- Disallow dynamic updates and zone transfers.
- Cache management options can be used based on server resources and caching policies.

- Keep caching servers updated with security patches and upgrades as they are exposed to cache poisoning and other "man-in-the-middle" attacks. This is discussed in the next chapter.
- Configure trusted or managed keys if DNSSEC validation is desired (details in Chapter 13)
- Other internal DNS servers will forward queries they cannot resolve through configuration or cache to these Internet caching servers.

Caching Server Configuration Example. An example named.conf configuration for this type of server follows:

```
acl internal-nets { 10.0.0.0/8; 172.16.0.0/12;
    2001:db8:4af0::/48; } ;
options {
  directory "/opt/named/dns/etc";
  recursion yes;
  version "hidden";
  allow-query { internal-nets; };
  allow-transfer { none; };
  allow-update { none; };
};
zone "." {
      type hint;
      file "Internet-root-hints.file";
};
```

The "Internet-root-hints.file" file should be the standard NIC root hints file pointing to the Internet root DNS servers. As this server builds up its cache, it will respond to internal queries using the cache first, then querying down the domain tree as appropriate starting with the root servers.

Resulting Internal Server Configuration Changes. Given the change in strategy from escalating nonauthoritative resolutions to Internet (or internal) roots to the use of caching servers, the following configuration changes are required for all Internal–Internal Category server configurations we've discussed thus far.

- Remove the following root zone statement block referring to the hints file

```
zone "." {
    type hint
    file root-hints.txt
}
```

- Enable forwarding to the caching servers instead of using the hints file. This is accomplished by inserting the following statements into the options{} block of each server's named.conf file

```
options {
. . .
    forwarders { 172.16.1.5; 172.16.1.6;};
    forward only;
. . .
}
```

This configuration instructs the DNS server to forward all queries to our caching servers. Forwarding can be configured at the global level as illustrated above, at a per-zone level and at a global level with zone-level exceptions by entering a blank forwarders statement (forwarders {};) within the respective zone statement block.

Considering our 172.16.40.5 slave server configuration, we can update its named. conf file by removing the root zone block and adding our two forwarding statements as described above. Then we can exempt the ipamworldwide.com zone from forwarding by inserting our blank forwarders statement within the zone block as follows:

```
zone "ipamworldwide.com" {
    type slave;
    forwarders { };
    masters { 172.16.30.5 ; };
    file "bak.ipamworldwide.com";
};
```

With this configuration, queries for resource records within the ipamworldwide.com domain will be resolved by the server itself; other queries will be forwarded to our Internet caching servers.

Another twist on this configuration involves retaining the root zone and hints file configuration on each server while changing the forward only; statement to forward first; within the named.conf file. This configures the server to attempt to resolve the query initially using forwarding, but failing resolution, to use alternative means such as resolving via the root servers. The forward only; statement instructs the server to forward as the first and last resort for resolution.

11.6.3 Extranet Resolution Servers

This scenario includes configuring internal DNS servers to resolve queries from internal clients for extranet partner information. This configuration is the complement of the extranet scenario we discussed in the External–Internal Category. In this particular scenario, there are three configuration possibilities.

Extranet Forward Zone. Building on our discussion of forwarding from the previous section, we can define queries bound for the partner's domain as a zone of type forward. All queries received by the internal DNS servers for resolutions within the partner's domain would be forwarded to the specified partner DNS servers. To implement this scenario for our partner's domain, let's say partner.net, we declare this zone within our named.conf file as follows:

```
zone "partner.net" {
    type forward;
    forwarders { 192.168.100.5; 192.168.200.5; };
    forward only;
};
```

Extranet Stub Zone. A stub zone is a special form of a slave zone whereby only the NS and glue records for the zone are transferred and maintained on the server, not the entire zone resource record contents. Like a stub resolver, a stub zone is configured with "who to ask" for queries regarding the given zone and not to provide the answer directly as a slave zone would. In the particular case of an extranet link, a stub zone could be created for our partner domain, partner.net.

```
zone "partner.net" {
    type stub;
    masters { 192.168.249.11; };
};
```

Extranet Delegation Via Internal Root. If you're using internal root servers, you can define the partner.net zone as delegation only and refer to the partner's DNS server(s) by configuring corresponding NS and glue records. In our prior internal root zone file example, we referred to an internal set of DNS servers to resolve queries to the partner.net domain. These referenced servers would need to configure this zone as forward or stub; alternatively, the root zone file could point directly to the partner's servers, though this may become a maintenance issue if your partner changes server IP addresses or hostnames.

11.7 CROSS-ROLE CATEGORY

11.7.1 Split View DNS Servers

The views feature of BIND 9 enables deployment of multiple versions of a zone to a DNS server. The server can filter the query based on an address match list on the query source and destination and whether the query is recursive or not. This filtering determines which version or view of the zone will be searched for resolution of the query. Each view is configured with its respective version of the zone file. A common example of using views is for "split DNS," or providing internal versus external versions of an organization's name space. While deployment of a single set of DNS servers to handle both internal and external queries is not recommended, it is a more practical approach for smaller organizations. But views can also be used on internal name space to restrict access to certain host resolutions to particular resolver clients.

In the example that follows, we'll define a new subdomain, `hr.ipamworld-wide.com`, defining two versions of the domain, and then associate these versions with corresponding views on the DNS server. The concept is to provide general access to the hr portal server (hostname `portal`), but restrict access to other hosts within the `hr.ipamworldwide.com` subdomain to only HR users on the network.

The first thing we'll consider is the zone files themselves. Let's create our general or default domain version in a zone file called `db.hr.ipamworldwide.com.default` and another file with broader visibility for HR clients called `db.hr.ipam-worldwide.com.hr`. Note that if the `hr` subdomain is not delegated, two versions of the parent zone file would be needed, one for each view of the subdomain.

Our `db.hr.ipamworldwide.com.default` file would contain a limited number or even just an A record (beyond the SOA, NS and glue records for the zone):

```
portal      IN    A     172.16.4.24
```

Whereas the `db.hr.ipamworldwide.com.hr` file would contain more resource records such as

```
payroll     IN    A     172.16.4.10
benefits    IN    A     172.16.4.14
empdb       IN    A     172.16.4.22
portal      IN    A     172.16.4.24
promo       IN    A     172.16.4.30
```

Note that two versions of the `4.16.172.in-addr.arpa.` domain are required as well, each corresponding to the IP addresses and hostnames exposed in each view. We can use the same `default` and `hr` suffix on the db file names.

```
db.172.16.4.default file excerpt:

. . .

24          IN    PTR   portal.hr.ipamworldwide.com.

. . .

db.172.16.4.hr file excerpt:

. . .

10          IN    PTR   payroll.hr.ipamworldwide.com.
14          IN    PTR   benefits.hr.ipamworldwide.com.
22          IN    PTR   empdb.hr.ipamworldwide.com.
```

```
24            IN    PTR   portal.hr.ipamworldwide.com.
30            IN    PTR   promo.hr.ipamworldwide.com.
. . .
```

Now that we've created our zone files for each version, we can associate them with the corresponding views on the DNS server. Let's use `hrdns.hr.ipamworldwide.com` as our master DNS server. Here's a partial example `named.conf` file for this server:

```
acl human-res {172.16.4.0/23; } ;

view "hr" {
       match-clients { "human-res"; };
       match-destinations { localnets; };

       zone "hr.ipamworldwide.com." {
             type master;
             file "db.eng.ipamworldwide.com.hr";
       };

       zone "4.16.172.in-addr.arpa." {
             type master;
             file "db.172.16.4.hr";
       };
};

view "default" {
       match-clients { any; };

        zone "hr.ipamworldwide.com." {
           type master;
           file "db.hr.ipamworldwide.com.default";
        };

        zone "4.16.172.in-addr.arpa." {
        type master;
        file "db.172.16.4.default";
        };
};
```

Note that the order of view statements within named.conf is important! The first view matching the query will be used to determine which zone file's information will be accessed. Hence we define our default view, which matches all client queries, after the more discriminating `hr` view statement. We stated that this was a partial definition. Special handling is required to properly perform zone transfers to slave servers likewise configured with these views. After all, an update to a resource record related to the portal. hr.ipamworldwide.com host could be interpreted as falling into either view; which one should be updated?

Assuring notifies, updates, and transfers among the correct views requires manipulation of the match-clients ACL as well as the use of query-source, notify-source, and transfer-source statements. By defining the source IP address for each of these functions and applying a corresponding ACL, interserver communications can be funneled to the correct view. In expanding on our example above, we need to modify our "human-res" ACL to also negate the IP address(es) used in the default view's source statements. That is, notifies from the master for the default view need to be blocked from the human-res view, given the importance of order. Likewise transfer requests from the slave for the default view need to be blocked from the human-res view. In addition, the query-source on both sets of servers should likewise be configured.

This is illustrated in Figure 11.8. Using letters to symbolize the *-source* options on each server for brevity, we can visualize that a notify regarding a zone update for View 2

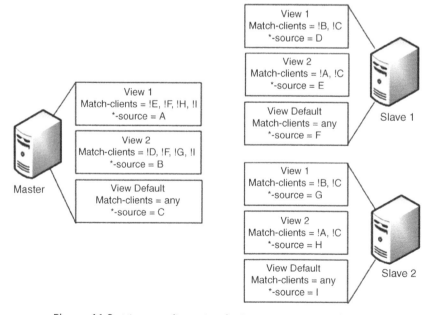

Figure 11.8. Views configuration for interserver communications.

from the Master to Slave 1, would first be matched against View 1 on the slave. The notify from View 2 will use source IP address B. On Slave 1, B is negated within the match-clients portion of the view definition, but falls within the match criteria of View 2 and is thence applied. Likewise, a transfer request from Slave 2 sourced on IP address I for the Default View to the Master would be negated within View 1 and View 2, but applied to the Default View correctly.

Applying this model to our simpler configuration example above with a master name server using IP source addresses 172.16.4.101 (e.g., address A in Figure 11.8) and 172.16.4.102 (address C), and a single slave using source addresses 172.16.5.201 (address D) and 172.16.5.202 (address F) we arrive at the following for the master:

```
acl human-res {!{!172.16.4.0/23; any;}; !172.16.5.202; };

view "hr" {
      match-clients { "human-res"; };
      match-destinations { localnets; };
      query-source address 172.16.4.101;
      zone "hr.ipamworldwide.com." {
           type master;
           notify-source 172.16.4.101;
           file "db.eng.ipamworldwide.com.hr";
      };

      zone "4.16.172.in-addr.arpa." {
          type master;
          notify-source 172.16.4.101;
          file "db.172.16.4.hr";
      };
};

view "default" {
      match-clients { any; };
      query-source address 172.16.4.102;
```

---

[*] That is, query-source and notify-source options on the master and query-source and transfer-source on each slave.

```
    zone "hr.ipamworldwide.com." {
            type master;
            notify-source 172.16.4.102;
            file "db.hr.ipamworldwide.com.default";
    };


    zone "4.16.172.in-addr.arpa." {
            type master;
            notify-source 172.16.4.102;
            file "db.172.16.4.default";
    };
};
```

The following reflects the corresponding slave server's view configuration:

```
acl human-res-slave {!{!172.16.4.0/23;any;}; !172.16.4.102; };

options {
        directory "/opt/dns/etc";
};

view "hr" {
        match-clients { "human-res-slave"; };
        match-destinations { localnets; };
            query-source address 172.16.5.201;
            zone "hr.ipamworldwide.com." {
                    type master;
                    notify-source 172.16.5.201;
                    masters { 172.16.4.101; };
            };

            zone "4.16.172.in-addr.arpa." {
                    type master;
                    notify-source 172.16.5.201;
                        masters { 172.16.4.101; };
            };
};
```

```
view "default" {
      match-clients { any; };
      query-source address 172.16.5.202;
      zone "hr.ipamworldwide.com." {
            type master;
            notify-source 172.16.5.202;
            masters { 172.16.4.102; };
      };

      zone "4.16.172.in-addr.arpa." {
            type master;
            notify-source 172.16.5.202;
            masters { 172.16.4.102; };
      };
};
```

11.7.2 Deploying DNS Servers with Anycast Addresses

Configuring DNS servers with anycast addresses enables multiple DNS servers to utilize a common IP address. Recall that an anycast address is an address assigned to multiple interfaces, typically on different nodes. Anycast is used when attempting to reach any one of the anycast addressable hosts without caring which host is reached. The routing infrastructure handles routing metric updates to track reachability and routing to the nearest host configured with the destination anycast address. Figure 11.9 illustrates an example with three DNS servers configured with anycast address 10.4.23.1.

As depicted in Figure 11.9, Router 1 has three routes to anycast address 10.4.23.1/32, corresponding to our three servers. The closest server is that homed on Router 2 and is two hops from Router 1. The next closest server is home on Router 5 and is reachable in three hops via Router 4. Lastly, the server connected to Router 6 is reachable in four hops via either Router 2 or 4. The logical view from Router 1's perspective is illustrated in Figure 11.10, where the anycast IP address is considered a single destination, reachable via multiple paths.

Anycast Benefits. Deploying anycast provides a number of benefits:

- Simplified resolver configuration
- Improved resolution performance

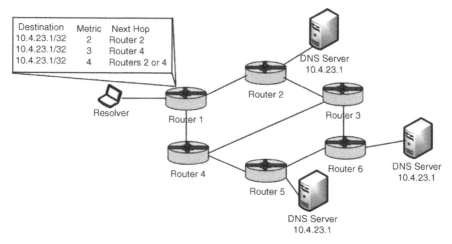

Figure 11.9. Anycast routing table example.

- High availability DNS services
- Resilience from DNS denial of service attacks

Resolvers configured with the DNS servers' anycast address would have their queries routed to the nearest DNS server configured with that anycast address. Thus, regardless of where the resolver host connects to the network, the same anycast IP address may be used by the resolver to locate a DNS server. This localized query process can also improve performance of the resolution process. A query to a DNS anycast address should be routed to the closest DNS server, thereby reducing the round trip delay portion of the overall query process.

The outage of a DNS server can be communicated (by absence of communication) to the routing infrastructure in order to update routing tables accordingly. This requires the

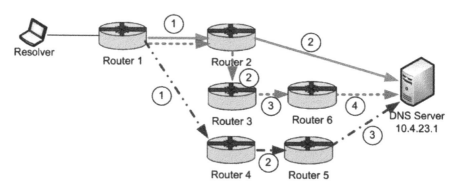

Figure 11.10. Logical routing perspective from Router 1 showing hop counts.

DNS server run a routing daemon using the routing protocol of choice to communicate reachability to the local router. Participation in routing protocol updates enables the local router to update its routing table with an appropriate metric and to pass this on to other routers via the routing protocol. Depending on the deployment of the DNS server, internal or external, a corresponding interior or exterior routing protocol would need to be running on the DNS server. The server simply needs to communicate that its anycast address is reachable. This is typically performed by assigning one of the server loopback addresses[*] as the anycast address and running a routing daemon on one or more ports advertising reachability to the anycast address. It would be especially useful if this routing update was linked to the status of the DNS daemon or service on the server, though application status is not generally considered when communicating IP address reachability.

Deploying anycast affords mitigation against denial of service attacks as evidenced by the distributed denial of service (DDoS) attack on multiple root servers on February 6, 2007 (136). Of the six root servers targeted, the two most severely affected were those that had not yet implemented anycast. The other four root servers, having deployed anycast, enabled the spreading of the attack across more physical servers. Thus, a DDoS attack on the I-root server, which did not have anycast in place, severely impacted the ability of the server to respond to legitimate queries, while the attack on the F-root server, which had over 40 servers sharing the F-root anycast address, distributed the impact of the attack across these servers. This form of load sharing enabled the F-root server(s) to continue processing legitimate queries while suffering a barrage of artificial requests.

Anycast Caveats. While anycast provides many benefits, consider the constraints and caveats of deploying anycast. Because resolvers may query any DNS server configured with the anycast address at a given time, it's important that the resolution information configured on the server be consistent. For example, the implementation on Internet root servers consists of a set of master servers with static information. These root servers do not accept dynamic updates. If anycast is desired for dynamic zones, then each server must have a unicast address in addition to its anycast address[†]. This enables updates to be directed to the master's unicast address, which may in turn notify its slaves via their respective unicast addresses. A hidden master configuration can be used with the slaves configured with anycast addresses.

Another consideration is the requirement to run a route daemon on your DNS servers configured with anycast addresses. While routing of packets to anycast addresses is primarily a routing function, the unreachability of a DNS server host may result in lost query attempts. Such would be the case if static routes are used to configure routers with fixed metrics for the DNS servers configured with a common anycast address. Should a server become unavailable, the serving router has no way to detect this and would not reroute packets destined for the anycast address. Therefore, incorporating a routing

---

[*] The term "loopback address" here refers to the software loopback address commonly implemented in routers and servers as the "box address" reachable on any of its interfaces.

[†] Every anycast server will require a unicast address for administration, but to support dynamic zones, an additional unicast address is required to provide an interface for updates, notify's and zone transfers.

daemon on the DNS server improves overall robustness. Should a server fail, the local router will determine that it is no longer reachable and will update its routing table and those of other routers via routing protocol updates. Internet root servers support BGP, given their deployment on the global Internet, though deployment within organizations will likely require support for OSPF, IGRP, or the interior routing protocol of choice.

Lastly, troubleshooting is a little more challenging when using anycast. Debugging a bogus response from a server's anycast address is difficult given the server ambiguity. To identify which anycast-addressed server is troublesome, it's a good idea to configure the server identification with the BIND server-id option. You can define a string identifier or just use the hostname argument to use the server's hostname. This value is retrievable by issuing a query with qname="ID.SERVER", qtype=TXT with qclass=CHAOS. Using the dig utility, this looks like

dig id.server chaos txt @<anycast-address>

Perhaps a better way is to use the dig +nsid argument with a query so you can correlate a bad response with the server identification in one transaction.

dig +nsid <query> @<anycast-address>

For more details on anycast configurations, see Refs (137) and (138).

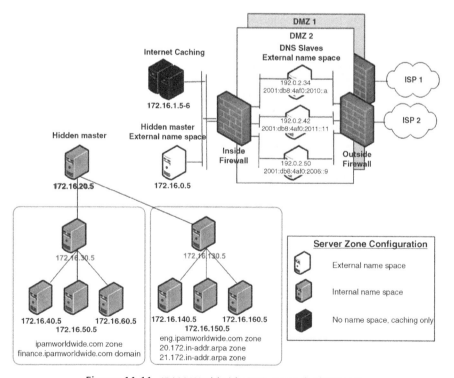

Figure 11.11. IPAM Worldwide DNS server deployments.

11.8 PUTTING IT ALL TOGETHER

We've presented numerous building block scenarios in this chapter addressing a wide variety of configurations, each targeted at addressing a specific DNS resolution purpose. Depending on the size and scale of your IP network, you may choose to implement several building block scenarios for different applications on your network. Just remember that there are no true cookie-cutter answers; each of these scenarios should be evaluated based on your individual needs. The intention here is to provide some guidelines in a modular fashion to help simplify the overall deployment design process.

We've intentionally defined each of these scenario building blocks with its own set of discrete DNS servers. This role-based approach facilitates modularity but also helps with troubleshooting and in managing security policies. Instead of having a common server handle both internal and external resolutions for example, segregating these functions across multiple servers provides physical and functional separation.

Most organizations will deploy at minimum the external DNS scenario (External–External Category) and the internal DNS (Internal–Internal) building blocks. Those with partners may also add the extranet scenarios covering both inbound and outbound query resolutions. Internet caching servers may be deployed to enable funneling of outbound Internet resolutions and to build up rich cache information over time. Views and/or anycast may also be configured based on your needs. The potential number of scenario combinations is endless. Figure 11.11 illustrates one possible incarnation of a holistic DNS infrastructure for IPAM Worldwide.

12

SECURING DNS (PART I)

12.1 DNS VULNERABILITIES

As we've seen, DNS is fundamental to the usability of nearly every IP network application, from web browsing, email, to multimedia applications and more. An attack that renders the DNS service unavailable or which manipulates the integrity of the data contained within DNS can effectively render an application or network unreachable. Clearly protection of DNS data and DNS communications throughout the resolution process is critical. This chapter will focus on potential security vulnerabilities within DNS in general. Specific DNS server implementations may contain additional vulnerabilities, so as with any network service or application, monitoring of operating system, and associated software vulnerabilities is a fundamental operational process.

It's instructive in discussing DNS security vulnerabilities to consider the data sources and data flow within the DNS, depicted in Figure 12.1. Starting in the upper right-hand corner of the figure, DNS servers are initially configured with configuration and zone file information. This configuration step may be performed using a text editor or an IPAM system. For Microsoft implementations, the "IPAM system" may be the Microsoft Management Console (MMC). Configuration of server parameters and associated zones is required.

IP Address Management: Principles and Practice, by Timothy Rooney
Copyright © 2011 the Institute of Electrical and Electronics Engineers, Inc.

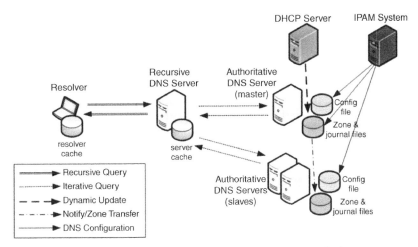

Figure 12.1. DNS data stores and update sources (11).

For BIND implementations, this configuration consists of a named.conf file and associated zone files on the master server. While a server may be master for some zones and slave for others, we'll use the master server terminology in assessing the vulnerability of a particular zone's information. Configuration of slave servers requires creation of the configuration file only, which defines the server's configuration parameters and its authority for particular zones. Slaves transfer zone information from corresponding masters.

Zone information may be updated by external sources as well, particularly DHCP servers. Dynamic updates can be accepted for clients obtaining dynamic IP addresses requiring DNS updating of address-to-name mappings. These updates will typically originate from the DHCP server assigning the address and will be directed to the server acting as master for the given zone. The master will add the update to its journal file and may then notify its slaves of the update, who may request an incremental zone transfer to capture the updated zone information.

Thus, authoritative zone information can be configured on a name server via zone file editing directly or by an IPAM system, and via zone transfers and dynamic updates, yielding several potential data sources and data update communications paths.

Beyond the configuration information and zone files, the third information repository within a DNS server is its cache. Cache information is accumulated through the query resolution process. As query answers are sought and received, corresponding answers are cached by the server. The cached information may be obtained not only from the Answer section of the DNS protocol message, but also from the Authority and Additional sections. These sections supply authoritative server information and information purportedly supplemental to the Answer. This information may include the authoritative servers for the relevant zone and other information related to the query (e.g., the A/AAAA "glue" record for an NS query).

The query resolution flow, beginning on the left of Figure 12.1, begins with the client resolver initiating a recursive query to its recursive server. Recall that the target server to query is defined in the client's resolver configuration, managed manually or via DHCP. The recursive server will issue iterative queries as necessary through the domain tree to resolve the query, generally ending with a name server that is authoritative for the zone corresponding to the query. The master or any of the slaves are authoritative with the zone information. The authoritative server responds with the answer and potentially related information, for example, in the Additional section of the response. The recursive server will generally cache this information, as will the resolver. This cache will be relied upon for similar future queries to improve resolution performance. So it's important to assure data integrity of information returned to both the resolver and recursive server (i.e., both resolvers, the stub resolver in the client and the resolver within the recursive server).

Now let's look at the vulnerability of this information and communications model. RFC 3833 (139) thoroughly discusses various vulnerabilities to the DNS protocol and information integrity. We'll summarize those and some other vulnerabilities here, and then address mitigation strategies.

12.1.1 Resolution Attacks

- *Packet Interception or Spoofing.* Like other client/server applications, DNS is susceptible to "man-in-the-middle" attacks where an attacker responds to a DNS query with false or misleading additional information. The attacker spoofs the DNS server response, leading the client to resolve and cache this information. This can result in hijacking resolvers and hence applications to incorrect destinations, for example, web sites.

- *ID Guessing or Query Prediction.* Another form of malicious resolution is ID guessing. The ID field of the DNS packet header is 16 bits in length, as is the UDP packet header ID. If an attacker can provide a response with the correct ID field and UDP port number, the resolver will accept the response. This enables the attacker to provide falsified results, assuming the query type, class, and name are known or guessed by the attacker. This attack can potentially redirect the host to an illicit site. Guessing a 2^{32} number is relatively easy even with brute force methods.

- *Name Chaining or Cache Poisoning.* This packet interception style attack features an attacker providing supplemental resolution information usually within the Additional or even Authority section of the DNS response packet, thereby poisoning the cache with malicious query information. This may for example attempt to falsify information for a popular web site such as cnn.com, google.com or the like, so when such a query is requested, the resolver will rely on this falsified cached information. When the resolver is asked to resolve such a query, it will access its cache and utilize the malicious information to essentially redirect the client to the attacker's intended destination. An alternative approach to forcing the resolver to access the poisoned cache data is to provide an email link, which when followed, will resolve to the intended poisoned hostname. The so-called Kaminsky DNS vulnerability is a cache poisoning type of attack.

- *Resolver Configuration Attack*. The resolver on the client must be configured with at least one DNS server IP address to which DNS queries can be issued. This configuration may be performed manually by hard-coding the DNS server IP address in the TCP/IP stack, or automatically via DHCP or PPP. This type of attack may alternatively originate from an attacker launching it via a web plug-in, for example. This type of attack seeks to redirect the resolver to an attacker's DNS server to resolve to malicious data.

12.1.2 Configuration and Server Attacks

- *Dynamic Updates*. An attacker may attempt to inject or modify data in a DNS zone by attempting a dynamic update to the server. This type of attack attempts to redirect resolutions from clients for the intended destination to an attacker-specified destination.
- *Zone Transfers*. Impersonating a slave and attempting to perform a zone transfer from a master is a form of attack that attempts to map or footprint the zone. That is, by identifying host to IP address mappings, as well as other resource records, the attacker attempts to identify targets for direct attacks. Attacking a particular host using its hostname as a clue ("payroll," for example) provides an easy target to attempt access or denial of service (DOS).
- *Server Configuration*. An attacker may attempt to gain access to the physical server running the DNS service. Requiring a login and password to access the server locally or remotely is highly recommended to defend against direct server access. Use of secure shell (SSH) is also recommended for remote access. When using an IPAM system, verify that IPAM-to-DNS server communications are secure. Beyond being able to manipulate named and zone information, an attack of this type certainly enables the use of the server as a stepping stone to other targets, especially if this server happens to be trusted internally.
- *Control Channel Attack*. Access to ndc or rndc channels provides powerful remote control capabilities, such as stopping/halting named, reloading a zone, and more. Accessing the control channel and stopping the service thereby denies the service to querying servers and resolvers.
- *Buffer Overflows and Operating System Attacks*. An attacker may attempt to gain access to the server by overflowing the code execution stack or buffer. Without going into details, such an attack calls a subroutine that returns to the main program at a point defined by the attacker. This is one example of several similar types of OS level attacks, exploiting OS vulnerabilities on which the DNS service is running.
- *Configuration Errors*. While typically not malicious (though most attacks are initiated from internal sources), misconfiguring the DNS service and/or zone information may lead to improper resolution or server behavior.

12.1.3 Denial of Service Attacks

- *Denial of Service.* DNS, like other network services, is vulnerable to denial of service attacks, which features an attacker sending thousands of packets to a server in hopes of overloading the server, causing it to crash or become otherwise unavailable to other queriers. The service is rendered unavailable and thus denied to others.
- *Distributed Denial of Service.* A variant of this type of attack is the use of multiple distributed attack points and is referred to as a distributed denial of service (DDOS) attack. The intent is the same, though the scale is larger, potentially impacting several servers.
- *Reflector Attack.* This form of attack attempts to use DNS servers to launch massive amounts of data at a particular target, thereby denying service for the target machine. The attacker issues numerous queries to one or more DNS servers using the target machine's IP address as the source IP address in each DNS query. Querying for records with large quantities of data such as NAPTR, EDNS0, and DNSSEC queries magnifies this attack. Each responding server responds with the data to the "requestor" at the spoofed IP address to inundate this target with a large data flow.

12.2 MITIGATION APPROACHES

Strategies for addressing these vulnerabilities are summarized in the following table. In general, you should keep tabs on vulnerability reports from vendors and perform fixes and upgrades when they become available. Deployment strategies for hidden masters and generally deploying role-based DNS servers are also effective in mitigating attacks as discussed in Chapter 11. We'll discuss DNSSEC in detail in the next chapter.

Vulnerability	Mitigation
Packet interception/ spoofing	DNSSEC provides effective mitigation of this vulnerability by providing: • Origin authentication: verification of the data source • data integrity verification - data received is the same as the data published in the zone file • authenticated denial of existence - a sought resource record does not exist
ID guessing/query prediction	DNSSEC effectively mitigates this vulnerability; in addition, BIND 9 randomizes DNS header message IDs to reduce the chance of guessing its value in a fake response. Since mid July, 2008, BIND also randomizes UDP port numbers on outbound queries to reduce the risk of this vulnerability.

(continued)

(Continued)

Vulnerability	Mitigation
Name chaining/cache poisoning	DNSSEC provides origin authentication and data integrity verification to resist these vulnerabilities; Additional BIND directives for cache and additional section cache enabling and cleaning intervals can also help; transaction ID and UDP port randomization also help reduce the risk of this vulnerability
Resolver configuration attack	Configure DNS servers via DHCP; monitor or periodically audit clients for misconfigurations or anomalies
Illicit dynamic update	Use ACLs on allow-update, allow-notify, notify-source. ACLs may also be defined as requiring transaction signatures for added origin authentication
Illicit zone transfer	Use ACLs with TSIG on allow-transfer; and use transfer-source IP address and port to use a nonstandard port for zone transfers
Server attack/hijack	• Use hidden masters to inhibit detection of the zone master • Disallow recursive queries on masters and on ALL external DNS servers • Keep server operating system up to date • Limit port or console access • Implement chroot
Control channel attack	Use ACLs within the controls statement to restrict who can perform rndc commands; require rndc key
Buffer overflows and OS level attacks	Keep OS updated, limit cache, acache sizes and define cached cleaning intervals
Named service misconfiguration	Use checkzone and checkconf utilities, as well as an IPAM system with error checking; keep fresh backups for reload if needed
Denial of service	• Limit communications using rate limiting and such parameters as recursive-clients, max-clients-per-query, transfers-in, transfers-per-ns, cache and acache sizes; • Consider anycast deployment
Reflector attacks	• Use allow-query/allow-recursion ACLs • Use views if appropriate • Require TSIG on queries if possible

12.3 NON-DNSSEC SECURITY RECORDS

We'll cover DNSSEC in the next chapter but we conclude our pre-DNSSEC security chapter with a discussion of other security-oriented resource record types.

12.3.1 TSIG—Transaction Signature Record

Transaction signature (TSIG), defined in RFC 2845 (102), utilizes shared secret keys to establish a trust relationship between two DNS entities, whether two servers or a client and a server. TSIG provides endpoint authentication and data integrity checking and can be used to sign dynamic updates and zone transfers. TSIG keys must be kept secure and manually configured on each end of the communications.

TSIG keys are used to sign a transaction by including a meta-resource record of type "TSIG" within the Additional section of a DNS message. A meta-resource record, similar to the OPT resource record type used for EDNS0, is used to pass additional information during a query/resolution transaction and is not included in a zone file per se. As such, these resource records are not cached and are computed dynamically for messages requiring signature.

The format of the TSIG meta-resource record is as follows:

Owner	TTL	Class	Type	RData								
Key Name	TTL	ANY	TSIG	Alg. Name	Time Signed	Fudge	MAC Size	MAC	Orig ID	Error	Other Len.	Other Data
k1-k2 ipamww.com.	0	ANY	TSIG	HMAC-MD5.SIG-ALG.REG.INT	232903 32	600	32	p19...	5076	0	0	

The RData fields within the TSIG meta record are defined as follows:

- *Algorithm Name.* The name of the hashing algorithm in domain name format. Currently defined algorithms are defined by IANA as follows:
  - HMAC-MD5.SIG-ALG.REG.INT (HMAC-MD5)
  - GSS-TSIG
  - HMAC-SHA1
  - HMAC-SHA224
  - HMAC-SHA256
  - HMAC-SHA384
  - HMAC-SHA512
- *Time Signed.* The time of signature in seconds since January 1, 1970 UTC.
- *Fudge.* Number of seconds of drift permitted in the Time Signed field.
- *MAC Size.* Length of the MAC in octets.
- *MAC.* The Message Authentication Code that contains a hash of the message being signed.
- *Original ID.* The ID number of the original message. If an update if forwarded, the message ID in the forwarded message could differ from the original. This enables the recipient to utilize the original message ID in reconstructing the original message for signature validation.
- *Error.* Encodes TSIG-related errors (see Table 9.1).
  - BADSIG: invalid key

   ◦ BADKEY: unknown key

   ◦ BADTIME: time signed outside of fudge range

- *Other Length*. Length in bytes of the Other Data section.
- *Other Data*. Blank unless Error = BADTIME, where the server will include its current time in this field.

The TSIG meta-resource record is constructed based on the message to be signed. A digest is created by applying the specified hash algorithm to the message and using this output as the Message Authentication Code field of the TSIG resource record. The TSIG meta-resource record is added to the Additional section of the DNS message.

12.3.2 SIG(0)—Signature Record with Empty Type Covered

Another form of transaction signature utilizes a special case of the SIG resource record, which was devised as part of the initial incarnation of DNSSEC. It has since been replaced by the RRSIG resource record in DNSSEC*bis*. Nevertheless, a special case of the SIG resource record may be used independently of DNSSEC to sign updates and zone transfers. The format of the SIG resource record is shown below.

  The notation SIG(0) refers to the use of the SIG resource record with an empty (i.e., 0) Type Covered field. In addition, RFC 2931 (118) recommends setting the owner field to root, the TTL to 0, and class to ANY as shown in the example below.

Owner	TTL	Class	Type					RData				
RRSet Domain	TTL	ANY	SIG	Type Cov.	Alg	Labels	Orig. TTL	Expire	Inception	Key tag	Signer	Signature
	0	ANY	SIG	0	3	3	86400	20080515 133509	2008011 5133509	30038	ipamww. com.	q8o1...

12.3.3 KEY—Key Record

The KEY record was defined with the initial definition of DNSSEC, but was superseded by the DNSKEY resource record. However, in the meantime, the KEY record was also utilized within SIG(0) to identify public keys used to decode signatures within the SIG(0) record. The KEY record has the same format as the DNSKEY record.

Owner	TTL	Class	Type			RData	
Key name	TTL	IN	KEY	Flags	Protocol	Algorithm	Key
K3941.ipamww.com.	86400	IN	KEY	256	3	1	12S9X-weE8F(le...

12.3.4 TKEY—Transaction Key Record

While RFC 2845 (102) specifies the TSIG standard, which utilizes shared secret keys, it does not provide for a key distribution or maintenance function. The Transaction Key (TKEY) meta-resource record was developed in order to support this key maintenance functionality. This process starts with a client or server sending a signed[*] TKEY query including any corresponding KEY records. A successful response from a server will include a TKEY resource record including an appropriate key. Depending on the mode specified in the TKEY record, both parties may now determine the shared secret. For example, if the Diffie–Hellman mode is specified, Diffie–Hellman keys are exchanged and both parties derive the shared secret that is then used to sign messages with TSIG.

The format of the TKEY meta-resource record is as follows:

Owner	TTL	Class	Type	RData								
Key Name	TTL	ANY	TKEY	Alg. Name	Inception	Expiration	Mode	Err	Key Size	Key Data	Other Len.	Other Data
k1-k2.ipam ww.com.	0	ANY	TKEY	HMAC-MD5.SIG-ALG.REG.INT	232903 32	23300 6564	2	0	2048	9k)2 …	0	

The RData fields within the TKEY meta record are defined as follows:

- *Algorithm Name.* The name of the hashing algorithm in domain name format. Currently defined algorithms are defined by IANA as follows:
  - HMAC-MD5.SIG-ALG.REG.INT (HMAC-MD5)
  - GSS-TSIG
  - HMAC-SHA1
  - HMAC-SHA224
  - HMAC-SHA256
  - HMAC-SHA384
  - HMAC-SHA512
- *Inception.* The time of inception or beginning of validity of the key in seconds since January 1, 1970 UTC.
- *Expiration.* The time of expiration or ending of validity of the key in seconds since January 1, 1970 UTC.
- *Mode.* The form or scheme of key assignment, which may have the following values:
  - 0 = Reserved
  - 1 = Server assignment

---

[*] Yes, that's signed as in TSIG or SIG(0), so the initial condition requires a key, though TKEY provides a means to delete or update keys.

- ○ 2 = Diffie–Hellman exchange
- ○ 3 = GSS-API negotiation
- ○ 4 = Resolver assignment
- ○ 5 = Key deletion
- ○ 6–65,534 = Available
- ○ 65,535 = Reserved
- *Error.* Encodes TKEY-related errors (see Table 9.1)
  - ○ BADSIG: invalid key
  - ○ BADKEY: unknown key
  - ○ BADTIME: time signed outside of inception/expiration range
  - ○ BADMODE: specified mode not supported
  - ○ BADNAME: invalid key name
  - ○ BADALG: specified algorithm not supported
- *Key Size.* Size of the key data field in octets.
- *Key Data.* The key.
- *Other Length.* Not used.
- *Other Data.* Not used.

13

SECURING DNS (PART II): DNSSEC

When I sign a letter or check, I inherently demonstrate my approval and authorization by virtue of my signature.[*] When I sign more important documents, such as a mortgage note, I need to have my signature validated, typically through a notary public. The notary verifies my identity and also validates my signature generally by comparing it with a driver's license or passport signature. By stamping my mortgage note, the notary confirms that it is I that signed the document and therefore my signature is trusted. DNSSEC works in a loosely analogous fashion. A resolver, or recursive server resolving on behalf of a stub resolver receives resolution data along with a signature on the data. As long as I trust the signer, I can validate the data using the signature. The element of trust requires some initial configuration of trust information from the signer in the form of trusted keys, which are used to verify the trustworthiness of the signer of the data received. If I don't trust the signer directly, I need to seek signature validation by seeking an entity that I trust that will "vouch for" the signer. Not that my mortgage company doesn't trust me, but they required validation of my signature!

DNS security extensions, DNSSEC, originally defined in RFC 2535 (140), was modified and recast as DNSSEC*bis*, defined in RFCs 4033–4035 (114, 141, 142). This

---

[*] This basic introduction is from Chapter 9 of Ref. 11 and the high level description therein is expanded in more detail in this chapter.

IP Address Management: Principles and Practice, by Timothy Rooney
Copyright © 2011 the Institute of Electrical and Electronics Engineers, Inc.

recasting was due to scalability issues with the original specification. While still being tweaked to some degree, DNSSEC*bis*, hereafter referred to simply as DNSSEC, provides a means to authenticate the origin of resolution data within DNS and to verify the integrity of that data. DNSSEC also provides a means to authenticate the nonexistence of DNS data, allowing the signature of "not found" resolutions (e.g., NXDOMAIN) as well. Thus, DNSSEC enables detection of packet interception, ID guessing, and cache poisoning attacks on both resolution data and on "not found" resolutions. DNSSEC provides these services through the use of asymmetric public key cryptography technology to perform data origin authentication and end-to-end data integrity verification.

13.1 DIGITAL SIGNATURES

We introduced the concept and process for digital signature generation and verification in Chapter 10 within the context of DKIM, but we'll review it briefly here for convenience. Digital signatures enable the originator of a given set of data to sign the data using a private key such that those receiving the data and the signature, along with a corresponding public key for deciphering the signature, can perform data origin and integrity verification. DNSSEC uses an asymmetric key pair (private key/public key) model. In such a model, data signed with a private key can be validated by deciphering the data with the corresponding public key. The private key and public key form a key pair. Conceptually, the private/public key pairs provide a means for holders of the public key to verify that data was signed using the corresponding private key. This provides authentication that the data verified was indeed signed by the holder of the private key. Digital signatures also enable verification that the data received matches the data published and was not tampered with in transit.

Refer to Figure 13.1. The data originator, shown on the left of the figure, generates a private key/public key pair and utilizes the private key to sign the data. The first step in signing the data is to produce a hash of the data, sometimes also referred to as a digest. Hashes are one-way functions[†] that scramble data into a fixed length string for simpler

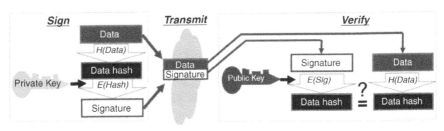

Figure 13.1. Digital signature creation and verification process (11).

[†] A one-way function means that the original data is not uniquely derivable from the hash. That is, one can apply an algorithm to create the hash, but there is no inverse algorithm to perform on the hash to arrive at the original data.

manipulation, and represent a "fingerprint" of the data. This means that it is very unlikely that another data input could produce the same hash value. Thus, hashes are often used as checksums but don't provide any origin authentication (anyone knowing the hash algorithm can simply hash arbitrary data). Common hash algorithms include HMAC-MD5, RSA-SHA-1, and RSA-SHA-256. The hash is encrypted using the private key to produce the signature. The encryption algorithm is fed the hash and the private key to produce the signature.

Both the data and its associated signature are transmitted to the recipient. Note that the data itself is not encrypted, merely signed. The recipient must have access to the public key that corresponds with the private key used to sign the data. In some cases a secure (trusted) public key distribution system such as a public key infrastructure (PKI) is used to make public keys available. In the case of DNSSEC, public keys are published within DNS, along with the resolution information and corresponding signature.

The recipient computes a hash of the received data, as did the data originator. The recipient applies the encryption algorithm to the received signature using the originator's public key. This operation is the inverse of the signature production process and produces the original data hash as its output. The output of this decryption, the original data hash, is compared with the recipient's computed hash of the data. If they match, the data has not been modified and the private key holder signed the data. If the private key holder can be trusted, the data can be considered validated.

13.2 DNSSEC OVERVIEW

DNSSEC utilizes this asymmetric key pair cryptographic approach to provide data origin authentication and end-to-end data integrity assurance. Any attempt to spoof or otherwise modify data en route to the destination will be detected by the recipient, that is, the resolver or more typically, its recursive/caching DNS server on its behalf. This feature makes DNSSEC an effective mitigation strategy against man-in-the-middle and cache poisoning attacks.

The original DNSSEC*bis* specifications do not account for a secure key distribution system, so one or more trusted keys have to be manually configured on the resolver or recursive name server.[‡] However, a subsequent specification, RFC 5011 (141), defines a means to ease this process by authenticating new and revoked trusted keys based on a manually configured initial key. This initial key serves as the "initial condition" in rolling forward over time with new, revoked, and deleted keys. We'll talk about this automated trusted key update process a bit later. Whether configured manually or updated automatically, each trusted key identifies the public key corresponding to a given trusted zone as authorized by the zone administrator.

This is analogous to the bank notary being trusted by the bank to validate my identity. After all, any imposter may sign invalid zone data with a private key and publish the

---

[‡] Pragmatically, the term "resolver" in the context of DNSSEC refers to the resolver function of the recursive server, which resolves the queried information and verifies signatures as well. Considering our deployment example from Chapter 11, the Internet Caching servers would perform this signature validation function.

corresponding data, signatures, and public key. Thus, the recursive server must be configured *a priori* with a key or set of keys that are trusted corresponding to trusted signed zones. The current public key in use by the trusted zone administrator must be conveyed to the resolver administrator out of band, or using a mechanism other than DNS. With the automed key update process just mentioned, an initial key must be configured for each trusted zone; however, ongoing key updates are performed using the DNS protocol.

A given trusted zone can authenticate a child zone's public key, extending the trust model from just the trusted zone to the trusted zone and its authenticated child zones. Likewise, these child zones can authenticate their children and so on, forming a *chain of trust* from the trusted zone to all signed delegated zones. With the Internet root zone now signed and major TLDs signed or soon to be signed, the chain of trust will emanate from the root trust anchor to TLDs, to lower level signed zones down the domain tree.

Configuration of trusted keys requires creation of a trust relationship with a zone administrator to obtain his/her public key. With a signed root and TLDs, this simplifies the trust model, requiring trust of the root zone and configuration of the root zone trust anchor. In lieu of (really as a predecessor to) using root zone keys, ISC has also created a trusted key registry (dlv.isc.org) as a repository of trusted keys for registered domains to enable "lookaside" validation in acting as a "parent zone proxy," reducing the requirement impact of forming individual relationships with each domain administrator.

While not explicitly required by DNSSEC specifications, operational experience has led to the recommendation that two keys be used per zone a zone signing key (ZSK) and a key signing key (KSK).[†] As we will see later, this streamlines the complex key rollover process while trading off key length security and complexity against nimbly changing zone signing keys as needed. At this point, suffice it to say that the ZSK is used to sign the data within the zone and the KSK is a longer term key that signs the ZSK. Both the ZSK and KSK are each comprised of a public and private key pair. The private keys are used to sign zone information and must be secured, ideally on a secure server or host. The corresponding public keys are published within the zone file in the form of DNSKEY resource records.

The public KSK of the trusted zone is the trusted key[‡] configured in each recursive server, which should match the corresponding KSK DNSKEY resource record published in the respective zone file. The resolved data's signature is validated using the zone's ZSK, and the ZSK is signed by and its signature is thereby validated by the trusted KSK.

If this KSK is not trusted, an attempt is made to check if the parent zone is signed or if lookaside validation is configured. If signed, this parent zone (or lookaside registry) signs its delegation to the child by signing the child's public KSK in the form of a delegation signer (DS) record (or DNSSEC Lookaside Validation, DLV record) in the parent zone. This delegation in turn is signed with the parent's ZSK which itself is signed with the

---

[†] The motivation for this recommendation and discussion of other DNSSEC operational practices are discussed in RFC 4641 (167).

[‡] A trusted key is synonymous with a trust anchor, which is also known as a Secure Entry Point (SEP) into the DNS domain tree.

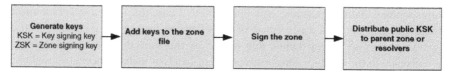

Figure 13.2. Basic DNSSEC implementation steps (11).

parent's KSK. Once again, if these signatures are valid and the KSK matches a trusted key, the resolution is complete and secure. Otherwise, the process continues with the parent's parent zone and so on.

The validation process works up the chain of trust to a matching trusted key, which if found, deems the resolution data validated. Otherwise, it will be considered insecure.

13.3 CONFIGURING DNSSEC

The process of implementing DNSSEC involves creating private/public key pairs, adding the public key information to the zone file to be signed, signing the zone with the corresponding private keys, and distributing the public KSK information to either parent zone administrators or to resolver administrators who trust you and your zone information. Figure 13.2 illustrates the basic process.

Let's now illustrate this basic process looking at the mechanics for implementing DNSSEC. We'll illustrate the process using manual and automated[*] BIND methods and utilities (144), which support DNSSEC*bis* today. Microsoft supports DNSSEC*bis* in its Windows Server 2008 R2 release. We'll demonstrate the implementation of DNSSEC by signing the ipamworldwide.com zone file after we review these steps in more detail.

13.3.1 Generate Keys

Our first step is to generate keys that will be used to sign our zone information. BIND ships with the `dnssec-keygen` utility which provides a simple command line to generate a private/public key pair. It even creates the DNSKEY record! To create a ZSK key pair for our ipamworldwide.com zone, we use the `dnssec-keygen` command:

```
dnssec-keygen –a RSA-SHA-1 –b 1024 –n ZONE –c IN –e ipamworldwide.com
```

This utility is used not only to create DNSSEC keys, but can also be used to create TSIG keys and KEY records. The arguments, all of which are optional unless otherwise specified, within the `dnssec-keygen` utility include

- -a *algorithm*: (required) where algorithm for DNSSEC keys may be
  o RSA-SHA-1

---

[*] BIND 9.7.0 introduced several new key and signature management features to automate many of these steps as we will describe.

    o RSA-SHA-256

    o RSA-SHA-512

    o NSEC3-RSA-SHA-1 (RSA-SHA-1 algorithm with a signal that the zone signed with this key may use NSEC3)

    o DSA (Digital Signature Algorithm)

    o NSEC3DSA (DSA algorithm with a signal that the zone signed with this key may use NSEC3)

    o RSA-MD5

- -b *keysize*: (required) specifies the number of bits in the key. Valid keysizes for each algorithm are

    o RSA-SHA keys 512–2048 bits

    o DSA keys. 512–1024 bits, divisible by 64

- -n *nametype*: (required) identifies the type of key owner. Valid values include ZONE (default, for DNSKEY), HOST, ENTITY, USER, or OTHER.

- -3: use an NSEC3-capable key generating algorithm (NSEC3-RSA-SHA-1 is used if no –a argument is specified). RSA-SHA-256 and RSA-SHA-512 are also NSEC3-capable.

- -A *date/offset*: sets the activation date of the key. The date/offset field is an absolute date/time when expressed in either YYYYMMDD or YYYYMM-DDHHMMSS format (or none to unset) or as an offset from the present time when a " + " or "−" prefix is used with either of these date formats. When not set, and –G is not set, the default is "now."

- -C: option to generate the private key without any metadata relating to creation, publication, and/or activation dates, which may be incompatible with older BIND versions.

- -c *class*: class of the DNS resource record containing the key.

- -D *date/offset*: defines the date or offset from the present time when this key is to be deleted from the zone. The date/offset field is an absolute date/time when expressed in either YYYYMMDD or YYYYMMDDHHMMSS format (or none to unset) or as an offset from the present time when a " + " or "−" prefix is used with either of these date formats. At the specfied time, the key will be removed from the zone, though it will remain in the key repository.

- -e: command option to use a large exponent when using the RSA-MD5 or RSA-SHA-1 algorithms.

- -E *engine*: command option to use crypto hardware (OpenSSL engine) for random number generation as well as key generation when supported. The default is pkcs11 when compiled with PKCS #11 support or none otherwise.

- -f *flag*: sets the Flags field in the DNSKEY (or KEY) resource record; currently, *flag* = KSK is used to create a KSK (sets the SEP bit in the DNSKEY record); flag = REVOKE sets the Revoke flag for this key.

- -g *generator*: specifies a key generator value for the DH algorithm.
- -G: generates a key which is not to be published or used for signing.
- -h: prints a help summary for this command.
- -I *date/offset*: sets the date/offset when the key is to be retired. The date/offset field is an absolute date/time when expressed in either YYYYMMDD or YYYYMMDDHHMMSS format (or none to unset) or as an offset from the present time when a "+" or "−" prefix is used with either of these date formats. When retired, the key remains in the zone but is no longer used to sign the zone.
- -k: indicates that a KEY record is to be created, not DNSKEY; deprecated in favor of the −T option.
- -K *directory*: defines the directory in which the key files will be placed.
- -p *protocol*: sets the Protocol field in the resource record. For DNSSEC, the default value of 3 is used.
- -P *date/offset*: sets the date/offset when the key is to be published in the zone file, though not used to sign the zone. The date/offset field is an absolute date/time when expressed in either YYYYMMDD or YYYYMMDDHHMMSS format (or none to unset) or as an offset from the present time when a "+" or "−" prefix is used with either of these date formats.
- -q: quiet mode, which suppresses output, including indication of progress.
- -r *randomsource*: indicates a source or random data such as a file or character device such as the keyboard.
- -R *date/offset*: defines the date when the key is to be revoked. The date/offset field is an absolute date/time when expressed in either YYYYMMDD or YYYYMMDDHHMMSS format (or none to unset) or as an offset from the present time when a "+" or "−" prefix is used with either of these date formats. When revoked, the "revoke" bit is set in the corresponding DNSKEY resource record, though it will remain in the zone and be used to sign the zone.
- -s *strength*: specifies the strength value of the key, though not relevant to DNSSEC.
- -t *type*: indicates the use of the key to authenticate data (AUTH) and/or to encrypt data (CONF). AUTHCONF supports both functions, while NOAUTH, NOCONF, and NOAUTHCONF negate respective functions.
- -T *rrtype*: specifies an RRType to use for public key creation in resource record format. Valid values of *rrtype* include DNSKEY (default) or KEY.
- -v *level*: sets the debug level.
- *keyname*: (required) the name of the key, generally the zone name, which serves as the owner field of the DNSKEY record.

The five date/offset based options are new in BIND 9.7.0 and provide timing meta data for the key being generated and hence when it is to be used in the zone signing process. Thus, keys can be staged and rolled through their entire lifecycle, consisting of publication in the zone, use for signing zone information, revocation, retirement, and deletion. To summarize these options and their use through a key's lifecycle

- -P. Defines the time when the key being generated is to be published in the zone file, though not used in signing.
- -A. Defines the activation time, when this key being generated is to be used to sign zone data. If this is a KSK and the update-check-ksk option is set to yes, this key will sign the DNSKEY RRSet only. Otherwise, it will be used to sign all zone RRSets, allowing for cases where a single zone key is implemented.
- -R. Defines the time when this key is to be revoked. This defines the date when the revoke flag will be set in the corresponding DNSKEY record. This key (with the revoke bit set) will still be used to sign zone data but resolvers will be on notice that this key is revoked.
- -I. Defines the retire time for the key, after which this key will not be used to sign zone data, though the key will remain in the zone file.
- -D. Defines the time when the key will be deleted from the zone file.

These timing options enable you to define the entire key lifecycle at key generation time!

An alternative key file generation utility first included with the BIND 9.6.0 distribution allows use of the PKCS#11[*] API to interface to a cryptographic token generating hardware device. The dnssec-keyfromlabel utility gets keys from the cryptographic hardware device and generates the public and private key files. This utility accepts the following arguments in exactly the same format as dnssec-keygen plus a new required parameter, indicating the key label.

- -a *algorithm*: (required) same values as dnssec-keygen
- -3: same meaning as dnssec-keygen
- -c *class*: same values as dnssec-keygen
- -C—: same meaning as dnssec-keygen
- -E *engine*: same values as dnssec-keygen
- -f *flag*: same values as dnssec-keygen
- -G: same meaning as dnssec-keygen
- -C—: same meaning as dnssec-keygen
- -h: same meaning as dnssec-keygen
- -k: same meaning as dnssec-keygen
- -K *directory*: same meaning as dnssec-keygen
- -l *label*: (required) label for keys on the PKCS#11 device
- -n *nametype*: same values as dnssec-keygen

---

[*] PKCS#11 is among the family of Public-Key Cryptography Standards published by RSA Laboratories.

- -p *protocol*: same values as `dnssec-keygen`
- -t *type*: same values as `dnssec-keygen`
- -v *level*: same values as `dnssec-keygen`
- -y: allows creation of DNSSEC key files even if the key ID collides with an existing key
- *keyname*: (required)

The meta data timing options discussed above are also supported. Both `dnssec-keygen` and `dnssec-keyfromlabel` return the key name. In our example, the result was

Kipamworldwide.com. + 005 + 14522

The format of the key name follows this convention

- K (for key)
- Keyname (ipamworldwide.com.)
- Key creation algorithm (005 = RSA-SHA-1 in this case)
- Key tag or identity of the key (14522)

The key tag provides a convenient way to refer to keys as we'll see a bit later. Two files were created by `dnssec-keygen` or `dnssec-keyfromlabel` using this name one with extension `.private` indicating the private key and the other with extension `.key`, containing the public key in the form of a DNSKEY record. In our example, the two key files were named

```
Kipamworldwide.com.+005+14522.private
Kipamworldwide.com.+005+14522.key
```

The `Kipamworldwide.com.` + 005 + 14522.private file contains the private key details including the format, algorithm, modules, exponents, primes, and coefficient values such as that shown below for the output of the `dnssec-keygen` command (blank lines inserted for improved readability).

```
Private-key-format: v1.2

Algorithm: 5 (RSASHA1)

Modulus:
x6QAwJiz6hHa/eUI2pGz6rvwEYpJdi1TJH8Uj41DPTmzseCOgFEqB3/dZB0Q
  5LEs1ZetAJJEk4F+WccRKwqnIcGkvIKfTC8hn+gbiBAnadQRFLxNMBs6KB0e+
  yqiNK60sbrn22F8AYRiG3n2rTQndVtkaZep9jbcCqfu/DagB10=

PublicExponent: AQAAAAE=

PrivateExponent:
CWheqbbkIx3kRIa7NyDbdwZYGA83uBtdfnBTu8QyV8/h419T3fyWrWfKo4wi
  Vys9q10Xmumwy/hSLmZJJrzxS6SVwaM/iEunsyyiHedeVKiMeYVlOlvJ3+
  OweKy/59y3drJS+qAm+cbtrhWZheXtzgR78wp2IK+4kHAhZTCYGAE=
```

Prime1:
8YuU4sicmKmu5Cz4IUjvE2kQit5pJPV3yUK04nPz9P0MJFKyCIAdsw2A5HoRn3++
  I5BtDjeQxkD0aFGA4S0fKXQ==

Prime2:
05ZzyiaiZK1JqQMCgT977NZkEuKgXI4seTUL1Wu7Z/FRs/7xHE4oSJrx7siwLOx
  WJKcc4Fo+4erVRHioiOadhAQ==

Exponent1:
Hpy1z37UsfdONCV7Kd/8xu07PslhtbX7EFVGRno/dOrWNp5p64hVhF5tbnNBVz
  ZHRQ+5IZzwMfQ3A3+GjY8QQQ==

Exponent2:
jfw+s9zt8uVMwubwowwxOsjX32GO3VrSPk68+CisiAVxYS8EdTOqvpYps6Vz+
  rJNnnk45urnlqDbWCx2tugyAQ==

Coefficient:
uUC/aKgEvOQymCmMukC4ExTm/7ly2w31V/NMOF2GzC7fc1gYvDZEOX6YNnz5e8
  PRD2bQXCTgsMorRs7PJYI2Cg==

The Kipamworldwide.com.+005+14522.key file is a bit easier to digest, containing our DNSKEY resource record

ipamworldwide.com. IN DNSKEY 256 3 5
      BQEAAAABx6QAwJiz6hHa/eUI2pGz6rvwEYpJdilTJH8Uj41DPTmzseCO
      gFEqB3/dZB0Q5LEs1ZetAJJEk4F+WccRKwqnIcGkvIKfTC8hn+gbiBAn
      adQRFLxNMBs6KB0e+yqiNK60sbrn22F8AYRiG3n2rTQndVtkaZep9jbc
      Cqfu/DagB10=

The interpretation or format of the DNSKEY resource record is depicted below.

Owner	TTL	Class	Type		RData			
Zone name	TTL	IN	DNSKEY	Flags	Proto	Alg	Key	
ipamworldwide.com.	86400	IN	DNSKEY	256	3	5	BQEAAA...	

The owner field defines the zone name. The RData consists of the following subfields

- *Flags*. Indicates that this key is a zone key (value = 256). Currently defined values for the Flags field are as follows. Using the decimal values below, we can see that a ZSK will have a flags value of 256, while a KSK will have an odd value, likely 257.
  - ○ Bit 7. ZSK (Decimal = 256)
  - ○ Bit 8. Revoke Signature (Decimal = 128)
  - ○ Bit 15. KSK or secure entry point (SEP) (Decimal = 1)
  - ○ Other bits. Unassigned
- *Protocol*. Must have a value of "3" indicating DNSSEC (this is the only value currently defined).

- *Algorithm*. Defines the algorithm used in key generation. Algorithms currently supported are encoded as follows
  - Value = 1. RSA-MD5, which is not recommended according to RFC 4034.
  - Value = 2. Diffie–Hellman
  - Value = 3. DSA-SHA-1
  - Value = 4. Reserved for Elliptic Curve
  - Value = 5. RSA-SHA-1, which is mandatory according to RFC 4034.
  - Value = 6. DSA-NSEC3-SHA1
  - Value = 7. RSASHA1-NSEC3-SHA1
  - Value = 8. RSA-SHA-256
  - Value = 10. RSA-SHA-512
  - Value = 12. GOST R 34.10-2001
  - Value = 252. Indirect
  - Values 253–254. Private
  - Values = 0, 255. Reserved
  - Other values. Unassigned
- *Key*. The public key (ZSK or KSK).

We can now repeat the dnssec-keygen command, this time using the −f KSK argument, along with a longer key size, to create our KSK pair.

```
dnssec-keygen −a RSASHA1 −b 2048 −n ZONE −c IN −e −f KSK ipamworldwide.
com.
```

The command line response to this command is the key pair name, Kipamworld-wide.com. + 005 + 06082.

The resulting DNSKEY record was created

```
ipamworldwide.com. IN DNSKEY 257 3 5
    AwEAAdSAwGoUBhtjpE8GLGN4ryt8yEq71DqdE+ij3boe9lmvpM02YZ1/
    AQxoHbyA7NqRr+8dsTM8OrF2yFRbcPly0/9q37T0PqxL5HjAZ8HrDoW9
    R/pC3XyRe9pMzRNr4as+c/xEISfhxzvR84CndF5XvFeh3H0kVDeTb+7Q
    RrG7hnph4P8w4SMg76tBvxHLFmj3OdP8vIUpRAnexEAdclamj1ZSPjLc
    dICzpDvQB/LLsYxx8wx2h0vTvhxZklqmyldPBtIZu2A551VIrU0xgCJx
    DjJGCgBbrplC01tYSdqlA1I2HCL8eV7io/CxnCuSThPlXaPLySojJpXU
    gDomWgVYeo0=
```

Notice the Flags field value is 257 for the KSK versus 256 for the ZSK due to the setting of the SEP flag. We'll refer to the KSK by its keyid = 06082 (from the generated key name) and the ZSK by its keyid = 14522.

13.3.2 Add Keys to the Zone File

Before we sign the zone, we need to include our two DNSKEY resource records within the zone file. Since the key files contain our DNSKEY resource records, you can either cut from the file and paste into the zone or simply use a $INCLUDE statement for each file

```
$INCLUDE Kipamworldwide.com.+005+14522.key
$INCLUDE Kipamworldwide.com.+005+06082.key
```

Don't forget to increment your serial number too. It's a good idea to run `named-checkzone` first, before signing the zone with the `dnssec-signzone` utility.

13.3.3 Sign the Zone

The zone signature process utilizes another BIND utility, `dnssec-signzone`, which performs a number of functions to sign the zone. First, it canonically orders the resource records within the zone. This essentially alphabetizes the resource records within the zone. This facilitates grouping of resource records with common owner name, class, and type into resource record sets (RRSets) for signature application. The other reason for canonically ordering resource records is to identify gaps between RRSets within the zone file and population with Next SECure resource records, which provide authenticated denial of existence of a given resource record within a zone. An NSEC3PARAM resource record must be present in the zone file to generate NSEC3 records during the zone signature process.

After canonical ordering and insertion of NSEC[3] records, `dnssec-signzone` signs the RRSets within the zone file, including DNSKEY RRSets (previously $INCLUDE'd in our example) and NSEC[3] RRSets. The signed zone file contains the original RRSets, canonically ordered and signed with resource record signature (RRSIG) records. The file also includes an NSEC[3] record and its corresponding RRSIG record for each RRSet within the file. The only records not signed within the zone file are NS records for child zones. The child zone is authoritative for this information, not the parent; therefore, the parent does not authenticate their accuracy.

Fortunately the `dnssec-signzone` utility performs all of these steps automatically canonical ordering, NSEC[3] insertion, and RRSIG creation and insertion to render a signed zone. Here's the dnssec-signzone command we'll use to sign the ipamworldwide.com. zone.

```
dnssec-signzone -k Kipamworldwide.com.+005+06082 -l dlv-registry.
net -g -o ipamworldwide.com. -t db.ipamworldwide.com Kipamworld-
wide.com.+005+14522.key
```

The arguments within the dnssec-signzone utility include

- `-3 salt`: generate an NSEC3 chain when signing this zone using the specified *salt* value. The salt is specified in hex and a dash (-3 -) indicates that no salt should be used when generating the NSEC3 chain.
- `-a`: verify all generated signatures.

- -A: set the OPTOUT flag on all NSEC3 records when generating an NSEC3 chain, and do not generate NSEC3 records for unsigned child zones (insecure delegations).
- -c *class*: class of the DNS zone.
- -C: compatibility mode with older versions of dnssec-signzone; generates *−zonename* keyset in addition to dsset-*zonename* upon signing the *zonename* zone.
- -d *directory*: look in the specified directory for the dsset or keyset files to sign the zone.
- -e *end_time*: specifies the date and time when the generated resource record set signature records expire. The end_time may be specified relative to the current time using $+N$, where N is the number of seconds from the current time, or in absolute time using the format YYYYMMDDHHMMSS in Coordinated Universal Time (UTC). When this argument is omitted, the default end_time is 30 days from the start_time by default (see −s).
- -E *engine*: command option to use crypto hardware (OpenSSL engine) for zone signing using keys from a secure keystore when supported. The default *engine* is pkcs11 when compiled with PKCS #11 support or none otherwise.
- -f *file*: specifies the name of the file of the signed zone. If omitted, the default is the current zone file name appended with signed.
- -g: indicates that delegation signer resource records, which authenticate signed child zones, should be created; the resulting ds-set keyset can be provided to the parent zone's administrator for inclusion in the parent zone for signature.
- -h: prints help summary of this command.
- -H *iterations*: when generating an NSEC3 chain (when specifying the -3 option), use *iterations* iterations.
- -i *interval*: when resigning a zone (passing a previously signed zone in as input), the interval specifies the time interval from the current time for which any signature records expiring before the interval will be regenerated. Thus, if signature (RRSIG) records are set of expire within five days and the zone is resigned with an interval of six days, the signature records will be regenerated; otherwise, the current signatures will be retained.
- -I *input-format*: defines the *input-format* of the zone file to sign, either text (the default) or raw. Setting this option to raw facilitates signing of raw zone data, which includes dynamic updates and thus adds little value for static zones.
- -j *jitter*: enables specification of a window used to randomize RRSIG signature expiration times to reduce the impact of several simultaneous expirations, each of which would require signature regeneration when the signed zone is passed for resigning.
- -k *key*: the *key* specified is a KSK; multiple −k arguments may be provided.
- -K *directory*: defines the directory in which the key files are located.
- -l *domain*: generate a DLV keyset file; this keyset can be registered with the DLV registry to validate "delegation" for this zone.

- -n *threads*: specifies the number of CPU threads to use when performing this operation.
- -N *serial-format*: specifies the format of the SOA record serial number of the signed zone to either
    - keep: do not modify the serial number of the zone file input.
    - increment: increment the serial number in accordance with RFC 1982 serial number arithmetic.
    - unixtime: set the serial number to the number of seconds since epoch (since midnight UTC January 1, 1970 not counting leap seconds).
- -o *origin*: specifies the zone origin for the zone being signed.
- -O *output-format*: specifies the *output-format* of the signed zone as either text (the default) or raw.
- -p: use pseudorandom data when signing the zone, which is faster but less secure than using real random data per the –r argument.
- -P: disables the default postsigning verification tests, which include verifying that a valid nonrevoked KSK exists for each algorithm in use, that all revoked KSKs are self-signed and that all records in the zone are signed for each algorithm.
- -r *randomsource*: indicates a source of random data such as a file or character device such as the keyboard.
- -s *start_time*: specifies the date and time when resource record set signature records (RRSIG) become valid. The start_time may be specified relative to the current time using $+N$, where N is the number of seconds from the current time, or in absolute time using the format YYYYMMDDHHMMSS in Coordinated Universal Time (UTC). When this argument is omitted, the default start_time is 1 h prior to the current time to allow for clock skew.
- -S: "smart signing" leveraging key meta data, configured using the timing options of dnssec-keygen; searches the key repository for keys matching the zone being signed, includes them within the zone file in accordance with respective meta data and timing then signs the zone. Keys where the current date is past the activation or revocation dates but prior to retirement or deletion (or if no meta data exists), are used to sign the zone; keys where the current date is past the publish date but prior to other dates are published but not used to sign the zone.
- -t: print statistics upon completion of the signature process.
- -T *ttl*: defines the TTL value to use with DNSKEY records imported into the zone file from the key repository (if the TTL is not specified on any extant DNSKEY records in the zone), as part of smart signing (see –S).
- -u: update the NSEC[3] chain within the zone; also enables switching from a NSEC chained zone to an NSEC3 chained zone and vice versa depending on the presence of the NSEC3PARAM record in the zone file.
- -v *level*: sets the debug level.
- -x: sign the zone's DNSKEY RRSet with KSKs not additionally ZSKs.

- -z : ignore the KSK flag (SEP flag bit) when determining what to sign; that is, use the KSK [and ZSK] to sign zone RRSets.
- zone_file : the name of the zone file to sign.
- key : the keys to use to sign the zone data.

The output of the dnssec-signzone utility is the signed zone which uses the same name as the original unsigned zone, concatenated with a ".signed" suffix. Following our example, you can see below that the db.ipamworldwide.com.signed file is much larger than our original zone file. Consider our initial db.ipamworldwide.com file prior to signing

```
$TTL86400

ipamworldwide.com. 1D IN  SOA extdns1.ipamworldwide.com.
      dnsadmin.ipamworldwide.com. (
                       204 ; serial
                       3H  ; refresh
                       15  ; retry
                       1w  ; expire
                       3h  ; minimum
                   )
ipamworldwide.com.  86400 IN NS  extdns1.ipamworldwide.com.
                    86400 IN NS  extdns2.ipamworldwide.com.
                    86400 IN NS  extdns3.ipamworldwide.com.

extdns1.ipamworldwide.com. 86400  IN  A  192.0.2.34
                    86400  IN  AAAA 2001:db8:4af0:2010::a
extdns2.ipamworldwide.com.86400  IN  A  192.0.2.42
                    86400  IN  AAAA 2001:db8:4af0:2011::11
extdns3.ipamworldwide.com.86400  IN  A  192.0.2.50
                    86400  IN  AAAA 2001:db8:4af0:2006::9

eng.ipamworldwide.com. 1w  IN  NS  ns1.eng.ipamworldwide.com.
                       1w  IN  NS  ns2.eng.ipamworldwide.com.
ns1.eng.ipamworldwide.com.  1w  IN  AAAA 2001:db8:4af0:2007::7
ns1.eng.ipamworldwide.com.  1w  IN  AAAA 2001:db8:4af0:2009::12

$ORIGIN ipamworldwide.com.
           1D  IN MX 10 smtp1.ipamworldwide.com.
           1D  IN MX 20 smtp2.ipamworldwide.com.
```

```
www            1D  IN  A 192.0.2.37
               1D  IN  AAAA 2001:db8:4af0:2010::25
               1D  IN  A 192.0.2.53
               1D  IN  AAAA 2001:db8:4af0:2006::5
w3             1D  IN  CNAME www.ipamworldwide.com.

smtp1          1D  IN  A 192.0.2.36
               1D  IN  AAAA 2001:db8:4af0:2010::1b
smtp2          1D  IN  A 192.0.2.45
               1D  IN  AAAA 2001:db8:4af0:2011::2b
ftp-support 1D  IN  A 192.0.2.44
               1D  IN  AAAA 2001:db8:4af0:2011::2c


$INCLUDE Kipamworldwide.com.+005+14522.key
$INCLUDE Kipamworldwide.com.+005+06082.key
```

Contrast this with the signed version:

```
ipamworldwide.com. 86400   IN SOA extdns1.ipamworldwide.com.
dnsadmin.ipamworldwide.com. (
                        204        ; serial
                        10800      ; refresh (3 hours)
                        15         ; retry (15 seconds)
                        604800     ; expire (1 week)
                        10800      ; minimum (3 hours)
                        )
           86400   RRSIG  SOA 5 2 86400 20100305135354 (
                        20100203135354 14522 ipamworldwide.com.
                        OQS+AaE57+ffRfz+SaMHOJI6b4l2bNnsSDIK
                        mIIMdmXOw8cylCMieaUBz8ek64FyMWLGh2c5
                        HogVxtt7s9cHICosxqhqZNXYT7GP+YpRRVO4
                        uCGgq6uoqCpgj1L39tqnSQ1da8pT5a6DRCIJ
                        fqsS5ubrmA/20cc02c15XFTlAik= )
           86400   NS     extdns1.ipamworldwide.com.
           86400   NS     extdns2.ipamworldwide.com.
           86400   NS     extdns3.ipamworldwide.com.
           86400   RRSIG  NS 5 2 86400 20100305135354 (
```

```
                     20100203135354 14522 ipamworldwide.com.
                     qVdOx6s9IAL4YWz2hPB1Q5aVNPcPbIsREenD
                     PP/7GyXbQKxAdDDugaWPHoKEvPA9f1SBWomZ
                     h4pGOKJaA5Pk9okF3FkHLHclTFVGfhTEdrVj
                     Dk6a8eRNoU+CMHWwmfJtNFpYpVVd6Ch1LWdw
                     ZJ27Z80HZrHtwZ8XmubPzu8MZlE= )
     86400   MX      10 smtp1.ipamworldwide.com.
     86400   MX      20 smtp2.ipamworldwide.com.
     86400   RRSIG   MX 5 2 86400 20100305135354 (
                     20100203135354 14522 ipamworldwide.com.
                     dR4kJtp5DyvCHTF7+uCNloKCRNVx5jM/XOd9
                     H5F7OhnDUIgPWKYnuCbL3PBhx1iK9OnrrL1g
                     ZvEuTAvifzzax4n8CSPCB0CbrMWWUXQ44vKG
                     IOWOLwzQKJX1PGHzGiG+6dktfqOnBgppXekA
                     QWBJA6nOAeGKtqQMtKUa75uqs2Y= )
     10800   NSEC    eng.ipamworldwide.com. NS SOA MX RRSIG
                       NSEC DNSKEY
     10800   RRSIG   NSEC 5 2 10800 20100305135354 (
                     20100203135354 14522 ipamworldwide.com.
                     WyZl4AduBUWdED01Ckc+I0nSArek5n3r6rKX
                     m26H5Sjow/RSpgmPJfGOH/9gjyEwnGoqrKbh
                     5s7kxtnvF3xVYFE1If7zv5bHxSvBqMDqdNXq
                     ChY9BJ9kOemQ0L7N1preadXfyVXBthl5jaPC
                     vKLSwAjmNAzbtV4f6S+CIDK288w= )
     86400   DNSKEY 256 3 5 (
                     BQEAAAABx6QAwJiz6hHa/eUI2pGz6rvwEYpJ
                     di1TJH8Uj41DPTmzseCOgFEqB3/dZB0Q5LEs
                     1ZetAJJEk4F+WccRKwqnIcGkvIKfTC8hn+gb
                     iBAnadQRFLxNMBs6KB0e+yqiNK60sbrn22F8
                     AYRiG3n2rTQndVtkaZep9jbcCqfu/DagB10=
                     ) ; key id = 14522
     86400   DNSKEY 257 3 5 (
                     AwEAAdSAwGoUBhtjpE8GLGN4ryt8yEq71Dqd
                     E+ij3boe9lmvpM02YZ1/AQxoHbyA7NqRr+8d
                     sTM8OrF2yFRbcP1y0/9q37T0PqxL5HjAZ8Hr
                     DoW9R/pC3XyRe9pMzRNr4as+c/xEISfhxzvR
```

```
                           84CndF5XvFeh3H0kVDeTb+7QRrG7hnph4P8w
                           4SMg76tBvxHLFmj3OdP8vIUpRAnexEAdclam
                           j1ZSPjLcdICzpDvQB/LLsYxx8wx2h0vTvhxZ
                           klqmy1dPBtIZu2A551VIrU0xgCJxDjJGCgBb
                           rp1C01tYSdqlA1I2HCL8eV7io/CxnCuSThPl
                           XaPLySojJpXUgDomWgVYeo0=
                           ) ; key id = 6082
         86400    RRSIG    DNSKEY 5 2 86400 20100305135354 (
                           20100203135354 14522 ipamworldwide.com.
                           V0bEwZmY56OrGQb02B/Pf17RAcFyPZAvPT/W
                           Rm/+nluSOYMVqdzRaKM/ae47KslioXm3tNcy
                           GF3uBvBql7xPzIOuIy3COoorXmbsshbuANo7
                           YfQsyXWuX2BIjjLAVRRLQolVcdDyyleoA0E7
                           BebPM+fQQtvN2C2IjrcacJyeUlc= )
         86400    RRSIG    DNSKEY 5 2 86400 20100305135354 (
                           20100203135354 6082 ipamworldwide.com.
                           e8jCEVY6C1lSImGqjgzVWAgp7cC4AWuntFvc
                           oCCO+2BwGxe7+zxP2r02CCSOCIrTqtgwpNRd
                           5aH4xBrYmZh0IFQ7OxTFSGBvQ4DxC8ZDdQVS
                           uTYCBSzN7kXRJZopZv3chhf7/9uyz3gqtQnl
                           5RyUVATMOG5eu+ewBFqGIsXJv5XMNG7ZTO15
                           rtRd8zF/7MIY7TlSbHULGP7OJxcNFtyt8wnc
                           /dObfcxril4tOwLPVF4QnLnLxAHvdWt+QPVQ
                           z23WIc0U+rg6U6FsSjoi0U2QAxVFebenTJED
                           U2juAdqEE8I1Y9oOvNQVtYFFjXFgi1vDLGCG
                           zM8i4fI9uGZUHvzKng== )
ns1.eng.ipamworldwide.com. 604800 IN AAAA 2001:db8:4af0:2007::7
ns2.eng.ipamworldwide.com. 604800 IN AAAA 2001:db8:4af0:2009::12
eng.ipamworldwide.com. 604800 IN NS  ns1.eng.ipamworldwide.com.
         604800   IN NS    ns2.eng.ipamworldwide.com.
         10800    NSEC     extdns1.ipamworldwide.com. NS RRSIG NSEC
         10800    RRSIG    NSEC 5 3 10800 20100305135354 (
                           20100203135354 14522 ipamworldwide.com.
                           dWwY0rZRfW5aYgBsbRuCxot6CGGG8hfgHId7
                           84IZIYi9HHgr02saBdlzmzqJCGre0pGSDBvf
```

```
                        ZpJP1BVUS1NuMycEBFBUIS8IUASDTxcLGjrT
                        169vIqiyXjICzrsu2fzKL1QNwUOFMGiedglh
                        1jkUJ1jKKs9yr4XFZBwP/y8OpoQ= )
extdns1.ipamworldwide.com. 86400 IN A 192.0.2.34
        86400    RRSIG  A 5 3 86400 20100305135354 (
                        20100203135354 14522 ipamworldwide.com.
                        IwNfRz7m6Rneh6hpacdIpTHGRftsU8e931OP
                        bjC0Dfw92DXn51uHghiCoE+rrO4zK1wYFP5L
                        CoKF43whVX1EXOt7UFGuAebr4587DnDqhKol
                        9XivKc35HvPz1ErniZHuUIsZCjvuziwvGIXS
                        72PkoHzNw/lxv+nDriemFn7tWxE= )
        86400 AAAA      2001:db8:4af0:2010::a
        86400 RRSIG     AAAA 5 3 86400 20100305135354 (
                        20100203135354 14522 ipamworldwide.com.
                        aNzJgdLi4DTttIUj+Y+9FLI2eAu5iRX9yewN
                        jvFG3aJ4moO4fWwhKFynltcfJFpKjHyq4eCD
                        PamIS/9fDOn8OdX1g8CkfKNQIszUoAkhSQXH
                        6avko1jwgP0lqHwjRNhdcW2UuE+pjyvgNlTW
                        ZOgb65nR+UjSJQXRQnHpyhyD+nk= )
        10800 NSEC      extdns2.ipamworldwide.com. A AAAA RRSIG
                          NSEC
        10800 RRSIG     NSEC 5 3 10800 20100305135354 (
                        20100203135354 14522 ipamworldwide.com.
                        ipB8eo8GLPvbCCzUF6ETXBiXsRXZiWu8y21z
                        uEoxJn+3T9dYXFEFFpdyj5Qnhl/gnvwpc1mP
                        sFyg0+P5mNziXO/Aj3LQF2HJMnQxT34dQdJb
                        Ze/6KBJZO6KZXwXrQXxVGrbFHY9xY5Q0gfs4
                        J2MUAZB074KWOVZKUzLUczgrwhI= )
extdns2.ipamworldwide.com. 86400 IN A 192.0.2.42
        86400 RRSIG     A 5 3 86400 20100305135354 (
                        20100203135354 14522 ipamworldwide.com.
                        ax6Umlog3DSn+KxIQSvbQjES9CwuaYZ+G0yT
                        NHOIwVOrV4cjP7LA2Pc2p7bQjwoTMkXK5uoU
                        Or8Mnd7/boJyQUrBF62pbhOqJ9mKbvrYD1ud
                        SivEiDnxAv0FTwagCe22Vvd3DNTjXUhizBt7
                        DlIbA921SCiNHqeFT/OljqcW+Z0= )
```

```
            86400 AAAA    2001:db8:4af0:2011::11
            86400 RRSIG   AAAA 5 3 86400 20100305135354 (
                          20100203135354 14522 ipamworldwide.com.
                          aQO0ipvwjtAS0DZiXJoTot9iPAToI5rqrkMD
                          lXRNimxuT/ED0+S94OUg5rA5a/XS80aDFSyD
                          uqLIVIiZC4Zd5jHazPxEjJR7YyJ0sx8kIy5Q
                          85LBJQhVsiADcoKz7NZ8TRFzSEGQNKMLVYIx
                          kVx8JpJcGWLeXBekk5J46OeacfE= )
           10800 NSEC     extdns3.ipamworldwide.com. A AAAA RRSIG
                            NSEC
           10800 RRSIG    NSEC 5 3 10800 20100305135354 (
                          20100203135354 14522 ipamworldwide.com.
                          J8j82DSNwUc0M2dd2vPzkTlOnjxrrTeKIWH2
                          h13hjbH3xr18WLQdJQiqJpXapXSKGX/57+C8
                          EO+OBbsqNMpwf+bNhxdnJazB7elYdk7KI8Xp
                          TmpyV9zRTJjr3U3l6pw2GjaCMkBDw8JD1+6w
                          LJjib4JgHg3pDswvo6ShXxpnezk= )
extdns3.ipamworldwide.com. 86400 IN A192.0.2.50
            86400 RRSIG   A 5 3 86400 20100305135354 (
                          20100203135354 14522 ipamworldwide.com.
                          a6IVQOXfc0UgsIfCJA/yGDvPdXUrXH2HJzS9
                          h/DGEIdu3ZBNcEwtKVvd4ph/rHXknX2Ito2m
                          4/1OLtvFdriZjhbpIERCatl45ySxhvugbZlb
                          EAjEWa1kixmPoOtXZ+pAS+7cLCxkodr5Np2t
                          f9Ppdv5bx4/a9BfM8abrUwrT988= )
            86400 AAAA    2001:db8:4af0:2006::9
            86400 RRSIG   AAAA 5 3 86400 20100305135354 (
                          20100203135354 14522 ipamworldwide.com.
                          AMeurMSeauKG/w0KSgo9tKWToMDXEOtArCmu
                          l3VKDUDN22Y7yfIUX+nwcUJuLRU4tLfeiLBT
                          E8IIjsJ3Qu9SQmCBB/4VCHjNax98c4+/RBym
                          M9sKuprQK9MEzV5kqqYyHdVuPFzSWCp0QXCO
                          AWrWGWfkO3oXS6oj+gqK3hHnAsQ= )
           10800 NSEC     ftp-support.ipamworldwide.com. A AAAA
                            RRSIG NSEC
           10800 RRSIG    NSEC 5 3 10800 20100305135354 (
```

```
                          20100203135354 14522 ipamworldwide.com.
                          nfQMcp6s2IyVItiCmb89DiSKYmdurlBo0Nx3
                          0IQYcoMvZVVXMa4ynCoq3lKdebjhGrW8e6NG
                          c5SyPYrBzjw1NVEPIr1mNoVN2EEBqquPYluC
                          z9f0M5N534yThP01yCsjee7FpIXGKYObhb5+
                          i5wLH10NrIpLJEAw3oWsXNPxkhQ= )
ftp-support.ipamworldwide.com. 86400 INA 192.0.2.44
            86400 RRSIG  A 5 3 86400 20100305135354 (
                          20100203135354 14522 ipamworldwide.com.
                          umyIYTUI2YaFXcRp9xATrAK7YnOz/PCbzOSF
                          xJLL9CLNzmtdPEvFW7iO9oeC8C+R3WfYafhV
                          aWiT/BYPbwqvxHaxRWFJ7hIO87n5PHfAHxyE
                          dIr1lLZO5f0IKK8oIgawIyHbE/XeqYHVeZpY
                          zJSGGMBiyTI/VGKluud17+/EDh4= )
            86400 AAAA    2001:db8:4af0:2011::2c
            86400 RRSIG   AAAA 5 3 86400 20100305135354 (
                          20100203135354 14522 ipamworldwide.com.
                          A43jiBaDMIhL9KtqP2uE2iG+sn5SZBVhqK9Q
                          ChRR0512pZJ5WGPip0KjgcJxaVnMbbBuyM7v
                          lzW6G1PerBwtbaX/zi2YnW+O0XyBYGlXjXPC
                          bHjM3I7Z07WgHD/I4jrHZVQczUDSmZCJQBIK
                          zEYlTt+su4K6EIfxw3uBlrheAAc= )
            10800 NSEC    smtp1.ipamworldwide.com. A AAAA RRSIG
                            NSEC
            10800 RRSIG   NSEC 5 3 10800 20100305135354 (
                          20100203135354 14522 ipamworldwide.com.
                          v/LRbW7drv03r+F5XasqZ2bjdGXQ7VP6kvOa
                          gt3s/gT5W/c8aLfTeA3lmwwEk3DrNEB9U+MV
                          XE9YdI1iLySu8J07hF9qJfSiCSIkZgmf5UDZ
                          BUUKifIXZVRHUy8uD2pXP3btZOrhR9CXU5oE
                          EfrvaGv7++yC+IhRJN7pbg+WEU0= )
smtp1.ipamworldwide.com. 86400   IN A    192.0.2.36
            86400 RRSIG   A 5 3 86400 20100305135354 (
                          20100203135354 14522 ipamworldwide.com.
                          lSISPwoCpLdSfWFFjhfuASY72DoA06dMPAic
                          5vhRJWQfoUbisWrGt29z7r7S7XYIwgRARURO
```

```
                            JDUSe93z7TzbjxO4UPDbuheFDYI7r+vDXLj2
                            cQgKT4gPJ6UCi2kawWaVbAzPz+ZzV2gfxJfc
                            fsjARB5rbNDk1BOO6IDI3pfPYh0= )
         86400 AAAA    2001:db8:4af0:2010::1b
         86400 RRSIG   AAAA 5 3 86400 20100305135354 (
                            20100203135354 14522 ipamworldwide.com.
                            Jap9zaU4gWcxHzXmtkK8NtCKGUCE/AdPf+/d
                            yWJC5PG7ClildQsxCIhbvgLHdQ0YfFMN5nvd
                            abt3fybBoTtbNATZeBqFDalMnF3IBzyhChA+
                            0DC1R27LGk7iyOZ5zsq055ZgROpkBbML3o9k
                            M7Y+Lx+nM3j44zj6YoUDsAUvP1s= )
         10800 NSEC    smtp2.ipamworldwide.com. A AAAA RRSIG
                            NSEC
         10800 RRSIG   NSEC 5 3 10800 20100305135354 (
                            20100203135354 14522 ipamworldwide.com.
                            x1YlFJQBUhSOTB/T7nrntcaB7x96AK+AAJZT
                            787XIryUwg5boDkA5MOGNxAoL6nurtbi3+6f
                            GLDoG4HYLsEmJlamw9+IANm1u2yLsg5q2viL
                            1ymroI0AlpeXNptDevgZ5+CiRiRKkNw0+BZ1
                            YCrdNJTBUo8pYfZDxdBpihi87EU= )
smtp2.ipamworldwide.com. 86400   IN A   192.0.2.45
         86400 RRSIG   A 5 3 86400 20100305135354 (
                            20100203135354 14522 ipamworldwide.com.
                            a+qfAnPTIcI7nBNRhg6BDZrFuQvBbiLZUPXA
                            kSXeLNkwtK5bodr+j0nZQqUFsCvHw/Gj2FH7
                            7L2ROcDto0QHE9WwKy3AjNtvRGg/GK54uO2v
                            A4NEx8C0sgIyWPkIC9Nbndp4bE2zV1r3O4Wr
                            UkAGYtD/ZMv79vhB8AsLKyfS+yM= )
         86400 AAAA    2001:db8:4af0:2011::2b
         86400 RRSIG   AAAA 5 3 86400 20100305135354 (
                            20100203135354 14522 ipamworldwide.com.
                            jQrvFnE/4JqFSfl6b/GR8j2hv/B+4XmuslCM
                            4P2D6YRYGNhZCeOw4DY3U9fGsg+B8gZii7U+
                            Rc9Qe8RyzV+wu8gy+65uvbSl9sb6zfGOrOp2
                            P+ZsAy7R0ZtPjzEdMLAIJdea4LdAgUO9IqNo
                            Q5ro79H9GAHptAw2epa+1XAp+wc= )
```

```
            10800 NSEC    w3.ipamworldwide.com. A AAAA RRSIG NSEC
            10800 RRSIG   NSEC 5 3 10800 20100305135354 (
                          20100203135354 14522 ipamworldwide.com.
                          gKXAbEocdwlnPIo9YtwLwOatBlamwpQTEM+e
                          rKjgibrjYPlymBiRwOs8lnrfXxCbv6v3ix6Q
                          IQcQrzKPugVEaIxUl6kqqHOLsXYwgbixppQX
                          Lcn1z9Wfmdv23Z6njQrdR+DmF6aQZPlUaiTn
                          SPtE26w59U1rtcyhm2p0vqic5l8= )
w3.ipamworldwide.com.  86400  IN CNAME www.ipamworldwide.com.
            86400 RRSIG   CNAME 5 3 86400 20100305135354 (
                          20100203135354 14522 ipamworldwide.com.
                          PTRpKmkZhBw18c1ZscxIlCL7P23fYgZBsEX9
                          DKrawjkyMZ5B+EqQaGNdsfgvmvirrcxCzv/K
                          MaMaeWBGI4Bb9gykm72thXneud5gHi5zLjsK
                          4uK/r3EdWcurQ89R44Q7pTUOy4yzCdpH/KDE
                          Qjd6P/JrWLnO/WW0gxurwHPFiBE= )
            10800 NSEC    www.ipamworldwide.com. CNAME RRSIG NSEC
            10800 RRSIG   NSEC 5 3 10800 20100305135354 (
                          20100203135354 14522 ipamworldwide.com.
                          W0jcsvdSJfLuJ6l7fAUdfnat9fd45OE6toO7
                          GHwkjRPWm1Q9C83W0Bgc161gZ4r/q1ZKoE6b
                          FvFOIIxz4NhPiJVb2bUbSL6A1K0vwD4KUGL4
                          ExKfuPM16/gLOE/Tqczcp/2ETXm5yksOkoPJ
                          ynOMoLpBIyNlHeJwtPBaHlbE+B0= )
www.ipamworldwide.com. 86400  IN A    192.0.2.37
            86400 IN A    192.0.2.53
            86400 RRSIG   A 5 3 86400 20100305135354 (
                          20100203135354 14522 ipamworldwide.com.
                          xjwhHWIy25aOvLP2E1y9aaN6GRcGUxoN4o+P
                          eZ0Wc05zjlDu6o1ZOCXivrbIOP4LVS7pqMX3
                          bg4SQDmzmRDQ0H/+Q8Fzxbf1UFQNcVB2uhtV
                          6R8DfNwRwIugoL+33qE2MOrrxWz16JutI2qo
                          vkYogNqDj1MNiiKkoGgmJQmiHYc= )
            86400 AAAA    2001:db8:4af0:2010::25
            86400 AAAA    2001:db8:4af0:2006::5
            86400 RRSIG   AAAA 5 3 86400 20100305135354 (
                          20100203135354 14522 ipamworldwide.com.
```

```
                          1RoCDp+0y/HM/xyEdciqO5cDWcRzxmQCwPbs
                          GKrCe+OoYHfTFnSBCAEReY4tneb/HMwYbqxV
                          SRp5oW2FPDi5GZunL7tLp7gF0tF7M9XlJVmi
                          9PDg9wiNzDxw/CgbsN/wbtsRpgbPxQwkACiP
                          eRsNDL3Y5EAxLi24yFw+Qay6uEc= )
```

```
    10800 NSEC   ipamworldwide.com. A AAAA RRSIG NSEC
    10800 RRSIG  NSEC 5 3 10800 20100305135354 (
```
```
                          20100203135354 14522 ipamworldwide.com.
                          auNzMg6x34+oradbjFKoQquKmB8sAmKg44FF
                          8FCuh7FI/mrKNHVuvlYmVNXNK/ZHA1JpVYzH
                          fpe4KxPGh8IcDftEfqd52Z0LsetYeRvxNzxQ
                          sAS+OzClCIiTiEpUNte6siExj7YvhBlPN4e4
                          pnkzTKPULWat489Juzo2U77XysA= )
```

Needless to say, signing a zone increases its size tremendously! It also increases resolution packet sizes, given the extra RRSIG and NSEC information with each RRSet, not to mention the potential for additional message traffic to validate the chain of trust back to a trust anchor.

Referring back to our discussion of the digital signature process, the original resolution data is of course the "data" from Figure 13.1 to be signed. The data actually consists of the entire RRSet which is hashed then signed using the private key of the key pair. The resulting signature comprises the signature field of each RRSIG record. Thus, at the beginning of our signed file, we have our original SOA record, followed by its corresponding signature (RRSIG). Then our three NS records are listed. This RRSet comprised of these three records is signed per the following RRSIG record. Likewise, the MX RRSet is listed and signed. Notice the RRSIG records indicate signature using the ZSK, per the key tag field value of 14522. The DNSKEY RRSet is itself signed by both the KSK and ZSK as evidenced by the two RRSIG records with respective KSK and ZSK key tags. Usually the KSK only signs the DNSKEY RRSet with the ZSK signs all zone RRSets. Notice also that the ns1 and ns2.eng.ipamworldwide.com glue records are not signed as these records are authoritative in the eng.ipamworldwide.com zone, not the ipamworldwide.com zone.

The NSEC record listed next provides a canonical ordering of records to identify and authenticate a negative answer for a non-existent resource record. This particular record indicates that the next owner is eng.ipamworldwide.com. This NSEC record also is signed. Each of the remaining RRSets includes an NSEC record and RRSet signature (RRSIG record).

13.3.4 Link the Chain of Trust

Now that the zone has been signed, you should determine its place in the chain of trust. That is, determine if the parent zone is signed or not. If the parent zone is not signed and the newly signed zone is the top-level domain, that is, signed (i.e., *zone apex*; e.g., `com` is not signed as of this writing.), recursive resolvers querying on behalf of stub resolvers must be configured with the zone's public KSK as a *trusted key*. This informs the resolver that zone information signed with this key is to be trusted. For those resolvers, which trust our ipamworldwide.com zone administrators' data, the KSK 06082 public key can be configured within the respective trusted-keys statement in each recursive server's named. conf file as per the following

```
trusted-keys {
"ipamworldwide.com." 257 3 5
  "AwEAAdSAwGoUBhtjpE8GLGN4ryt8yEq71DqdE+ij3boe9lmvpM02YZ1/
  AQxoHbyA7NqRr+8dsTM8OrF2yFRbcP1y0/9q37T0PqxL5HjAZ8HrDoW9
  R/pC3XyRe9pMzRNr4as+c/xEISfhxzvR84CndF5XvFeh3H0kVDeTb+7Q
  RrG7hnph4P8w4SMg76tBvxHLFmj3OdP8vIUpRAnexEAdclamj1ZSPjLc
  dICzpDvQB/LLsYxx8wx2h0vTvhxZklqmy1dPBtIZu2A551VIrU0xgCJx
  DjJGCgBbrp1C01tYSdqlA1I2HCL8eV7io/CxnCuSThPlXaPLySojJpXU
    gDomWgVYeo0=";
};
```

Within the recursive server configuration, we have declared a trust anchor or SEP at the ipamworldwide.com zone. Note that a trusted key entry with the corresponding KSK public key is required for each trust anchor you wish to configure. As we'll discuss later, the more trust anchors you configure, the more keys you need to manage during each zone's key rollover process. With the signed root and TLD zones, only one trust anchor need be maintained.

Automated trust anchor update capabilities reduce the manual management of trust anchor rollovers. For such trust anchors, instead of using the `trusted-keys` statement, the `managed-keys` statement can be used. In the following example, we use the public KSK from our trust anchor as the initial key. This key serves as the trusted key initially, but as the zone administrator for the ipamworldwide.com zone publishes, activates, revokes, retires, and deletes keys in accordance with the timing capabilities and automation of BIND 9.7 and above, this recursive server will remain in step and keep its own repository of current trust anchor keys per trust anchor. Hence, when this initial key is revoked and another key activated, signature of the DNSKEY RRSet by both the newly activated and this now-revoked key validates the transition to the newly active key.

```
managed-keys {
"ipamworldwide.com." initial-key 257 3 5
    "AwEAAdSAwGoUBhtjpE8GLGN4ryt8yEq71DqdE+ij3boe9lmvpM02YZ1/
    AQxoHbyA7NqRr+8dsTM8OrF2yFRbcP1y0/9q37T0PqxL5HjAZ8HrDoW9
    R/pC3XyRe9pMzRNr4as+c/xEISfhxzvR84CndF5XvFeh3H0kVDeTb+7Q
```

RrG7hnph4P8w4SMg76tBvxHLFmj3OdP8vIUpRAnexEAdclamj1ZSPjLc
dICzpDvQB/LLsYxx8wx2h0vTvhxZklqmy1dPBtIZu2A551VIrU0xgCJx
DjJGCgBbrp1C01tYSdqlA1I2HCL8eV7io/CxnCuSThPlXaPLySojJpXU
gDomWgVYeo0='';
};

Now if the zone just signed is a child zone of a signed parent zone, the parent zone administrator must include the delegation signer record in the parent zone file to link the chain of trust. In this manner, the parent zone can vouch for this signed child zone. Thus, trust anchors need not be configured in resolvers or recursive servers for this zone, just its parent or an even higher level ancestor signed zone.

The −g option on the dnssec-signzone utility automatically created our DS records for the zone in a dsset-ipamworldwide.com. file. The file contains two DS records, one of which may be chosen based on the preferred digest type. The integer shown before the digest in the examples below indicates the digest type. Type 1 is SHA-1 and type 2 is SHA-256. The digest follows which is computed as a hash using the corresponding digest type or algorithm of the signed zone's KSK DNSKEY resource record owner and RData fields (i.e., the KSK DNSKEY record, omitting the TTL, class and type).

```
ipamworldwide.com.
INDS6082515F696637B085D8F5CBFD0C8B9E031CB6CB07159B
ipamworldwide.com. IN DS 6082 5 2
7FFD9203E916B5D49F631D060FAFD05D26974BEFCED25AACB88122722E4A7AA9
```

In terms of authenticating records or their nonexistence in signed child (delegated) zones, the delegation signer resource record type provides the link from a parent to a delegated child zone's key as a link within the chain of trust. We'll walk through how this works within the resolution process next. The DS resource record has the following format

Owner	TTL	Class	Type	RData			
Delegated domain	TTL	IN	DS	Key tag	Alg.	Type	Digest
ipamworldwide.com.	86400	IN	DS	6082	5	1	5F695D8F5BFD0C...

The RData portion of the DS record identifies the key tag or id of the child zone's public KSK, while the Algorithm matches the Algorithm field in the referenced DNSKEY record. The Digest Type indicates the type of hash or digest which is conveyed in the Digest field. Valid Digest Type values are 1 (SHA-1) or 2 (SHA-256). The Digest field contains the digest or hash of the corresponding child zone public KSK DNSKEY resource record owner field concatenated with the same DNSKEY record's RData field.

The parent zone administrator would add the DS RRSet to the parent zone and sign it to authenticate its origin and integrity.

In BIND 9.6, a new utility, dnssec-dsfromkey, was introduced. This utility enables generation of DS resource records without having to re-sign the zone using dnssec-signzone. This utility is available with the following parameters

- -1: use SHA-1 as the digest algorithm
- -2: use SHA-256 as the digest algorithm
- -a *algorithm*: where algorithm may be
  o SHA-1
  o SHA-256
- -A: include ZSKs along with KSKs for generation of DS records; if omitted, only DS records for KSKs are created.
- -c *class*: identifies the class (default is IN).
- -d *directory*: directory location of the keyset files.
- -f *file*: specifies a zone file name in lieu of specifying the keyfile name.
- -l *domain*: generate a DLV set instead of a DS set and append *domain* to each record in the set.
- -K *directory*: defines the directory in which the key files are located.
- -s: command argument is a domain name not a keyfile name.
- -v *level*: specifies the debug level.

The dnssec-dsfromkey utility can generate DS or DLV records based on a keyfile or a domain name; the –s argument defines the argument as a domain name

```
dnssec-dsfromkey -s [-v level] [-1] [-2] [-a algorithm] [-l domain]
keyfile
```

The omission of –s identifies the argument as a keyfile name.

```
dnssec-dsfromkey [-v level] [-1] [-2] [-a algorithm] [-l domain] [-K
directory] [-c class] [-f file] [-A] domainname
```

13.4 THE DNSSEC RESOLUTION PROCESS

Now let's review how the resolution and verification process works. Configuring the trusted or managed keys statement above into our recursive server configuration (named. conf), we have declared ipamworldwide.com as a trusted zone. When I issue a query for a host within the ipamworldwide.com zone, for example, ftp-support. ipamworldwide.com, my resolver will set the DNSSEC OK (DO) bit in the EDNS0 extended Rcode field. DNSSEC requires EDNS0 to support this extended Rcode field and also for the generally large response packets likely exceeding the nominal 512-byte UDP packet limit. The packet length increase is due to the response by the server configured with the authoritative signed zone with not only the resolution data requested, the A record(s) for `ftp-support.ipamworldwide.com`, but the associated signature record associated with the A record set.

13.4.1 Verify the Signature

The signature process signs resource record sets, which are groupings of resource records with common owner name, class, and type. The signature is created using the private key referenced by the key tag parameter and is placed within the signature field of the RRSIG resource record.

The RRSIG resource record has the following format

Owner	TTL	Class	Type	RData							
RRSet Owner	TTL	IN	RRSIG	Type Cov.	Alg.	Labels	Orig. TTL	Expire	Inception	Key tag	Signer	Signa-ture
ftp-support. ipamworld wide.com.	86400	IN	RRSIG	A	5	3	86400	2010030 5215354	2010020 3215354	14522	ipam world wide. com.	umyI...

The RData fields within the RRSIG record are defined as follows.

- *Type Covered.* The type of the resource record set covered by this signature. In our example, the A record type is covered by this signature which signs our two-resource record RRSet with owner ftp-support.ipamworldwide.com.
- *Algorithm.* The algorithm used in generating the key, which is encoded in the same manner as the Algorithm field of the DNSKEY resource record type (see DNSKEY above).
- *Number of Labels.* Indicates the number labels within the owner field. For example, ftp-support.ipamworldwide.com has three labels. This field is used to reconstruct the original owner name used to create the signature in the case where the owner name returned by the server has a wildcard label (*).
- *Original TTL.* The TTL of the signed RRSet as defined in the authoritative zone, used to validate a signature. This field is needed because the TTL field returned in the original response is normally decremented by a caching resolver and use of the TTL field may lead to erroneous calculations.
- *Signature Expiration.* The date and time of the expiration of this signature expressed as either the number of seconds since January 1, 1970 00:00:00 UTC or in the form of YYYYMMDDHHmmSS where

- o YYYY is the year (within 68 years of the present date to prevent numerical wrapping of this field)
- o MM is the month, 01–12
- o DD is the day of the month, 01–31
- o HH is the hour in 24 h notation, 00–23
- o mm is the minute, 00–59
- o SS is the second, 00–59
- o Signatures are not valid after this date/time.
- *Signature Inception.* The date and time of the inception of this signature formatted in the same manner as the Signature Expiration field. Signatures are not valid before this date/time.
- *Key Tag.* Provides an association with the corresponding key (DNSKEY resource record(s)) by key id or tag.
- *Signer's Name.* Identifies the owner name of the DNSKEY resource record that was used to create this signature.
- *Signature.* The cryptographic signature covering the RRSIG RData (excluding this Signature field itself) concatenated with the resource records comprising the RRSet identified by the RRSIG owner, class, and covered type fields.

Thus, the response to our query includes the A records and the associated RRSIG record as indicated by this response captured with the dig utility below. The server will set the Authentic Data (AD) bit in the DNS header in the response only if it has authenticated (cryptographically verified) all included resource records in the Answer section and all included negative response resource records in the Authority section. Note that if you query the server which is authoritative for the issued query, the AD bit will not be set. This server simply returns the answer and leaves validation rightly to the querier. If you query your recursive server which is not authoritative for the queried information, it will perform the resolution and DNSSEC validation, which if successful, will set the AD bit in the result. We'll review the details of the dig utility, which is very useful in verifying and troubleshooting zone configurations in Chapter 14.

```
$ dig +dnssec A ftp-support.ipamworldwide.com. @127.0.0.1

; ≪ ≫ DiG 9.6.2 ≪ ≫ +dnssec A ftp-sf.ipamworldwide.com. @127.0.0.1
; (1 server found)
;; global options: printcmd
;; Got answer:
;; ->>HEADER<<- opcode: QUERY, status: NOERROR, id: 462
```

```
;; flags: qr aa rd ra; QUERY: 1, ANSWER: 3, AUTHORITY: 2, ADDITIONAL: 3


;; OPT PSEUDOSECTION:
; EDNS: version: 0, flags: do; udp: 4096
;; QUESTION SECTION:
;ftp-sf.ipamworldwide.com.    IN    A


;; ANSWER SECTION:
ftp-sf.ipamworldwide.com. 86400 IN    A    10.1.32.9
ftp-sf.ipamworldwide.com. 86400 IN    A    10.1.32.5
ftp-sf.ipamworldwide.com. 86400 IN    RRSIG A 5 3 86400 20100525173519
   20100425173519 14522 ipamworldwide.com.owHoS6b1xTNKuzJjgJs3nL4Kwr-
   LehnfixVjAF2T6 RHu4dVmq4w1p+FNC Oji2BkWKOhjY3+7jU4doFr/RNioe8vmsqyn
   R5YeSSRzzFy/d63Riz3bQ5BANbGRqpTn6Q9HQlm+KYSpwY5CrjqOQnP+Ynme4nhT9
   +z8h5ahdwtK9 EtI=


;; AUTHORITY SECTION:
ipamworldwide.com.    86400  IN   NS   ns.ipamworldwide.com.
ipamworldwide.com.      86400   IN RRSIG   NS 5 2 86400 20100525173519
20100425173519  14522 ipamworldwide.com. OLonIvBmJZDEZoRRvOiq7GnlWnr-
   8LTWHtKSR60CJN13hd23Vvkbq/EkV 46wp6OK6Q0qNtJGE+YqFW9xml7d6kQRZO-
   qIyCiDZqHQinV7LlAa0Da8z5+UGduD3gVLceES7lvGZpLlbyUm9kFGf5FhPZ/
   JciPF4qKUdAvfEeitu/aY=


;; ADDITIONAL SECTION:
ns.ipamworldwide.com. 86400  IN   A   10.1.32.4
ns.ipamworldwide.com. 86400  IN    RRSIG A 5 3 86400 20100525173519
20100425173519 14522 ipamworldwide.com. IHtLJaWam57mVoYCgFqlEPC9N9p7n-
   Wicy7MBvdQP6PgNfhnOTOg2vQHR rQRDdBWBmgaSRoiWSdF2IQTEfH4T16591-
   OEjtBnPR/7zRAxU9abnkUDvGCZsAFfqKfWxBZFrxUTbxloekEhMC98FqCnvaRIsL-
   NYbiP/0KhehWmBF nlA=
```

The recursive server or resolver, having received the RRSet (data) and the RRSIG (signature) may then issue a DNSKEY query to obtain the DNSKEY RRSet if it is not already cached or provided with the response in the Additional section. The signature in the RRSIG record is processed with the key of tag 14522 and compared with a hash of the RRSIG RData (less the signature) concatenated with the resource records within the RRSet. If the comparison yields a match, the signature is validated successfully. Next, the RRSIG of the DNSKEY RRSet is used to validate the ZSK itself. Performing a similar calculation as just described to validate the A RRSet, the resolver or recursive server validates the DNSKEY RRSet with respect to the public KSK signature. Given a successful match as well as the fact that the public KSK matches a configured trusted-key, we have therefore successfully validated the A RRSet data.

13.4.2 Authenticated Denial of Existence

What if I mistyped the hostname I intended to query? Without DNSSEC, I'd receive an error (NXDOMAIN) indicating the record was not found. Just as an affirmative answer may be spoofed, "not found" answers may be too. To address this potential vulnerability, DNSSEC incorporates the Next SECure (NSEC) resource record to provide a means to authenticate the nonexistence of a record matching the query. The NSEC record essentially points from one RRSet to the next within the zone file, identifying gaps between RRSets. The format of the NSEC record is as follows.

Owner	TTL	Class	Type	RData	
RRSet Owner	TTL	IN	NSEC	Next RRSet Owner	Type Bit Maps
ns1.ipamww.com.	86400	IN	NSEC	ns2.ipamww.com.	A AAAA RRSIG NSEC

In this example, the NSEC record associated with owner ns1.ipamww.com indicates that the next owner name in canonical order is ns2.ipamww.com, and this owner (ns1) exists with resource records of type A, AAAA, RRSIG, and NSEC. This record indicates that there aren't any records canonically between ns1.ipamworldwide.com and ns2.ipamworldwide.com, such as ns1a.ipamworldwide.com, for example. Each NSEC RRSet is also signed with the private ZSK, which in turn is validated against a trusted KSK.

NSEC3 provides similar authenticated denial of existence indication for RRSets, but it also obfuscates trivial enumeration of RRSets in the zone, which can be considered an information security risk. Because the NSEC3 record uses hashed owner names along with a salt value, which further complicates the hash dictionary creation function, it is much more computationally expensive to enumerate the zone. As such it is also computationally expensive when signing the zone and when validating query resolutions indicating record nonexistence.

13.4.3 Parent Delegation in a Chain of Trust

Now let's expand our example to illustrate the role of the DS record in generating an inter-zone chain of trust to a trust anchor. Consider Figure 13.3, where we will work our way up from the resolved data to the trust anchor. Let's assume the public KSK of the ipamworldwide.com. zone (key id = 06082) is configured as a trust anchor in my recursive server. When I issue an A record query for host.child.ipamworldwide.com., name resolution follows the traditional domain tree traversal to obtain a cached or authoritative answer. Assuming I had set the DO bit, the resolution RRSet along with the

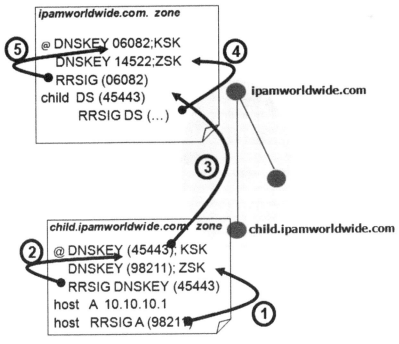

Figure 13.3. DNSSEC chain of trust traversal.

corresponding RRSIG record will be returned. The recursive server can validate the RRSIG with the child.ipamworldwide.com's ZSK (key id = 98211), shown as the arrow labeled "1" in Figure 13.3. In turn the ZSK can be validated against the zone's KSK (key id = 45443), per step 2. Given that I do not have this KSK configured as a trust anchor, I cannot trust this data. However, the recursive server queries the parent zone, ipamworldwide.com., for a DS record to determine if the parent can authenticate this zone's data. This is shown as step 3 in the figure.

If the DS record digest matches the corresponding child.ipamworldwide.com zone's KSK DNSKEY data, I can conclude that the ipamworldwide.com. zone has signed the delegation to child.ipamworldwide.com. The recursive server then validates the signature on the DS record against ipamworldwide.com's ZSK (key id = 14522) and in turn its KSK (key id = 06082), which is configured as a trusted key. Therefore, I have confirmed the original data resolved as trusted via the chain of trust back to a configured trust anchor! This same process could be repeated for any number of parent–child iterations up the domain tree to the signed root using the root zone trust anchor. I ultimately must have a trusted key configured for the zone or one of its ancestor zones within which my query applies. Considering the wide variety of zones for which queries need to be authenticated, including reverse zones, this set of trust anchors could quickly become very large!

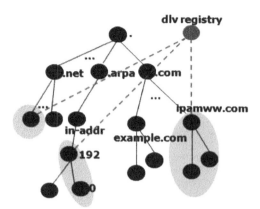

Figure 13.4. DLV chain of trust.

DNSSEC Lookaside Validation was defined to help keep the set of trust anchors to a manageable level in the time before the root zone was signed. DLV utilizes a centralized registry of signed zone public keys. By configuring the DLV registry as a trust anchor, you thereby trust the DLV registry and all "child" zones to which it authenticates. These zones are not actual child zones of the DLV, but are zones that the DLV authenticates. Zone administrators may register their signed zone keys with the DLV registry in a secure manner to maintain this "lookaside" or "sideways" chain of trust, as opposed the domain tree parent–child chain of trust we just discussed.

Figure 13.4 illustrates this concept. Without root and TLD zone signing, trusted keys had to be configured for each trusted zone. In the figure, these are illustrated as the ipamww.com, 192.in-addr.arpa and a .net zones. By using the DLV concept, the DLV signs the DS-equivalent DLV record to authenticate the KSK of the each "child" zone. The benefit of a DLV registry is to reduce the number of keys being managed in each recursive server in your organization. If the DLV signs three zone keys as illustrated in Figure 13.4, you need only be concerned with the DLV's key rollover, not the constituent three keys'. The DLV registry must be trusted fully, as zones for which it authenticates are not selectively accepted by registry users.

A trusted keys statement must be entered for the DLV registry and only one DLV registry may be so referenced. The DLV is identified in the recursive name server by configuring its public KSK in the `trusted-keys` statement block as we illustrated earlier. When building a chain of trust during name resolution, the recursive server will attempt to build the chain back to a configured trust anchor; should a valid chain not exist, it will attempt to validate the chain of trust through the DLV. The DLV registry must be able to authenticate its registered zones, much like the manner in which a parent zone validates its children's KSKs. The DLV resource record is used for this purpose, and its format is identical to the DS resource record type. It performs an equivalent function, though not in the traditional parent–child delegation chain.

Owner	TTL	Class	Type				RData
DLV domain	TTL	IN	DLV	Key tag	Algorithm	Type	Digest
ipamww.com.dlv_reg.net.	86400	IN	DLV	32284	5	1	90df80DF89lLe....

When the recursive server issues its last resort attempt to validate data in a zone, it seeks the DLV record corresponding to that zone in question within the DLV registry. The DLV registry is identified in the recursive server via the dnssec-lookaside statement, configured within the options block of named.conf. This statement identifies the branch of the domain tree for which escalations to the DLV registry are valid, as well as a reference to the trust anchor identified in the trusted-keys statement. For example, the statement below indicates that resolutions within the gov. domain could be escalated to dlv.us. and trusted as long as the dlv.us public KSK matches the configured dlv.us trusted key.

```
dnssec-lookaside "gov" trust-anchor "dlv.us";
```

13.5 KEY ROLLOVER

The most administratively intensive task with DNSSEC deals with the process of key rollover, particularly KSK rollover. Like passwords, keys must be periodically changed. It's best to provide a moving target to would-be attackers! The use of separate key-signing versus zone-signing keys helps the administration of this process. This is due to the fact that any zone administrator can simply resign his/her zone using a ZSK without affecting anyone else. Whatever ZSK is used, it is ultimately signed by the KSK, which may be configured as a trust anchor or referenced by a DS or DLV resource record. Thus, ZSKs can be changed at will. However, because KSKs are configured as trust anchors and are potentially referenced by other zones' DS or DLV records, they do impact other administrators and require a fairly tight integration process.

The two basic methods used for key rollover are preseeding the key, which is effective for rolling over ZSKs and the dual-key signature approach, which can be used to rollover KSKs. The key issue (no pun intended) with rollover relates to the updating of cached resolution and signature information in recursive servers and resolvers. When a resolver obtains authenticated resolution information, it will cache this information, including the DNSKEY records containing ZSKs and KSKs, for the duration of the original record TTL. After the TTL expires, the resolver must issue a new query for the corresponding information. If a zone administrator performs a flash cut of a new key for an old key, resolvers and recursive servers having performed queries with the old key, still valid per its TTL, will be unable to authenticate data resolved within the zone that was signed with the new key. This time impact is illustrated in Figure 13.5. Therefore, maintaining a window during which key updates can be propagated and two or more keys are valid comprise the basic rollover techniques.

Let's discuss and compare the two common rollover strategies by first considering Figure 13.6. Note that ZSK and KSK rollover should occur independently of one another

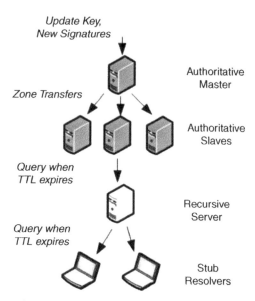

Figure 13.5. Zone information propagation.

if possible. We'll assume the preseed strategy is applied to ZSK rollover, while the dual-signature approach is applied to KSK rollover. Examining first ZSK rollover, our initial condition features a zone signed with ZSK [key tag] 14522 and KSK 6082 as indicated by the pen icon. At time t_0, the preseed time, a second, "passive" ZSK, 28004, is created using the dnssec-keygen utility or via BIND 9.7+ automation and its corresponding DNSKEY resource record is included in the zone file along with the active ZSK 14522. After ZSK 28004 has been inserted or included in the zone file, the zone must be resigned, still using ZSK 14522. The passive ZSK is itself signed by the active keys and made available for resolver and recursive server caching, but is not yet used to sign zone data.

Once published, both keys should remain in the zone file until all slave servers obtain the zone file via zone transfers plus the key expiration time. The key expiration time should be longer than the zone or resource record TTLs. When this time has passed at time t_1, the rollover time, the zone can be resigned, this time using the now formerly passive ZSK 28004. The formerly active ZSK can be left in the zone for the equivalent interval until time t_2, then removed from the zone file. Depending on the frequency of

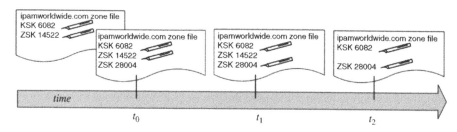

Figure 13.6. DNSSEC preseed key rollover strategy (11).

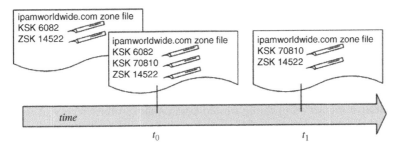

Figure 13.7. DNSSEC dual-signature key rollover strategy (11).

ZSK rollover, the time t_2 may correspond to t_0 in the next key rollover cycle, where the zone would always have two ZSKs, one active and one passive. Otherwise, at this point only the active ZSK exists within the zone.

Now let's examine the dual-signature rollover method, shown in Figure 13.7. This process starts with the same initial conditions as in our prior example. At rollover time, t_0, a new KSK (70810) is created using the dnssec-keygen utility with the –k option. Now sign the zone using the dnssec-signzone utility using *both* the current and new KSK and the active ZSK. Recall that dnssec-signzone permits specification of multiple KSKs. The public key of the new KSK must then be communicated to all resolvers/recursive servers that utilize this zone as a trust anchor. In addition, the parent zone that authenticates this zone must be updated.

An output of the dnssec-signzone utility when using the –g option includes a dsset-<zonename> file containing the corresponding DS resource record(s) that can be included in the parent's zone file. The –l option creates a dlvset-<zonename> file containing the corresponding DLV resource records. The parent zone or DLV administrator must copy or include these DS or DLV records, respectively and resign the parent zone. Given the manual configuration required to perform these tasks on the parent zone and resolvers/recursive servers, this time frame is less deterministic than the preseed method. Once this time has elapsed and the parent zone and trust anchor configurations have been updated, the old KSK may be removed from the zone file and the zone resigned using only the newly current KSK as shown at time t_1.

Emergency rollover procedures should be devised in the event of compromise of a private key corresponding to an active KSK or ZSK. Should an attacker obtain the private key, he/she could forge zone data and sign it with the private key. Resolvers and recursive servers would authenticate the falsified data based on the corresponding published public key. As we've seen, the ZSK can be changed autocratically and should be changed immediately. Changing the KSK however, does require broader involvement and coordination. We recommend documenting a process for emergency rollovers that includes the parent zone administrator and DLV registry contacts, as well as a means to communicate to users who have configured the KSK as a trust anchor. This could be via a registered email list and secure web site posting.

One other aspect of key updating is algorithm rollover. This involves the use of a new key-generation algorithm, for example, as a result of an algorithm compromise or upgrade. As with changing the key itself, the dual signature process described above can be used to generate keys using new algorithms and roll them into production.

13.5.1 Automated Trust Anchor Rollover

RFC 5011 (143) defines a means to automate trust anchor rollover to reduce the administrative impact on updating trusted keys on all resolvers/recursive servers that utilize this zone as a trust anchor. This automation requires an initial configuration of the current public KSK for the trust anchor zone. But unlike manual configuration, it need not be manually updated every time the trust anchor KSK is changed. Automated trust anchor updates can be configured in a recursive BIND server using the `managed-keys` statement in BIND 9.7 and above. The initial trusted key will be used to validate future key transactions communicated using the DNS protocol. The resolver must periodically query the trust anchor for its DNSKEY RRSet to check for updates. If a new key is added correctly, it will be automatically considered a valid trust anchor key for the zone if signed by the current trusted key. If the current trusted key is revoked and is signed by the zone's trusted key(s), the trusted key will automatically be removed from processing. Hence the initial-key configured in the `managed-keys` statement is used as the trust anchor initial condition only; this key may be revoked in the future, and the DNS server automatically tracks the status of current trusted keys.

Figure 13.8 provides a state diagram of trusted keys from the resolver's perspective based on key states retrieved via validated (signed by current trusted key(s)) DNSKEY queries. When a new SEP key (trust anchor) is retrieved by the server within the DNSKEY RRSet, the key enters the Add Pending state. This state helps mitigate the case where an attacker has compromised the trusted key and seeks to convince the resolver to use the attacker's new key. If the resolver does not see the pending key in the DNSKEY

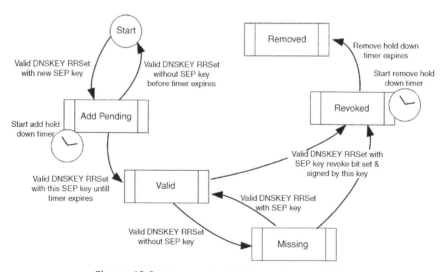

Figure 13.8. Trust anchor (SEP) state diagram (143).

RRSet at any time during the duration of the *add hold down* timer, the key will be considered invalid. It would be very challenging for an attacker to correctly respond to every DNSKEY query during this interval. Once the hold down timer expires, the trusted key enters the Valid state and is considered a valid trusted key for the zone. In this state if the key is missing from the DNSKEY RRSet, it will be considered Missing but will be reinstated to Valid state upon reappearance with valid signatures.

When the zone administrator desires to revoke the key due to its age in its lifecycle or because it was compromised, the key will be published in the zone with the Revoke bit set in the DNSKEY Flags field. This key must be used to sign the DNSKEY RRSet in addition to any other active or pending trusted keys. In this case, the key will be considered Revoked. This state may be entered from either the Valid or Missing states. The server begins a *remove hold down* timer, which upon expiration, stimulates removal of the trusted key from the server configuration.

13.5.2 DNSSEC and Dynamic Updates

You may be wondering given that the zone signing process requires the canonical ordering of a zone, then signature, how does one insert a new resource record into the zone securely? Fortunately, zone signing does not require reprocessing of the entire zone. Individual RRSets are signed, enabling a more modular process. However, the NSEC[3] records must be adjusted to account for the update, effectively inserting the update by adjusting the canonical ordering.

When dyamically updating a secure zone, the update itself must be secure. The server should require signatures on update messages and should define which servers or networks may perform updates. When an update has been received and authenticated, it remains within the journal file. To fully sign the zone with the update, the server must temporarily freeze dynamic updates, when using pre-BIND 9.6, via the `rndc freeze` command. This shuts off acceptance of dynamic updates. Once frozen, the zone must be resigned using the `dnssec-signzone` functionality. Then, dynamic updates may be reenabled using the `rndc thaw` command.

This manual freeze-sign-thaw process has been obviated in BIND 9.6 and above which has added an automated signing mechanism for dynamic updates, vastly simplifying this process. Along with its normal integration of journal updates into the zone file, BIND signs each update using the ZSK along with the corresponding "before" and "after" NSEC[3] records to canonically insert the record into the zone. BIND 9.6 also periodically examines the zone for signatures nearing expiration. It will then automatically generate new signatures in such cases. To perform this automated signature process, BIND must have access to the ZSK private key to sign or resign records.

13.5.3 DNSSEC Deployment Considerations

BIND provides several utilities for the creation of keys and for signing zones to simplify the DNSSEC implementation process. However, consider the following carefully when deciding to deploy DNSSEC

- Decide which zones you want to sign. In general, the first and perhaps only zones to consider signing are your public or external zones. These enables users resolving your public name space to do so securely and reduces the probability of an attacker "impersonating" your zone. Partner connections via the Internet should likewise be considered. Otherwise, internal resolution of internal information can usually be trusted within most organizations.
- As we've seen the size of a signed zone file is much larger than that of a corresponding unsigned zone file. This may affect required server memory for large zones as well as zone loading time.
- Signing your zones protects the integrity of your name space but not your DNS caches. Consider configuring DNSSEC validation on your Internet-querying DNS servers.
- The resolution response for a given query would also grow larger, given the attachment of RRSIG records and potentially DNSKEY records corresponding to the query. This could adversely affect query response time and performance.
- The resolution process performance may also be further adversely impacted by the trust anchor confirmation process, where keys and delegation signer records are validated up to the trust anchor zone or DLV registry.
- DNSSEC introduces the requirement for time synchronization given the absolute time references denoting valid and expiration times in RRSIG records
- Zone footprinting by hopping NSEC records is a potential information over-exposure though the NSEC3 record makes this process more difficult. Consider whether zone footprinting is really an issue for you (generally information published in DNS is public information!) due to the computational complexity and potentially time for generating NSEC3 records within a signed zone.
- Key update procedures for initialization and rollover must be devised to provide authenticated access to updated KSKs via an out of band mechanism if your trusting resolvers are not using the automated trust anchor update feature. The KSK public key update must be communicated to all who trust your zone as well as your parent zone or DLV, if any, in the form of a DS or DLV record, respectively.
- DNSSEC performs data origin authentication, data integrity verification, and authenticated denial of existence. It does not protect against other vulnerability types introduced in Chapter 12. Don't forget to implement the mitigation tactics discussed in that chapter to protect against other vulnerabilities.

PART IV

IPAM INTEGRATION

Having discussed the constituent components of IPAM in the previous three parts of this book, Part IV brings together the integrated management tasks for these components. We'll start with overall IPAM techniques in Chapter 14. Then we'll discuss IPv6 implementation in an IPv4 network and coexistence strategies in Chapter 15.

14

IP ADDRESS MANAGEMENT PRACTICES

In the Preface of this book, we stated that the practice of IP address management (IPAM) entails the application of network management disciplines to IP address space and associated network services. Because IP addresses and associated DHCP and DNS functions are so foundational to IP services and applications running over a network, these functions must be prudently managed, much as other critical network infrastructure elements are managed. It's a small leap to consider DNS and DHCP servers as network elements, as they provide critical IP services to clients on an IP network. While not in-band or on the data path for user IP traffic like traditional network elements, they provide necessary services required to make such in-band data paths possible and usable. From a telephony Intelligent Network analogy, DNS and DHCP are akin to Network Control Points in providing lookup and addressing infromation. So it follows that centralized management of these servers is equally wise and beneficial[*].

---

[*] Much of the content of this chapter mirrors that of similarly titled Chapter 6 of Ref. 11.

The most commonly applied network management approach is that of the FCAPS[*] model for network management. The Information Technology Infrastructure Library, ITIL®, has emerged as a popular set of guidelines for managing enterprise IT infrastructures. Developed by the U.K. Office of Government and Commerce (OGC), ITIL is a best practices framework with the perspective of the IT organization as a service provider to the enterprise. We'll discuss common IP address management tasks within the context of the FCAPS model, then relate functional mapping of these tasks to ITIL process areas toward the end of the chapter.

14.1 FCAPS SUMMARY

The FCAPS model covers the following key functions within the practice of network management:

- *F = Fault Management.* Involves monitoring and detection of network faults with the ability to diagnose, isolate, and resolve them. As network elements such as routers, servers, and switches are monitored to detect faults or outages, DHCP and DNS services should likewise be monitored. Appropriate workaround mechanisms such as providing for high availability services may also be implemented.
- *C = Configuration Management.* Entails accurate configuration and backups of network elements, including DHCP and DNS servers. Accurate and timely configuration of network elements reduces provisioning errors and time intervals within change management windows.
- *A = Accounting Management.* Involves tracking and policing of usage of network resources with respect to business quotas or customer entitlements. Aspects of IP management regarding access control policies, address utilization with respect to business parameters, and monitoring service level agreement (SLA) compliance fall within accounting management.
- *P = Performance Management.* Deals with tracking performance of network elements and services, along with resource utilization. Tracking of IP address utilization and DHCP/DNS server performance are key requirements for effective IP address management.
- *S = Security Management.* Includes the securing of information regarding the network and its users, providing access controls, as well as audit logging and security breach detection. Security management for IP address management includes IP address access policies, auditing, DNS and DHCP security, and rogue or illicit device detection on the network.

---

[*] FCAPS is defined in ITU standard M.3400 (192) as part of the Telecommunications Management Network (TMN) framework for managing data networks.

14.2 COMMON IP MANAGEMENT TASKS

Using the basic FCAPS functional categorization, we'll discuss the most common IP management tasks, starting with "configuration," then move on to the other categories. Some functions may likely require the use of multiple management systems depending on your IP management system capabilities. For example, if your IP management system consists of a spreadsheet, you'll need another tool to perform fault management functions. Likewise for commercial IP management systems, varying subsets of functions and tasks will be available natively within the system, while others will require supplemental systems.

14.3 CONFIGURATION MANAGEMENT

When most people think of IPAM, they primarily consider it a configuration management mechanism. Early IPAM systems in fact focused solely on configuration management, though many have expanded into other aspects of FCAPS over time. Nevertheless, configuration management remains a fundamental function of IPAM. In this section, we'll discuss common tasks required when managing IP address space and DHCP/DNS server configurations. These tasks relate to the day-to-day activities of an IP address planner with respect to moves, adds, and changes for IP addresses, subnets, address space, domains, and other aspects of DHCP and DNS configuration.

Configuration management within the context of IPAM entails the configuring of DHCP and DNS servers for lease and parameter assignment and name resolution, respectively. This involves at minimum, configuration of IPAM-related information, that is, address pools and associated parameters and DNS configuration and zone files. The configuration process may also entail configuration of high availablilty deployments and server level configuration parameters, for server-based or appliance-based DHCP/DNS servers.

The result of the configuration management function is that each of the DHCP and DNS servers within the network is configured with its files or parameters necessary to perform its respective role in the network, for example, primary DHCP server for a set of address pools, failover DHCP configuration, DNS zones, parameters, and options. From this perspective, the goal is to base each DHCP and DNS server's configuration on its type (e.g., ISC, Microsoft, etc.), its role in deployment, and the portion of the network it is serving. The portion of the network relates to the association of a set of DNS domains, subnets, and address pools assigned to each server, and should align with the overall IPAM plan for address space and domains.

Configuration of routers with new, moved, or deleted subnets, as well as relay agent information regarding which DHCP servers to which to relay DHCP packets is another function closely tied to IP management. Few IPAM systems on the market perform this level of router integration natively. Historically, the IP or server teams were distinct from router teams, so inter-team automation was discouraged; after all, if a router ended up being misconfigured, it would come back to the router team. Some IPAM systems enable automation of this process nonetheless, natively or via an API call, which can "hook" the output of an IPAM system subnet allocation to the input of a router configuration tool. The brute force method likely entails sending an email to the router team after a subnet has been allocated in the IP inventory database or spreadsheet.

14.3.1 Address Allocation Tasks

Address Block Allocation. Starting at the top of the IPAM food chain, consider the tasks required to perform top-level block allocations using the processes we discussed in Chapter 3. Allocation of address space hierarchically from the top-down, planning address space allocations must consider business requirements with respect to address capacity for each application and user community at each site from the bottom-up. Ultimately, each site will be served from the respective allocation, so capacity planning should incorporate addressing needs at each current and planned future site.

If you don't have time or resources to conduct a full capacity analysis, one rule of thumb for enterprise organizations is to consider the number of employees at each location and multiply this number by four. This quantity provides a rough estimate and accounts for each employee's devices as well as infrastructure devices like routers and servers. On the other hand, if you have plentiful address space for the size of your organization, you may just want to allocate uniformly, as we illustrated in Chapter 3.

Once address capacity has been quantified per site, consider the routing topology and how to best model the addressing hierarchy. Using a core-regional-access router topology as with IPAM Worldwide lends itself to a corresponding mapping of addressing hierarchy. Such a topology features a backbone or core network feeding regional networks, which in turn feed access or local networks. Routers serve as topological interfaces and provide aggregation of downstream networks. Now integrate the capacity data with the topology to identify the roll-up of address space at each hierarchy level.

Let's illustrate this integration by example. IPAM Worldwide's topology features a core network serving the global continental level. The regional level subdivides the continents of North America and Europe. With 17,000 employees mapping to roughly 75,000 IP addresses, our 10.0.0.0/8 network should provide plenty of capacity with over 16 million IP addresses, let alone our IPv6 space. Thus, IPAM Worldwide's IP planners decide to utilize a *uniform* allocation strategy as much as possible. The largest distribution center is in Norristown with about 450 employees and the largest branch office of Quincy is planning expansion up to 200 employees. Hence, each distribution center will receive a /23 allocation (510 usable IP addresses) per application[*] and each branch office will receive a /24 (254 usable addresses) per application. This provides ample address space for each site with room for growth.

The region with the most offices, North America East, contains 8 distribution centers and 9 branch offices. The corresponding address space rollup per application (8 /23s + 9 /24s) is roughly a /19[†]. To provide adequate address capacity for growth, IPAM

---

[*] If we were to assign one monolithic block to these sites, we'd likely require a quantity of IP addresses totaling four times the number of employees, but we're allocating multiple like-sized blocks instead.

[†] Eight /23s = one /20, and eight /24s = one /21. One /20 + one /21 + one /24 is over 3/4 of a /19.

Worldwide's IP planner allocates a /18 for each application in each region. After these sizing guidelines have been defined, the execution process detailed in Chapter 3 for IPAM Worldwide may ensue.

A more intensive strategy may alternatively be employed to allocate to each site only what is needed. This *as-needed* approach requires more precise determination and tracking over time of IP address capacity requirements at each site to assure adequate capacity deployment. This approach is more intensive but makes for better utilization of the address space, which may be required for larger organizations or service providers. The same process is used for block allocation, though the math and tracking requirements become a bit more rigorous, especially with a mix of differently sized allocations. The requirement to proactively monitor address utilization increases when allocations are "right-sized" to conserve address space, where extra "fudge factors" in allocations are kept to a minimum.

Based on the selected DHCP and DNS server deployment strategy and needs of the expansion, you should map out server sizing regarding the number of servers of a given size of each type needed and target locations. Based on this plan, procurement of the servers, shipping/receiving, then base level server configuration can ensue. While we haven't added any suballocations yet at this point in the process, this base DHCP/DNS configuration would include basic policy definitions, as well as zones corresponding to the domain plan for the additional address space.

For base and subsequent address block allocations, updating the address plan is a necessary first step. But there's more to be done. To implement the plan, the allocated address space should be configured in the core routers to enable dynamic updating of routing tables. Updating of relay agent information in routers to relay to the DHCP server(s) is another required task, though this is more commonly performed during the subnet allocation task. Additional housekeeping tasks may be necessary to add the newly allocated address space to server access control lists (ACLs) at the network interface level and also at the DNS service level regarding "allow" options such as allow-query, allow-recursion, and so on, as well as view definitions if appropriate.

In summary, the task of address block allocation includes the following subtasks:

- Identify sites requiring IP space and quantities of users or IP devices required per site.
- Determine the routing topology in terms of address aggregation requirements.
- Identify the minimum allocation at each level of the topology considering growth plans, and employ allocation policies such as a uniform or as-needed strategy.
- Identify free address space within the IP address inventory and allocate a block of the selected size.
- Design, procure, install, and configure DHCP and DNS servers as required.
- Update router configurations with the allocated network and relay agent information.
- Update DHCP and DNS ACL configurations if appropriate.

- Manage the overall allocation process to track locations and servers coming on line. Subnet allocations per location are covered next.

Subnet Allocation. After the baseline address allocation has been deployed, the foundation is in place for subnet allocations that support individual IP addresses for routers and hosts. Business initiatives will likely drive subnet allocations: new sites requiring IP addresses due to expansion of the business, plans for new service offerings such as voice over IP, and even a merger or acquisition each can heavily impact the IP address plan. A similar process with respect to sizing up expected capacity requirements, mapping capacity rollups to the supporting routing topology, and consideration of free address capacity and allocation policies can be used for subsequent allocations.

This basic task of subnet allocation involves the determination of a subnet that is available which rolls up with the address allocation plan for the given location and application, and assignment of the subnet in the IP address plan "database." For example, if IPAM Worldwide decides to open a new distribution center in Portland, Oregon, IP planners would access our IP inventory spreadsheet to identify available address space. The address allocation breakdown of North America West data space (10.32.128.0/18) was illustrated in Chapter 3 and is shown below.

N.A. West Data	10.32.128.0/18 **00001010 00100000 10**000000 00000000
San Fran. Site	10.32.128.0/23 **00001010 00100000 1000000**0 00000000
Denver Site	10.32.130.0/23 **00001010 00100000 1000001**0 00000000
Vancouver Site	10.32.132.0/23 **00001010 00100000 1000010**0 00000000
Phoenix Site	10.32.134.0/23 **00001010 00100000 1000011**0 00000000
Calgary Site	10.32.136.0/24 **00001010 00100000 10001000** 00000000
Albuquerque Site	10.32.137.0/24 **00001010 00100000 10001001** 00000000
Salt Lake City Site	10.32.138.0/24 **00001010 00100000 10001010** 00000000
Boulder Site	10.32.139.0/24 **00001010 00100000 10001011** 00000000
Edmonton Site	10.32.140.0/24 **00001010 00100000 10001100** 00000000
Sacramento Site	10.32.141.0/24 **00001010 00100000 10001101** 00000000
Anaheim Site	10.32.142.0/24 **00001010 00100000 10001110** 00000000
Free Space	10.32.143.0/24 **00001010 00100000 10001111** 00000000
Free Space	10.32.144.0/20 **00001010 00100000 1001**0000 00000000
Free Space	10.32.160.0/19 **00001010 00100000 101**00000 00000000

As we discussed in Chapter 3, by using a best-fit approach, we should consider the smallest free block for allocation. We see from this table that we have a /24 available, but this is too small for our Portland distribution center, which requires a /23. We'll look to the next smallest block, 10.32.144.0/20 and allocate our /23 from this block. We thus allocate 10.32.144.0/23 to Portland, and the remainder of the original /20 block consists of 10.32.152.0/21, 10.32.148.0/22, and 10.32.146.0/23 as shown in the resultant table below.

N.A. West Data	10.32.128.0/18	**00001010 00100000 10**000000 00000000
San Fran. Site	10.32.128.0/23	**00001010 00100000 1000000**0 00000000
Denver Site	10.32.130.0/23	**00001010 00100000 1000001**0 00000000
Vancouver Site	10.32.132.0/23	**00001010 00100000 1000010**0 00000000
Phoenix Site	10.32.134.0/23	**00001010 00100000 1000011**0 00000000
Calgary Site	10.32.136.0/24	**00001010 00100000 10001000** 00000000
Albuquerque Site	10.32.137.0/24	**00001010 00100000 10001001** 00000000
Salt Lake City Site	10.32.138.0/24	**00001010 00100000 10001010** 00000000
Boulder Site	10.32.139.0/24	**00001010 00100000 10001011** 00000000
Edmonton Site	10.32.140.0/24	**00001010 00100000 10001100** 00000000
Sacramento Site	10.32.141.0/24	**00001010 00100000 10001101** 00000000
Anaheim Site	10.32.142.0/24	**00001010 00100000 10001110** 00000000
Portland Site	10.32.144.0/23	**00001010 00100000 1001000**0 00000000
Free Space	10.32.143.0/24	**00001010 00100000 10001111** 00000000
Free Space	10.32.146.0/23	**00001010 00100000 1001001**0 00000000
Free Space	10.32.148.0/22	**00001010 00100000 1001010**0 00000000
Free Space	10.32.152.0/21	**00001010 00100000 10011**000 00000000
Free Space	10.32.160.0/19	**00001010 00100000 101**00000 00000000

Note that our free 10.32.143.0/24 block is now enclosed or surrounded by assigned blocks. A future requirement for a /24 or smaller block can use this space, but otherwise it is unusable. Applying a best-fit approach seeks to minimize these "orphaned" blocks, though as we see, they still may be rendered.

In addition to identifying and recording the allocated subnet, the subnet allocation process requires provisioning of the subnet address on the appropriate router interface. Some individual IP addresses on the subnet need to be assigned to infrastructure devices like routers and servers. Defining and updating DHCP server configurations is also required to account for address pool(s) and corresponding DHCP options and/or client class parameters needed for devices that will require DHCP on the allocated subnet.

Devices to be assigned addresses on the subnet now and in the future will likely require name resolution information in DNS. At a minimum, this information applies to a forward domain for domain name-to-IP address lookup and a reverse domain for the IP address-to-name lookup. This requires defining and updating DNS server configurations with domain updates (e.g., in-addr.arpa and ip6.arpa domain(s)) and resource record updates for name servers and statically assigned addresses. Of course, these domains must exist or must be provisioned and configured on the respective DNS server.

Depending on your domain topology, adding a new subnet to a location may utilize an existing domain, though this is not necessarily the case. A new domain may need to be defined and configured as a subdomain or as a new zone on the appropriate DNS servers. In the same way, the reverse domain corresponding to the subnet address may need to be added as well, unless a higher layer in-addr.arpa or ip6.arpa zone will host the corresponding PTR resource records.

The subnet allocation process illustrates the tight interrelationship among address allocation, assignment, and DHCP and DNS server configuration tasks. Depending on your business processes, subnets may be allocated or reserved prior to address assignment and DHCP/DNS configuration. Nonetheless, this complete set of steps will typically be required to bring a subnet into production:

- Identify free address space within the scope of the topology where the subnet is needed.
- Allocate a subnet of the required size from the appropriate address space and record the allocation in the IP address plan.
- Update router configurations regarding the allocated network.
- Assign and provision manually assigned addresses for routers, servers or other subnet infrastructure devices.
- Design and configure DHCP address pools if necessary to serve dynamic hosts on the subnet. This may require association of options, directives and client classes based on requirements of devices planned for use of the address pool(s).
- Define new DNS domains required to serve hosts on the subnet, define resource records for infrastructure or static devices within new or existing domains and configure appropriate DNS servers.[*]
- Complete the allocation process by confirming provisioning and reachability of the subnet, as well as by verifying corresponding DHCP and DNS configurations.

IP Address Assignment. Assigning, deassigning, and reassigning IP addresses to individual hosts is usually the most frequent IP management activity in most organizations. This is typically associated with deployment, redeployment, or decommissioning of devices, including routers, servers, printers, and the like. In terms of address assignment, the IP address inventory database must be consulted to identify an available IP address. If possible, it would be useful to ping the IP address to be assigned just to verify accuracy of the inventory, though we'll discuss the process of overall inventory assurance as a separate task. The IP address to be assigned should then be denoted as assigned to the given device in the inventory database.

The actual physical IP address assignment may be performed by manually (statically) configuring the device, by autoconfiguration, or by using DHCP (in this case, we'll assume Manual DHCP is used to assign the designated IP address to the corresponding host). In the static assignment case, the assigned address must be configured directly on the device,

---

[*] In some networks, pre-seeding of resource records for DHCP addresses is required to permit users of these addresses to appear in DNS (e.g., to facilitate VPN connections, which require the presence of a PTR record) without performing dynamic updates.

so unless the IP address assigner is also responsible for the physical assignment, this process would entail an email or phone call to the device owner conveying the assigned IP address information to be entered. With autoconfiguration, this bottom-up assignment process is more of a detection issue than top-down assignment. When using Manual DHCP, an entry in the appropriate DHCP server(s) configuration file would be necessary to map the device's hardware address to the assigned IP address.

Most devices with IP addresses will require corresponding DNS resource records to enable reachability by name. Using the DHCP method of address assignment, the DHCP server can be configured to update a master DNS server upon assignment of the IP address. This update would affect the forward domain for domain name-to-IP address (A/AAAA) lookup and the reverse domain for the reverse (PTR) lookup. A similar DNS update task would be required if assigning the address manually. Updating DNS with this new host information may entail editing or updating the corresponding zone files on the server or by sending dynamic updates.

You may not want an autoconfigured device to update DNS on its own, at least on an enterprise network, though this may be suitable for a community or ad hoc network. Identifying the presence of a newly autoconfigured device to manually update DNS presents its own challenge! If such devices require resolution information in DNS, use of a router log or subnet snooping utility may be necessary to identify the IPv6 address.

In summary, the task of IP address assignment includes the following subtasks:

- Determine how the device will obtain its IP address: via manual configuration, autoconfiguration, or via DHCP.
  - o If Dynamic DHCP or Automatic DHCP, determine if current address pools, if any, on the subnet have capacity to support the device; if so, this task completes; if not, configure an address pool of the corresponding DHCP type on the DHCP server along with necessary option parameters.
  - o If Manual DHCP, identify a free IP address within the subnet where the device is located and assign the address to the device by configuring the DHCP server to reserve or assign a Manual DHCP address for the device's MAC address.
  - o If manually configured on the device, identify a free IP address within the subnet where the device is located and assign the address to the device. Have the assigned static IP address configured on the device manually.
  - o In all cases, update the IP address plan with the assigned address, whether a spreadsheet or other IPAM tool.
- Determine if DNS resource records need to be manually created and updated. This would generally be the case for statically assigned addresses. For DHCP-assigned devices, the DHCP server can be configured to perform dynamic updates, though in some cases where dynamic updates are not feasible or allowed by policy, manual updating of corresponding resource records may be required.
- Verify completion of the address assignment process by pinging the address successfully and verifying its resource records in DNS. For devices assigned an

address via an address pool, verification may not be needed; however, if it is, the address may not be known *a priori*. Locating the device's MAC address in the DHCP lease file, followed by a ping of the corresponding address confirms its assignment in this case.

14.3.2 Address Deletion Tasks

As we've illustrated, address allocation is a top-down process, with allocation of hierarchical blocks, from which subnets can be allocated, from with IP addresses can be assigned. Deletion of address space requires the inverse operation and is necessarily bottom-up. Deleting an address block before the underlying blocks, subnets, and IP addresses have been deleted would strand these underlying elements, so unless you enjoy mass chaos, a more controlled process is warranted.

Deleting IP Addresses. Deleting an IP address is relatively straightforward: delete or free up the IP address in the IP inventory, removing the M-DHCP entry from DHCP if appropriate releasing the lease, and removing associated DNS resource records. However, care must be taken to assure the address has been relinquished by the device and that DHCP and DNS updates have been completed before assigning the address to another device. For example, simply deleting a lease on a DHCP server does not force the client holding that lease to relinquish it. The DHCP Force-Renew message was designed to force a DHCP client to enter the Renewing state to enable a server to potentially NAK the client's attempt to renew the lease, thereby freeing the address. However, Force-Renew has not been widely implemented.

Denoting the address as in a state of "pending deletion" or something similar would alert other administrators not to assign that address to another device until confirmation is received of its availability. This confirmation process entails pinging the address, perhaps successively over several days, and confirming the deletion of its associated data in DNS and DHCP servers.

Deleting Subnets. Deleting a subnet may be required when closing a site or consolidating address space. Devices with IP addresses on the subnet to be deleted should be moved or decommissioned such that the subnet is free of address assignments (other than perhaps subnet-serving routers). After all IP addresses have been verified as free, the subnet may be reclaimed into the free address space for future allocation.

Upon freeing up of a subnet, it may be possible to join the freed space with a contiguous free address block, creating a larger free block. Following our IPAM Worldwide North America West Data block example from the Subnet Allocation section above, if IPAM Worldwide decides to close the Anaheim branch office, its address space, 10.32.142.0/24, now considered free, is contiguous with the 10.32.143.0/24 block. We could join these two blocks into a single free block, 10.32.142.0/23. Doing so now makes it clear that this /23 could be assigned to a future distribution center for example.

Deleting Blocks. Address block deletion may result from the withdrawal from a major business market or consolidation of sites, among other reasons. Generally all downstream IP addresses, subnets, address pools, resource records, and domains should first be decommissioned before the macro level block can be freed up for future assignment consideration. Thus, after the individual delete IP address tasks and delete subnet tasks within the target block have been completed, the block itself may be freed up. As with a modest to large allocation task, project planning resources may be required to verify deletions up the hierarchy. As in the delete subnet task, freed block space may be joined with contiguous free space. As with block allocations, additional housekeeping tasks related to DHCP and DNS ACL configurations should be considered with respect to address pools, domains, ACLs, and resource records.

14.3.3 Address Renumbering or Movement Tasks

Moving, or renumbering of address blocks, subnets or individual addresses combines the allocation process with the deletion process. The allocation process, as described above, should be performed from a top-down perspective to allocate space to which underlying subnets and IP addresses will be moved. The deletion process frees up address space from the bottom-up as addresses are moved to the target allocated space. In essence, the size of the scope of the addresses to be moved must be allocated to accommodate the addresses to be moved, temporarily doubling the address space associated with this set of devices. As addresses are moved, the former address space can be freed up, returning address allocations to previous levels.

IP Address Moves. Moving an IP address can be considered a combination of assigning an IP address on the destination subnet and deleting the IP address on the current subnet. Depending on the method of address assignment and the type of move, different tactics can be used. The type of move relates to physical movement of a device to a different subnet (physical move) versus the reassignment of the IP address on the same or a different subnet (logical move). A physical move of a nonmobile IP device will typically involve a "reboot" of each IP device, which affords more control of the address assignment process.

PHYSICAL MOVES. Physical moves imply powering down, moving, then powering up devices at the destination location. For Dynamic DHCP and Automatic DHCP assigned devices, if an entire pool is being moved, the destination pool should be setup on a [same or different] DHCP server. Make sure the router(s) serving the destination subnet are configured to relay DHCP packets to the DHCP server configured with the new pool. When these devices power up, they will likely attempt to renew the most recent lease they possessed on the old subnet. Make sure any Automatic DHCP devices issue DHCPRE-QUESTs upon power up and don't just continue using their old IP lease; if they assume the old [infinite] is valid, manual intervention will be required to reset the device's address. Otherwise, the DHCP server will NAK the DHCPREQUEST attempt by each client. Clients will revert to the Init-Reboot state and issue a DHCPDISCOVER packet to obtain a new lease. The DHCP server obliges with a lease within the new destination pool. A similar process may be used for DHCPv6 clients. Once all devices have physically moved, the pool serving the old subnet may be decommissioned.

Physical movement of a M-DHCP device entails creating the M-DHCP entry in the DHCP server serving the new subnet and deleting the entry on the former DHCP server. If the same DHCP server is being used, simply edit the IP address associated with the device's MAC address. When the device powers up on the new subnet, it should follow a similar process to Dynamic DHCP and Automatic DHCP, with a DHCPREQUEST attempt, which the DHCP server NAKs, followed by reversion to issuing a DHCPDIS-COVER and address reassignment using the standard DHCP process.

Moving a device that autoconfigures its IPv6 address will lead to the device detecting its new subnet via router discovery along with corresponding subnet policies including the availability of DHCPv6 services. If autoconfiguring its address, the device auto-configures then verifies its uniqueness through duplicate address detection. If using DHCPv6, the normal DHCPv6 process is followed to obtain an IPv6 address and associated parameters. In some cases (i.e., when the O bit is set in the router adver-tisement), both autoconfiguration and DHCPv6 may be used.

Updating of DNS resource records may be performed by the DHCP server or manually if dynamic updates are prohibited for these DHCP cases.

Physical moves of manually configured devices requires assignment of an address from the IP inventory, and manually configuring the new IP address in the device as it powers up on the new subnet. At this point, the old address can be freed up, though an interim "pending delete" state may be useful in preventing premature reassignment of the corresponding address prior to verification of address availability. DNS resource records should be updated as well to reflect the device's new IP address.

In all of these cases, the IP inventory should be utilized to identify free address(es) on the destination subnet or pool, and to free up addresses on the old subnet as well as corresponding DNS resource records as device moves are confirmed.

LOGICAL MOVES. Logical moves are a bit more challenging as they do not necessarily involve a device reinitializing. For DHCP devices, an address pool containing the destination IP addresses should be configured on the [same or different] DHCP server. The lease time for the pool or device should be stepped down in advance of the move date. For example, if a normal lease time is 1 week, it should be lowered to 1 day for example during the week leading up to the move and to 2–6 h on the day of the move. A device may have renewed a weeklong lease just before you changed the lease time to days, so it will not attempt to renew until halfway through the week (or based on your T1 time option setting). Thus if your nominal lease time is 2 weeks, ratchet down the lease time 2 weeks before the planned move. On the day of the move, set the lease time to a minimum[*] time if it's important that all devices move at nearly the same time. If move coincidence is not critical, leaving lease times on the order of hours should yield a complete move within a few hours.

In this scenario, it's recommended that the DHCP server perform DNS updates if possible to more closely map DNS information updates with address changes. Manual

---

[*] Minimum time can be on the order of minutes or hours depending on network traffic and server performance considerations. The shorter the lease time, the more DHCP packets will be sent but the more time-aligned the move of DHCP clients can be orchestrated.

intervention of A-DHCP devices may be necessary unless they do adhere to lease renewal policies despite possessing infinite leases.

Movement of manually addressed devices follows the same process as in physical movement. A destination IP address is assigned from the IP inventory, and the new IP address is configured on the device. Once confirmed, the old address can be freed up. DNS resource records should be updated as well to reflect the device's new IP address.

Logical movement of an autoconfigured device can be performed by configuring the router serving the corresponding subnet to ratchet down the preferred and valid address lifetime values it advertises during the neighbor (router) discovery process. Shortening these timer values for the address prefix from which the device is being moved while introducing the new prefix with a "normal" address lifetimes will enable autoconfigured devices to perform this logical move automatically. Once all devices have moved and the valid lifetime of the former prefix expires, the prefix can be removed.

Subnet Moves. Moving a subnet could involve one of two results: movement of the subnet and its assigned IP addresses to another router interface, preserving the current address assignment or movement to another router interface, requiring a new subnet address. We'll include the subnet renumbering task with the latter case as it too results in a new subnet address though without necessarily moving the subnet to another router interface. The first case requires consideration of address space rollup within the hierarchy but generally consists of modifying and verifying router provisioning compliance with the plan, as well as updates to routing tables and DHCP Relay addresses as necessary.

Movement of a subnet due to a physical move or a higher level renumbering requires a bit more work. A physical movement where devices are physically moved, for example, when an office is moved, is inherently disruptive. The destination subnet may be allocated and provisioned on the destination router interface, along with the other tasks described above related to reserving static addresses and updating DHCP and DNS configurations. When each moved device plugs in, it will need to be manually readdressed with the new address and/or obtain a DHCP lease on a pool relevant to the subnet as described above for IP address moves. Logical subnet moves or renumbering likewise follows the logical IP address move process for each device.

After all devices have been moved from the old subnet to the new, the old subnet may be freed up following the delete subnet process.

Block Moves. Moving macro level blocks with underlying subnets and IP addresses requires careful project planning and execution. The allocation of the destination block should follow those tasks outlined for block allocation. Assuming a move is for renumbering only, a like-sized destination block should be allocated. If the move is motivated by or otherwise spurs the opportunity for address consolidation or expansion, the destination allocation should be sized based on underlying capacity requirements and topology architecture as discussed in the Block Allocation section. Once the allocation has been made, sub-allocations and subnet allocations may begin. IP addresses and pools can then be moved following the process described for IP address moves. As IP addresses and subnets completely move from their old assignments, these can be decommissioned or freed up when moves have been confirmed and their corresponding resource records removed.

14.3.4 Block/Subnet Splits

Splitting an address block entails the creation of two or more smaller sized blocks from a given source block. Splits may be necessary to free up address space or even as a means of suballocation of address space. In the former case, the addresses within a subnet may be consolidated to the first half of the subnet, freeing up assignments in the second half. In this scenario splitting the block yields an occupied subnet (first half) and a free subnet (second half). Some organizations have historically allocated regional blocks, then split them to assign sub-blocks and subnets lower in the address hierarchy. In some sense this is a form of block allocation.

Note that splitting a block in two will render two formerly usable addresses generally unusable as the former single network with one network and one broadcast address now has two of each. For example, the 192.168.24.0/24 network has network address 192.168.24.0 and broadcast address 192.168.24.255. Splitting this block into two /25s, 192.168.24.0/25 and 192.168.24.128/25, renders formerly usable address 192.168.24.127 as the new first network's broadcast address and 192.168.24.128 as the second network's network address.

Be cognizant of DNS reverse zone impacts when splitting blocks. If DNS administrative authority for the two resulting subnets remains consolidated under one set of administrators, the original in-addr.arpa or ip6.arpa zone probably does not require modification. However, if a resulting split block or subnet will have its devices administered in DNS by a separate delegated authority, then the original reverse domain will require splitting as well. This entails creation of two reverse zones corresponding to the resulting split subnets and notification to the parent reverse zone administrator of the split in responsibility to properly delegate down the reverse zone tree to the proper set of DNS servers for authoritative information.

Splitting a block need not be restricted to only splitting in half, say a /24 into two /25s. A split may be used to carve out a /23 from a /20, as we did when assigning address space to our new Portland distribution center in the section regarding subnet allocation. This split yielded a /23, which we assigned to Portland, and free space consisting of a /23, a /22, and a /21. In this example, we preserved large blocks following our optimal allocation strategy. Alternatively, we could have simply split our /20 into eight /23s, though this may be wasteful unless same-sized allocations are used by policy, which is the uniform allocation policy, as opposed to the as-needed allocation strategy.

In summary, the process of splitting a block is similar to that of allocating a block. The block to be split is successively divided until the desired block size is attained. Remaining free blocks are either retained or also split to the same size as the desired block to render a uniform block split. DNS implications on the reverse zone tree and administrative delegation must be considered. And keep in mind that each network resulting from the split results in an additional network and broadcast address.

14.3.5 Block/Subnet Joins

A join combines two contiguous same-sized address blocks or subnets into a single block or subnet. We saw an example of joining blocks in the block deletion section. After freeing up the Anaheim block, 10.32.142.0/24, we joined it to a contiguous free block, 10.32.143.0/24 to create a single 10.32.142.0/23 block. Successive joins may be performed to consolidate smaller chunks of contiguous address space. Joins are only valid for contiguous blocks of the same size. Joining a /25 and a /24 is not valid as the "other /25" not included in the join must remain uniquely identified. However, two contiguous /25s and a neighboring /24 can be joined to form a /23. The two /25s would be joined first to form a /24; then this and the other /24 can be joined to create a /23.

Rolling up of joined blocks may also require an updating of DNS reverse zones to consolidate underlying device resource records into a "joined" reverse zone reflecting the resulting consolidated subnet.

14.3.6 DHCP Server Configuration

DHCP server configuration is a key IPAM task as we covered in Part II of this book. As we've discussed, the address management tasks covered so far have major impact on DHCP server configurations. DHCP server configuration goes beyond address pool creation, movement, and deletion, though the extent of additional functions is constrained by the capabilities of the DHCP server vendor. Key among DHCP server configuration parameters are

- *DHCP Address Pools.* Address ranges and associated DHCP options and server policies for Dynamic, Automatic, and Manual DHCP clients.
- *Client Classes.* Parameter match values (e.g., vendor-class-identifier = "Avaya 4600") and associated allow/deny pools and DHCP options and server policies.
- High availability parameter settings for primary/failover or split scopes.
- Configuration of server activities such as dynamic DNS updates and other server directives and parameters.

The actual server configuration syntax and interface will depend on the server type. For example, ISC DHCP servers can be configured by editing the dhcp.conf file while Microsoft DHCP can be updated using a Windows MMC interface. Both of these and other DHCP vendors also provide command line interfaces or APIs to perform configuration updates. DHCP deployment, covered in Chapter 7, also plays a role in each server's configuration. For these and other products, please consult your vendor's documentation.

Address Assignment/DHCP and IP Address Management. Individual static IP address assignments need to be recorded to assure uniqueness. Within allocated subnets, DHCP address pools should be tracked to provide an overall view of address assignments within the subnet, whether statically or dynamically assigned. While tracking of individual DHCP leases within a spreadsheet is not readily performed, allocation of address pools within the spreadsheet or database should be performed at the least. This will help assure unique address assignments over time.

This consolidated address assignment data store provides the known level of IP address inventory. The IPAM Worldwide team has assigned a consistent set of IP addresses on each subnet for static devices such as routers, switches and servers. The team has also defined a number of Manual DHCP addresses for printers and address pools for sharing among DHCP client devices like laptops and VoIP phones. We've created a new tab for each site (this spreadsheet is getting quite large!) to inventory individual address as well as address pool assignments. Additional "comment" information is useful to track as well for certain devices, such as vendor contact, support information, asset information, and the like.

In addition to tracking IP address assignments, configuration of the corresponding DHCP server(s) must be performed to enable DHCP clients to obtain addresses. Configuration of the DHCP server entails configuring it with the address ranges corresponding to those assigned within the address plan. In Figure 14.1, we've allocated addresses 10.16.128.50-10.16.129.240 as a DHCP pool, so this range must be defined on a DHCP server. In addition, client class information, options, and other configuration parameters need to be configured on the DHCP server to properly configure different types of clients. This configuration operation may be performed using a text editor for ISC's DHCP server, using Microsoft Management Console (MMC) for Microsoft DHCP servers or using an IPAM tool that supports automated DHCP server configuration for DHCP server types deployed in your network. The main advantages of using an IPAM tool are that IP inventory information readily enables definition of DHCP pools and much of the DHCP server configuration information can be defined in the IPAM system and then applied across multiple DHCP servers, instead of defining this iteratively on multiple servers.

14.3.7 DNS Server Configuration

Like DHCP, DNS server configuration is a critical IPAM function as per Part III of this book. DNS configuration is tightly linked with address allocation, assignment, moves, and deletions as we've seen. These tasks discussed previously affect DNS domains, resource records, and possibly server configuration parameters. Key among DNS server configuration parameters are

- *Domains.* Adding, modifying, or deleting domains/zones on DNS servers.
- *Resource Records.* Adding, modifying, or deleting resource records.
- *Server, View, and Zone Configurations.* Setting and modifying option parameters affecting ACLs, server configuration, and so on.

The actual DNS server configuration syntax will depend on the server type. ISC BIND servers can be configured by editing the named.conf and associated zone files on the

Location	Address Block/Subnet	IP Addresses	Address and Device Type	Comments
San Francisco				
	10.16.128.0/23	10.16.128.1	Static—Router	SanFran VoIP subnet router 1
		10.16.128.2	Static—Router	SanFran VoIP subnet router 2
		10.16.128.3	Static—Router	SanFran VoIP subnet router HSRP address
		10.16.128.4	Static—DNS Server	Contact Fred Jones for support
		10.16.128.5	Static—FTP Server	
		10.16.128.6	Static—File Server	San Fran secondary
		10.16.128.7	Static—File Server	Backup for Seattle
		10.16.128.8	Static—File Server	Backup for Phoenix
		10.16.128.9		Save for growth
		10.16.128.10	Static—IPPBX	IP PBX-SF1
		10.16.128.11	Static—IPPBX	IP PBX-SF2
		...		
		10.16.128.20	Engineering Lab Server	Contact Engineering for assistance
		10.16.128.21	Engineering Lab Server	Contact Engineering for assistance
		10.16.128.22	Engineering Lab Server	Contact Engineering for assistance
		...		
		10.16.128.50- 10.16.129.240	VoIP DHCP Pool	Contact Mary Smith for support
		...		

Figure 14.1. Sample inventory table for IP addresses.

server. DNS servers that support DDNS may also support resource record updates in this manner. The use of `nsupdate` or similar DDNS mechanism provides a means to perform incremental updates without having to manually edit zone text files and reload respective zones, for example, using rndc. DDNS updates apply to resource record adds/changes/deletes only, so any zone or server configuration parameter changes or zone additions or deletions would still require text file editing and reloading of named.conf and/or affected zones. The deployment model for your DNS servers also plays a role in server configuration as we discussed in Chapter 11.

DNS and IP Address Management. Given the direct relationship between IP addresses and reverse domains, hostnames and other host information, it's clear that DNS is a key component of IP address management. Hosts on an IP network are assigned hostnames to facilitate human comprehension and IP addresses to enable communications via IP packets. DNS provides the critical linkage between hostnames and IP addresses, making IP applications easier to use.

From an IP address management perspective, clearly reverse DNS domains have a direct association with IP address block and subnet allocations. These domains are derived directly from their corresponding IP addresses. IPAM Worldwide has secured the ipamworldwide.com domain name from its ISP or domain registry. In so doing, IPAM Worldwide supplied three DNS server addresses to which iterative queries seeking resolution for ipamworldwide.com suffixes can be directed. Assigning web, email, and related Internet-facing servers, this domain suffix can help IPAM Worldwide create a global Internet presence.

Within the organization, this domain name is also used on the intranet. Subdomains are to be defined for the Corporate, Sales, Engineering, and Logistics team. The Engineering subdomain (eng.ipamworldwide.com) has been delegated to Engineering team DNS administrators, while the remaining subdomains will be centrally administered within the IT group. The Engineering team may further create subdomains below eng.ipamworldwide.com without impacting the IT team's administration effort. By delegating the eng subdomain, the IT team is empowering the Engineering team to manage the resolution of all eng subdomain hosts as well as its subdomains.

In keeping with the philosophy of centralizing IP address inventory, it follows that tracking hostnames and resource records associated with each IP address should be performed. Building on our IP inventory spreadsheet we just reviewed for IPAM Worldwide's San Francisco office, we can track this information for individual devices by simply inserting an FQDN column in our spreadsheet as shown in Figure 14.2.

In the above example, we're tracking only the FQDN for each statically defined host. Hosts obtaining leases from the DHCP address pool can have their hostname information updated in DNS via Dynamic DNS. We need to assure that we properly transcribe this inventory information into the DNS server configurations. From this "database," we can derive the A, AAAA, and PTR records corresponding to each host. We could expand the columns on the spreadsheet to track additional resource records associated with given hosts such as CNAME, MX, and so on.

14.3.8 Server Upgrades Management

New versions of DHCP and DNS server software are published periodically to address security vulnerabilities, provide bug fixes, or offer new features. The urgency to perform an upgrade is usually dictated by what's being addressed, with security vulnerabilities certainly being of highest urgency. The upgrade process is typically vendor specific and may require alignment of which hardware platforms and operating systems the upgraded version has been certified to run on. Hopefully the underlying operating system requirements would change only for new feature introductions and not security or bug fixes, but this is governed by vendor policy.

Most vendor DHCP/DNS appliance upgrades roll in the operating system upgrades as necessary within an overall upgrade package. Because the appliance vendor typically provides the operating system with the hardware platform, they should publish

Address Block/Subnet	IP Addresses	Address Type	FQDN	Comments
10.16.128.0/23	10.16.128.1	Static — Router	router-sf01.ipamworldwide.com.	SanFran VoIP subnet router 1
	10.16.128.2	Static — Router	router-sf10.ipamworldwide.com.	SanFran VoIP subnet router 2
	10.16.128.3	Static — Router	router-sf11.ipamworldwide.com.	SanFran VoIP subnet router HSRP address
	10.16.128.4	Static — DNS Server	ns-sf01.ipamworldwide.com.	Contact Fred Jones for support
	10.16.128.5	Static — FTP Server	ftp-sf.ipamworldwide.com.	
	10.16.128.6	Static—File Server	filecab-sf.ipamworldwide.com.	San Fran secondary
	10.16.128.7	Static—File Server	file-dr.ipamworldwide.com.	Backup for Seattle
	10.16.128.8	Static—File Server	file-phx.ipamworldwide.com.	Backup for Phoenix
	10.16.128.9			Save for growth

Figure 14.2. Sample inventory table with FQDNs.

	10.16.128.10	Static—IP PBX	denalo1.corp.ipamworldwide.com.	IP PBX-SF1
	10.16.128.11	Static—IP PBX	denalo2.corp.ipamworldwide.com.	IP PBX-SF2
	...			
	10.16.128.20	Engineering Lab Server	eng-sf1.eng.ipamworldwide.com.	Contact Engineering for assistance
	10.16.128.21	Engineering Lab Server	eng-sf2.eng.ipamworldwide.com.	Contact Engineering for assistance
	10.16.128.22	Engineering Lab Server	eng-sf3.eng.ipamworldwide.com.	Contact Engineering for assistance
	...			
	10.16.128.50-10.16.129.240	DHCP Pool for VoIP Phones		Contact Mary Smith for support
	...			

Figure 14.2. (*continued*)

compatibility upgrades as necessary for newer versions of their DHCP and DNS services. Most appliance solutions enable centralized staging of upgrade packages, with deployment to distributed appliances, vastly simplifying the upgrade process over a software-based upgrade process.

If you're running ISC, Microsoft, or other vendor DHCP or DNS daemons on your own hardware, you'll need to keep apprised of not only DHCP/DNS security updates but also those affecting the corresponding operating system running on the hardware.

14.4 FAULT MANAGEMENT

Fault management encompasses not only fault detection, but alert notification, trouble isolation capabilities, trouble tracking, and problem resolution processes. Monitoring of DHCP and DNS servers for faults and events enables a proactive means of minimizing services outages. In a well-designed network services architecture, clients should be able to obtain leases and resolve domain names despite an individual DHCP or DNS server outage. Nevertheless, detection of such an outage is important as the outage reduces the number of servers that clients may use to obtain these services thereby raising the vulnerability to service outage in the event of an additional server failure. For example, in a DHCP failover deployment, failure of one server will leave just one server available to service DHCP clients. In such a scenario, detection of the failed server facilitates timely, though not panicked, resolution of the server outage.

14.4.1 Fault Detection

Fault detection may be performed using a variety of methods depending on the capabilities supported by deployed DHCP and DNS servers. These range from proprietary polling or notification, to syslog scanning and/or forwarding, to SNMP polling and trap detection by SNMP-based network management systems. In addition, some commercial IP management systems offer intrasystem or proprietary monitoring, particularly for appliance-based products. Since appliances are fully self-contained solutions, incorporating not only DHCP and DNS services but a hardware platform and operating system, the vendor has the ability to fully access fault information related to the appliance at the hardware, operating system, and DHCP/DNS levels.

In addition to monitoring the state of DHCP and DNS servers, as reported by the servers, it's a good idea to monitor for hung services. This may occur if a service is running but is in a state where it is unable to perform its role in providing leases or resolving DNS queries. This can be detected by analyzing successive polls for lease or query trasactions received and processed, and verifying differential counts greater than zero, assuming normal transaction rates at that particular time of day are nonzero.

An alternative, on-demand form of service testing involves sending the server a DNS query or DHCPDISCOVER (or SOLICIT) packet and verifying receipt of a proper response. This tactic provides some assurance that the services are not only running, but are responding to clients. The bottom line is that some form of service functional fault detection can provide a truer mapping to what an end user may consider a fault or outage.

In addition to monitoring DHCP and DNS servers, monitoring of the IP management system itself provides benefits of assuring access to IP address and DHCP and DNS server configuration information that may otherwise be prevented by an outage. At a minimum, backup or distribution of the data store provides a snapshot to reconstruct the information in the event of a site outage or disaster.

Monitoring of networking equipment and communications links is a common practice for general network monitoring and can provide insights to outages affecting the ability of clients to reach DHCP or DNS servers. This added information can be very helpful in troubleshooting a particular problem or fault.

Fault correlation is the analysis of individual faults received from multiple network elements or management systems to help isolate the root cause of a set of faults. For example, faults from a layer 2 switch, a router, and a WAN access device can be analyzed collectively to suggest that these three faults are related and the likely root cause is a link outage. Fault correlation is a common feature of large scale network management systems and if your IP management system provides alarm feeds, it may be able to feed into a higher level alert correlation function. Whether fault correlation is performed automatically by a network management system or manually by comparing information from multiple systems, this process exposes a broader set of data for fault analysis with the goal of isolating a fault to a given server, link, or network element.

Fault management capability is an important consideration for those responsible for managing an IP network, and critical DHCP and DNS network services should be among those elements monitored. Mitigation of the impacts of faults may be achieved through deployment of highly available configurations to minimize end user impacts of an outage of any individual component.

14.4.2 Troubleshooting and Fault Resolution

IP Address Troubleshooting. A variety of tools are available to troubleshoot IP assignment, DNS and DHCP faults, some of which may even be provided by your IPAM vendor. To verify or identify IP address assignments, intentional or otherwise, a variety of discovery techniques will prove beneficial. Ranging from a simple ICMP Echo request, ping, traceroute, nmap, or SNMP, a variety of tools may be used to attempt to contact individual hosts or view router or switch ARP tables. Many IPAM systems incorporate at least one form of discovery to provide verification of IP address assignments or to assist in troubleshooting.

DNS Troubleshooting. Beyond server reachability and server/service status checks, troubleshooting of DNS resolution is a key function required to diagnose and resolve DNS issues. ISC provides a pair of configuration-checking utilities that are useful as a syntax check prior to loading network configuration or zone files.

CONFIGURATION FILE CHECK. The named-checkconf (144) command performs syntax checking of the named.conf file. The syntax of this command is

named-checkconf [-v] [-j] [-t *directory*] [*filepath*] [-z]

The command parameters are defined as follows:

- -v: prints the version of named-checkconf
- -j: read the journal file if it exists when loading a zone file
- -t *directory*: change root (chroot) to *directory* in order to process include directives
- *filepath*: path to the named.conf file, defaults to/etc/named.conf
- -z: load the master zone files as defined in named.conf to verify proper loading

ZONE FILE CHECK. The named-checkzone (144) utility provides syntax checking for a particular zone file. The syntax of this command is

named-checkzone [-v] [-j] [-d] [-q] [-c *class*] [-k *mode*] [–n *mode*] [-o *filename*]
[-t *directory*] [-w *directory*] [-D] [*zonename*] [*filepath*]

The command parameters are defined as follows:

- -v: prints the version of named-checkzone
- -j: read the journal file if it exists when loading the zone file
- -d: enable debugging
- -q: quiet mode, 1=errors, 0=no errors
- -c `class`: specify zone `class`; default is IN
- -k `mode`: perform check-name checks on hostnames with `modes` of `fail`, `warn` (default) or `ignore`
- -n `mode`: check if NS records improperly use IP addresses as Rdata with `modes` of `fail`, `warn` (default) or `ignore`
- -o `filename`: write zone output to `filename`
- -t `directory`: change root (chroot) to `directory` in order to process include directives
- -w `directory`: change the current working directory to `directory` in order to process include directives
- `zonename`: domain name of the zone being checked
- `filepath`: path to the zone file

NAME SERVER LOOKUP. Among the most popular DNS diagnostic tools are nslookup (name server lookup) and dig (domain information groper). Nslookup is included with Windows DNS installations and both nslookup and dig ship with the BIND software distribution. Nslookup (145) is a simple utility that enables querying of a DNS server. Today, most administrators prefer dig, which provides much more detail and control over the query formulation, resolver configuration override, output formatting and more. To perform a single lookup using nslookup, simply type

```
nslookup lookup-value [name server]
```

where `lookup-value` is the host domain name or IP address to lookup and the `name server` is the server name or IP address to query. Additional options, specified below, may be included preceding the `lookup-value` with each option name prefixed with a hyphen (e.g., `-timeout=5`). Interactive mode for nslookup may be invoked by either entering nslookup with no arguments or entering nslookup followed by a hyphen, space character, and name server hostname or IP address like

```
nslookup- 172.18.71.105
```

Interactive mode enables entry of commands to formulate and perform queries. The following interactive mode commands are available:

- `host` [`nameserver`]: lookup the `host` on the specified `nameserver` or default server. This is similar to the command line format described above.

- `server` *domain*: lookup *domain* using the current [default] server and change the default server to that authoritative for the *domain* or the IP address specified in the *domain* field.
- `lserver` *domain*: lookup *domain* using the current [default] server and change the current server to that authoritative for the *domain* or the IP address specified in the *domain* field.
- `exit`: exits interactive mode.
- `set` *option*[=*value*]: set options to influence lookup behavior; the following may also be used in noninteractive mode by prefixing the option name with a hyphen on the nslookup command line.
  - `all`: displays current option values and current [default] server and host.
  - `class=`*value*: sets the Qclass within the query; valid *value*s are IN, CH, HS or ANY.
  - `[no]debug`: `debug` enables display of full response packet and `nodebug` disables this display.
  - `[no]d2`: `d2` turns on debugging and `nod2` turns off debugging display.
  - `domain=`*name*: sets the domain search list to domain *name*.
  - `[no]search`: `search` configures use of the domain search resolver configuration to append such domains to nonfully qualified searches containing at least one dot. `nosearch` disables use of search list.
  - `port=`*value*: sets the TCP/UDP port number to *value*; the default is 53.
  - `querytype=`*value*: sets the Qtype to a resource record type to query.
  - `type=`*value*: same as `querytype`.
  - `[no]recurse`: `recurse` issues a recursive query and `norecurse` does not.
  - `retry=`*number*: sets the *number* of query retries.
  - `timeout=`*seconds*: sets the number *seconds* to wait for a reply.
  - `[no]vc`: `vc` instructs nslookup to use TCP and `novc` to use UDP.
  - `[no]fail`: `nofail` sets nslookup to try the next name server if a SERVFAIL or a referral is received; `fail` does not try the next server.

DOMAIN INFORMATION GROPER. Dig (146) enables the formulation of a DNS query using standard DNS messages, emulating a resolver or recursive server. Dig provides granular control of the format of a query that can be sent to a DNS server in order to analyze the resulting response.

A common example usage of the dig command simply requests a resolution for a hostname:

```
dig @ns1.ipamworldwide.com A ftp-sf.ipamworldwide.com
```

This example would result in the issuance of an A record query for ftp-sf.ipamworldwide.com to the DNS server ns1.ipamworldwide.com. Valid possible arguments for the dig utility include

- @*server*: where *server* is the domain name or IP address of the DNS server to which to issue the query. If this parameter is not specified, dig will query the DNS servers listed in the client's resolver configuration.
- -b *address*: sets the source IP address of the query to *address*. This is useful for testing ACLs or views.
- -c *class*: class of the DNS resource record to query; the default is Internet.
- -f *filename*: enables issuance of successive queries as listed one per line in the specified *filename*. Format each line of the file as you would a dig command for the given query (without specifying "dig" on each line). This facilitates automated testing of a set of queries for critical resolutions in one step. Don't forget the boss' favorite resolutions.
- -k *filename*: signs the query and validates response signatures using TSIG, transaction signatures specified in *filename*. The TSIG key must match that defined in the DNS server's named.conf configuration.
- -p *port*: specifies the destination UDP (or TCP) port to use for the query; if not specified, the default DNS port, 53 is used.
- -q *name*: explicitly identifies the owner *name* to use in the query instead of using the "bare" name argument. That is, dig -q sf-ftp1 = dig sf-ftp1.
- -t *type*: explicitly identifies the query type to use instead of using the "bare" type argument. The default type is "A" unless –x is specified, indicating a PTR lookup.
- -x *address*: specifies a PTR lookup for the specified *address*. This option enables entry of an IPv4 or IPv6 address whereas if using –t with type PTR the name must be formatted as an .arpa. name.
- -y [*hmac:*]*name:key*: specifies an explicit TSIG key (instead of referring to a file with the –k option). The *hmac* field indicates key algorithm, HMAC-MD5 by default, the *name* field is the TSIG key name and *key* is the key itself. Care should be taken when using the –y option as the key can be visible from the output or command shell history. The TSIG key must match that defined in the DNS server's named.conf configuration.
- -4: send query using IPv4 transport.
- -6: send query using IPv6 transport.
- name: the owner name to query. Dig supports Internationalized Domain Names (IDN), so non-ASCII names may be specified.
- type: the query type to request in the query. The default type is A.
- class: the class of resource record to query. The default class is Internet.

- -h: prints help summary of the command; if no parameters are specified with the dig command, the help summary is provided.
- Query options: dig provides a number of options that can be specified to include or explicitly exclude query features. The plus sign is used to indicate each option and the no keyword indicates negation of the specified feature. The description of each option is written as if entered in the affirmative (without no). Note that a space is shown in this list between the optional no keyword and the option name where appropriate for readability. However, when entering respective commands, omit the space, for example, +notcp to negate the +tcp option.

TRANSPORT OPTIONS

- +bufsize=*bytes*: sets the UDP message buffer size to *bytes* bytes; valid values range from 0 to 65,535.
- +[no] fail: instructs dig to not try the next candidate server upon receiving a SERVFAIL result. This is the default behavior of dig, which is opposite that of a resolver.
- +[no] ignore: ignore any truncation resulting from a UDP query; normally such a UDP truncation scenario would lead to reissuing the query using TCP (which occurs when using +noignore) but using the +ignore setting instructs dig to not reissue the query using TCP.
- +[no] tcp: query using TCP; by default TCP is used for AXFR or IXFR queries and UDP is used for all other queries.
- +time=*time*: sets the query timeout to *time* seconds (default = 5, minimum = 1).
- +tries=*n*: sets the number of times, *n*, a UDP query will be sent in the absence of an answer (default = 3, minimum = 1).
- +retry=*n*: sets the number of times, *n*, a UDP query will be resent after the first query in the absence of an answer (default = 2, minimum = 1). To clarify, +tries specifies the total attempts while +retry specifies the number of attempts after the initial attempt.
- +[no] vc: query using TCP (vc = virtual circuit); by default TCP is used for AXFR or IXFR queries and UDP is used for all other queries.

RESOLVER CONFIGURATION OVERRIDE OPTIONS

- +domain=*domainname*: sets the domain search list exclusively to the specified *domainname*.
- +ndots=*m*: specifies the number of dots (m) in the name to be considered fully qualified; that is, when fewer dots are entered in the name field, dig will append domain names specified in the domain or search parameter within the resolver configuration.

- + [no] search: enables domain search list processing based on the searchlist or domain directive specified in the resolver client.
- + [no] defname: Deprecated—equivalent to + [no] search.
- + [no] showsearch: display intermediate search results.

DNS HEADER SETTING OPTIONS

- + [no] aaonly: sets the Authoritative Answer (AA) bit in the header of the query to indicate desire for an authoritative (noncached) answer.
- + [no] aaflag: equivalent to + [no] aaonly.
- + [no] adflag: sets the Authentic Data (AD) bit in the header of the query. This option is provided "for completeness" though it has no meaning. The AD bit is normally set by a server to indicate that the query response data has been verified via DNSSEC validation.
- + [no] cdflag: sets the Checking Disabled (CD) bit in the header of the query to instruct the queried DNS server to disable DNSSEC signature validation for this query.
- + [no] dnssec: sets the DNSSEC OK (DO) bit in the EDNS0 OPT record to indicate DNSSEC processing is desired.
- + edns=*version*: sets the EDNS version to *version*.
- + noedns: clears the EDNS *version* set with + edns.
- + [no] recurse: sets the Recursion Desired (RD) bit in the header of the query. Dig queries set the RD bit by default to request recursion except when the + nssearch or + trace options are specified.

OUTPUT OPTIONS

- + [no] all: displays the results in the default format; setting + noall suppresses all results.
- + [no] cmd: displays the first line of dig output showing the version of dig and the applied query options. This line displays by default.
- + [no] comments: dig normally displays results organized in DNS message format, organized by Header, Question, Answer, Authority, and Additional sections. These "sections" of the response along with blank lines are considered comments in the output that improve readability. Setting + nocomments suppresses these lines in the output. The output will still contain the query time, server, time stamp, and message size, though this can be surpressed using + nostats.
- + [no] identify: when used with + short, also displays the IP address and port number of the DNS server that provided each answer.
- + [no] multiline: displays complex resource record (e.g., SOA) results in multiline format; the default is to display each on a single line.

- + [no]nssearch: display the SOA record of the name servers authoritative for the zone specified in the name field (or −n parameter).
- + [no] short: display a terse answer. For example, when issuing an A query for a given name, only the resolved IP address(es) would be displayed.
- + [no] stats: displays the query time, responding name server, time stamp, and message size.
- + [no]trace: display the delegation path from the root servers to the authoritative name servers for the queried name. Dig will issue iterative queries to each server down the delegation path, displaying answers from each along the way. This is very helpful in identifying lame (broken) delegations in the domain tree.

DNS MESSAGE OPTIONS

- + [no] additional: displays the Additional section of the response (the default is to display the Additional section contents).
- + [no] answer: displays the Answer section of the response (the default is to display the Answer section contents).
- + [no] authority: displays the Authority section of the response (the default is to display the Authority section contents).
- + [no] besteffort: displays the contents of malformed messages (the default is to not display malformed responses).
- + [no] cl: displays the resource record class in dig results for this query.
- + [no] nsid: include the EDNS NSID request option to request the name server identity from the server.
- + [no] qr: displays the query as it was sent to the DNS server, organized by Header and Question fields by default.
- + [no] question: displays the Question section of the response (the default is to display the Question section contents).
- + [no] ttlid: displays the resource record TTL in dig results for this query.

DNSSEC SIGNATURE VALIDATION

- + [no] sigchase: chase DNSSEC signature chains; requires dig be compiled with the -DDIG_SIGCHASE switch.
- + trusted-key=filename: identifies a filename containing trusted keys to be used with +sigchase; requires dig be compiled with the -DDIG_SIGCHASE switch.
- + [no] topdown: perform top-down validation when chasing DNSSEC signature chains used with +sigchase; requires dig be compiled with the -DDIG_SIGCHASE switch.

The dig utility for BIND 9 allows entry of multiple queries on a single command line simply by concatenating successive query name-type-parameters-options strings. For example, the following illustrates running a query for a PTR lookup for IP address 10.0.3.43 including display of the query along with a CNAME query for "ftp" while setting the resolver domain suffix to ipamworldwide.com.

dig –x 10.0.3.43 + qr ftp CNAME + domain=ipamworldwide.com

DHCP Troubleshooting. Testing DHCP transactions can be performed using DHCP client capabilities like ipconfig for Windows or ifconfig commands for Unix or Linux. These commands provide that ability to perform DHCP releases, renews, and set user class. For example, using `ipconfig` on a Microsoft Windows command line enables display of the IP configuration using the following arguments:

- `/all`: displays IP configuration information for each interface including
  - IPv4 address and subnet mask
  - Additional IP addresses including IPv6 addresses
  - MAC address(es)
  - Interface description
  - DNS domain suffix
  - Default gateway
  - DHCP server from which the lease was obtained along with dates/times the lease was obtained and that the lease expires
  - DNS servers for resolver configuration
  - WINS servers to query for NetBIOS lookups if configured
- Omitting the /all argument displays the IP addresses, subnet mask, domain suffix and default gateway only.
- `/?`: displays help in the form of a command summary.
- `/displaydns`: displays contents of the resolver's cache.
- `/showclassid` *adapter*: displays the user class configured for the specified interface adapter.

`ipconfig` also provides the following commands:

- `/release` [*adapter*]: Issues a DHCPRELEASE to release the lease for all or the specified interface adapter.
- `/renew` [*adapter*]: Issues a DHCPRENEW to renew all leases or that for the specified interface adapter.
- `/registerdns`: Issues a DHCPRENEW to renew all leases and updates DNS A record(s) directly (client to DNS server, not DHCP server to DNS).

- /flushdns: Clears the resolver cache.
- /setclassid *adapter class*: Sets the user class name for the specified interface adapter.

14.5 ACCOUNTING MANAGEMENT

Accounting management basically intends to keep everyone honest. Are those assigned addresses still in use? Are any unassigned addresses actually being used? Did the new subnet get provisioned on the router yet? Thus accounting management enables verification of successful configuration, as well as overall adherence to the IP addressing plan. Techniques for accounting management functions include discovery analysis of IP addresses, router subnets, switch port mappings, DNS resource records, and DHCP lease files.

Analysis of discovered information is necessary in order to compare this information with the IP inventory "plan of record." Such discrepancy reporting and comparison is difficult work, but provides a level of assurance of inventory accuracy. Without such a function, rogue users could access free service or otherwise infiltrate the network. In addition, planned network changes yet unimplemented may cause downstream process delays and violation of internal or external service level agreements on provisioning intervals.

14.5.1 Inventory Assurance

Each of the common IP management tasks we've covered so far relies on accurate IP address inventory to enable the allocation, deletion, and movement of blocks, subnets, IP addresses, and DHCP and DNS server configurations. Accuracy is absolutely essential for these address management tasks. But accurate inventory is also essential for general troubleshooting. Should a remote site be unreachable due to a network outage, it may be necessary to identify IP addresses, resource records, or other IPAM-related data for devices at the site. Only by maintaining an accurate IP inventory can such information be accessed when it may be needed most and when it cannot be obtained directly from the network.

In this section, we'll review steps you can take to assure the accuracy of your IP inventory. This includes controlling who can make certain changes to certain IPAM information, to discovering actual network data, reconciling the actuals with the inventory, and finally reclaiming address space.

Change Control and Administrator Accountability. As we've seen in reviewing these IP management tasks, a change in IP inventory often affects other network elements, including routers and DHCP and DNS servers. If different individuals or teams manage these different elements, it's a good idea to convene a planning or change control meeting periodically or as needed to review and schedule upcoming planned addressing changes. A little rigor can add some discipline to the process and keep those potentially affected by changes in the loop.

One way to help assure accuracy of IP inventory itself is to limit write access to the inventory to those whom are authoritative for and keenly knowledgeable of the IP addressing plan. Using a single password-protected spreadsheet that the one and only IP planner can modify is one approach to protecting the IP inventory from inadvertent or erroneous changes. However, for even modestly sized organizations, this approach is unwieldy. With the organization reliant on a single individual for the entire IP address plan, the individual must work around the clock and should he or she leave the organization, recovery of access to the inventory may be very difficult unless a successor is groomed in advance.

Support of multiple simultaneous administrators is a key feature of most IPAM systems on the market, and most allow some level of scope control so that certain administrators can only perform certain functions on certain devices or portions of the network. Make sure your chosen system supports administrator logging should you need to investigate "who did what" on the system.

As important as disciplined multi-administrator scoped access to the IP inventory is to delegating accountability, arbitrary changes to IP address assignments, DNS resource records, subnet addresses can be made outside of the scope of the IP inventory. For example, manual configurations can be mistyped, subnets can be provisioned on the wrong router interface, and client or DHCP updates to DNS can all contribute to IP inventory drift from reality. The IP inventory is a model of the IP address plan, and IPAM tasks rely on the accuracy of the plan. Therefore, it's prudent to take "pulse readings" from the IP network itself. Periodically polling and comparing the actual assignments on the network with the inventory is key to assuring inventory accuracy.

Network Discovery. A variety of methods are available to gather network actuals data, from ping, to DNS lookups, to SNMP polls. Pinging enables detection of an occupant of an IP address and provides a basic method to determine which IP addresses are in use for comparison with the respective portion of the IP inventory. Ping is very useful but be aware that some routers or firewalls will drop ping packets or even some devices can be configured to ignore pings. Setting up remote ping agents to perform local pinging on command can help avert the router/firewall traversal issue.

Nmap, freely available at insecure.org/nmap, is a particularly useful tool at the right price. It combines several discovery mechanisms to gather a variety of information from devices connected to the IP network, including ping sweeps, DNS lookups, and port scanning. When sweeping a subnet, nmap can perform these tasks in one command, issuing a ping to each address, looking up a corresponding PTR record in DNS, and attempting connections to various TCP and UDP ports to identify the device's operating system. From an IPAM perspective, ping results help identify IP address occupancy, DNS lookups help corroborate hostname-to-IP address mapping between DNS servers and the IP inventory and port scanning can provide additional information about the type of device occupying each IP address.

SNMP is another means of discovering IP inventory-related information. While most end devices like laptops or VoIP phones don't natively enable SNMP, most infrastructure elements like routers, switches, and servers do. Of particular interest within router MIBs are the Interfaces, IpAddresses, and Arp tables. If your infrastructure devices support MIB-II, the interpretation of these tables *should* be consistent across different products. Just be aware of minor variations, even among different products from the same vendor. The information in these tables enables collection of the interfaces and subnets per interface provisioned as reported by the router. This provides useful validation of inventory in general, but can also be polled when in the process of allocating, moving, or deleting blocks and subnets.

Polling router ARP cache tables can provide a definitive mapping of MAC addresses to IP addresses on recent subnet communications. Even if a device refuses to respond to a ping, it must use the address resolution protocol (ARP) to formulate a layer 2 (e.g., Ethernet) frame in which to envelop its intended IP packet. As implied by the fact that this is cached information, it is transient and must be polled frequently.

Pinging of an IPv6 subnet is impractical given the sheer size of 2^{64} possible IP addresses on a /64 subnet. Polling of a router's Neighbor Discovery table, for example, ipv6NetToMedia SNMP MIB is a more effective means to perform IPv6 host discovery.

IP Inventory Reconciliation. Network discovery information provides a reality check on actual subnet allocations, IP address assignments and associated resource records. By comparing discovered information with the IP inventory database, discrepancies can be identified and investigated. While this comparison may require "eyeballing" the differences between the inventory spreadsheet and the discovery output, the effort can prove beneficial for several reasons. For example, database discrepancies can be identified that may be the result of

- *Incorrect Router Provisioning.* Incorrect subnet, mask, router interface, and so on.
- *Incomplete Router Provisioning.* Planned change not yet implemented.
- *Device Reachability Issue.* If a device should be at a given IP address and no response is received. This could result from a device outage, a transient outage (reboot), address reassignment, or network unreachability.
- *Incorrect IP Address Assignment.* Manually configured address is incorrect or device obtains a DHCP address from an unintended pool or address.
- *Actual IP Address Assignment.* For autoconfigured devices, the IP address is selected by the device. Also in some decentralized scenarios, the installer of a device on the subnet may select an IP address. Discovery can be used to update the IP inventory for these cases.
- *Incomplete IP Address Assignment.* All aspects of the assignment process, whether manual or DHCP, are incomplete. This issue is particularly applicable to manually assigned addresses where manual effort is needed to configure the assigned IP address, to detect autoconfigured devices and to update DNS.
- *Rogue Device Presence.* An unknown or unauthorized device has obtained an IP address. This provides an effective post-access control mechanism to complement and audit a network access control solution.

In addition to detecting discrepancies, analyzing discovery information can confirm completion of allocation or assignment tasks, as well as delete tasks. Discovery data is indispensible when moving blocks, subnets, and IP addresses. Since moves require allocation of the new address(es), movement, then deletion of the old address(es), confirmation of move completion is essential prior to deleting the old address(es) from the IP inventory. These addresses should not be deleted before the move completes so they are not unknowingly reassigned to other devices or subnets prior to their actual relinquishment.

In summary, network discovery is essential to assuring the accuracy of the IP inventory. It is also beneficial to monitoring provisioning or assignment progress and time frames, managing the completion of tasks requiring multiple related subtasks, and detecting incorrect assignments as well as potentially rogue devices.

14.5.2 Address Reclamation

Another benefit of network discovery and reconciliation discussed above is the detection of device reachability issues. If a server has been provisioned and has historically responded on a given IP address, but now no longer does so, such an event should stimulate further investigation. If there were no plans to move or decommission the device or there are no network problems reaching other devices on the subnet, the device may be suffering an outage, may be rebooting, may have been moved or disconnected, or may have been readdressed. If the server is providing critical services or applications, hopefully you're monitoring its status via a network management system[*] that can corroborate the outage theory and trigger corrective actions. If the IP address is discovered on the next attempt, perhaps it was simply rebooting. If it does not respond for the next n attempts, perhaps it is no longer physically (or at least electrically!) there. Unfortunately people don't always inform the IP planning team that a device has been removed or moved elsewhere, even in the tightest of organizations. A quick phone call to the site to check on the device's status may prove fruitful, but it's often difficult and time-consuming to identify the device's "owner" to verify status.

Nevertheless, the key point to assessing the possible fate of the device is that it may take multiple discovery attempts to determine if a device was there and no longer is, suffered a transient outage or disconnect, or was borrowed and has now been returned. Tracking a succession of discovery attempts may be difficult. A running log or spreadsheet can be used to log discrepancies or "missing" IP addresses as they are [not] detected. Reviewing this log over time may help determine if an IP address recorded as in use actually isn't.

In reviewing such a log, if a given IP address had been successfully discovered until a month ago, when it was last reachable after so many attempts, for example, 30, it may be confirmed as available for future assignment, or *reclaimable*. The concept of reclaim

---

[*] Or if the server is a DHCP or DNS server, it may be monitored via the IP management system.

entails identifying IP addresses that are denoted as in-use in the IP inventory, but are in reality not in-use, nor have they been in-use in recent history. Analyzing multiple discovery results provides a more robust sample set on which to base a reclaim decision, essentially deleting the device from the inventory and freeing it up for assignment to another device.

Besides providing robust confirmation of a device deletion from the IP inventory, reclaim may likewise be applied to subnets. When deleting a subnet, it's generally advisable to verify that all IP address occupants have been deleted and are no longer using IP addresses on the subnet[*]. Analyzing discovery results from all addresses on a given subnet can provide assurance that the subnet may be deleted. But like IP address reclaim, multiple sample sets provide more robust confirmation of the reclaimable disposition. Just keep in mind that you'll rarely see zero responses on a subnet, at least while it's still provisioned on a router interface, so you'll want to check successive discovery results ignoring routers, switches, and perhaps other device types.

14.6 PERFORMANCE MANAGEMENT

Performance management involves the monitoring functions of the IP management system and more importantly, the DHCP and DNS servers operating in the network. It's useful to track basic server statistics such as CPU utilization, memory, disk, and network interface input/output (I/O). Such monitoring enables tracking of the hardware's ability to support the DHCP and DNS (and any other services) running on the server. Trending analysis in this regard is beneficial as well to enable proactive planning of future hardware procurements to enable load distribution among more servers.

14.6.1 Services Monitoring

Monitoring of the DNS service helps assure adequate DNS horsepower to meet the demands for name resolution, and to help identify any exception conditions. BIND supports flexible logging of a variety of event types to a configurable set of output destinations or channels, including syslog, file, null, or stderr (the operating system's standard error output destination). Microsoft supports the DNS server event viewer with settable severity level reporting and counters for total queries/second received and responses/second sent. DHCP servers likewise provide logging to monitor overall service health and statistics, typically to a log file, syslog, or an event log.

These measures enable collection of performance data from the server's perspective. However, they don't convey the services performance as experienced by DHCP clients and DNS resolvers. Measuring client performance requires the remote issuance of a DNS

---

[*]Ignoring the router IP address's occupancy since it will typically identify itself on the subnet.

query or DHCPDISCOVER (or SOLICIT) packet and measuring the response time for receipt of a proper response[*]. This remote issuance could originate from services probes deployed in various locations to generate these "synthetic transactions," and measure and store response time results. Analyzing historical data from different probes can provide keen insight into DNS/DHCP services and network performance.

14.6.2 Address Capacity Management

Overall IP address capacity monitoring is another key performance management function within the scope of IPAM. Tracking address utilization from devices manually addressed, as well as those obtaining addresses via DHCP, enables proactive management of address space. Address allocations are initially based on estimated forecasts, which hopefully are accurate. Even when the forecast is perfect however, IP network dynamics due to employee movement, large events, subscriber growth, and unplanned address demands can consume the entire capacity of a subnet and its address pools. Periodic monitoring of utilization levels on pools and subnets, with historical tracking and trending can provide forewarning of a capacity crunch to trigger a supplemental allocation to expand capacity before it runs out.

Many DHCP server products enable monitoring of lease levels by command line, scripts or SNMP. Microsoft DHCP also provides a general 90% alerting threshold, providing notification should an address pool reach 90% capacity. Other servers and IP management systems provide similar or additional alert threshold definition and application. It's usually better to be notified by an IP management or network monitoring system than by irritated customers or end users attempting to access the network.

14.6.3 Auditing and Reporting

Most management systems in general provide some level of auditing of "who did what" and varying levels of reporting. These functions, which could just as easily be categorized under Accounting Management, enable administrators to track and troubleshoot activity and to convey status information in report format. Auditing of IP address usage, that is, who had a given IP address at a certain point in time is valuable information when troubleshooting a network issue or investigating potential illicit activity. Likewise, if you are attempting to track the history of IP address occupancy for a given device, reporting by hardware address is also beneficial.

Performing such auditing without an IP management system may be difficult except for the smallest of networks. Iterative dumps of DHCP lease data to track dynamically addressed clients over time are necessary. The ability to search for a given IP address requires access to a single (or two if failover or split scopes is in effect) DHCP server's lease history, while the search by hardware address necessitates searching across all DHCP servers, assuming the device is capable of mobility.

---

[*] As mentioned in the Fault Management section, the absence of a response may indicate a services outage and should be investigated if it persists.

Common reports of interest for IP address planning include the following, though your system may provide different or additional reports.

- *Address Utilization Report.* By pool, subnet, block, rollups through hierarchy.
- *Address Assignment Report.* Summary of assigned addresses by subnet or block as current snapshot and/or history.
- *Address Discrepancy Report.* Highlights of discrepancies between the IP inventory and discovered IP address information.
- *DHCP Performance Report.* Summary and details of DHCP protocol messages by type and/or client and server key metrics summary.
- *DNS Performance Report.* Summary and details of queries by type, by querier, by question and server key metrics summary.
- *Audit Reports.* Administrator activity, by subnet, by IP address, by hardware address, by resource record, by server.

14.7 SECURITY MANAGEMENT

Several IP management vendors have attempted to join the "NAC" bandwagon, enabling IP planners to restrict IP address assignments only to valid devices or users, as determined by DHCP MAC address filtering or user login. Such a solution needs to provide exception reporting and ideally alerting, should a number of access attempts by a device or user fail. One failed access attempt can likely be attributed to mistyping, but several failures may indicate an attacker attempting to crack the system to access the network. Of course, if the attacker knows the subnet address, he/she could manually configure an IP address to access the network, bypassing DHCP. This process is discussed in detail along with alternative approaches in Chapter 8.

Chapters 8, 12 and 13 address securing the information on and transactions with DHCP and DNS severs, respectively. Securing the IP inventory and DHCP and DNS configuration data is also important, as this information is critical and should be protected from sabotage. Protecting IP data requires administrator access controls, enabling at least password-protected access to the information. If your organization has more than two or three administrators, a more sophisticated administrator security approach may be warranted with the use of an IP management system. Most systems go beyond minimal password entry to enable scoping of administrator access by system function, by portions or certain elements of the network, by access type, for example, super user versus read-only access and more. The sophistication of access controls will be driven by the number of administrators, their respective roles and responsibilities, and organizational security policies.

14.8 DISASTER RECOVERY/BUSINESS CONTINUITY

Business continuity practices seek to maintain the operation of the enterprise in the face of a major outage. A major outage or "disaster," implies that the sheer magnitude of the outage goes beyond a handful of servers or network devices. Automated and manual procedures must be documented in advance to reconfigure or redeploy resources to maintain operation of the network and applications, or at least the critical services and applications. We've discussed a variety of approaches for deploying and configuring redundant DNS and DHCP services in Chapters 7 and 11. Once deployed and configured, redundancy features should provide network services continuity in the event of an individual server outage. On top of these technologies, deployment of DHCP and DNS appliances may provide an added layer of availability. While typically providing intrasite hardware redundancy, this deployment model is not normally considered for disaster recovery solutions due to co-location requirements. Appliance redundancy nevertheless provides a viable redundancy option especially for critical servers, such as master DNS servers.

Business continuity of IPAM operations will likely require deployment of multiple IPAM databases. Deployment of multiple active databases or primary/backup configurations will depend on your selected vendor. Vendors implement a wide variety of approaches to facilitate redundancy such as full database copies and transfer, multimaster databases that require some level of network partitioning, to deployment of database replication technologies using storage area networks or SQL or LDAP replication capabilities. Operations tasks required to perform a disaster recovery will likewise vary per vendor.

Evaluation of vendor disaster recovery capabilities will depend on your business objectives, budget and polices, but three key questions should be considered:

1. Is the IPAM database involved in name resolution or address assignment? For example, some systems route dynamic updates from DHCP to the IPAM database for uniqueness checks prior to routing to DNS. If the IPAM database is in such a "critical path," redundancy and high availability are paramount.

2. How frequently do your administrators make changes to IPAM data? The more frequent the rate of change, the more data changes may be lost between data synchronizations between the primary and backup database(s). A daily database backup may be acceptable in cases where changes are made infrequently whereas a subdaily or transactional replication process may be required for high rate-of-change environments.

3. What is the process to perform invocation of the backup system? Some vendors provide a relatively simple recovery procedure, while others require more manual intervention. Some small level of manual intervention is probably desirable given the broad impact of a disaster recovery failover. Intermittent issues may lead to false positives and potentially disruptive failovers, so initiating the failover manually can eliminate a disaster caused by the solution. Hopefully disasters occur infrequently if never, but when needed, the failover process should be executable by staff on hand within time constraints defined by policy.

These basic questions are interdependent. If the answers to questions 1 and 2 are "yes" and "frequently," respectively, then the answer to question 3 should probably be "single step" or at least "very streamlined."

14.9 ITIL PROCESS MAPPINGS

The IT Infrastructure Library[*] is a documented set of best practices for use by an IT organization desiring to manage, monitor, and continually improve IT services provided to the enterprise organization. ITIL was developed by the U.K. Office of Government and Commerce, and its IT service-oriented approach has been deployed by a number of organizations. The most common drivers for ITIL implementation include

- Costs reduction of IT services delivery to the organization.
- Risk management through disciplined planning and evaluation of potential service-affecting changes.
- IT service level consistency and improvements.
- Efficiencies in utilizing documented processes and continual improvement.

Many of the functions within these process areas are identical or similar to those discussed earlier in the chapter, so we'll simply summarize these within their respective mappings to ITIL process areas.

14.9.1 ITIL Process Areas

ITIL processes are split into two areas: service delivery and service support. Service delivery involves the planning, development, and deployment of IT services, while service support entails service operations in managing service levels and support. The service desk is a third process area that integrates with both service delivery and service support to provide a unified interface for IT to the rest of the organization. ITIL version 3 builds upon these sets of processes, with a couple additions and functional splits.

Service Delivery. *Service level management* is a service delivery process area that encompasses the specification of service levels for various services provided by the IT organization. This is akin to a service level agreement. Service level management also includes measurement of service delivery against these specifications to monitor adherence to and measuring the level of service that IT provides.

From an IPAM perspective, service level management can involve definition and measurement of the level of service provided to those requesting IPAM-related services, whether it be end users requesting an IP address or the business needing to open a new retail office. Treating the end user or the business in these cases as customers, this process seeks to gauge whether service delivery is meeting defined service levels, such as timeliness of completion of these requests. Automating IPAM-related service delivery, whether solely IPAM impacting or involving IPAM as part of a larger IT service such as

---

[*] Details are available at the ITIL web site, http://www.itil-officialsite.com/home/home.asp (168). Functional mappings in the section are based on those initially discussed in (174).

VoIP deployment, facilitates timely and accurate services delivery. An example metric is the time frame by which a subnet or an IP address will be assigned.

Financial management naturally includes accounting, similar to accounting management in the FCAPS model, though the financial management area addresses actual dollars and cents as well. This process area also deals with any chargebacks or cost allocations for certain departments under an IT funding or cost allocation model.

Some firms do implement cost chargebacks for IP address usage. In such a scenario, the financial management processes would need to account for tracking of IP address usage along with the corresponding user and chargeable entity (e.g., department). Depending on the billing or chargeback cycle, this IP address use information will need to be stored for the current cycle and more to enable archiving or dispute resolution. Audits and history data in your IPAM system can also be a big help in justifying cost allocations.

Capacity management simply involves assuring adequate IT resources of the proper type are available for the business to conduct its work. Considering the application of this concept to IPAM, certainly IP address capacity management springs to mind, but one should also consider DHCP and DNS server load capacity. In the former case, capacity management requires monitoring of addresses and address pools to provide enough IP addresses for employees to get an address and access the network. Monitoring for trends is helpful, and enabling alerting for low pools is also recommended for tightly allocated networks. Of course, given the magnitude of IPv6 address space, this will likely not be an issue for IPv6 space for the foreseeable future.

With respect to server capacity management, monitoring each server's network, memory and CPU utilization over time can provide insights into its performance. Such performance tasks may in fact be required as a linkage to service level management in terms of percentage of transaction completion (lease or resolution) as well as response times. Regardless, excessive loads on servers can have detrimental impacts on the availability of DNS and DHCP services, so server monitoring and perhaps even probe-like transactional monitoring can provide effective measures of service levels and capacity.

Availability management is a service delivery process area focused on making sure IT services are available to end users. High availability, a common goal for applications including DHCP and DNS, requires deployment of redundant configurations and the ability to leverage these configurations to provide continuous service in the face of a component outage.

As discussed in Chapters 7 and 11, deployment of redundant appliances can provide localized clustering, which with implementation of DHCP failover or split-scopes and multi-server DNS deployments, provides an additional layer of redundancy. Redundant IPAM database deployments through LDAP or replicated relational databases can also assure availability of the IPAM application for managing IP space. Monitoring of the availability of each of these redundant components enables proactive detection of outages to facilitate rapid outage resolution (mean time to repair) while redundant components shoulder the load.

Continuity management is related to availability management in that it deals with providing continuously available services. For example, in the event of a disaster, this process area would require a disaster recovery plan be in place. As discussed in the Business Continuity section earlier, a variety of strategies are available based on the criticality and scope requirements of the organization for particular DHCP/DNS servers and IPAM systems.

Service Desk. Serving as the interface to the user community, the service desk filters input to the IT organization for incident reporting, change requests and even new service requests. It serves to filter and direct user requests or problems to any one of the other ITIL areas, providing end users with a helpdesk function.

The policies and culture of the organization will drive whether the service desk performs traditional "level 1" support only by logging troubles with subsequent follow-up, or higher support levels up front to perform a level of diagnosis. In the case of level 1 support, little more is needed than a ticketing system with the ability to assign tickets to those responsible for other process areas depending on the caller's issue. A service desk staffed to perform some trouble diagnosis will require access to status monitoring tools to try to "see what the caller sees" with respect to the issue.

For IP address or name resolution-related calls, providing service desk personnel access to IP inventory information may prove beneficial. For instance, if a person located in the Philadelphia Headquarters office is not able to get an IP address, the service desk needs to know the address plan for Headquarters in order to focus the problem and trouble resolution process on that particular subnet, associated routers or DHCP/DNS servers.

The service desk is the interface not only for trouble reports, but for change requests, such as IP subnet or address assignments. Providing service desk personnel with basic access to the IPAM system to request such changes, or better yet, enable end users themselves to register such service requests to an automated IT portal can increase end users' satisfaction with IT services through rapid fulfillment.

Service Support. *Incident management* is a service support process area that involves tracking and resolving incidents. In ITIL version 2, it also deals with change requests, whereas in version 3, these are split into separate process areas. As described above, the service desk receives incident and change requests from the end user community directly. Through network monitoring IT can also detect and troubleshoot network issues proactively. Regardless of the means of detection for a given incident, access to IP inventory data is indispensible to troubleshooting and incident resolution. In addition, monitoring of server states with thresholds, alerts, logging information, and audits can provide a head start to incident detection and management.

Service requests can be handled by service request tickets initiated via the service desk or IT web portal as described in the Service Desk section.

Problem management calls for the tracking of known problems and resolutions in a known problem database. If someone calls into the service desk with an incident, for example, it could get bumped over to problem management to identify whether this incident has been reported and addressed in the past. If so, the defined resolution path can be followed to quickly troubleshoot and resolve the issue.

While IPAM systems traditionally don't store problem histories with resolution annotations, some can provide a database of problem information through logging history, as well as inventory change audits. Network management system integration through APIs can provide a holistic view of problem history by providing IPAM data through the API to a trouble ticketing system for example. IPAM is a key part of the overall network or IT service management approach, but it's not comprehensive; no system is. Having that integration is a key to having a holistic view of the problem management scope.

Configuration management within ITIL is similar to the FCAPS configuration management functionality in terms of identifying, recording, and controlling configuration parameters affecting IT services. And as we discussed extensively in this chapter, configuration management functions are a large focus area of IPAM processes. This includes configuring new address pools from a DHCP perspective, zones and resource records in DNS, IP addresses for subnets on routers, and so on, which all fall into the realm of configuration management. The IPAM database can be considered a configuration management database (CMDB) component of an IT's confederation of CMDBs for network configuration inventory.

Administrator controls need to be considered for organizations with more than one IPAM administrator to ensure that changes to DHCP and DNS configurations are done with the appropriate scope and permissions. For instance, you may want administrators to be able to make changes, but not actually deploy them on the DHCP and DNS servers—restricting that function to a higher level of administrator. On the back end, audit information is key for accountability tracking and reporting.

Possessing accurate IP configuration information is needed to provide a solid foundation on which future configuration changes can be planned. A corollary requirement leads to the necessity of validating that inventory against network actual data. IP inventory tracked on a spreadsheet is fine but requires constant updating. Having the ability to collect information from the network and then compare it with the plan is very important. Audits go hand in hand with inventory information collection. Arming the service desk with this information can provide a solid first line of defense for addressing calls immediately, or to at least moving them through the process more quickly.

Change management provides controls on the implementation of changes in the IT infrastructure. This involves assuring that all affected parties are in agreement with respect to the scope and implementation timing of the proposed change. In terms of IPAM, the scope of change management commonly affects IPAM components, such as the addition of an address pool, deployment of a new DHCP/DNS server in the network, or upgrading a server to a new software version. Basically, anything affecting any part of the infrastructure, whether it's physical or software or even underlying appliance operating system, falls under the change management process, which seeks to assure all appropriate approvals are in place and corresponding back-out plans are available.

Release management is a service support process area that provides controls on deployed releases for hardware and software versions, not only for operating systems, but also for applications and appliances. This process area is responsible for making those versions available and accessible on the IT network and making sure there's an authorized set of releases and versions available that can be deployed appropriately.

Release planning and upgrade management for DHCP and DNS servers via a central location can be a big timesaver. The alternative requiring on-site upgrades of operating system, patches, and application software is costly and time-consuming. Release management of the IPAM system also falls within this category.

CONCLUSION

FCAPS and ITIL are similar in that they both advocate documented processes with disciplined execution. The importance of IPAM to an organization should drive application of FCAPS or ITIL principles to the practice of IPAM within the organization. This chapter has presented a detailed perspective of key IPAM process steps in the context of an FCAPS framework, as well as a suggested mapping to ITIL.

15

IPv6 DEPLOYMENT AND IPv4 COEXISTENCE

15.1 INTRODUCTION

IPv6[*] was originally specified in the mid-1990s to address a then-urgent need to supplement the rapidly diminishing IPv4 address space. At the time work begun in earnest on defining IPv6 or IPng (IP next generation) as it was initially named, the Internet was just starting to catch on with the general public. More and more enterprises were expanding their internal networks to enable connection to the global Internet. Since every reachable host required a unique public IPv4 address, the demand for addresses skyrocketed.

While these events spurred the development of IPv6, they also stimulated the development of other technologies that prolonged the life expectancy of IPv4 address space. As we discussed in Chapter 1, classless interdomain routing (CIDR) enabled Regional Internet Registries and ISPs to allocate address space more efficiently than with former classful-only allocation methods.

Another IPv4 allocation strategy discussed in Chapter 1 that vastly reduced the amount of address space required by organizations from RIRs or ISPs was the allocation

---

[*]The material in this chapter is based on and adds more detail to Chapter 8 of Ref. 11 and on Ref. 147.

IP Address Management: Principles and Practice, by Timothy Rooney
Copyright © 2011 the Institute of Electrical and Electronics Engineers, Inc.

of private address space. Defined in RFC 1918, the allocation of private networks enabled every organization to use the same address space for their internal networks. Communicating to Internet hosts or among organizations still required public addresses, but the use of network address translation (NAT) firewalls provided private-to-public address translation for internal hosts accessing the Internet.

One could also argue that DHCP itself enabled better utilization of address space, with its ability to share addresses among a number of users on an as-needed basis. While predominantly configured with private address space within organizations having little impact on public space, DHCP is also used by broadband and wireless service providers to enable Internet access for their respective subscriber bases.

These growing subscriber bases are still driving increasing IPv4 address consumption, diminishing available capacity. And in many parts of the world, current allocations of IPv4 address space are inadequate. For example, Asia has been allocated about 20% of IPv4 allocations yet supports half of the world's population! Asia has been among the leaders in deployments of IPv6, followed by Europe. While North America has enjoyed relatively plentiful IPv4 address space, many organizations are evaluating a move to IPv6, especially among government and service provider organizations.

When we discuss IPv6 "migration," we're referring to an initial state of an IPv4-only network, in which IPv6 nodes and networks are added or overlaid over time, resulting in an IPv6-only network, or more likely in most cases, a predominantly IPv6 network with continued IPv4 support.

15.1.1 Why Implement IPv6?

On May 22, 2007, the American Registry of Internet Numbers (ARIN—one of the RIRs) board issued a public statement "advis[ing] the Internet community that migration to IPv6 numbering resources is necessary for any applications which require ongoing availability from ARIN of contiguous IP numbering resources." This in essence stated that IPv4 numbering resources (including IPv4 addresses) are becoming more scarce and that entities (LIRs, ISPs) requiring additional addresses over time need to plan for IPv6. All RIRs have also issued similar statements. Some estimates predict depletion of IPv4 space at the RIR level around 2012.[*] In fact Dr. Geoff Huston of APNIC has published enlightening analysis updated daily at www.potaroo.net/tools/ipv4 lending evidence to these dire predictions.[†]

Upon this final RIR allocation of IPv4 space in 2012 or whenever this occurs, ISPs will still have space to allocate; the last block allocated by an RIR will exhaust RIR space, but this allocated ISP block is still available for ISP allocation. ISP space will deplete when the ISP customer base fully consumes their allocatable space, which could take a year or so after that. Enterprises that haven't submitted nor have plans to submit requests

---

[*] While one can surmise the exhaustion date of IPv4 address space from this analysis, the intent of Dr. Huston's analysis focuses more on identifying when RIR policies must be in place to deal with the new RIR role for managing IPv4 address resources.

[†] Perhawps this "doomsday scenario" is what the Mayans had in mind!

for IP addresses in the foreseeable future may conclude that IPv6 won't affect them. But at the point in time where only IPv6 space is available, new ISPs or organizations seeking to expanding address space will generate end users with IPv6-only connectivity. This will drive IPv4-only organizations to implement IPv6 on external (Internet-facing) web, email, and other public servers as this IPv6-only population grows.

In addition, like many IP network changes such as those driven by wireless and PDA adoption within organizations, IPv6 may end up being driven by employees connecting to the network via next generation cell phones, PDAs, or even with Windows Vista (or 7) via network or home connections! In this case, the requirement to manage IPv6 address space may be thrust upon IT managers. Whether driven by external IPv6-only users or internal users, it's more prudent to proactively plan now for IPv6, whether you plan to fully migrate your network or plan to deal with individual IPv6 devices attempting to connect. Many service providers are already well along the path towards IPv6 deployment within their IP networks.

15.1.2 IPv4–IPv6 Coexistence Technologies

Numerous technologies are available to facilitate the migration of devices to IPv6. We use the term "coexistence" since the "migration" will likely be a very lengthy process. We'll discuss these approaches according to the following basic categories:

- *Dual Stack.* Support of both IPv4 and IPv6 on network devices.
- *Tunneling.* Encapsulation of an IPv6 packet within an IPv4 packet for transmission over an IPv4 network or vice versa.
- *Translation.* IP header, address, and/or port translation such as that performed by gateway or NAT devices.

The selected strategy requires effective coordination of the following:

- IPv4 and IPv6 network and subnet allocations, existing and planned.
- Validating network infrastructure and application compatibility with IPv6
- DNS resource record configuration corresponding to appropriate name resolution to address(es) for desired tunneling or translation.
- Compatible client/host and router support of selected tunneling mode as appropriate.
- Deployment of translation gateway(s) as appropriate.

Example IPv6 implementation scenarios are provided later in this chapter for service providers and enterprises, but first, let's discuss the key coexistence technologies.

15.2 DUAL-STACK APPROACH

The dual-stack approach consists of implementing both IPv4 and IPv6 protocol stacks on devices requiring access to both network layer technologies, including routers, other infrastructure devices, application servers, and end user devices. Such devices would be configured with both IPv4 and IPv6 addresses, and they may obtain these addresses via methods defined for the respective protocols as enabled by administrators. For example, an IPv4 address may be obtained via DHCPv4, while the IPv6 address may be autoconfigured.

Implementations may vary with dual-stack approaches with respect to the scope of the stack, which is shared versus what is unique to each IP version. Ideally, only the network layer would be dualized, using a common application, transport, and data link layer. This is the approach implemented in Microsoft Vista and 7, as opposed to the XP implementation, which utilized dual transport and network layers, requiring in some cases, redundant configuration of each stack. Other approaches may span the entire stack, down to the physical layer requiring a separate network interface for IPv6 versus IPv4. This approach, while contrary to the benefits of a layered protocol model, may be intentional and even desirable, especially in the case of network servers with multiple applications or services, some of which intentionally support only one version or the other.

15.2.1 Deployment

Deployment of dual-stacked devices sharing a common physical network interface implies the operation of both IPv4 and IPv6 over the same physical link. After all, Ethernet and other layer 2 technologies support either IPv4 or IPv6 payload thanks to protocol layering. Dual-stacked devices require routers supporting such links to be dual stacked as well. This overlay approach is expected to be very common during the transition and is depicted in Figure 15.1. This diagram can be extended beyond a physical LAN to a multihop network where routers support IPv4 and IPv6 and route IPv4 packets among native IPv4 hosts and IPv6 packets among IPv6-capable hosts.

While it's generally anticipated that routers would be among the first IP elements to be upgraded to support both protocols, RFC 4554 (193) is an informational RFC describing an innovative approach using VLANs to support an overlay configuration without requiring immediate router upgrades. This approach relies on VLAN tagging to

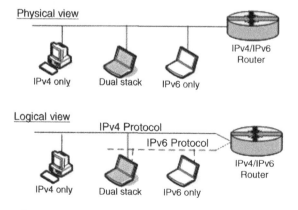

Figure 15.1. Dual-stacked network perspectives (11).

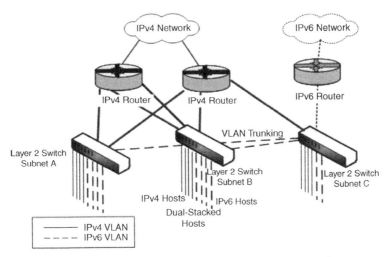

Figure 15.2. Dual-stack deployment using VLANs (147).

enable layer 2 switches to broadcast or trunk the Ethernet frames containing IPv6 payload to one or more IPv6 capable routers. By upgrading one router to support IPv6, for example, the gateway to an IPv6 network, the switch ports to which its interfaces are connected can be configured as the "IPv6 VLAN." Other IPv6 or dual-stacked devices could then be configured as members of the IPv6 VLAN, and multiple such VLANs could be likewise configured. An example of this deployment is displayed in Figure 15.2.

15.2.2 DNS Considerations

As we shall see, DNS plays a crucial role in proper operation of each transition technology; after all, it provides the vital linkage between end user naming, for example, web site address at the application layer and the destination IP address, whether IPv4 or IPv6 at the network layer. End users attempting to access a dual-stack device will query DNS, which can be configured by administrators with an A resource record corresponding to the node's IPv4 address and a AAAA resource record corresponding to its IPv6 address. The owner field of the resource record may have a common host domain name corresponding to the device as per the following example.

```
dual-stack-host.ipamworldwide.com.86400 IN A    10.200.0.16
dual-stack-host.ipamworldwide.com.86400 IN AAAA 2001:DB8:2200::A
```

Resolution of IP-address-to-host domain name may also be configured in DNS within the appropriate .arpa domain

```
16.0.200.10.in-addr.arpa. 86400 IN PTR dual-stack-host.ipamworld-
   wide.com.
A.0.0.0.0.0.0.0.0.0.0.0.0.0.0.0.0.0.0.0.0.0.0.2.2.8.B.D.0.1.0.0.2.
   ip6.arpa. 86400
IN PTR dual-stack-host.ipamworldwide.com.
```

A dual-stack node itself must be able to support receipt of A and AAAA records during its own DNS resolution processing, and communicate with the intended destination using the address and protocol corresponding to the returned record. Some resolver configurations may enable definition of the preferred network protocol when both an A and AAAA record are returned from the query, not to mention the protocol to use when issuing DNS queries themselves. In addition, as we shall see, some automatic tunneling technologies utilize specific IPv6 address formats, so addresses corresponding to one or more tunneled address formats may also be returned and may be used to the extent that the resolving host supports the corresponding tunneling technology. Resolving corresponding PTR records requires traversal down the corresponding .arpa. tree, which in some cases can be tricky as we'll discuss.

In terms of IP version used in the transport of DNS queries and answers, RFC 3901 (Internet Best Current Practice 91) (148) recommends that each recursive DNS server should support IPv4-only or dual-stack IPv4/IPv6. The RFC also recommends that every DNS zone should be served by at least one IPv4-reachable authoritative DNS server. These recommendations were set forth to provide backward compatibility for IPv4-only resolvers which will be around for quite some time.

15.2.3 DHCP Considerations

The mechanism for using DHCP under a dual-stack implementation is simply that each stack uses its corresponding version of DHCP. That is, to obtain an IPv4 address, use DHCP; to obtain an IPv6 address or prefix, use DHCPv6. However, additional configuration information is provided by both forms of DHCP, such as which DNS or NTP server to use. The information obtained may lead to incorrect behavior on the client, depending on how the information from both servers is merged together. For example, if DNS server addresses are provided by both DHCP transactions, preferences of IPv4, IPv6, or mixed preference ordering cannot be conveyed. This remains an ongoing area of concern, as documented in RFC 4477 (149), but the current standard is to use a DHCP server for IPv4 and a DHCPv6 server for IPv6, possibly implemented on a common physical server.

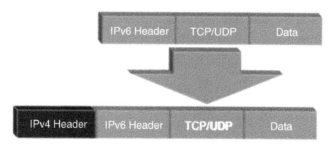

Figure 15.3. IPv6 over IPv4 tunneling (11).

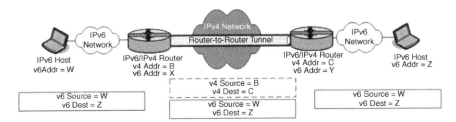

Figure 15.4. Router-to-router tunnel (11).

15.3 TUNNELING APPROACHES

A variety of tunneling technologies have been developed to support IPv4 over IPv6 and IPv6 over IPv4 tunneling. These technologies are generally categorized as *configured* or *automatic*. Configured tunnels are predefined, whereas automatic tunnels are created and torn down on the fly. We'll discuss these two tunnel types after reviewing some tunneling basics.

In general, tunneling of IPv6 packets over an IPv4 network entails prefixing an IPv6 packet with an IPv4 header as illustrated in Figure 15.3. This enables the tunneled packet to be routed over an IPv4 routing infrastructure; the IPv6 packet is simply considered payload within the IPv4 packet. The entry node of the tunnel, whether a router or host, performs the encapsulation. The source IPv4 address in the IPv4 header is populated with that node's IPv4 address and the destination address is that of the tunnel endpoint. The Protocol field of the IPv4 header is set to 41 (decimal) indicating an encapsulated IPv6 packet. The exit node or tunnel endpoint performs decapsulation to strip off the IPv4 header and routes the packet as appropriate to the ultimate destination via IPv6.

15.3.1 Tunneling Scenarios for IPv6 Packets Over IPv4 Networks

Using this basic tunneling approach, a variety of scenarios based on tunnel endpoints have been defined. Probably the most common configuration is a router-to-router tunnel, depicted in Figure 15.4, which is the most common approach for configured tunnels.

In this figure, the originating IPv6 host on the left has IPv6 address of W (for simplicity and brevity for now). A packet* destined for the host on the far end of the diagram with IPv6 address of Z is sent to a router serving the subnet. This router, with IPv4 address of B and IPv6 address of X, receives the IPv6 packet. Configured to tunnel packets destined for the network on which host Z resides, the router encapsulates the IPv6 packet with an IPv4 header. The router uses its IPv4 address (B) as the source IPv4 address and the tunnel endpoint router, with IPv4 address of C, as the destination address as depicted by the dashed rectangle beneath the IPv4 network in the center of Figure 15.4. The tunneled packets are routed like "regular" IPv4 packets to the destination tunnel

---

* This packet is crudely identified in the figure as the solid-line rectangle beneath the originating host displaying the packet's IPv6 source address of W and destination address of Z. The tunnel header is shown as the dotted-line rectangle in this and subsequent tunneling figures.

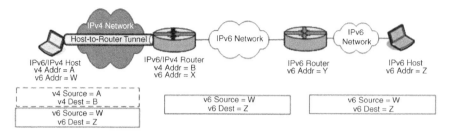

Figure 15.5. Host-to-router tunneling configuration (11).

endpoint router. This endpoint router decapsulates the packet, stripping off the IPv4 header and routes the original IPv6 packet to its intended destination, Z.

Another tunneling scenario features an IPv6/IPv4 host, capable of supporting both IPv4 and IPv6 protocols, tunneling a packet to a router, which in turn decapsulates the packet and routes it natively via IPv6. This flow and packet header addresses are shown in Figure 15.5. The tunneling mechanism is the same as in the router-to-router case, but the tunnel endpoints are different.

The router-to-host configuration is also very similar, as shown in Figure 15.6. The originating IPv6 host on the left of the diagram sends the IPv6 packet to its local router, which routes it to a router closest to the destination. The serving router is configured to tunnel IPv6 packets over IPv4 to the host as shown in the figure.

The final tunneling configuration is one that spans end-to-end, from host-to-host. If the routing infrastructure has not yet been upgraded to support IPv6, this tunneling configuration enables two IPv6/IPv4 hosts to communicate via a tunnel as shown in Figure 15.7. In this example, the communications is IPv4 from end-to-end.

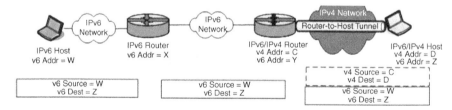

Figure 15.6. Router-to-host tunnel configuration (11).

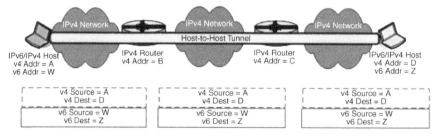

Figure 15.7. Router-to-host tunnel configuration (11).

15.3.2 Tunnel Types

As mentioned, tunnels are either configured or automatic. Configured tunnels are predefined by administrators in advance of communications. In the scenarios described above, configuration of the respective tunnel endpoints is required to configure the device regarding when to tunnel IPv6 packets, that is, based on destination, along with other tunnel configuration parameters that may be required by the tunnel implementation.

An automatic tunnel does not require tunnel preconfiguration, though enablement of tunneling configuration may be required. Tunnels are created based on information contained within the IPv6 packet, such as the source or destination IP address. The following automatic tunneling techniques are described in this section.

- *6to4*. Automatic router-to-router tunneling based on a particular global address prefix and embedded IPv4 address.
- *ISATAP*. Automatic host-to-router, router-to-host, or host-to-host tunneling based on a particular IPv6 address format with inclusion of an embedded IPv4 address.
- *6over4*. Automatic host-to-host tunneling using IPv4 multicasting.
- *Tunnel Brokers*. Automatic tunnel setup by a server acting as a tunnel broker in assigning tunnel gateway resources on behalf of hosts requiring tunneling.
- *Teredo*. Automatic tunneling through NAT firewalls over IPv4 networks.
- *Dual-stack transition mechanism*. Enables automatic tunneling of IPv4 packets over IPv6 networks.

6to4. 6to4 is an IPv6 over IPv4 tunneling technique that relies on a particular IPv6 address format to identify 6to4 packets and to tunnel them accordingly. The address format consists of a 6to4 prefix, 2002::/16, followed by a globally unique IPv4 address for the intended destination site. This concatenation forms a 48 prefix per the diagram below.

The unique IPv4 address, 192.0.2.131 in our example of Figure 15.8, represents the IPv4 address of the 6to4 router terminating the 6to4 tunnel. The 48-bit 6to4 prefix serves as the global routing prefix, and a Subnet ID can be appended as the next 16 bits, followed by an Interface ID to fully define the IPv6 address. Routers with 6to4 tunneling support (6to4 routers) must be employed, and IPv6 hosts that are to send/receive via 6to4 tunnels must be configured with a 6to4 address and are considered 6to4 hosts.

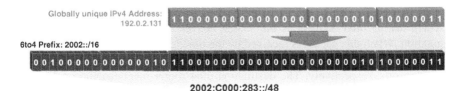

2002:C000:283::/48

Figure 15.8. 6to4 address prefix derivation (147).

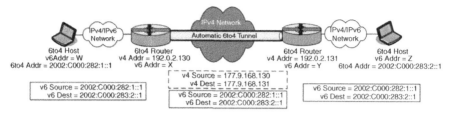

Figure 15.9. 6to4 tunneling example (147).

Let's consider an example, two sites containing 6to4 hosts desire to communicate and are interconnected via 6to4 routers connected to a common IPv4 network; this could be the Internet or an internal IPv4 network. Per Figure 15.9 the IPv4 addresses of the routers' IPv4 interfaces (facing each other) are 192.0.2.130 and 192.0.2.131, respectively. Transforming these IPv4 addresses into 6to4 prefixes we arrive at 2002:C000:282::/48 and 2002:C000:283::/48, respectively. These prefixes now identify each site in terms of 6to4 reachability. Our 6to4 host on the left is on Subnet ID = 1 and for simplicity has Interface ID = 1. Thus, this host's 6to4 address is 2002:C000:282:1::1. This address would be configured on the device manually or automatically (autoconfiguration based on the devices' interface ID and the router's advertisement of the 2002: C000:282:1::/64 prefix). Similarly, the 6to4 host at the other site resides on subnet ID = 2 and interface ID = 1, resulting in a 6to4 address of 2002:C000:283:2::1.

The AAAA and PTR resource records corresponding to these 6to4 addresses should also be added to DNS within the appropriate domains. When tunneling through the Internet, the destination AAAA and PTR records are maintained by each organization managing the corresponding 6to4 devices and resolution may require traversal down each domain subtree. The AAAA record follows normal "forward domain" resolution, but the PTR record is less straightforward. Since the PTR domain tree is based on the corresponding IPv6 address, which in the 6to4 case is "self-configured" by an organization based on its IPv4 address space and not by an upstream IPv6 address registry, the ip6.arpa delegation is unlinked from an authoritative upstream domain parent. A special registrar was established to handle delegations from the 2.0.0.2.ip6.arpa zone: the Number Resource Organization (NRO). Our administrators for the ip6.arpa domain corresponding to the 2002:C000:283::/48 prefix in our example would register the 3.8.2.0.0.0.0.C.2.0.0.2.ip6.arpa zone with 6to4.nro.net along with corresponding authoritative name servers.

Getting back to the packet flow, when our host on the left wishes to communicate with the host on the right, a DNS lookup would resolve to its 6to4 address. The sending host will use its 6to4 address as the source and the destination 6to4 address as the destination. When this packet is received by the 6to4 router, the router will encapsulate the packet with an IPv4 header using its (source) and the other 6to4 router's (destination) IPv4 addresses, respectively. The destination 6to4 router receiving the packet would decapsulate it and transmit the packet on its 2002:C000:283:2::/64 network to the destination 6to4 host.

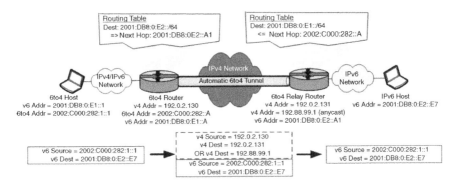

Figure 15.10. 6to4 host communicating with a native IPv6 host (147).

6to4 can provide an efficient mechanism for IPv6 hosts to communicate over IPv4 networks. As IPv6 networks are incrementally deployed, *6to4 relay routers*, which are IPv6 routers that also support 6to4, can be used to relay packets from hosts on "pure" IPv6 networks to IPv6 hosts via IPv4 networks.

The same addressing and tunneling scheme applies, however, the 6to4 router requires knowledge of the 6to4 relay routers to map global unicast (native) IPv6 addresses to a 6to4 address for tunneling. There are three ways these relay routers can be configured

1. Configure routes to destination native IPv6 networks with the 6to4 relay router as the next hop. This is illustrated in Figure 15.10.

2. Utilize normal routing protocols, enabling the 6to4 relay router to advertise routes to IPv6 networks. This scenario would apply when advertising routes to migrated or internal IPv6 networks. If the pure IPv6 network in Figure 15.10 is the "IPv6 internet," the following default route option is likely a better alternative.

3. Configure a default route to the 6to4 relay router to reach IPv6 networks. This scenario may apply where an IPv6 Internet connection is reachable only through a IPv4 network internally to the organization and few or no pure IPv6 networks exist within the organization.[*]

In walking through Figure 15.10, we have a 6to4 host on an IPv4/IPv6 network on the left of the diagram with a native IPv6 address and a 6to4 address. This host sets out to communicate with a native IPv6 host with IP address 2001:DB8:0:E2::E7 on the right side of the diagram. This IPv6 address is returned within a AAAA resource record response from a DNS server when queried for the IP address of the destination host. Thus,

---

[*] A variant on this scenario calls for the definition of the default route next hop as the 6to4 relay router anycast address for IPv6 networks. This variation supports the scenario with multiple 6to4 relay routers. RFC 3068 (194) defines an anycast address for 6to4 relay routers: 2002:C058:6301::/48. This address corresponds to the IPv4 address of 192.88.99.1. This variant is also illustrated in Figure 15.10.

our 6to4 host on the left formulates an IPv6 packet using either its IPv6 or 6to4 (shown) address as the source IP address based on host address selection policies, and the destination host's IPv6 address as the destination.

This packet then arrives at the 6to4 router on the left of the IPv4 network cloud. The router would need to have a routing table entry in order to route to the destination 2001: DB8:0:E2::/64 network, pointing to the 6to4 relay router's 6to4 address as shown in the figure. The 6to4 router then creates an automatic tunnel to the corresponding IPv4 address contained in bits 17–48 of the 6to4 address found in the routing table. Note that as just discussed, this routing table entry could alternatively be a default route for IPv6 packets to the 6to4 relay router's 6to4 unicast address or the 6to4 anycast address.

While not shown in the router's routing table in Figure 15.10, the tunneled packet headers depicted below the IPv4 network cloud indicate that the destination IPv4 address encapsulating the IPv6 packet could be the IPv4 unicast address or the IPv4 address corresponding to the 6to4 anycast address. The 6to4 relay router, upon receiving the IPv4 packet, would decapsulate it, then transmit the native IPv6 packet to the intended recipient.

In the reverse direction, use of the recipient's 6to4 address as the destination IPv6 address would inform the 6to4 relay that this packet requires 6to4 tunneling to the corresponding 6to4 router. However, if the destination address is a native IPv6 address, the routing table within the 6to4 relay router must contain a mapping of the 6to4 address of the corresponding 6to4 router as the next hop toward the IPv6 host.

Intrasite Automatic Tunneling Addressing Protocol (ISATAP). ISATAP is

an experimental protocol providing automatic IPv6 over IPv4 tunneling for host-to-router, router-to-host, and host-to-host configurations. ISATAP IPv6 addresses are formed using an IPv4 address to define its Interface ID. The Interface ID is comprised of ::5EFE:a.b.c.d, where a.b.c.d is the dotted decimal IPv4 notation. So an ISATAP interface ID corresponding to 192.0.2.131 is denoted as ::5EFE:192.0.2.131. The IPv4 notation provides a clear indication that the ISATAP address contains an IPv4 address without having to translate the IPv4 address into hexadecimal. This ISATAP Interface ID can be used as a normal interface ID in appending it to supported network prefixes to define IPv6 addresses. For example, the link local IPv6 address using the ISATAP Interface ID above is FE80::5EFE:192.0.2.131.

Hosts supporting ISATAP are required to maintain a *potential router list* (PRL) containing the IPv4 address and associated address lifetime timer for each router advertising an ISATAP interface. ISATAP hosts solicit ISATAP support information from local routers via router solicitation over IPv4. The solicitation destination needs to be identified by the host by prior manual configuration, by looking up the router in DNS with a hostname of "isatap," or using a DHCP vendor-specific option indicating the IPv4 address(es) of the ISATAP router(s). The DNS technique requires administrators to create resource records for ISATAP routers using the isatap hostname.

An ISATAP host would encapsulate the IPv6 data packet with an IPv4 header as shown in Figure 15.11, using the IPv4 address corresponding to the chosen router from the PRL.

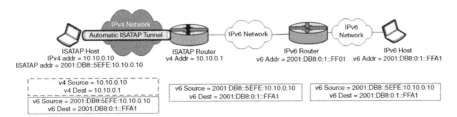

Figure 15.11. ISATAP host-to-router example (147).

ISATAP hosts can autoconfigure their ISATAP Interface IDs using configured IPv4 addresses, whether the IPv4 address is defined statically or is obtained via DHCP. Microsoft XP and 2003 server perform such autoconfiguration if configured with IPv6. Microsoft Vista and 7 clients and Windows 2008 servers support ISATAP auto-configuration by default. The ISATAP interface ID is appended to a 64-bit global network prefix and subnet ID provided by solicited ISATAP routers in their router advertisements.

Following Figure 15.11, the host on the left of the diagram identifies the destination host's IP address, in this case an IPv6 address, using DNS. An IPv6 packet would be formed by the host, using its ISATAP IPv6 address as its source address, and the destination IPv6 host address as the destination address. This packet is encapsulated in an IPv4 header, thereby forming an automatic tunnel. The tunnel source address is set to the ISATAP host's IPv4 address, the destination address is set to the ISATAP router's IPv4 address, and the protocol field in the IP header is set to decimal 41, indicating an encapsulated IPv6 packet. The ISATAP router need not be on the same physical network as the host, and the tunnel can span a generic IPv4 network (zero or more hops) between the host and the ISATAP router. The ISATAP router strips off the IPv4 header and routes the remaining IPv6 packet to the destination host using normal IPv6 routing.

The destination host can respond to the originating host using the originating host's ISATAP address. Since the ISATAP address contains a globally unique network prefix/ Subnet ID, the destination packet coming back is routed to the serving ISATAP router. Upon processing the Interface ID, the ISATAP router can extract the IPv4 address of the destination host and encapsulate the IPv6 packet with an IPv4 header to the original host. In a similar manner, the native IPv6 host to the right of Figure 15.11 could have initiated the communication to the ISATAP host. Going from right to left, the ISATAP router in this case would create the ISATAP tunnel to the host.

Host-to-host ISATAP tunnels, similar to that displayed in Figure 15.7, can be initiated by ISATAP hosts residing on an IPv4 network, where a link local (same subnet) or global network prefix can be prefixed to each host's ISATAP interface ID. In Figure 15.7, IPv6 addresses W and Z would represent ISATAP addresses formed from IPv4 addresses A and D, respectively.

6over4. 6over4 is an automatic tunneling technique that leverages IPv4 multicast. IPv4 multicast is required and is considered a *virtual link layer* or *virtual Ethernet* by 6over4. Because of the virtual link layer perspective, IPv6 addresses are formed using a link local scope (FE80::/10 prefix). A host's IPv4 address comprises its 6over4 Interface ID portion of its IPv6 address. For example, a 6over4 host with IPv4 address of 192.0.2.85 would formulate an IPv6 interface ID of ::C000:255, and thus, a 6over4 address of FE80::C000:255. 6over4 tunnels can be of the form host-to-host, host-to-router, and router-to-host, where respective hosts and routers must be configured to support 6over4. IPv6 packets are tunneled in IPv4 headers using corresponding IPv4 multicast addresses. All members of the multicast group receive the tunneled packets, thus the analogy of virtual link layer, and the intended recipient strips off the IPv4 header and processes the IPv6 packet. As long as at least one IPv6 router also running 6over4 is reachable via the IPv4 multicast mechanism, the router can serve as a tunnel endpoint and route the packet via IPv6.

6over4 supports IPv6 multicast as well as unicast, so hosts can perform IPv6 router and neighbor discovery to locate IPv6 routers. When tunneling IPv6 multicast messages, for example, for neighbor discovery, the IPv4 destination address is formatted as 239.192.Y.Z, where Y and Z are the last two bytes of the IPv6 multicast address. Thus an IPv6 message to the all-routers link-scoped multicast address, FF02::2 would be tunneled to IPv4 destination 239.192.0.2. The Internet Group Membership Protocol (IGMP) is used by 6over4 hosts to inform IPv4 routers of multicast group membership.

Tunnel Brokers. Tunnel brokers provide another technique for automatic tunneling over IPv4 networks. The tunnel broker manages (brokers) tunnel requests from dual-stack clients and tunnel broker servers, which connect to the intended IPv6 network. Dual-stack clients attempting to access an IPv6 network can optionally be directed to a tunnel broker web portal for entry of authentication credentials, to authorize use of the broker service. The tunnel broker may also manage certificates for authorization services. The client also provides the IPv4 address for its end of the tunnel, along with the desired FQDN of the client, the number of IPv6 addresses requested, and whether the client is a host or a router.

Once authorized, the tunnel broker performs a number of tasks to broker creation of the tunnel

- assigns and configures a tunnel server and informs the selected tunnel server of the new client;
- assigns an IPv6 address or prefix to the client based on the requested number of addresses and client type (router or host);
- registers the client FQDN in DNS; and
- informs the client of its assigned tunnel server and associated tunnel and IPv6 parameters including address/prefix and DNS name.

Figure 15.12 illustrates the client-tunnel broker interaction at the top of the figure, and the resulting tunnel between the client and the assigned tunnel server below. RFC 5572 (150) formalizes the Tunnel Setup Protocol (TSP) to promote common tunnel setup messages and component interactions.

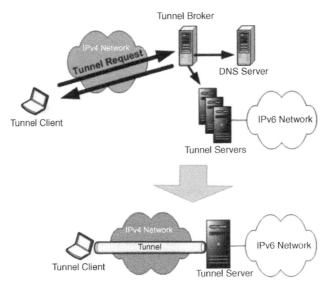

Figure 15.12. Tunnel broker interaction (147).

Teredo. Tunneling through firewalls that perform network address translation can be challenging if not impossible by design. Teredo is a tunnel broker technology that enables NAT traversal of IPv6 packets tunneled over UDP over IPv4 for host-to-host automatic tunnels. Teredo incorporates the additional UDP header (see Figure 15.13) in order to facilitate NAT/firewall traversal. Many NAT/firewall devices will not allow traversal of IPv4 packets with the packet header protocol field set to 41, which is the setting for tunneling of IPv6 packets as mentioned previously. The additional UDP header further "buries" the tunnel to enable its traversal through NAT/firewall devices, most of which support UDP port translation.

Teredo is defined in RFC 4380 (151) to provide "IPv6 access of last resort" due to its overhead and will be used less and less as 6to4-enabled or IPv6-aware firewall routers are deployed. Teredo requires the following elements as shown in Figure 15.14.

- Teredo client
- Teredo server
- Teredo relay

The Teredo tunneling process starts with a Teredo client performing a qualification procedure to discover a Teredo relay closest to the intended destination IPv6 host and identify the type of NAT firewall that is in place. The Teredo relay is the Teredo tunnel endpoint serving the intended destination host. Teredo hosts must be preconfigured with this Teredo server IPv4 addresses to use, which help establish Teredo connections.

Determining the closest Teredo relay entails sending an IPv6 ping (ICMPv6 echo request) to the destination host. The ping is encapsulated with a UDP and IPv4 header and

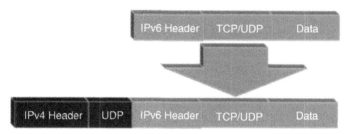

Figure 15.13. Teredo tunnels add UDP then IPv4 headers (151).

sent to the Teredo server, which decapsulates it and sends the native ICMPv6 packet to the destination. The destination host's response will be routed via native IPv6 to the nearest (routing-wise) Teredo relay, then back to the originating host. In this manner, the client determines the appropriate Teredo relay's IPv4 address and port by virtue of its IPv4 and UDP [tunnel] headers. Figure 15.14 illustrates the case with a Teredo client communicating to a native IPv6 host.

NAT Types. The type of NAT being traversed drives the need to perform an additional step to enable the NAT device to initialize table mappings for the data exchanged between the Teredo client and the IPv6 host. The following NAT types have been defined as follows:

- *Full Cone.* All IP packets from the same internal IP address and port are mapped to a corresponding external address and port. External hosts can communicate with the host by transmitting to the mapped external address and port.
- *Restricted Cone.* All IP packets from the same internal IP address and port are mapped to a corresponding external address and port. An external host can communicate with the internal host only if the internal host had previously sent a packet to the external host.
- *Port Restricted Cone.* All IP packets from the same internal IP address and port are mapped to a corresponding external address and port. External hosts can communicate with the internal host only if the internal host had previously sent a packet to the external host using the external host's address and the same port number.

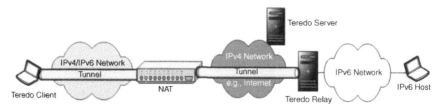

Figure 15.14. Teredo client to IPv6 host connection (147).

- *Symmetric.* All IP packets from a given internal IP address and port to a specific external IP address and port are mapped to a particular IP address and port. Packets from the same host IP address and port to a different destination IP address or port results in a different external IP address and port mapping. External hosts can communicate with the internal host only if the internal host had previously sent a packet to the external host using the external host's address and the same port number.

Table 15.1 illustrates these different NAT types. Based on outgoing traffic shown for each case, the NAT will map the internal address and port to an assigned external address and port; this in turn drives the corresponding permitted incoming traffic shown in the right-hand column of the table. First considering the full cone example, an internal host with IP address 10.10.0.1 initiates a session through the NAT using source port 10081. The NAT maps the original 10.10.0.1 source IP address to 192.0.2.1 on the outgoing packet from the NAT. The NAT also assigns port number 43513 on the outgoing packet and assigns port number 42512 (any high numbered port) for the internal leg back to the IPv4 internal host. Hence, the NAT terminates the first connection and bridges it to another; the first connection is (10.10.0.1:10081 ↔ NAT IP address:42512) while the second is (192.0.2.1:43513 ↔ Destination IP address from original packet: Destination port from original packet).

Based on this internally initiated communiqué, any external host may initiate a packet to IP address 192.0.2.1 and thereby connect to the 10.10.0.1 host internally. This is

TABLE 15.1. NAT Types

Outgoing Traffic					Permitted Incoming Traffic	
Internal Host → External Host			NAT Mapping		External Host → Internal Host	
Full Cone	Source	Destination	Internal	⇔External	Source	Destination
IP Addr	10.10.0.1	Any	10.10.0.1	192.0.2.1	Any	192.0.2.1
Port	10081	Any	42512	43513	Any	Any
Restricted Cone	Source	Destination	Internal	⇔External	Source	Destination
IP Addr	10.10.0.1	203.0.113.8	10.10.0.1	192.0.2.1	203.0.113.8	192.0.2.1
Port	10081	Any	42512	43513	Any	Any
Port Restricted Cone	Source	Destination	Internal	⇔External	Source	Destination
IP Addr	10.10.0.1	203.0.113.8	10.10.0.1	192.0.2.1	203.0.113.8	192.0.2.1
Port	10081	80	42512	43513	80	Any
Symmetric	Source	Destination	Internal	⇔External	Source	Destination
IP Addr	10.10.0.1	203.0.113.8	10.10.0.1	192.0.2.1	203.0.113.8	192.0.2.1
Port	10081	80	42512	43513	80	43513

denoted on the right of the table under permitted incoming traffic. In the full cone case, an incoming packet from an external host may come from any IP address or port (source address and port = any) and the destination IP address of 192.0.2.1 on any port will be accepted.

Contrast this with the symmetric case at the bottom of the table, where an internal host on IP address 10.10.0.1 uses source port 10081 to initiate a connection to destination IP address 203.0.113.8 port 80. The NAT terminates this connection and initiates an external connection to the given destination address and port, mapping the source IP address to 192.0.2.1 and port to 43513. In this case, the only accepted incoming traffic permitted to traverse the NAT will have a source IP address and port of 203.0.113.8:80 and destination 192.0.2.1:43513, which the NAT had mapped based on the communications from the originating host.

The restricted cone configuration maps the original destination IP address as permitted as a subsequent incoming source IP address from the external space (203.0.113.8) when the corresponding destination IP address is the NAT-mapped address, 192.0.2.1 in this example. The port restricted scenario adds port validity checking by permitting the original destination address and port as permitted as subsequent incoming IP address and port from the external space (203.0.113.8:80) when the corresponding destination IP address and port match the NAT-mapped 192.0.2.1 address in this example.

To communicate using Teredo, the NAT type drives the Teredo initialization process in order to establish the firewall traversal. Identification of the NAT as full cone requires no further qualification because any external host may initiate communications to its external address. But either of the restricted cone scenarios do require further qualification to properly map the source and destination addresses corresponding to those within the NAT. To complete the mapping within the NAT of the internal host communiqué with the destination host, a *bubble packet* is sent by the Teredo client to the destination host. A bubble packet is an IPv6 header with no payload, itself encapsulated in the Teredo tunnel IPv4/UDP header. It enables the NAT to complete the mapping of internal and external IP addresses and internal and external port numbers for the port restricted cone scenario.

Generally the bubble packet is sent directly from the source Teredo client to the destination host. But if the destination host is also behind a firewall, the bubble packet may be discarded since this is an unsolicited external packet. In this case, the Teredo client times out and sends the bubble packet via the Teredo server, which is identified by the intended destination Teredo formatted IPv6 address, which encodes the Teredo IPv4 address. The Teredo server then forwards the packet over a Teredo tunnel to the destination host, which has its own IPv4 address also encoded in the Teredo IPv6 address.

Assuming the destination host is also a Teredo client, it will receive the packet, having been initialized by a prior ping it sent to this Teredo server during client configuration. The destination host will then respond to the originating host directly, completing the NAT mapping (on both sides). Figure 15.15 illustrates this scenario with two Teredo clients communicating via a common Teredo relay. Teredo does not support automatic traversal of symmetric NAT devices.

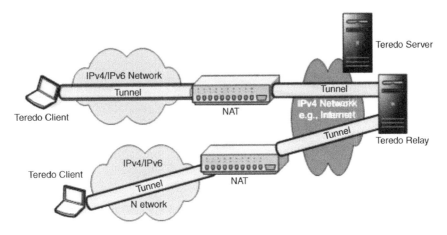

Figure 15.15. Two Teredo clients communicating via the IPv4 Internet (147).

As we've seen, the Teredo IPv6 address is formatted with the client and its server Teredo server IPv4 addresses. The Teredo IPv6 address is of the format depicted in Figure15.16.

The Teredo prefix is a predefined IPv6 prefix: 2001::/32. The Teredo server IPv4 address comprises the next 32 bits. Flags indicate the type of NAT as either full cone (hex value = 8000) or restricted or port restricted (hex value = 0000). The client port and client IPv4 address fields represent obfuscated values of these respective values by reversing each bit value.

15.3.3 Tunneling Scenarios for IPv4 Packets Over IPv6 Networks

During an IPv6 implementation, some IPv6 clients on IPv6 networks may still need to communicate with IPv4 applications or hosts on IPv4 networks, such as the Internet. Tunneling of IPv4 packets over the IPv6 network provides a means to preserve this communications path.

Dual-Stack Transition Mechanism (DSTM). DSTM provides a means to tunnel IPv4 packets over IPv6 networks, ultimately to the destination IPv4 network and host. The host on the IPv6 network intending to communicate with the IPv4 host would require a dual stack, as well as a DSTM client. Upon resolving the hostname of the intended destination host using DNS to only an IPv4 address, the client would initiate the DSTM process, which is very similar to the tunnel broker approach. The

Figure 15.16. Teredo IPv6 address format (151).

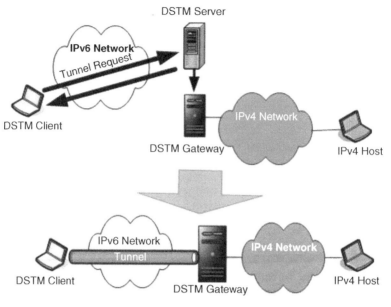

Figure 15.17. DSTM tunnel setup (147).

process begins with the DSTM client contacting a DSTM server to obtain an IPv4 address preferably via the DHCPv6 protocol,[*] as well as the IPv6 address of the DSTM gateway. The IPv4 address is used as the source address in the data packet to be transmitted. This packet is encapsulated with an IPv6 header using the DSTM client's source IPv6 address and the DSTM gateway's IPv6 address as the destination. The next header field in the IPv6 header indicates an encapsulated IPv4 packet with this "4over6" tunneling approach.

A variant of DSTM supports VPN based access from a DSTM client outside of the native network, for example, a home-based worker. In this scenario, assuming the DSTM client obtains an IPv6 address but no IPv4 address, it can connect to the DSTM server to obtain an IPv4 address. This access should require authentication to establish a VPN between the DSTM client and DSTM gateway.

15.3.4 Tunneling Summary

The following table summarizes the applicability of tunneling based on the source host capabilities/network type and the destination address resolution and network type.

---

[*] While the DSTM RFC drafts (152) denote DHCPv6 as the preferable method to obtain an IPv4 address, DHCPv6 does not currently define assignment of IPv4 addresses natively or via an option setting.

	To					
From	IPv4 Destination on IPv4 Network	Dual-Stack Destination on IPv4 Network Resolved to IPv4 Address	Dual-Stack Destination on IPv4 Network Resolved to IPv6 Address	Dual-Stack Destination on IPv6 Network Resolved as IPv4 Address	Dual-Stack Destination on IPv6 Network Resolved as IPv6 Address	IPv6 Destination on IPv6 Network
IPv4 client on IPv4 network	Native IPv4	Native IPv4		Native IPv4 → IPv4-compatible		
Dual-stack client on IPv4 network	Native IPv4	Native IPv4	Host-to-host IPv6 over IPv4[a]	Native IPv4 → IPv4-compatible	Host-to-router IPv6 over IPv4[a]	Host-to-router IPv6 over IPv4[a]
Dual-stack client on IPv6 network	DSTM → Native IPv4	DSTM → Native IPv4	Native IPv6 → Router-to-host IPv6 over IPv4[a]	DSTM	Native IPv6	Native IPv6
IPv6 client on IPv6 network			Native IPv6 → IPv6 over IPv4[a]		Native IPv6	Native IPv6

[a] Resolution to an IPv6 address could be a native IPv6 address, or a 6to4, ISATAP, Teredo, 6over4 or IPv4-compatible address. The host must select the destination address based on its support of the corresponding technology.

The cells in the upper left and lower right of the table indicate use of a native IP version from end-to-end. Any intervening networks of the opposite protocol must be either tunneled through via a router-to-router tunnel or translated at each boundary using a translation technology, discussed in the next section.

The other cells indicate a tunneling scenario. The " $\rightarrow$ " symbol represents a transition point or tunneling endpoint within the network that converts the corresponding native protocol to a tunneled protocol or vice versa.

The blank cells indicate an invalid connection option via tunneling. However, translation technologies could be employed to bridge these gaps as we'll discuss next.

15.4 TRANSLATION APPROACHES

Translation techniques perform IPv4-to-IPv6 translation (and vice versa) at a particular layer of the protocol stack, typically network, transport, or application. Unlike tunneling, which does not alter the tunneled data packet but merely appends a header or two, translation mechanisms do modify or translate IP packets commutatively between IPv4 and IPv6. Translation approaches are generally recommended in an environment with IPv6-only nodes communicating with IPv4-only nodes; that is, for the blank cell scenarios in the summary table above. In dual-stack environments, native or tunneling mechanisms are preferable.[*]

15.4.1 Stateless IP/ICMP Translation (SIIT) Algorithm

The common algorithm for translating IPv4 and IPv6 packets is the Stateless IP/ICMP Translation (SIIT) algorithm. SIIT provides translation of IP packet headers between IPv4 and IPv6. SIIT resides on an IPv6 host or gateway and converts outgoing IPv6 packet headers into IPv4 headers, and incoming IPv4 headers into IPv6. To perform this task, the IPv6 host must be provided an IPv4 address, either configured on the host or obtained via a network service unspecified in RFC 2765 (153). When the IPv6 host desires to communicate with an IPv4 host, the SIIT algorithm would convert the IPv6 packet header into IPv4 format. The SIIT algorithm recognizes such a case when the IPv6 address is an IPv4-mapped address, formatted as shown in Figure 15.18. The mechanism to convert the resolved IPv4 address into an IPv4-mapped address is provided by bump-in-the-stack (BIS) or bump-in-the-API (BIA) techniques described later.

Based on the presence of the IPv4-mapped address format as the destination IP address, SIIT performs header translation as described next to yield an IPv4 packet for transmission via the data link and physical layers. The source IP address for an IPv6 node uses a different format, that of the IPv4-translated format, shown in Figure 15.19, though RFC 2765 does not specify how this address is initially configured.

---

[*] Per RFC 2766 (156).

Figure 15.18. IPv4 mapped address format (12).

Figure 15.19. IPv4 translated address format used within SIIT (153).

A potential protocol stack view of the SIIT algorithm is shown in Figure 15.20. The basic header translation process is summarized below for both directions.

IPv4 → IPv6 Header Translation	IPv6 → IPv4 Header Translation
Version = 6	*Version* = 4
Traffic Class = IPv4 header TOS bits	*Header Length* = 5 (no IPv4 options)
Flow Label = 0	*Type of Service* = IPv6 header Traffic Class field
Payload Length = IPv4 header total length value − (IPv4 header length + IPv4 options length)	*Total Length* = IPv6 header payload length field + IPv4 header length
	Identification = 0
Next Header = IPv4 header protocol field value	*Flags* = Don't fragment = 1, more fragments = 0
Hop Limit = IPv4 TTL field value − 1	*Fragment Offset* = 0
Source IP Address = 0:0:0:0: FFFF::/96 concatenated with IPv4 header source IP address	*TTL* = IPv6 hop limit field value − 1
	Protocol = IPv6 next header field
Destination IP Address = 0:0:0:0:0:FFFF::/96 concatenated with IPv4 header destination IP address	*Header Checksum* = Computed over the IPv4 header
	Source IP Address = low order 32 bits of IPv6 Source IP Address field (IPv4-translated address)
	Destination IP Address = low order 32 bits of IPv6 Destination IP Address field (IPv4-mapped address)
	Options = None

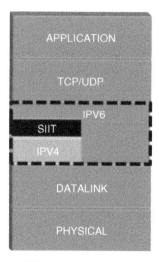

Figure 15.20. SIIT stack example (153).

Now let's look at some techniques that employ the SIIT algorithm to translate IPv4 and IPv6 packets.

15.4.2 Bump in the Stack (BIS)

BIS (154) enables hosts using IPv4 applications to communicate over IPv6 networks. BIS snoops data flowing between the TCP/IPv4 module and link layer devices (e.g., network interface cards) and translates the IPv4 packet into IPv6. The components of BIS are shown in Figure 15.21.

The Translator component translates the IPv4 header into an IPv6 header according to the SIIT algorithm. The Extension Name Resolver snoops DNS queries for A record types; upon detecting such a query, the Extension Name Resolver component creates an additional query for the AAAA record type for the same host domain name (Qname) and class (Qclass). If no affirmative answer is received from the AAAA query, the communications ensues using IPv4; if the AAAA query is successfully resolved, the Extension Name Resolver instructs the Address Mapper component to associate the returned IPv4 address (A record) with the returned IPv6 address (AAAA record). If only a AAAA response is received, the Address Mapper assigns an IPv4 address from an internally configured pool of addresses.

The IPv4 address is needed in order to provide a response up the stack to the application requesting resolution to the A query. Thus, the Address Mapper maintains the association of the real or self-assigned IPv4 address with the IPv6 address of the destination. Any data packets destined to that IPv4 address are then translated by the Translator into IPv6 packets for transmission via IPv6 networks.

In the case of the BIS host receiving an IPv6 packet initiated from an external host that is not already mapped, the Address Mapper will assign an IPv4 address from its internal pool and translate the IPv6 header into IPv4 for communication up the stack.

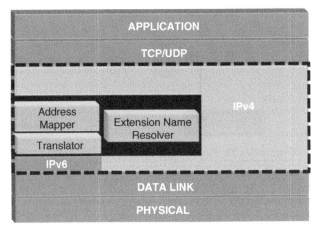

Figure 15.21. Bump- in-the-stack (BIS) components (154).

15.4.3 Bump in the API (BIA)

The bump-in-the-API (BIA) (155) strategy enables the use of IPv4 applications, while communicating over an IPv6 network. Unlike IP header modification provided by BIS, the BIA approach translates between IPv4 and IPv6 APIs. BIA is implemented between the application and TCP/UDP layer of the stack on the host and consists of an API Translator, an Address Mapper, Name Resolver, and Function Mapper as depicted in Figure 15.22.

When the IPv4 application sends a DNS query to determine the IP address of a destination host, the Name Resolver intercepts the query and creates an additional query requesting AAAA records. A DNS reply with an A record will provide the answer with

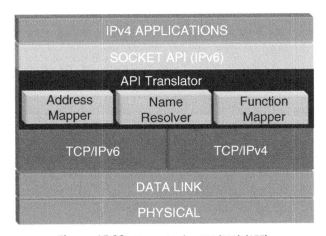

Figure 15.22. Bump in the API (BIA) (155).

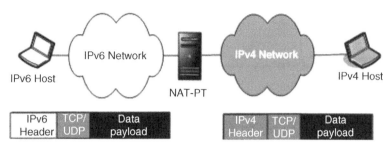

Figure 15.23. NAT-PT deployment (deprecated) (147).

the given IPv4 address. A reply with only a AAAA record stimulates the name resolver to request an IPv4 address from the Address Mapper to map to the returned IPv6 address. The Name Resolver utilizes the mapped IPv4 address to return an A record response to the application. The Address Mapper maintains this mapping of IPv6 addresses to those assigned from an internal address pool consisting of the unassigned IPv4 address space (0.0.0.0/24). The Function Mapper intercepts API function calls and maps IPv4 API calls to IPv6 socket calls.

15.4.4 Network Address Translation with Protocol Translation (NAT-PT)—DEPRECATED

As the name implies, the NAT-PT (156) process not only entails translating IPv4 addresses into IPv6 addresses like a familiar IPv4 NAT, but also performs protocol header translation as described in the SIIT section.[*] A NAT-PT device serves as a gateway between an IPv6 network and an IPv4 network and enables native IPv6 devices to communicate with hosts on the IPv4 Internet, for example. The NAT-PT device maintains an IPv4 address pool, and associates a given IPv4 address with an IPv6 address while the communications ensues. Figure 15.23 illustrates the architecture of a NAT-PT deployment. For numerous reasons enumerated in RFC 4966 (157), NAT-PT (and NAPT-PT described next) has been deprecated and should not be deployed.

15.4.5 Network Address Port Translation with Protocol Translation (NAPT-PT)—DEPRECATED

NAPT-PT enables IPv6 nodes to communicate with IPv4 nodes using a single IPv4 address. Thus, in Figure 15.23 above, instead of maintaining a one-to-one association of an IPv6 address and a unique IPv4 address as in NAT-PT, NAPT-PT maps each IPv6 address to a common IPv4 address with a unique TCP or UDP port value set in the corresponding IPv4 packet. The use of a single shared IPv4 address minimizes the possibility of IPv4 address pool depletion under the NAT-PT scenario.

---

[*] With the exception of the source and destination IP address fields which are governed by associations within the NAT-PT gateway.

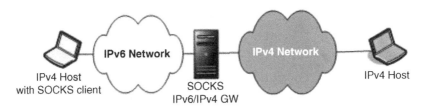

Figure 15.24. Basic SOCKS Gateway configuration (159).

15.4.6 SOCKS IPv6/IPv4 Gateway

SOCKS, defined in RFC 1928 (158), provides transport relay for applications traversing firewalls, effectively providing application proxy services. RFC 3089 (159) applies the SOCKS protocol for translating IPv4 and IPv6 communications. And like the other translation technologies already discussed, this approach includes special DNS treatment, termed *DNS name resolving delegation*, which delegates name resolution from the resolver client to the SOCKS IPv6/IPv4 gateway. An IPv4 or IPv6 application can be "socksified" to communicate with the SOCKS gateway proxy for ultimate connection to a host supporting the opposite protocol. Figure 15.24 illustrates the case of an IPv6 host configured with a SOCKS client connecting to an IPv4 host. A socksified IPv4 host could just as well communicate via the SOCKS gateway to an IPv6 host, from right-to-left.

15.4.7 Transport Relay Translator (TRT)

Much like the SOCKS configuration, TRT features a stateful gateway device that interlinks two "independent" connections over different networks. The TCP/UDP connection from a host terminates on the TRT, and the TRT creates a separate connection to the destination host and relays between the two connections. TRT requires a DNS-Application Layer Gateway, DNS-ALG,[*] which acts as a DNS proxy. TRT is specified to enable IPv6 hosts to communicate with IPv4 destinations. As such, the primary function of the DNS-ALG is to perform a AAAA resource record query as requested by IPv6 resolvers; if a AAAA record is returned, the reply is passed on to the resolver and the data connection may ensue as an IPv6 connection. If no AAAA records are returned, the DNS-ALG performs an A record query, and if an answer is received, the DNS-ALG formulates an IPv6 address using the IPv4 address contained in the returned A record. RFC 3142(160), which defines TRT as an informational RFC, specifies use of the prefix C6::/64 followed by 32 zeroes plus the 32-bit IPv4 address. However, IANA has not allocated the C6::/64 prefix. Thus, a locally configured prefix is required instead.

15.4.8 Application Layer Gateway (ALG)

ALGs perform protocol translation at the application layer and perform application proxy functions, similar to HTTP proxies. A client's application would typically need to be configured with the IP address of the proxy server, to which a connection would be

---

[*] Sometimes referred to as "trick or treat DNS-ALG" or totd.

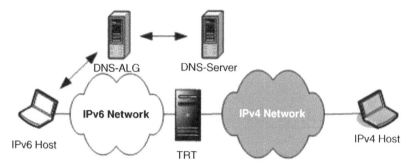

Figure 15.25. TRT configuration with DNS-ALG (160).

made upon opening the application, for example, web browser for the HTTP proxy case.
An ALG may be useful for web or other application-specific access to the IPv4 Internet
by hosts on an IPv6-only network.

15.5 APPLICATION MIGRATION

The *de facto* application programming interface (API) for TCP/IP applications is the
sockets interface originally implemented on BSD UNIX (on which BIND was also
originally implemented). The sockets interface defines program calls to enable
applications to interface with TCP/IP layers to communicate over IP networks.
Microsoft's Winsock API is also based on the sockets interface. Both sockets and
Winsock interfaces have been modified to support IPv6's longer address size and
additional features. In fact, most major operating system have implemented support for
sockets or Winsock including Microsoft (XP SP1, Vista, 7, Server 2003 & 2008),
Solaris (8 +), Linux (kernel 2.4 +), Mac OS (X.10.2), AIX (4.3 +), and HP-UX
(11i with upgrade). The updated sockets interface supports both IPv4 and IPv6 and
provides the ability for IPv6 applications to interoperate with IPv4 applications by use
of IPv4-mapped IPv6 addresses. Check with your applications vendors for IPv6
compatibility and requirements.

15.6 PLANNING THE IPv6 DEPLOYMENT PROCESS

15.6.1 Service Provider Deployment Options

Service providers, residential broadband service providers in particular, can implement
IPv6 within their networks and ultimately deploy IPv6 addresses to customers. Beyond
applying the various techniques discussed in this chapter, two additional alternatives
have been developed:

- *6rd.* IPv6 Rapid Deployment defines a modification to the 6over4 transition
  approach to enable provision of IPv6 addresses to end customers while continuing
  to support an IPv4 and IPv6 infrastructure.

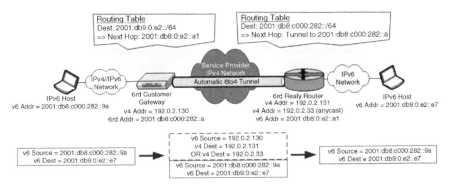

Figure 15.26. 6rd deployment example.

- *Dual-Stack Lite.* Provides a means for service providers to better utilize increasingly scare IPv4 addresses while deploying IPv6 out to customers' premises.

6rd (IPv6 Rapid Deployment). RFC 5569 (161) defines "IPv6 Rapid Deployment on IPv4 Infrastructures (6rd)," a technique to enable a service provider to provision IPv6 addresses to end customers while maintaining an IPv4 infrastructure. This method calls for tunneling of customer IPv6 traffic from the customer premises to an IPv6 destination via modified 6to4 technique. The modification entails use of the service provider's IPv6 prefix (/32) in lieu of the 6to4 prefix, 2001::/16.

Like 6to4, the next 32 bits of the IPv6 prefix consists of the IPv4 address of the 6to4 gateway, in this case the customer premises broadband router. Hence, a 6to4 prefix is defined as 2001:<32-bit IPv4 address>::/48, while the 6rd prefix is <32-bit service provider IPv6 prefix>:<32-bit IPv4 address>::/64.* This enables the service provider to provision a /64 to each customer, which comprises a single IPv6 subnet. Thus, a service provider with an RIR allocated IPv6 block 2001:db8::/32 would provision a customer gateway device with IPv4 address 192.0.2.130 with a 6rd subnet address of 2001:db8: c000:282::/64 as shown in Figure 15.26.

A device within the residence requiring an IPv6 address would be assigned an address from this subnet. For example in Figure 15.26, a PC is assigned IPv6 address 2001:db8:c000:232::9a. The 6rd customer gateway tunnels native IPv6 packets over IPv4 to a 6rd gateway. The other address related change between 6rd and 6to4 is that the anycast 6to4 address is fixed (192.88.99.1), while the 6rd anycast address is defined by the service provider themselves within its own address space. Each customer router must be provisioned with the 6rd relay agent or anycast address(es).

The 6rd relay router terminates the IPv4 tunnel, then routes the IPv6 packet natively to its destination. The use of the service provider's prefix enables 6rd-reachable destinations to be advertised along with the service provider's native IPv6 traffic.

---

*Use of a portion of the IPv4 address, say 24 lower order unique bits of a common 10.0.0.0 address allows a longer service provider prefix if desired.

Dual-Stack Lite. Dual-stack lite is a technology that enables a service provider to more efficiently utilize the diminishing pool of available public IPv4 addresses, while facilitating long-term support of IPv4 addresses assigned to customer network devices (162). Service providers typically assign an address to a customer router or gateway which interfaces directly to the broadband access network. The customer gateway performs DHCP server functions in assigning IP addresses to IP devices in the home network. It is expected that such home network devices will support only IPv4 for quite some time.

The components comprising a dual-stack lite implementation include the following:

- Basic Bridging BroadBand (B4) element bridges the IPv4 home network with an IPv6 network; the B4 function may reside on the customer gateway device or within the service provider network.
- Softwire IPv4-in-IPv6 tunnel between the B4 and the AFTR.
- Address Family Translation Router (AFTR) terminates the IPv4-in-IPv6 softwire tunnel with the B4 element and also performs IPv4–IPv4 network address translation functionality.

Figure 15.27 illustrates the inter-relationship of these three components within an end-to-end IP connection. Starting on the left of the figure, the IPv4 host obtains an IPv4 address, 10.1.0.2, from the DHCP server function of the customer gateway. Let's say this IPv4 host desires to connect to a web site, which has been resolved to IP address 192.0.2.21. The IPv4 host formulates an IP packet with source address 10.1.0.2 and source port of 1000, for example, and destination address 192.0.2.21 port 80. The host transmits this packet to its default route, the customer gateway.

The customer gateway in this example includes the B4 element, which sets up the softwire IPv4-in-IPv6 tunnel if it is not already established. The customer gateway has been assigned an IPv6 address on its WAN port (facing the service provider network) and it is over this connection that the tunnel is established. The customer gateway has also been configured with the AFTR IPv6 address manually or via DHCPv6. As shown in Figure 15.27, the B4 element encapsulates the original IPv4 packet with an IPv6 header and transmits it to the AFTR.

The AFTR terminates the tunnel and removes the IPv6 header. The AFTR then performs an IPv4–IPv4 NAT function. This is required to translate the original packet's

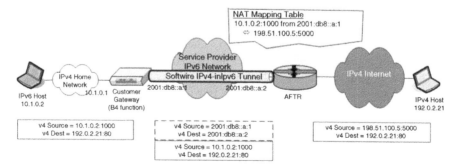

Figure 15.27. Dual-stack lite architecture (162).

private (RFC 1918) IPv4 source address into a public IPv4 address. Thus, the service provider must provision a pool of public IPv4 addresses which can be used as source IP addresses on packets destined for an IPv4 destination as in this case. This pooling enables the service provider to more efficiently utilize the increasingly scare public IPv4 address space. The AFTR also generally performs port translation as well and must track this mapping for each NAT operation in order to properly map IPv4 addresses and port numbers bidirectionally.

In Figure 15.27, the AFTR has mapped the customer's source IPv4 address and port, 10.1.0.2:1000 to 198.51.100.5:5000. Since all customers will utilize 10.0.0.0 address space, the NAT mapping table also tracks the tunnel over which the packet originated. The packet ultimately transmitted to the destination host includes this mapped IPv4 address and port, 198.51.100.5:5000. Return packets destined for this address/port are mapped to [destination] address 10.1.0.2:1000 and tunneled to 2001:db8::a:1.

Customers deploying native IPv6 or dual-stack hosts can have respective IPv6 addresses provided by DHCPv6 functionality implemented in the customer gateway or via autoconfiguration. IPv6 packets transmitted over the home network to the customer gateway would not utilize the softwire tunnel, but instead be routed natively over the service provider IPv6 access network.

15.6.2 Enterprise Deployment Scenarios

There's certainly no shortage of technology options when considering an IPv6 implementation approach. Having many options is good, but it can be intimidating. Selecting the right path will depend on your current environment in terms of end user devices and operating systems, router models and versions, as well as key applications, budget, and resources, as well as time frames. Given the proliferation of dual-stack support in leading operating systems and networking products, a dual-stack approach is likely to be the most prevalent approach. In this section, we'll review some basic IPv6 implementation scenarios to provide a flavor for various macro-level approaches. In reviewing these, let's use the basic diagram in Figure 15.28 as a baseline. In this figure, we have a client, in this case with IPv4 applications, IPv4 sockets API, and TCP/IPv4 stack, and a server with

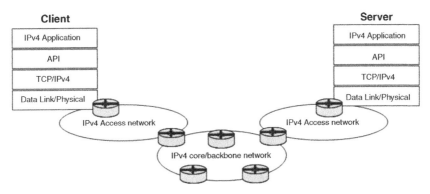

Figure 15.28. Base case for IPv4 network—initial state prior to migration (147).

a comparable configuration. We've split the interconnection network into access networks for the client and server, respectively and a core or backbone network.

Note that this basic diagram illustrates a pair-wise client–server connection. For a given use case, this could represent an internal client access to an internal server via an all-internal access and core network. But it could also represent an internal client and internal server communicating over the Internet, an internal client communicating to an Internet-based server, or an external client communicating via the Internet to an internal server. This convention simplifies the sheer number of unique use cases. Nuances among these variations will be pointed out as appropriate when describing the migration scenarios.

15.6.3 Core Migration Scenario

The first scenario involves initially supplementing the backbone or core network with IPv6. This scenario requires upgrading of all core routers to support IPv6 routing and routing protocols and for access-to-core boundary routers to support dual stacks. The core network could be an internal backbone or an IPv6 ISP network. A common implementation approach for the access-core boundary routers is to employ configured tunnels between them. This enables these boundary routers to advertise IPv4 routes and tunnel IPv4 packets across the IPv6 backbone. Alternatively, translation gateways could be used at these boundary points. Either way, this properly implemented approach should have little to no effect on the client or server devices or software, and could provide a starting point for IPv6 experimentation without affecting end users.

15.6.4 Server Side Migration

The next scenario assumes our base case as the initial state followed by upgrading servers and application hosts to dual-stack implementations. With the server still able to support IPv4 communications and applications, end clients should communicate as before via

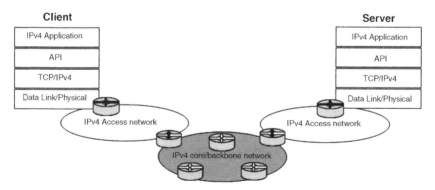

Figure 15.29. Core migration scenario (147).

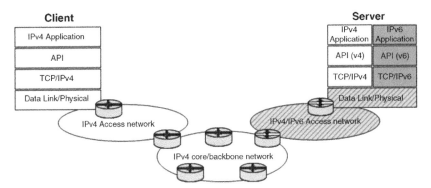

Figure 15.30. Server side migration scenario (147).

IPv4. However, the server would be able to serve IPv6 clients as well. This scenario may reflect the following use cases:

- Where the client and server in Figure 15.30 are within a common organization, the organization could upgrade just its servers to provide a means of overall readiness testing for IPv6 prior to upgrading and affecting end clients. End clients would not have access to any IPv6 applications in this case.
- This scenario may also reflect an interorganizational connection via an IPv4 network, for example, the IPv4 Internet.
  - o An organization migrating or having completed migration to IPv6 would likely implement a dual-stack server for Internet-facing IP applications, such as its web servers. In this case, an IPv4 browser client can access the web server via the Internet. The web server could serve both IPv4 clients and IPv6 browser clients. Depending on the ISP capabilities, the ISP could provide a translation gateway from an IPv6 access network, or tunneling could be used.
  - o An organization migrating or having completed migration to IPv6 that requires network connections to partners running IPv4-only would also map to this scenario. Implementation of configured tunnels would be a good approach for such an interorganizational link.
- If we ignore the IPv4 portion of the dual stack on the server and consider the server IPv6-only, this scenario could represent an IPv4-only client attempting to access an IPv6-only server. Such a scenario would require the use of one of the following techniques:
  - o An IPv4–IPv6 translation gateway bordering the IPv4–IPv6 networks, assuming the server access network is also IPv6-only.
  - o If the server access network is IPv4-only, the server must employ a host-based translation mechanism such as BIS or BIA to translate between IPv4 and IPv6 headers.

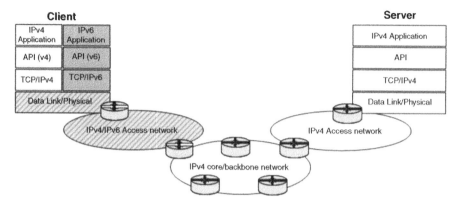

Figure 15.31. Client side migration scenario (147).

15.6.5 Client Side Migration

Figure 15.31 represents a scenario starting with our initial configuration of Figure 15.28, followed by the migrating of clients to dual-stack implementations, as well as access network routers. Existing IPv4 client devices would be supplemented with IPv6 applications, API and TCP/IP stack. Much of this is already provided when migrating to Windows XP SP1, Vista or 7, or Mac OS X. This scenario represents the following example cases:

- After a particular organization's complete migration to IPv6, continued use of dual stack would support access to IPv4 web sites. Hence, this may be a post-transition scenario in effect for a number of years, until Internet accessible applications complete the transition to IPv6. However, a more likely configuration for such a scenario is the complete migration to IPv6 within the organization and a translation gateway to the IPv4 Internet (ISP) link.

- Such a configuration within a given organization is deemed unlikely outside of those working on IPv6 projects having a need to access external IPv6 applications. Typically, client deployments on a wide scale within an organization would require requisite server side support.

- Ignoring the IPv4 portion of the client stack and considering the client IPv6-only, this scenario could depict a fully transitioned IPv6 user access an IPv4 application such as a web server. Such a scenario would typically feature a translation gateway on the IPv4 ISP connection, though 6to4, ISATAP, or Teredo tunneling could be employed as well.

15.6.6 Client–Server Migration

A commonly anticipated approach to IPv6 migration within an organization features upgrading of clients and servers at about the same time or on a rolling basis, including applications as appropriate. The use of dual-stack deployments facilitates the deployment to clients and servers over time. Special consideration must be given to application

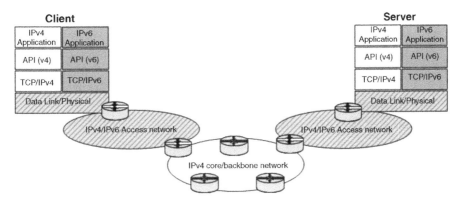

Figure 15.32. Dual-stack deployment scenario (147).

migration, especially for integrated enterprise applications accessed by a large user population. Support of mixed IPv4/IPv6 clients in transition is ideal but may not be practical.

This scenario reflects the intra-enterprise example described above, as well as a broader set of examples per the table below, considering also single-stack cases.

15.6.7 Overall IPv6 Implementation Planning

Despite substantial differences in address lengths and formats, among other aspects, IPv4 and IPv6 are both network layer protocols which enable application communications over a common layer 1 and 2 network. This facilitates coexistence of IPv4 and IPv6 during a transition interval over the same physical networks. However, layers above layer 3 will more likely be impacted, especially in terms of applications that display, utilize, or enable entry of IP addresses.

IPv6 implementation presents a number of challenges. Key among them are defining and organizing an overall plan for IPv6 network allocation and deployment. This is where the discipline of an IPAM system can help. While there are numerous detailed steps involved, the following four high-level steps are recommended for planning and performing such a transition.

1. Baseline your current environment; this step itself can be accomplished by implementing the practices we've discussed throughout this book.

   - Inventory and baseline the current IPv4 network environment in determining what IPv4 address spaces are in use, how they have been allocated, what individual IPv4 addresses have been assigned and are in use, and other IP-related information per device.

   - As a corollary to the prior step, inventory and baseline the associated Dynamic Host Configuration Protocol (DHCP) server configurations with respect to address pools and associated policies and options.

- Identify and record associated Domain Name Server (DNS) configurations and resource records associated with IPv4 devices.

- Inventory network devices (infrastructure and end user) to assess current and expected future IPv4/IPv6 level of support.

- Analyze applications for potential migration impacts and if so, plan for addressing these impacts.

2. Plan your IPv6 deployment

  - Map out a strategy for IPv6 implementation including consideration of the following:

    o Application migration and required upgrades

    o Networking/router migrations or upgrades

    o Selection of coexistence technologies from tunneling, translation, and/or dual-stack approaches and planning corresponding DNS impacts

    o Selection of IPv6 device configuration strategy, for example, stateless autoconfiguration, stateful configuration, or hybrid

  - Consider time frame requirements if any, analyze dependencies across affected elements, and determine budgeting requirements to derive a migration plan.

3. Execute the deployment process

  - Begin execution of the deployment plan based on the prior step and project manage the process with respect to schedules, budget, dependencies, and contingency plans.

  - Track the IP address inventory of baselined IPv4 space and associated IPv6 overlay space. Of course, growth and changes in the IPv4 space will most likely continue throughout the transition, so dovetail these updates into the plan as appropriate.

  - Update DNS and DHCP services to accommodate the transitioning environment, for example, to support both IPv4 and IPv6 hosts, as well as IPv4 and IPv6 transport.

4. Manage the IPv4–IPv6 Network

  - Manage IPv4 and IPv6 address space and corresponding DHCP and DNS services.

  - Based on your plan, some IPv4 space may be decommissioned. This can be done as portions of your network fully migrate to IPv6 or as a final decommissioning step across the network.

  - You may desire to leave IPv4 protocol operational throughout or on portions of your network depending on requirements to service external hosts which may be IPv4-only based on internal policies.

BIBLIOGRAPHY

1. J. Postel. *DoD Standard Internet Protocol*. IETF, January 1980. RFC 760.
2. J. Postel. *Internet Protocol*. IETF, September 1981. RFC 791.
3. Internet Systems Consortium (ISC). The ISC Domain Survey. *www.isc.org*. [Online] [Cited: May 15, 2010] www.isc.org/solutions/survey.
4. R. Hinden. *Applicability Statement for the Implementation of Classless Inter-Domain Routting (CIDR)*. IETF, September 1993. RFC 1517.
5. Y. Rekhter, T. Li. *An Architecture for IP Address Allocation with CIDR*. IETF, September 1993. RFC 1518.
6. V. Fuller, T. Li, J. Yu, K. Varadhan. *Classless Inter-Domain Routing (CIDR): an Address Assignment and Aggregation Strategy*. IETF, September 1993. RFC 1519.
7. Y. Rekhter, B. Moskowitz, D. Karrenberg, G. J. de Groot, E. Lear. *Address Allocation for Private Internets*. IETF, February 1996. RFC 1918.
8. IANA. *Special-Use IPv4 Addresses*. IETF, September 2002. RFC 3330.
9. M. Cotton, L. Vegoda. *Special Use IPv4 Addresses*. IETF, January, 2010. RFC 5735.
10. S. Deering, R. Hinden. *Internet Protocol, Version 6 (IPv6) Specification*. IETF, December 1998. RFC 2460.
11. T. Rooney. *Introduction to IP Address Management*. IEEE Press/Wiley, 2010.
12. R. Hinden, S. Deering. *IP Version 6 Addressing Architecture*. IETF, February 2006. RFC 4291.
13. Internet Assigned Numbers Authority (IANA). Internet Protocol Version 6 Address Space. *www.iana.org*. [Online] [Cited: May 3, 2010.] http://www.iana.org/assignments/ipv6-address-space/ipv6-address-space.xhtml.
14. R. Hinden, S. Deering, E. Nordmark. *IPv6 Global Unicast Address Format*. IETF, August 2003. RFC 3587.
15. R. Hinden, B. Haberman. *Unique Local IPv6 Unicast Addresses*. IETF, October 2005. RFC 4193.
16. B. Haberman, D. Thaler. *Unicast-Prefix-Based IPv6 Multicast Addresses*. IETF, August 2002. RFC 3306.
17. J.-S. Park, M.-K. Shin, H.-J. Kim. *A Method for Generating Link-Scoped IPv6 Multicast Addresses*. IETF, April 2006. RFC 4489.

18. M. Crawford, B. Haberman, Eds. *IPv6 Node Information Queries*. IETF, August 2006. RFC 4620.

19. Microsoft. IPv6 Address Autoconfiguration. *www.microsoft.com*. [Online] [Cited: October 19, 2009.] http://msdn.microsoft.com/en-us/library/aa917171.aspx.

20. D. Johnson, S. Deering. *Reserved IPv6 Subnet Anycast Addresses*. IETF, March 1999. RFC 2526.

21. J. Loughney, Ed. *IPv6 Node Requirements*. IETF, April 2006. RFC 4294.

22. M. Blanchet. *A Flexible Method for Managing the Assignment of Bits of an IPv6 Address Block*. IETF, April 2003. RFC 3531.

23. IANA. Number Resources. *www.iana.org*. [Online] [Cited: October 20, 2009.] http://www.iana.org/numbers/.

24. K. Hubbard, M. Kosters, D. Conrad, D. Karrrenberg, J. Postel. *Internet Registry IP Allocation Guidelines*. IETF, November 1996. RFC 2050.

25. AfriNIC. AfriNIC Home Page. *www.afrinic.net*. [Online] [Cited: October 20, 2009.] http://www.afrinic.net/.

26. APNIC. APNIC Home Page. *www.apnic.net*. [Online] [Cited: October 20, 2009.] http://www.apnic.net/.

27. ARIN. ARIN Home Page. *www.arin.net*. [Online] [Cited: October 20, 2009.] http://www.arin.net/.

28. LACNIC. LACNIC Home Page. *www.lacnic.net*. [Online] http://www.lacnic.net/.

29. RIPE NCC. RIPE Network Coordination Centre Home Page. *www.ripe.net*. [Online] [Cited: October 20, 2009.] http://www.ripe.net/.

30. C. Huitema. *The H Ratio for Address Assignment Efficiency*. IETF, November 1994. RFC 1715.

31. A. Durand, C. Huitema. *The Host-Density Ratio for Address Assignment Efficiency: An Update on the H Ratio*. IETF, November 2001. RFC 3194.

32. R. Droms. *Dynamic Host Configuration Protocol*. IETF, March 1997. RFC 2131.

33. S. Alexander, R. Droms. *DHCP Options and BOOTP Vendor Extensions*. IETF, March 1997. RFC 2132.

34. B. Croft, J. Gilmore. *Bootstrap Protocol (BOOTP)*. IETF, September 1985. RFC 951.

35. Internet Systems Consortium. *dhcpd.conf man*. Redwood City, CA: Internet Systems Consortium, Inc. (ISC), 2010.

36. T. Lemon, S. Cheshire, B. Volz. *The Classless Static Route Option for Dynamic Host Configuration Protocol (DHCP) Version 4*. IETF, December 2002. RFC 3442.

37. R. Droms, K. Fong. *NetWare/IP Domain Name and Information*. IETF, November 1997. RFC 2242.

38. G. Stump, R. Droms, Y. Gu, R. Vyaghrapuri, A. Demirtjis, B. Beser, J. Privat. *The User Class Option for DHCP*. IETF, November 2000. RFC 3004.

39. C. Perkins, E. Guttman. *DHCP Options for Service Location Protocol*. IETF, June 1999. RFC 2610.

40. S. Park, P. Kim, B. Volz. *Rapid Commit Option for the Dynamic Host Configuration Protocol Version 4 (DHCPv4)*. IETF, March 2005. RFC 4039.

41. M. Stapp, B. Volz, Y. Rekhter. *The Dynamic Host Configuration Protocol (DHCP) Client Fully Qualified Domain Name (FQDN) Option*. IETF, October 2006. RFC 4702.

42. M. Patrick. *DHCP Relay Agent Information Option*. IETF, January 2001. RFC 3046.

43. C. Monia, J. Tseng, K. Gibbons. *The IPv4 Dynamic Host Configuration Protocol (DHCP) Option for the Internet Storage Name Service.* IETF, September 2005. RFC 4174.

44. R. Droms. *Unused Dynamic Host Configuration Protocol (DHCP) Option Codes.* IETF, January 2004. RFC 3679.

45. D. Provan. *DHCP Options for Novell Directory Services.* IETF, November 1997. RFC 2241.

46. K. Chowdhury, P. Yegani, L. Madour. *Dynamic Host Configuration Protocol (DHCP) Options for Broadcast and Multicast Control Servers.* IETF, November 2005. RFC 4280.

47. R. Droms, W. Arbaugh, Eds. *Authentication for DHCP Messages.* IETF, June 2001. RFC 3118.

48. R. Woundy, K. Kinnear. *Dynamic Host Configuration Protocol (DHCP) Leasequery.* IETF, February 2006. RFC 4388.

49. M. Johnston, S. Venaas, Eds. *Dynamic Host Configuration Protocol (DHCP) Options for Intel Preboot eXecution Environment (PXE).* IETF, November 2006. RFC 4578.

50. S. Drach. *DHCP Option for The Open Group's User Authentication Protocol.* IETF, January 1999. RFC 2485.

51. H. Schulzrinne. *Dynamic Host Configuration Protocol (DHCPv4 and DHCPv6) Option for Civic Addresses Configuration Information.* IETF, November 2006. RFC 4776.

52. E. Lear, P. Eggert. *Timezone Options for DHCP.* IETF, April 2007. RFC 4833.

53. R. Troll. *DHCP Option to Disable Stateless Auto-Configuration in IPv4 Clients.* IETF, May 1999. RFC 2563.

54. C. Smith. *The Name Service Search Option for DHCP.* IETF, September 2000. RFC 2937.

55. G. Waters. *The IPv4 Subnet Selection Optoin for DHCP.* IETF, November 2000. RFC 3011.

56. B. Aboba, S. Cheshire. *Dynamic Host Configuration Protocol (DHCP) Domain Search Option.* IETF, November 2002. RFC 3397.

57. H. Schulzrinne. *Dynamic Host Configuration Protocol (DHCP-for-IPv4) Option for Session Initiation Protocol (SIP) Servers.* IETF, August 2002. RFC 3361.

58. P. Agarwal, B. Akyol. *The Classless Static Route Option for Dynamic Host Configuration Protocol (DHCP) Version 4.* IETF, December 2002. RFC 3442.

59. B. Beser, P. Duffy, Eds. *Dynamic Host Configuration Protocol (DHCP) Option for CableLabs Client Configuration.* IETF, March 2003. RFC 3495.

60. J. Polk, J. Schnizlein, M. Linsner. *Dynamic Host Configuration Protocol Option for Coordinate-Based Location Configuration Information.* IETF, July 2004. RFC 3825.

61. J. Littlefield. *Vendor-Identifying Vendor Options for Dynamic Host Configuration Protocol Version 4 (DHCPv4).* IETF, October 2004. RFC 3925.

62. L. Morand, A. Yegin, S. Kumar, S. Madanapalli. *DHCP Options for Protocol for Carrying Authentication for Network Access (PANA) Authentication Agents.* IETF, May 2008. RFC 5192.

63. H. Schulzrinne, J. Polk, H. Tschofenig. *Discovering Location-to-Service Translation (LoST) Servers Using the Dynamic Host Configuration Protocol (DHCP).* IETF, August 2008. RFC 5223.

64. P. Calhoun. *Control and Provisioning of Wireless Access Points (CAPWAP) Access Controller DHCP Option.* IETF, March 2009. RFC 5417.

65. G. Bajko, S. Das. *Dynamic Host Configuration Protocol (DHCPv4 and DHCPv6) Options for IEEE 802.21 Mobility Services (MoS) Discovery.* IETF, December 2009. RFC 5678.

66. B. Volz. *Reclassifying Dynamic Host Configuration Protocol Version 4 (DHCPv4) Options.* IETF, November 2004. RFC 3942.

67. D. Hankins. *Dynamic Host Configuration Protocol Options Used by PXELINUX.* IETF, December 2007. RFC 5071.

68. R. Droms, Ed., J. Bound, B. Volz, T. Lemon, C. Perkins, M. Carney. *Dynamic Host Configuration Protocol for IPv6 (DHCPv6).* IETF, July 2003. RFC 3315.

69. H. Schulzrinne, B. Volz. *Dynamic Host Configuration Protocol (DHCPv6) Options for Session Initiation Protocol (SIP) Servers.* IETF, July 2003. RFC 3319.

70. R. Droms, Ed. *DNS Configuration Options for Dynamic Host Configuration Protocol for IPv6 (DHCPv6).* IETF, December 2003. RFC 3646.

71. O. Troan, R. Droms. *IPv6 Prefix Options for Dynamic Host Configuration Protocol (DHCP) Version 6.* IETF, December 2003. RFC3633.

72. V. Kalusivalingam. *Network Information Service (NIS) Configuration Options for Dynamic Host Configuration Protocol for IPv6 (DHCPv6).* IETF, October 2004. RFC 3898.

73. V. Kalusivalingam. *Simple Network Time Protocol (SNTP) Configuration Option for DHCPv6.* IETF, May 2005. RFC 4075.

74. S. Venaas, T. Chown, B. Volz. *Information Refresh Time Option for Dynamic Host Configuration Protocol for IPv6 (DHCPv6).* IETF, November 2005. RFC 4242.

75. B. Volz. *Dynamic Host Configuration Protocol for IPv6 (DHCPv6) Relay Agent Remote-ID Option.* IETF, August 2006. RFC 4649.

76. B. Volz. *Dynamic Host Configuration Protocol for IPv6 (DHCPv6) Relay Agent Subscriber-ID Option.* IETF, June 2006. RFC 4580.

77. B. Volz. *The Dynamic Host Configuration Protocol for IPv6 (DHCPv6) Client Fully Qualified Domain Name (FQDN) Option.* IETF, October 2006. RFC 4704.

78. S. Zeng, B. Volz, K. Kinnear, J. Brzozowski. *DHCPv6 Relay Agent Echo Request Option.* IETF, September 2007. RFC 4994.

79. J. Brzozowski, K. Kinnear, B. Volz, S. Zeng. *DHCPv6 Leasequery.* IETF, September 2007. RFC 5007.

80. H. Jang, A. Yegin, K. Chowdhury, J. Choi. *DHCP Options for Home Information Discovery in MIPv6.* IETF, May 2008. draft-ietf-mip6-hiopt-17.

81. M. Stapp *DHCPv6 Bulk Leasequery.* IETF, February 2009. RFC 5460.

82. D. Jones, R. Woundy. *The DOCSIS (Data-Over-Cable Service Interface Specifications) Device Class DHCP (Dynamic Host Configuration Protocol) Relay Agent Information Sub-Option.* IETF, April 2002. RFC 3256.

83. K. Kinnear, M. Stapp, R. Johnson, J. Kumarasamy. *Link Selection Sub-Option for the Relay Agent Information Option for DHCPv4.* IETF, April 2003. RFC 3527.

84. R. Johnson, T. Palaniappan, M. Stapp. *Subscriber-ID Suboption for the Dynamic Host Configuration Protocol (DHCP) Relay Agent Option.* IETF, March 2005. RFC 3993.

85. R. Droms, J. Schnizlein. *Remote Authentication Dial-In User Service (RADIUS) Attributes Suboption for the Dynamic Host Configuration Protocol (DHCP).* IETF, February 2005. RFC 4014.

86. M. Stapp, T. Lemon. *The Authentication Suboption for the Dynamic Host Configuration Protocol (DHCP) Relay Agent Option.* IETF, March 2005. RFC 4030.

87. M. Stapp, R. Johnson, T. Palaniappan. *Vendor-Specific Information Suboption for the Dynamic Host Configuration Protocol (DHCP) Relay Agent Option.* IETF, December 2005. RFC 4243.

88. K. Kinnear, M. Normoyle, M. Stapp. *The Dynamic Host Configuration Protocol Version 4 (DHCPv4) Relay Agent Flags Suboption.* IETF, September 2007. RFC 5010.

89. J. Jumarasamy, K. Kinnear, M. Stapp. *DHCP Server Identifier Override Suboption.* IETF, February 2008. RFC 5107.

90. P. Valian. NetReg. *sourceforge.net.* [Online] [Cited: January 31, 2010.] http://netreg. sourceforge.net.

91. Cisco Systems, Inc., *Cisco Network Admission Control (NAC).* San Jose, CA: Cisco Systems, Inc., 2009.

92. Microsoft Corporation. *Introduction to Nework Access Protection.* Redmond, WA: Microsoft Corporation, 2008.

93. H. Eidnes, G. de Groot, P. Vixie. *Classless IN-ADDR.ARPA Delegation.* IETF, March 1998. RFC 2317.

94. P. Faltstrom, P. Hoffman, A. Costello. *Internationalizing Domain Names in Applications (IDNA).* IETF, March 2003. RFC 3490.

95. P. Hoffman, M. Blanchet. *Nameprep: A Stringprep Profile for Internationalized Domain Names (IDN).* IETF, March 2003. RFC 3491.

96. P. Hoffman, M. Blanchet. *Preparation of Internationalized Strings (stringprep).* IETF, December 2002. RFC 3454.

97. A. Costello. *Punycode: A Bootstring Encoding of Unicode for Internationalized Domain Names in Applications (IDNA).* IETF, March 2003. RFC 3492.

98. Internationalized Domain Names (IDN). *International Telecommunications Union.* [Online] [Cited: October 21, 2009.] http://www.itu.int/ITU-T/special-projects/idn/introduction. html.

99. P. V. Mockapetris. *Domain Names—Implementation and Specification.* IETF, November 1987. RFC 1035.

100. P. Vixie, Ed., S. Thomson, Y. Rekhter, J. Bound. *Dynamic Updates in the Domain Name System (DNS UPDATE).* IETF, April 1997. RFC 2136.

101. P. Vixie. *Extension Mechanisms for DNS (EDNS0).* IETF, August 1999. RFC 2671.

102. P. Vixie, O. Gudmundsson, D. Eastlake, 3rd, B. Wellington. *Secret Key Transaction Authentication for DNS (TSIG).* IETF, May 2000. RFC 2845.

103. D. Eastlake, 3rd. *Secret Key Establishment for DNS (TKEY RR).* IETF, September 2000. RFC 2930.

104. D. Eastlake, 3rd. *HMAC SHA TSIG Algorithm Identifiers.* IETF, August 2006. RFC 4635.

105. D. Eastlake, 3rd. *Domain Name System (DNS) IANA Considerations.* IETF, November 2008. RFC 5395.

106. Internet Assigned Numbers Authority, (IANA). Domain Name System (DNS) Parameters. *www.iana.org.* [Online] [Cited: August 10, 2010.] http://www.iana.org/assignments/ dns-parameters.

107. M. Crawford. *Non-Terminal DNS Name Redirection.* IETF, August 1999. RFC 2672.

108. C. F. Everhart, L. A. Mamakos, R. Ullmann, P. V. Mockapetris. *New DNS RR Definitions*. IETF, October 1990. RFC 1183.

109. M. Mealling. *Dynamic Delegation Discovery System (DDDS) Part Three: The Domain Name System (DNS) Database*. IETF, October 2002. RFC 3403.

110. M. Mealling. *Dynamic Delegation Discovery System (DDDS) Part Two: The Algorithm*. IETF, October 2002. RFC 3402.

111. P. Faltstrom, M. Mealling. *The E.164 to Uniform Resource Identifiers (URI) Dynamic Delegation Discovery System (DDDS) Application (ENUM)*. IETF, April 2004. RFC 3761.

112. M. Wong, W. Schlitt. *Sender Policy Framework (SPF) for Authorizing Use of Domains in E-Mail, Version 1*. IETF, April 2006. RFC 4408.

113. E. Allman, J. Fenton, M. Delany, J. Levine. *DomainKeys Identified Mail (DKIM) Author Signing Practices (ADSP)*. IETF, August 2009. RFC 5617.

114. R. Arends, R. Austein, M. Larson, D. Massey, S. Rose. *Resource Records for DNS Security Extensions*. IETF, March 2005. RFC 4034.

115. M. Andrews, S. Weiler. *The DNSSEC Lookaside Validation (DLV) DNS Resource Record*. IETF, February 2006. RFC 4431.

116. S. Josefsson. *Storing Certificates in the Domain Name System (DNS)*. IETF, March 2006. RFC 4398.

117. M. Richardson. *A Method for Storing IPsec Keying Material in DNS*. IETF, March 2005. RFC 4025.

118. D. Eastlake, 3rd. *DNS Request and Transaction Signatures (SIG(0)s)*. IETF, September 2000. RFC 2931.

119. C. Farrell, M. Schulze, S. Pleitner, D. Baldoni. *DNS Encoding of Geographical Location*. IETF, November 1994. RFC 1712.

120. C. Davis, P. Vixie, T. Goodwin, I. Dickinson. *A Means for Expressing Location Information in the Domain Name System*. IETF, January 1996. RFC 1876.

121. C. Allocchio, *Using the Internet DNS to Distribute MIXER Conformant Global Address Mapping (MCGAM)*. IETF, January 1998. RFC 2163.

122. M. Crawford, C. Huitema. *DNS Extensions to Support IPv6 Address Aggregation and Renumbering*. IETF, July 2000. RFC 2874.

123. S. Thomson, C. Huitema, V. Ksinant, M. Souissi. *DNS Extensions to Support IP Version 6*. IETF, October 2003. RFC 3596.

124. P. Koch. *A DNS RR Type for Lists of Address Prefixes*. IETF, June 2001. RFC 3123.

125. ATM Forum Technical Committee. *ATM Name System, V2.0*. ATM Forum, 2000. AF-DANS-0152.000.

126. M. Stapp, T. Lemon, A. Gustafsson. *A DNS Resource Record (RR) for Encoding Dynamic Host Configuration Protocol (DHCP) Information (DHCID RR)*. IETF, October 2006. RFC 4701.

127. P. Nikander, J. Laganier. *Host Identity Protocol (HIP) Domain Name System (DNS) Extensions*. IETF, April 2008. RFC 5205.

128. D. Eastlake, 3rd. *DSA KEYs and SIGs in the Domain Name System (DNS)*. IETF, March 1999. RFC 2536.

129. R. Atkinson. *Key Exchange Delegation Record for the DNS*. IETF, November 1997. RFC 2230.

130. B. Manning, R. Colella. *DNS NSAP Resource Records*. IETF, October 1994. RFC 1706.

131. B. Laurie, G. Sisson, R. Arends, D. Blacka. *DNS Security (DNSSEC) Hashed Authenticated Denial of Existence.* IETF, March 2008. RFC 5155.

132. S. Weiler. *Legacy Resolver Compatibility for Delegation Signer (DS).* IETF, May 2004. RFC 3755.

133. R. Gellens, J. Klensin. *Message Submission for Mail.* IETF, April 2006. RFC 4409.

134. A. Gulbrandsen, P. Vixie, L. Esibov. *A DNS RR for Specifying the Location of Services (DNS SRV).* IETF, February 2000. RFC 2782.

135. J. Schlyter, W. Griffin. *Using DNS to Securely Publish Secure Shell (SSH) Key Fingerprints.* IETF, January 2006. RFC 4255.

136. Internet Corporation for Assigned Names and Numbers (ICANN). Factsheet—Root server attack on 6 February 2007. *Internet Corporation for Assigned Names and Numbers. www. icann.org.* [Online] [Cited: October 22, 2009.] http://www.icann.org/announcements/fact-sheet-dns-attack-08mar07.pdf.

137. B. Woodcock.Best Practices in IPv4 Anycast Routing. *Packet Clearing House.* [Online] August 2002. [Cited: May 3, 2010.] http://www.pch.net/resources/papers/ipv4-anycast/ipv4-anycast.pdf.

138. T. Rooney. *DNS Anycast Addressing for High Availability and Performance.* Santa Clara, CA: BT INS, Inc., 2008.

139. D. Atkins, R. Austein. *Threat Analysis of the Domain Name System (DNS).* IETF, August 2004. RFC 3833.

140. D. Eastlake, 3rd. *Domain Name System Security Extensions.* IETF, March 1999. RFC 2535.

141. R. Arends, R. Austein, M. Larson, D. Massey, S. Rose. *DNS Security Introduction and Requirements.* IETF, March 2005. RFC 4033.

142. R. Arends, R. Austein, M. Larson, D. Massey, S. Rose. *Protocol Modifications for the DNS Security Extensions.* IETF, March 2005. RFC 4035.

143. M. StJohns. *Automated Updates of DNS Security (DNSSEC) Trust Anchors.* IETF, September 2007. RFC 5011.

144. Internet Systems, Consortium. *BIND 9 Administrator Reference Manual.* Redwood City, CA: Internet Systems Consortium, Inc. (ISC), 2010.

145. A. Cherenson. *nslookup man page (BIND Distribution).* Redwood City, CA: Internet Systems Consortium, Inc. (ISC), 2010.

146. Internet Systems, Consortium. *dig man page (with BIND Distribution).* Redwood City, CA: Internet Systems Consortium (ISC), 2010.

147. T. Rooney. *IPv4-to-IPv6 Transition and Co-Existence Strategies.* Santa Clara, CA: BT INS, Inc., March 2008.

148. A. Durand, J. Ihren. *DNS IPv6 Transport Operational Guidelines.* IETF, September 2004. RFC 3901.

149. T. Chown, S. Venaas, C. Strauf. *Dynamic Host Configuration Protocol (DHCP): IPv4 and IPv6 Dual-Stack Issues.* IETF, May 2006. RFC 4477.

150. M. Blanchet, F. Parent. *IPv6 Tunnel Broker with Tunnel Setup Protocol (TSP).* IETF, February 2010. RFC 5572.

151. C. Huitema. *Teredo: Tunneling IPv6 Over UDP Through Network Address Translations (NATs).* IETF, February 2006. RFC 4380.

152. J. Bound, L. Toutain, J. L. Richier. *Dual Stack IPv6 Dominant Transition Mechanism (DSTM)*. IETF, October 2005. draft-bound-dstm-exp-04.txt.

153. E. Nordmark. *Stateless IP/ICMP Translation Algorithm (SIIT)*. IETF, February 2000. RFC 2765.

154. K. Tsuchiya, H. Higuchi, Y. Atarashi. *Dual Stack Hosts Using the "Bump-in-the-Stack" Technique (BIS)*. IETF, February 2000. RFC 2767.

155. S. Lee, M.-K. Shin, Y.-J. Kim, E. Nordmark, A. Durand. *Dual Stack Hosts Using "Bump-in-the-API" (BIA)*. IETF, October 2002. RFC 3338.

156. G. Tsirtsis, P. Srisuresh. *Network Address Translation-Protocol Translation (NAT-PT)*. IETF, February 2000. RFC 2766.

157. C. Aoun, E. Davies. *Reasons to Move the Network Address Translator-Protocol Translator (NAT-PT) to Historic Status*. IETF, July 2007. RFC 4966.

158. M. Leech, M. Ganis, Y. Lee, R. Kuris, D. Koblas, L. Jones. *SOCKS Protocol Version 5*. IETF, March 1996. RFC 1928.

159. H. Kitamura. *A SOCKS-Based IPv6/IPv4 Gateway Mechanism*. IETF, April 2001. RFC 3089.

160. J. Hagino, K. Yamamoto. *An IPv6-to-IPv4 Transport Relay Translator*. IETF, June 2001. RFC 3142.

161. R. Despres. *IPv6 Rapid Deployment on IPv4 Infrastructures (6rd)*. IETF, January 2010. RFC 5569.

162. A. Durand, Ed. *Dual-Stack Lite Broadband Deployments Post IPv4 Exhaustion*. IETF, February 2010. draft-ietf-software-dual-stack-lite-03.txt.

163. J. Klensin, Ed. *Simple Mail Transfer Protocol*. IETF, April 2001. RFC 2821.

164. P. Resnick, Ed. *Internet Message Format*. IETF, April 2001. RFC 2822.

165. A. Drescher. Director, Technical Services. *Private Correspondence.* Throughout 2006–present.

166. T. Rooney. *IPv6 Addressing and Management Challenges*. Santa Clara, CA: BT INS, Inc., March 2008.

167. O. Kolkman, R. Gieben. *DNSSEC Operational Practices*. IETF, September 2006. RFC 4641.

168. Office of Government and Commerce (OGC). ITIL(R) Home. *Official ITIL(R) Website.* [Online] APM Group Limited. [Cited: September 16, 2009.] http://www.itil-officialsite.com/home/home.asp.

169. L. Delgrossi, L. Berger, Eds. *Internet Stream Protocol Version 2 (ST2) Protocol Specification – Version ST2 +*. IETF, August 1995. RFC 1819.

170. T. Bates, Y. Rekhter. *Scalable Support for Multi-Home Multi-Provider Connectivity*. IETF, January 1998. RFC 2260.

171. J. Abley, K. Lindqvist, E. Davies, B. Black, V. Gill. *IPv4 Multihoming Practices and Limitations*. IETF, July 2005. RFC 4116.

172. G. Huston. *Architectural Approaches to Multi-Homing for IPv6*. IETF, September 2005. RFC 4177.

173. E. Nordmark, T. Li. *Threats Relating to IPv6 Multihoming Solutions*. IETF, October 2005. RFC 4218.

174. T. Rooney. *Applying ITIL Best Practice Principles to IPAM*. Santa Clara, CA: BT Diamond IP, August 2008.

175. R. Johnson. *TFTP Server Address Option for DHCPv4*. IETF, June 2010. RFC 5859.

176. W. Townsley, O. Troan. *IPv6 Rapid Deployment on IPv4 Infrastructures (6rd) – Protocol Specification*. IETF, August 2010. RFC 5969.

177. K. Nichols, S. Blake, F. Baker, D. Black. *Definition of the Differentiated Services Field (DS Field) in the IPv4 and IPv6 Headers*. IETF, December 1998. RFC 2474.

178. M. Thomson, J. Winterbottom. *Discovering the Local Location Information Server (LIS)*. IETF, March 2010. draft-ietf-geopriv-lis-discovery-15.txt.

179. S. Lawrence, Ed., J. Elwell. *Session Initiation Protocol (SIP) User Agent Configuration*. IETF, June 2010. draft-lawrence-sipforum-user-agent-config-03.

180. R. Gayraud, B. Lourdelet. *Network Time Protocol (NTP) Server Option for DHCPv6*. IETF, June 2010. RFC 5908.

181. T. Huth, J. Freimann, V. Zimmer, D. Thaler. *DHCPv6 Options for Network Boot*. IETF, July 2010. draft-ietf-dhc-dhcpv6-opt-netboot-10.txt.

182. M. Crawford. *Binary Labels in the Domain Name System*. IETF, August 1999. RFC 2673.

183. R. Bush, A. Durand, B. Fink, O. Gudmundsson, T. Hain, Editors. *Representing Internet Protocol version 6 (IPv6) Addresses in the Domain Name System (DNS)*. *IETF, August 2002. RFC 3363*.

184. J. Klensin. *Internationalized Domain Names for Applications (IDNA): Definitions and Document Framework*. IETF, August 2010. RFC 5890.

185. J. Klensin. *Internationalized Domain Names for Applications (IDNA): Protocol*. IETF, August 2010. RFC 5891.

186. P. Faltstrom, Ed. *The Unicode Code Points and Internationalized Domain Names for Applications (IDNA)*. IETF, August 2010. RFC 5892.

187. H. Alvestrand, Ed. Right-to-Left Scripts for Internationalized Domain Names for Applications (IDNA). IETF, August 2010. RFC 5893.

188. J. Klensin. *Internationalized Domain Names for Applications (IDNA): Background, Explanation, and Rationale*. IETF, August 2010. RFC 5894.

189. R. Allbery. *DNS SRV Resource Records for AFS*. IETF, April 2010. RFC 5864.

190. J. Levine. *DNS Blacklists and Whitelists*. IETF, February 2010. RFC 5782.

191. R. Austein. *DNS Name Server Identifier (NSID) Option*. IETF, August 2007. RFC 5001.

192. ITU-T Study Group 4. *Series M: TMN and Network Maintenance: International Transmission Systems, Telephone Circuits, Telegraphy, Facsimile and Leased Circuits. TMN Management Functions*. ITU, 2001. ITU-T M.3400.

193. T. Chown. *Use of VLANs for IPv4-IPv6 Coexistence in Enterprise Networks*. IETF, June 2006. RFC 4554.

194. C. Huitema. *An Anycast Prefix for 6to4 Relay Routers*. IETF, June 2001. RFC 3068.

GLOSSARY

The key terms used throughout this book are summarized as follows:

- **DHCP (Dynamic Host Configuration Protocol):** automates IP address assignment to network hosts or devices. DHCP technology applies to both IPv4 and IPv6 address assignment, though "DHCP" typically refers to assignment of IPv4 addresses.

- **DHCPv6:** DHCP specifically for IPv6 addresses, not version 6 of the DHCP protocol.

- **DNS (Domain Name System):** The distributed database of Internet name, address, and other information.

- **DNSSEC:** DNS security extensions provide resolution data origin authentication (the source truly published this data), data integrity verification (the data was not modified en route), and authenticated denial of existence of data (the requested data truly does not exist in this zone).

- **FCAPS:** An initialism of the five major functional areas of network management, namely Fault, Configuration, Accounting, Performance, and Security as described in ITU Telecommunications Management Network standards.

- **Host:** An end device that communicates on an IP network, such as a server, laptop, and VoIP phone. We contrast an end device with network infrastructure devices such as routers and switches.

- **IP (Internet Protocol):** The network layer used across the Internet and all IP networks. IP generically refers to all IP versions, while IPv4 and IPv6 denote respective IP versions.

- **IPAM (IP address management):** The disciplined approach to managing IP address space and associated DHCP and DNS services.

- **ISC (Internet Systems Consortium):** Developer of a reference implementation of DHCP and DNS (BIND).

- **ITIL® (Information Technology Infrastructure Library):** Developed by the U.K. Office of Government and Commerce (OGC), is a best practices framework

IP Address Management: Principles and Practice, by Timothy Rooney
Copyright © 2011 the Institute of Electrical and Electronics Engineers, Inc.

with the perspective of the information technology (IT) organization as a service provider to the enterprise.

- **KSK (key signing key):** Used within DNSSEC to sign a zone signing key (ZSK), which in turn signs DNS zone data. The public KSK is published in a DNSKEY resource record within the corresponding secure zone. Resolvers or recursive servers configured to trust this zone's data must have a copy of the public KSK (or that of a parent zone's or lookaside validator's zone) configured as trust-anchors within their respective configurations.

- **NAT (network address translation):** A gateway or firewall that changes (translates) an IP address within the IP packet header prior to forwarding; commonly used in enterprise networks to translate internal private IP addresses to external public IP addresses.

- **TCP (Transmission Control Protocol):** The connection-oriented transport layer protocol within the TCP/IP protocol suite.

- **UDP (User Datagram Protocol):** The connectionless transport layer protocol within the TCP/IP protocol suite.

- **ZSK (zone signing key):** Used within DNSSEC to sign zone information, meaning each of the resource record sets within the zone.

RFC INDEX

This index lists the major IPAM-relevant Request for Comments (RFCs) documents as published by the Internet Engineering Task Force (IETF). RFC documents may be retrieved from www.ietf.org/rfc. Obsoleted RFCs are not listed. RFCs 3789–3796 are surveys of deployed IPv4 addresses and are not listed in the tables below but provide interesting insight to the mention and definition of IPv4 addresses for specific applications.

The Status column indicates the RFC status as Informational, Experimental, Standards Track, Draft Standard, Proposed Standard, Standard and Historic. RFCs that have been adopted as Best Current Practices (BCP) are enumerated by BCP number.

IPv4 PROTOCOL RFCs

RFC	Status	Title
791	Standard	Internet Protocol
1042	Standard	Standard for Transmission of IP Datagrams over IEEE 802 Networks
1546	Informational	Host Anycasting Service
1878	Historic	Variable Length Subnet Table for IPv4
2101	Informational	IPv4 Address Behaviour Today
2365	BCP 23	Administratively Scoped IP Multicast
3927	Proposed Standard	Dynamic Configuration of IPv4 Link Local Addresses
4116	Informational	IPv4 Multihoming Practices and Limitations
4632	BCP 122	Classless Interdomain Routing (CIDR): The Internet Address Assignment and Aggregation Plan

IP Address Management: Principles and Practice, by Timothy Rooney
Copyright © 2011 the Institute of Electrical and Electronics Engineers, Inc.

IPv6 PROTOCOL RFCs

RFC	Status	Title
1752	Proposed Standard	The Recommendation for the IP Next Generation Protocol
1881	Informational	IPv6 Address Allocation Management
1887	Informational	An Architecture for IPv6 Unicast Address Allocation
2375	Informational	IPv6 Multicast Address Assignments
2460	Draft Standard	Internet Protocol, Version 6 (IPv6) Specification
2526	Proposed Standard	Reserved IPv6 Subnet Anycast Addresses
2894	Proposed Standard	Router Renumbering for IPv6
3484	Proposed Standard	Default Address Selection for Internet Protocol Version 6 (IPv6)
3582	Informational	Goals for IPv6 Site-Multihoming Architectures
3587	Informational	IPv6 Global Unicast Address Format
3627	Informational	Use of /127 Prefix Length Between Routers Considered Harmful
3701	Informational	6bone (IPv6 Testing Address Allocation) Phaseout
3879	Proposed Standard	Deprecating Site Local Addresses
3956	Proposed Standard	Embedding the Rendezvous Point (RP) Address in an IPv6 Multicast Address
4007	Proposed Standard	IPv6 Scoped Address Architecture
4076	Informational	Renumbering Requirements for Stateless Dynamic Host Configuration Protocol for IPv6 (DHCPv6)
4177	Informational	Architectural Approaches to Multihoming for IPv6
4193	Proposed Standard	Unique Local IPv6 Unicast Addresses
4218	Informational	Threats Relating to IPv6 Multihoming Solutions
4291	Draft Standard	IP Version 6 Addressing Architecture
4294	Informational	IPv6 Node Requirements
4339	Informational	IPv6 Host Configuration of DNS Server Information Approaches
4489	Proposed Standard	A Method for Generating Link-Scoped IPv6 Multicast Addresses
4843	Experimental	An IPv6 Prefix for Overlay Routable Cryptographic Hash Identifiers (ORCHID)
4861	Draft Standard	Neighbor Discovery for IP Version 6 (IPv6)
4862	Draft Standard	IPv6 Stateless Address Autoconfiguration
4941	Draft Standard	Privacy Extensions for Stateless Address Autoconfiguration in IPv6
4968	Informational	Analysis of IPv6 Link Models for 802.16 Based Networks
5006	Experimental	IPv6 Router Advertisement Option for DNS Configuration
5156	Informational	Special-Use IPv6 Addresses
5157	Informational	IPv6 Implications for Network Scanning
5375	Informational	IPv6 Unicast Address Assignment Considerations
5453	Standards Track	Reserved IPv6 Interface Identifiers
5902	Informational	IAB Thoughts on IPv6 Network Address Translation

IPv4/IPv6 COEXISTENCE RFCs

RFC	Status	Title
2185	Informational	Routing Aspects of IPv6 Transition
2529	Proposed Standard	Transmission of IPv6 over IPv4 Domains Without Explicit Tunnels
2765	Proposed Standard	Stateless IP/ICMP Translation Algorithm (SIIT)
2767	Informational	Dual Stack Hosts Using the "Bump-in-the-Stack" Technique (BIS)
3053	Informational	IPv6 Tunnel Broker
3056	Proposed Standard	Connection of IPv6 Domains via IPv4 Clouds [6to4]
3068	Proposed Standard	An Anycast Prefix for 6to4 Relay Routers
3089	Informational	A SOCKS-based IPv6/IPv4 Gateway Mechanism
3142	Informational	An IPv6-to-IPv4 Transport Relay Translator
3338	Experimental	Dual Stack Hosts Using "Bump-in-the-API" (BIA)
3574	Informational	Transition Scenarios for 3GPP Networks
3750	Informational	Unmanaged Networks IPv6 Transition Scenarios
3904	Informational	Evaluation of IPv6 Transition Mechanisms for Unmanaged Networks
3964	Informational	Security Considerations for 6to4
3974	Informational	SMTP Operational Experience in Mixed IPv4/IPv6 Environments
4029	Informational	Scenarios and Analysis for Introducing IPv6 into ISP Networks
4038	Informational	Application Aspects of IPv6 Transition
4057	Informational	IPv6 Enterprise Network Scenarios
4213	Proposed Standard	Basic Transition Mechanisms for IPv6 Hosts and Routers
4215	Informational	Analysis of IPv6 Transition in Third Generation Partnership Project (3GPP) Networks
4241	Informational	A Model of IPv6/IPv4 Dual Stack Internet Access Service
4361	Proposed Standard	Node-specific Client Identifiers for Dynamic Host Configuration Protocol Version Four (DHCPv4)
4380	Proposed Standard	Teredo: Tunneling IPv6 over UDP through Network Address Translations (NATs)
4477	Informational	Dynamic Host Configuration Protocol (DHCP): IPv4 and IPv6 Dual-Stack Issues
4554	Informational	Use of VLANs for IPv4-IPv6 Coexistence in Enterprise Networks
4798	Proposed Standard	Connecting IPv6 Islands over IPv4 MPLS Using IPv6 Provider Edge Routers (6PE)
4852	Informational	IPv6 Enterprise Network Analysis—IP Layer 3 Focus
4942	Informational	IPv6 Transition/Coexistence Security Considerations

(Continued)

RFC	Status	Title
4966	Informational	Reasons to Move the Network Address Translator—Protocol Translator (NAT-PT) to Historic Status
4977	Informational	Problem Statement: Dual Stack Mobility
5181	Informational	IPv6 Deployment Scenarios in 802.16 Networks
5211	Informational	An Internet Transition Plan
5214	Informational	Intrasite Automatic Tunnel Addressing Protocol (ISATAP)
5569	Informational	IPv6 Rapid Deployment on IPv4 Infrastructures (6rd)
5747	Experimental	4over6 Transit Solution Using IP Encapsulation and MP-BGP Extensions

IP ADDRESS ALLOCATION RFCs

RFC	Status	Title
1219	Informational	On the Assignment of Subnet Numbers
1518	Historic	An Architecture for IP Address Allocation with CIDR
1900	Informational	Renumbering Needs Work
1715	Informational	The H Ratio for Address Assignment Efficiency
1918	BCP 5	Address Allocation for Private Internets
2008	BCP 7	Implications of Various Address Allocation Policies for Internet Routing
2050	BCP 12	Internet Registry IP Allocation Guidelines
2071	Informational	Network Renumbering Overview: Why Would I Want It and What Is It Anyway?
2908	Informational	The Internet Multicast Address Allocation Architecture
3177	Informational	IAB/IESG Recommendations on IPv6 Address Allocations to Sites
3194	Informational	The H-Density Ratio for Address Assignment Efficiency—An Update on the H ratio
3531	Informational	A Flexible Method for Managing the Assignment of Bits of an IPv6 Address Block
3819	BCP 89	Advice for Internet Subnetwork Designers
3849	Informational	IPv6 Address Prefix Reserved for Documentation
4147	Informational	Proposed Changes to the Format of the IANA IPv6 Registry
4192	Informational	Procedures for Renumbering an IPv6 Network Without a Flag Day
4779	Informational	ISP IPv6 Deployment Scenarios in Broadband Access Networks
4786	BCP 126	Operation of Anycast Services

(Continued)

(*Continued*)

RFC	Status	Title
5505	Informational	Principles of Internet Host Configuration
5684	Informational	Unintended Consequences of NAT Deployments with Overlapping Address Space
5735	BCP 153	Special Use IPv4 Addresses
5736	Informational	IANA IPv4 Spacial Purpose Address Registry
5737	Informational	IPv4 Address Blocks Reserved for Documentation
5771	BCP 51	IANA Guidelines for IPv4 Multicast Address Assignments
5887	Informational	Renumbering Still Needs Work

DHCP PROTOCOL RFCs

RFC	Status	Title
1534	Draft Standard	Interoperation Between DHCP and BOOTP
2131	Draft Standard	Dynamic Host Configuration Protocol
2132	Draft Standard	DHCP Options and BOOTP Vendor Extensions
2241	Proposed Standard	DHCP Options for Novell Directory Services
2242	Proposed Standard	NetWare/IP Domain Name and Information
2485	Proposed Standard	DHCP Option for The Open Group's User Authentication Protocol
2563	Proposed Standard	DHCP Option to Disable Stateless Autoconfiguration in IPv4 Clients
2610	Proposed Standard	DHCP Options for Service Location Protocol
2855	Proposed Standard	DHCP for IEEE 1394
2937	Proposed Standard	The Name Service Search Option for DHCP
3004	Proposed Standard	The User Class Option for DHCP
3011	Proposed Standard	The IPv4 Subnet Selection Option for DHCP
3046	Proposed Standard	DHCP Relay Agent Information Option
3074	Proposed Standard	DHC Load Balancing Algorithm
3118	Proposed Standard	Authentication for DHCP Messages
3203	Proposed Standard	DHCP Reconfigure Extension
3256	Proposed Standard	The DOCSIS Device Class DHCP Relay Agent Information Suboption
3361	Proposed Standard	Dynamic Host Configuration Protocol (DHCP-for-IPv4) Option for Session Initiation Protocol (SIP) Servers
3396	Proposed Standard	Encoding Long Options in the Dynamic Host Configuration Protocol (DHCPv4)
3397	Proposed Standard	Dynamic Host Configuration Protocol (DHCP) Domain Search Option

(*Continued*)

RFC	Status	Title
3442	Proposed Standard	The Classless Static Route Option for Dynamic Host Configuration Protocol (DHCP) Version 4
3456	Proposed Standard	Dynamic Host Configuration Protocol (DHCPv4) Configuration of IPsec Tunnel Mode
3495	Proposed Standard	Dynamic Host Configuration Protocol (DHCP) Option for CableLabs Client Configuration
3527	Proposed Standard	Link Selection Suboption for the Relay Agent Information Option for DHCPv4
3634	Proposed Standard	Key Distribution Center (KDC) Server Address Suboption for the Dynamic Host Configuration Protocol (DHCP) CableLabs Client Configuration (CCC) Option
3679	Informational	Unused Dynamic Host Configuration Protocol (DHCP) Option Codes
3825	Proposed Standard	Dynamic Host Configuration Protocol Option for Coordinate-based Location Configuration Information
3925	Proposed Standard	Vendor-Identifying Vendor Options for Dynamic Host Configuration Protocol Version 4 (DHCPv4)
3942	Proposed Standard	Reclassifying Dynamic Host Configuration Protocol Version 4 (DHCPv4) Options
3993	Proposed Standard	Subscriber-ID Suboption for the Dynamic Host Configuration Protocol (DHCP) Relay Agent Option
4030	Proposed Standard	The Authentication Suboption for the Dynamic Host Configuration Protocol (DHCP) Relay Agent Option
4039	Proposed Standard	Rapid Commit Option for the Dynamic Host Configuration Protocol Version 4 (DHCPv4)
4174	Proposed Standard	The IPv4 Dynamic Host Configuration Protocol (DHCP) Option for the Internet Storage Name Service
4243	Proposed Standard	Vendor-Specific Information Suboption for the Dynamic Host Configuration Protocol (DHCP) Relay Agent Option
4280	Proposed Standard	Dynamic Host Configuration Protocol (DHCP) Options for Broadcast and Multicast Control Servers
4361	Proposed Standard	Node-specific Client Identifiers for Dynamic Host Configuration Protocol Version Four (DHCPv4)
4388	Proposed Standard	Dynamic Host Configuration Protocol (DHCP) Leasequery
4390	Proposed Standard	Dynamic Host Configuration Protocol (DHCP) over InfiniBand
4578	Informational	Dynamic Host Configuration Protocol (DHCP) Options for the Intel Preboot eXecution Environment (PXE)
4702	Proposed Standard	The Dynamic Host Configuration Protocol (DHCP) Client Fully Qualified Domain Name (FQDN) Option

(*Continued*)

(*Continued*)

RFC	Status	Title
4703	Proposed Standard	Resolution of Fully Qualified Domain Name (FQDN) Conflicts among Dynamic Host Configuration Protocol (DHCP) Clients
4776	Proposed Standard	Dynamic Host Configuration Protocol (DHCPv4 and DHCPv6) Option for Civic Addresses Configuration Information
4833	Proposed Standard	Timezone Options for DHCP
5010	Proposed Standard	The Dynamic Host Configuration Protocol Version 4 (DHCPv4) Relay Agent Flags Suboption
5071	Informational	Dynamic Host Configuration Protocol Options Used by PXELINUX
5107	Proposed Standard	DHCP Server Identifier Override Suboption
5192	Proposed Standard	DHCP Options for Protocol for Carrying Authentication for Network Access (PANA) Authentication Agents
5223	Proposed Standard	Discovering Location-to-Service Translation (LoST) Servers Using the Dynamic Host Configuration Protocol (DHCP)
5417	Proposed Standard	Control and Provisioning of Wireless Access Points (CAPWAP) Access Controller DHCP Option
5460	Proposed Standard	DHCPv6 Bulk Leasequery
5678	Standards Track	Dynamic Host Configuration Protocol (DHCPv4 and DHCPv6) Options for IEEE 802.21 Mobility Services (MoS) Discovery
5859	Informational	TFTP Server Address Option for DHCPv4

DHCPv6 PROTOCOL RFCs

RFC	Status	Title
3315	Proposed Standard	Dynamic Host Configuration Protocol for IPv6 (DHCPv6)
3319	Proposed Standard	Dynamic Host Configuration Protocol (DHCPv6) Options for Session Initiation Protocol (SIP) Servers
3633	Proposed Standard	IPv6 Prefix Options for Dynamic Host Configuration Protocol (DHCP) Version 6
3646	Proposed Standard	DNS Configuration Options for Dynamic Host Configuration Protocol for IPv6 (DHCPv6)
3736	Proposed Standard	Stateless Dynamic Host Configuration Protocol (DHCP) Service for IPv6
3769	Informational	Requirements for IPv6 Prefix Delegation

(Continued)

RFC	Status	Title
3898	Proposed Standard	Network Information Service (NIS) Configuration Options for Dynamic Host Configuration Protocol for IPv6 (DHCPv6)
4075	Proposed Standard	Simple Network Time Protocol (SNTP) Configuration Option for DHCPv6
4242	Proposed Standard	Information Refresh Time Option for Dynamic Host Configuration Protocol for IPv6 (DHCPv6)
4580	Proposed Standard	Dynamic Host Configuration Protocol for IPv6 (DHCPv6) Relay Agent Subscriber-ID Option
4649	Proposed Standard	Dynamic Host Configuration Protocol for IPv6 (DHCPv6) Relay Agent Remote-ID Option
4703	Proposed Standard	Resolution of Fully Qualified Domain Name (FQDN) Conflicts Among Dynamic Host Configuration Protocol (DHCP) Clients
4704	Proposed Standard	The Dynamic Host Configuration Protocol for IPv6 (DHCPv6) Client Fully Qualified Domain Name (FQDN) Option
4776	Proposed Standard	Dynamic Host Configuration Protocol (DHCPv4 and DHCPv6) Option for Civic Addresses Configuration Information
4833	Proposed Standard	Timezone Options for DHCP
4994	Proposed Standard	DHCPv6 Relay Agent Echo Request Option
5007	Proposed Standard	DHCPv6 Leasequery
5192	Proposed Standard	DHCP Options for Protocol for Carrying Authentication for Network Access (PANA) Authentication Agents
5223	Proposed Standard	Discovering Location-to-Service Translation (LoST) Servers Using the Dynamic Host Configuration Protocol (DHCP)
5460	Proposed Standard	DHCPv6 Bulk Leasequery
5678	Standards Track	Dynamic Host Configuration Protocol (DHCPv4 and DHCPv6) Options for IEEE 802.21 Mobility Services (MoS) Discovery
5908	Standards Track	Network Time Protocol (NTP) Server Option for DHCPv6

DNS PROTOCOL RFCs

RFC	Status	Title
1034	Standard	Domain Names—Concepts and Facilities
1035	Standard	Domain Names—Implementation and Specification
1101	Unknown	DNS Encoding of Network Names and Other Types

(Continued)

(*Continued*)

RFC	Status	Title
1183	Experimental	New DNS RR Definitions
1464	Experimental	Using the Domain Name System to Store Arbitrary String Attributes
1480	Informational	The US Domain
1591	Informational	Domain Name System Structure and Delegation
1706	Informational	DNS NSAP Resource Records
1712	Informational	DNS Encoding of Geographical Location
1876	Experimental	A Means for Expressing Location Information in the Domain Name System
1982	Proposed Standard	Serial Number Arithmetic
1996	Proposed Standard	A Mechanism for Prompt Notification of Zone Changes (DNS NOTIFY)
2136	Proposed Standard	Dynamic Updates in the Domain Name System (DNS UPDATE)
2163	Proposed Standard	Using the Internet DNS to Distribute MIXER Conformant Global Address Mapping (MCGAM)
2181	Proposed Standard	Clarifications to the DNS Specification
2182	BCP 16	Selection and Operation of Secondary DNS Servers
2219	BCP 19	Use of DNS Aliases for Network Services
2308	Proposed Standard	Negative Caching of DNS Queries (DNS NCACHE)
2317	BCP 20	Classless IN-ADDR.ARPA delegation
2536	Proposed Standard	DSA KEYs and SIGs in the Domain Name System (DNS)
2539	Proposed Standard	Storage of Diffie–Hellman Keys in the Domain Name System (DNS)
2540	Experimental	Detached Domain Name System (DNS) Information
2671	Proposed Standard	Extension Mechanisms for DNS (EDNS0)
2672	Proposed Standard	Non-Terminal DNS Name Redirection
2673	Experimental	Binary Labels in the Domain Name System
2782	Proposed Standard	A DNS RR for Specifying the Location of Services (DNS SRV)
2870	BCP 40	Root Name Server Operational Requirements
2874	Experimental	DNS Extensions to Support IPv6 Address Aggregation and Renumbering
3123	Experimental	A DNS RR Type for Lists of Address Prefixes (APL RR)
3258	Informational	Distributing Authoritative Name Servers via Shared Unicast Addresses
3363	Informational	Representing Internet Protocol Version 6 (IPv6) Addresses in the Domain Name System (DNS)
3364	Informational	Tradeoffs in Domain Name System (DNS) Support for Internet Protocol Version 6 (IPv6)

(Continued)

RFC	Status	Title
3425	Proposed Standard	Obsoleting IQUERY
3467	Informational	Role of the Domain Name System (DNS)
3490	Proposed Standard	Internationalizing Domain Names in Applications (IDNA)
3491	Proposed Standard	Nameprep: A Stringprep Profile for Internationalized Domain Names (IDN)
3492	Proposed Standard	Punycode: A Bootstring Encoding of Unicode for Internationalized Domain Names in Applications (IDNA)
3596	Draft Standard	DNS Extensions to Support IP Version 6
3597	Proposed Standard	Handling of Unknown DNS Resource Record (RR) Types
3681	BCP 80	Delegation of E.F.F.3.IP6.ARPA.
3901	BCP 91	DNS IPv6 Transport Operational Guidelines
4074	Informational	Common Misbehavior Against DNS Queries for IPv6 Addresses
4159	BCP 109	Deprecation of "ip6.int"
4183	Informational	A Suggested Scheme for DNS Resolution of Networks and Gateways
4185	Informational	National and Local Characters for DNS Top Level Domain (TLD) Names
4290	Informational	Suggested Practices for Registration of Internationalized Domain Names (IDN)
4343	Proposed Standard	Domain Name System (DNS) Case Insensitivity Clarification
4367	Informational	What's in a Name: False Assumptions about DNS Names
4406	Experimental	Sender ID: Authenticating E-Mail
4406	Experimental	Purported Responsible Address in E-Mail Messages
4407	Experimental	Sender Policy Framework (SPF) for Authorizing Use of Domains in E-Mail, Version 1
4472	Informational	Operational Considerations and Issues with IPv6 DNS
4592	Proposed Standard	The Role of Wildcards in the Domain Name System
4690	Informational	Review and Recommendations for Internationalized Domain Names (IDNs)
4697	BCP 123	Observed DNS Resolution Misbehavior
4701	Proposed Standard	A DNS Resource Record (RR) for Encoding Dynamic Host Configuration Protocol (DHCP) Information (DHCID RR)
4892	Informational	Requirements for a Mechanism Identifying a Name Server Instance
5001	Proposed Standard	DNS Name Server Identifier (NSID) Option
5158	Informational	6to4 Reverse DNS Delegation Specification

(Continued)

(*Continued*)

RFC	Status	Title
5205	Experimental	Host Identity Protocol (HIP) Domain Name System (DNS) Extensions [HIP RR]
5395	BCP 42	Domain Name System (DNS) IANA Considerations
5507	Informational	Design Choices When Expanding the DNS
5679	Proposed Standard	Locating IEEE 802.21 Mobility Services Using DNS
5855	BCP 155	Nameservers for IPv4 and IPv6 Reverse Zones
5864	Standards Track	DNS SRV Resource Records for AFS
5890	Standards Track	Internationalized Domain Names for Applications (IDNA): Definitions and Document Framework
5891	Standards Track	Internationalized Domain Names for Applications (IDNA): Protocol
5892	Standards Track	The Unicode Code Points and Internationalized Domain Names for Applications (IDNA)
5893	Standards Track	Right-to-Left Scripts for Internationalized Domain Names for Applications (IDNA)
5894	Standards Track	Internationalized Domain Names for Applications (IDNA): Background, Explanation, and Rationale
5936	Standards Track	DNS Zone Transfer Protocol (AXFR)

DNS SECURITY-RELATED RFCs

RFC	Status	Title
2230	Informational	Key Exchange Delegation Record for the DNS
2845	Proposed Standard	Secret Key Transaction Authentication for DNS (TSIG)
2930	Proposed Standard	Secret Key Establishment for DNS (TKEY RR)
2931	Proposed Standard	DNS Request and Transactional Signatures (SIG(0)s)
3007	Proposed Standard	Secure Domain Name System (DNS) Dynamic Update
3110	Proposed Standard	RSA/SHA-1 SIGs and RSA KEYs in the Domain Name System (DNS)
3645	Proposed Standard	Generic Security Service Algorithm for Secret Key Transaction Authentication for DNS (GSS-TSIG)
3833	Informational	Threat Analysis of the Domain Name System (DNS)
4033	Proposed Standard	DNS Security Introduction and Requirements
4034	Proposed Standard	Resource Records for DNS Security Extensions
4035	Proposed Standard	Protocol Modifications for the DNS Security Extensions
4255	Proposed Standard	Using DNS to Securely Publish Secure Shell (SSH) Key Fingerprints

(*Continued*)

RFC	Status	Title
4398	Proposed Standard	Storing Certificates in the Domain Name System (DNS)
4431	Informational	The DNSSEC Lookaside Validation (DLV) Resource Record
4470	Proposed Standard	Minimally Covering NSEC Records and DNSSEC Online Signing
4471	Experimental	Derivation of DNS Name Predecessor and Successor
4509	Proposed Standard	Use of SHA-256 in DNSSEC Delegation Signer (DS) Resource Records (RRs)
4641	Informational	DNSSEC Operational Practices
4686	Informational	Analysis of Threats Motivating DomainKeys Identified Mail (DKIM)
4871	Proposed Standard	DomainKeys Identified Mail (DKIM) Signatures
4955	Proposed Standard	DNS Security (DNSSEC) Experiments
4956	Experimental	DNS Security (DNSSEC) Opt-In
4986	Informational	Requirements Related to DNS Security (DNSSEC) Trust Anchor Rollover
5011	Proposed Standard	Automated Updates of DNS Security (DNSSEC) Trust Anchors
5016	Informational	Requirements for a DomainKeys Identified Mail (DKIM) Signing Practices Protocol
5074	Informational	DNSSEC Lookaside Validation (DLV)
5155	Proposed Standard	DNS Security (DNSSEC) Hashed Authenticated Denial of Existence [NSEC3, NSEC3PARAM]
5358	BCP 140	Preventing Use of Recursive Nameservers in Reflector Attacks
5452	Standards Track	Measures for Making DNS More Resilient Against Forged Answers
5585	Informational	DomainKeys Identified Mail (DKIM) Service Overview
5617	Standards Track	DomainKeys Identified Mail (DKIM) Author Domain Signing Practices (ADSP)
5672	Standards Track	RFC 4871 DomainKeys Identified Mail (DKIM) Signatures—Update
5702	Proposed Standard	Use of SHA-2 Algorithms with RSA in DNSKEY and RRSIG Resource Records for DNSSEC
5782	Informational	DNS Blacklists and Whitelists
5863	Informational	DomainKeys Identified Mail (DKIM) Development, Deployment, and Operations
5933	Standards Track	Use of GOST Signature Algorithms in DNSKEY and RRSIG Resource Records for DNSSEC

DNS ENUM-RELATED RFCs

RFC	Status	Title
2916	Proposed Standard	E.164 number and DNS
3245	Informational	The History and Context of Telephone Number Mapping (ENUM) ...
3403	Proposed Standard	Dynamic Delegation Discovery System (DDDS) Part Three: The Domain Name System (DNS) Database [NAPTR RR]
3761	Proposed Standard	The E.164 to Uniform Resource Identifiers (URI) Dynamic Delegation Discovery System (DDDS) Applications (ENUM)
3762	Proposed Standard	Telephone Number Mapping (ENUM) Service Registration for H.323
3764	Proposed Standard	enumservice registration for Session Initiation Protocol (SIP) Addresses-of-Record
3824	Informational	Using E.164 numbers with the Session Initiation Protocol (SIP)
3953	Proposed Standard	Telephone Number Mapping (ENUM) Service Registration for Presence Services
3958	Proposed Standard	Domain-Based Application Service Location Using SRV RRs and the Dynamic Delegation Discovery System (DDDS)
4114	Proposed Standard	E.164 Number Mapping for the Extensible Provisioning Protocol (EPP)
4725	Informational	ENUM Validation Architecture
4759	Proposed Standard	The ENUM Dip Indicator Parameter for the "tel" URI
4848	Proposed Standard	Domain-Based Application Service Location Using URIs and the Dynamic Delegation Discovery Service (DDDS)
5067	Informational	Infrastructure ENUM Requirements
5483	Informational	ENUM Implementation Issues and Experiences
5526	Informational	The E.164 to Uniform Resource Identifiers (URI) DDDS Application for Infrastructure ENUM
5527	Informational	Combined User and Infrastructure ENUM in the e164.arpa Tree

MANAGEMENT OR OPERATIONAL RFCs

RFC	Status	Title
1713	Informational	Tools for DNS Debugging
1912	Informational	Common DNS Errors
2151	Informational	A Primer on Internet and TCP/IP Tools and Utilities
2606	BCP 32	Reserved Top Level DNS Names
3172	BCP 52	Management Guidelines and Operational Requirements for the Address and Routing Parameter Area Domain ("arpa")
5157	Informational	IPv6 Implications for Network Scanning

INDEX